BUILDING THE COUNTRYSIDE

Society for Libyan Studies Open Access Monograph 2

BUILDING THE COUNTRYSIDE

RURAL ARCHITECTURE AND SETTLEMENT IN TRIPOLITANIA DURING THE ROMAN AND LATE ANTIQUE PERIODS

Nichole Sheldrick

Society for Libyan Studies Open Access Monograph 2

Published in 2021 by:
The Society for Libyan Studies
c/o The British Academy
10-11 Carlton House Terrace
London SW1Y 5AH

www.societyforlibyanstudies.org

ISBN: 978-1-900971-77-5

Cover and interior design by Chris Bell, cbdesign

TABLE OF CONTENTS

List of Tables vii

List of Figures ix

Figure Acknowledgments xii

Acknowledgments xiii

A Brief Note on Arabic Place Names and Words xiv

1 Introduction 1

1.1 Regional Boundaries 2

1.2 Climate and Environment 3

1.3 Historical Context and Human Geography 4

1.4 Urban Settlement 7

2 Previous Work, Sources and Methodology 11

2.1 Before World War II 11

2.2 After World War II 12

2.3 Satellite Imagery and Remote Sensing 16

2.4 Methodology 17

3 Development and Chronology of Rural Settlement and Architecture 21

3.1 Pre-Roman and Indigenous Architecture and Settlement 21

3.1.1 Stone Huts 21

3.1.2 Fortified Hilltop Settlements 23

3.1.3 Non-Stone Architectures 25

3.2 Rural Settlement Chronology 26

3.2.1 Ceramics and Dating 26

3.2.2 Survey Evidence 27

4 Military Architecture and Settlement 35

4.1 Identifying Military Buildings 35

4.1.1 Epigraphy and Terminology 35

4.1.2 Appearance and Construction 37

4.1.3 Date 39

4.1.4 Location 39

4.1.5 Summary 39

4.2 Typology and Analysis 40
4.2.1 Major Forts 44
4.2.2 Marching Camp(?) 46
4.2.3 Minor Forts 46
4.2.4 Fortlets 48
4.2.5 Outposts 51
4.2.6 Observation Posts: Watchtowers and Clausurae 53
4.3 Military Settlements 55
4.4 Discussion 57

5 Unfortified Architecture and Settlement 59

5.1 Farms and Farm Buildings: Terminology 59
5.2 Physical Characteristics and Analyses 61
5.2.1 Form and Plan 61
5.2.2 Size 71
5.2.3 Use of Space: Presses, Crops and Animals 75
5.2.4 Materials and Construction Techniques 80
5.2.5 Decoration and Luxury 90
5.3 Unfortified Settlements and Other Rural Structures 94
5.3.1 Settlements 94
5.3.2 Other Structures 97
5.4 Discussion 100

6 Fortified Architecture and Settlement 107

6.1 Fortified Farmhouses, Forts and *Gsur*: Terminology 107
6.2 Physical Characteristics and Analyses 108
6.2.1 Form and Plan 108
6.2.2 Size 128
6.2.3 Use of Space: Presses, Crops and Animals 133
6.2.4 Materials and Construction Techniques 137
6.2.5 Inscriptions, Decoration and Luxury 148
6.3 Fortified Settlements and Other Rural Structures 153
6.3.1 Settlements 153
6.3.2 Other Structures 160
6.4 Discussion 161

7 Conclusions 167

Bibliography 171

Appendix Tables 193

Arabic Abstract 207

Appendix A: Military Buildings
Appendix B: Unfortified Buildings
Appendix C: Fortified Buildings
Appendix D: Inscriptions from Fortified Buildings

These Appendices are available as a pdf on the Society for Libyan Studies website, with the Open Access version of the book

LIST OF TABLES

Table 5.1: Number of unfortified buildings identified in each sub-region of Tripolitania. 61

Table 5.2: Frequency of unfortified building types by region. 64

Table 5.3: Minimum, maximum, mean and median total areas for all unfortified buildings and complexes, divided by region. 71

Table 5.4: Minimum, maximum, mean and median total areas for all open farm buildings (farmyard courtyard and undifferentiated), divided by region. 72

Table 5.5: Minimum, maximum, mean and median total areas for courtyard buildings, divided by region. 73

Table 5.6: Minimum, maximum, mean and median total areas for farmyard buildings, divided by region. 73

Table 5.7: Minimum, maximum and mean area for all open farm buildings in the pre-desert and Syrtica, divided by quartile. 74

Table 5.8: Minimum, maximum, mean and median total areas for open complexes, divided by region 75

Table 5.9: Minimum, maximum, mean and median total areas for buildings without yards, divided by region. 75

Table 5.10: Distribution of unfortified buildings with presses by region. 76

Table 5.11: Minimum, maximum, mean and median sizes of buildings with different numbers of presses. 77

Table 5.12: Distribution of construction techniques employed in unfortified buildings, divided by region. 85

Table 5.13: Frequency of construction techniques used in different unfortified building types across Tripolitania. 89

Table 5.14: Average size (m^2) of unfortified farm buildings in different regions, divided by construction technique. 90

Table 5.15: Frequency of unfortified buildings at which luxury elements were observed. 91

Table 5.16: Number of 'settlements' into which unfortified buildings can be grouped based on different distances. 95

Table 5.17: Average number of unfortified buildings in recorded settlements. 96

Table 6.1: Number of fortified buildings identified in each sub-region of Tripolitania. 109

Table 6.2: Frequency of fortified building types by region. 111

Table 6.3: Fortified buildings with ditches, divided by region and building type. 126

Table 6.4: Minimum, maximum, mean and median total areas for all fortified buildings, divided by region. 128

Table 6.5: Minimum, maximum, mean and median total areas for fortified tower buildings, divided by region. 130

Table 6.6: Minimum, maximum, mean and median total areas for fortified compound buildings, divided by region. 130

Table 6.7: Mean sizes of unfortified courtyard and fortified compound buildings, divided by region. 132

Table 6.8: Distribution of fortified buildings with presses by region. 134

Table 6.9: Minimum, maximum, mean and median sizes of fortified buildings with different numbers of presses. 136

Table 6.10: Distribution of construction techniques employed in fortified buildings, divided by region. 142

Table 6.11: Frequency of construction techniques used in different fortified building types and sub-types across Tripolitania. 146

Table 6.12: Average size (m^2) of fortified towers in different regions, divided by construction technique. 147
Table 6.13: Average size (m^2) of fortified compounds in different regions, divided by construction technique. 148
Table 6.14: Frequency of fortified buildings at which luxury elements were observed. 148
Table 6.15: Number of 'settlements' into which fortified buildings can be grouped based on different distances. 153
Table 6.16: Average number of fortified buildings in recorded settlements. 154
Table 6.17: Distribution of settlements associated with fortified structures, divided by building type, region and in total. 157
Table 6.18: Number and percentage of fortified settlement groups which intersect at least one unfortified group at different distances. 158
Table 6.19: Total number of unfortified and fortified buildings catalogued, divided by region. 161
Table 6.20: Number of unfortified (U) and fortified (F) buildings of known location and settlement groups. 162

LIST OF FIGURES

Figure 1.1: Approximate limits and main geographic features of ancient Tripolitania. 3

Figure 1.2: Distribution and density of urban settlements in *Africa Proconsularis*, Tripolitania and Cyrenaica, after the *Barrington Atlas* (Talbert 2000). 8

Figure 2.1: Areas of published (white) and new satellite surveys (red). 18

Figure 2.2: Distribution of all unfortified, fortified and military buildings recorded in the catalogue and regional divisions for analysis. 19

Figure 3.1: Examples of stone huts in the eastern pre-desert and Syrtica. 22

Figure 3.2: Examples of hillforts. 24

Figure 3.3: Approximate locations of six survey areas for which detailed chronological survey data were available. 28

Figure 3.4: Chronological distribution of ceramic evidence collected in six survey areas. 29

Figure 3.5: Chronological distribution of ceramic evidence collected in three survey areas with unfortified and fortified buildings separated. 31

Figure 3.6: Chronological distribution of ceramics recovered for all a) unfortified and b) fortified farm buildings in the *ULVS* area (after Mattingly & Dore 1996: 150, fig. 5.38 and 156, fig. 5.43a). 34

Figure 4.1: Military buildings with projecting towers from around the Roman Empire. 38

Figure 4.2: Civilian buildings in Tripolitania and Fazzan with projecting towers. 38

Figure 4.3: Buildings in Tripolitania with projecting towers previously identified as military but now thought to be (potentially) civilian. 38

Figure 4.4: Distribution of known and suspected military buildings and roads in Tripolitania. Numbers correspond to those used in Appendix A. 41

Figure 4.5: Ground area (m^2) of known military buildings in Tripolitania. 43

Figure 4.6: Major forts and marching camp. 45

Figure 4.7: Minor forts. 47

Figure 4.8: Fortlets. 49

Figure 4.9: Possible but unconfirmed fortlets. 51

Figure 4.10: Outposts. 52

Figure 4.11: Watchtowers. 53

Figure 4.12: The Tebaga *clausura* (western *gebel*). 54

Figure 4.13: Major forts with approximate settlement extents. 54

Figure 4.14: Outposts with settlements. 56

Figure 5.1: Distribution of all catalogued unfortified buildings (n=1,653). 62

Figure 5.2: Frequency of unfortified plan types, in total and divided by region. 64

Figure 5.3: Examples of farmyard buildings. 65

Figure 5.4: Examples of courtyard buildings. 66

Figure 5.5: Distribution of farmyard buildings. 67

Figure 5.6: Distribution of courtyard buildings. 67

Figure 5.7: Examples of open complexes. 68

Figure 5.8: Distribution of open complexes. 69
Figure 5.9: Distribution of range type buildings. 70
Figure 5.10: Mean sizes (m^2) of all open, courtyard and farmyard buildings, divided by region. 72
Figure 5.11: Distribution of unfortified buildings with presses, divided by number of presses recorded. 76
Figure 5.12: Mean sizes of unfortified buildings, divided by number of presses. 78
Figure 5.13: Ashlar masonry. 82
Figure 5.14: *Opus africanum* masonry. 82
Figure 5.15: Regular masonry (top, lower left) and the remains of irregular masonry (lower right). 83
Figure 5.16: Coursed rubble/drystone. 84
Figure 5.17: Ratios of construction techniques employed in unfortified buildings in different regions of Tripolitania (excluding the Southwest and eastern Syrtica for which there were no data). 85
Figure 5.18a: Geographical distribution of construction techniques used in unfortified buildings: ashlar and *opus africanum*. 86
Figure 5.18b: Geographical distribution of construction techniques used in unfortified buildings: large and small orthostats. 86
Figure 5.18c: Geographical distribution of construction techniques used in unfortified buildings: regular and irregular masonry. 87
Figure 5.18d: Geographical distribution of construction techniques used in unfortified buildings: Syrtica combination, mortared rubble and coursed rubble/drystone. 87
Figure 5.19: Ratios of construction techniques used in different unfortified building types. 89
Figure 5.20: Distribution of unfortified buildings with luxury elements. 91
Figure 5.21: Examples of (apotropaic?) phallic reliefs. 93
Figure 5.22: Proportions of settlements with one vs. two or more individual unfortified buildings recorded. 95
Figure 5.23: Wadi walls. 98
Figure 5.24: Examples of mausolea. 99
Figure 6.1: Distribution of all catalogued fortified buildings (n=810). 109
Figure 6.2: Frequency of fortified plan types, in total and divided by region. 112
Figure 6.3: Distribution of all tower-like fortified buildings. 112
Figure 6.4: Examples of 'central lightwell' towers. 113
Figure 6.5: Examples of 'range lightwell' towers. 113
Figure 6.6: Towers of non-rectangular shape. 114
Figure 6.7: Distribution of fortified compound buildings. 114
Figure 6.8: Examples of fortified courtyard compounds. 115
Figure 6.9: Examples of doubled fortified compounds. 116
Figure 6.10: Examples of irregular fortified compounds. 117
Figure 6.11: Distribution of fortified buildings with externally projecting towers. 118
Figure 6.12: Examples of fortified buildings with externally projecting towers. 119
Figure 6.13: Examples of fortified buildings with batters. 121
Figure 6.14: Distributions of fortified buildings with batters. 122
Figure 6.15: Distribution of fortified buildings with externally projecting yards. 122
Figure 6.16: Examples of fortified buildings with externally projecting yards. 123
Figure 6.17: Distribution of fortified buildings with external enceintes. 124
Figure 6.18: Examples of fortified buildings with external enceintes. 125
Figure 6.19: Distribution of fortified buildings with ditches. 126
Figure 6.20: Examples of wide, surrounding ditches. 127
Figure 6.21: Mean sizes of unfortified and fortified buildings. 129
Figure 6.22: Mean sizes (m^2) of all fortified buildings, towers and compounds. 130

Figure 6.23: Mean sizes of unfortified courtyard and fortified compound buildings, divided by region. 131
Figure 6.24: Distribution of fortified buildings with presses. 134
Figure 6.25: A fortified building with larger masonry in lower courses (possibly robbed/re-used from earlier buildings) and smaller masonry in upper courses. 138
Figure 6.26: Ashlar masonry. 139
Figure 6.27: Regular masonry 140
Figure 6.28: Irregular masonry. 140
Figure 6.29: Coursed rubble/drystone. 140
Figure 6.30: Very regular masonry. 141
Figure 6.31: Ratios of construction techniques employed in fortified buildings in different regions of Tripolitania. 142
Figure 6.32a: Geographical distribution of construction techniques used in fortified buildings: ashlar and *opus africanum*. 143
Figure 6.32b: Geographical distribution of construction techniques used in fortified buildings: very regular masonry. 143
Figure 6.32c: Geographical distribution of construction techniques used in fortified buildings: regular and irregular masonry. 144
Figure 6.32d: Geographical distribution of construction techniques used in fortified buildings: mortared rubble and coursed rubble/drystone. 144
Figure 6.33: Fortified structures with ashlar and rounded corners. 145
Figure 6.34: Proportions of different types of masonry used in fortified tower and compound buildings. 147
Figure 6.35: Distribution of fortified buildings with luxury features. 149
Figure 6.36: An example of an inscription above a sculpted doorway on a fortified building. 150
Figure 6.37: Sculpted doorframes. 151
Figure 6.38: Interior niches. 152
Figure 6.39: Proportions of settlements with one vs. two or more individual fortified buildings recorded. 154
Figure 6.40: Fortified buildings with closely clustered settlements. 155
Figure 6.41: Fortified buildings with dispersed settlements. 156
Figure 6.42: Fortified building with clustered settlement. 157
Figure 6.43: Distribution of fortified buildings with associated settlements. 158
Figure 6.44: Examples of fortified building settlement groups in close proximity to unfortified settlement groups. 159

FIGURE ACKNOWLEDGMENTS

Photographs from the *UNESCO Libyan Valleys Survey* (*ULVS*) Archive have been reproduced with permission from the Society for Libyan Studies, David Mattingly, and the School of Archaeology and Ancient History at the University of Leicester, where the archive is currently held. Photos from the *ULVS* Archive are referenced in the following format:

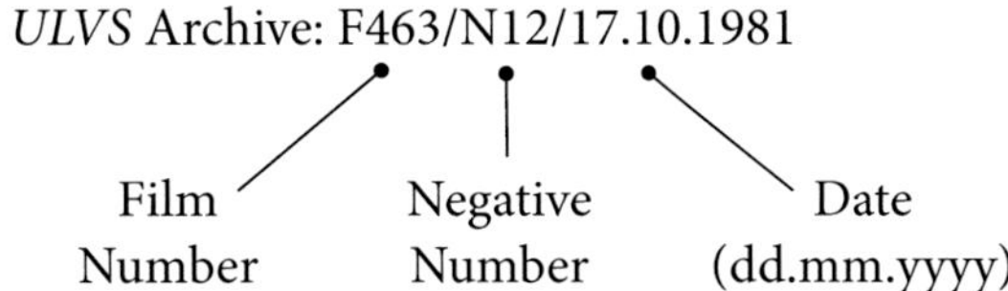

Photographs and reconstruction drawings from Barker 1996b, Brogan & Smith 1984, Scott, Dore, & Mattingly 1996, and Welsby 1992 reproduced with permission from the Society for Libyan Studies.

Photograph from Oates 1953 reproduced with permission from the British School at Rome.

Photograph from Ahmed 2010 reproduced with permission from Mftah A.M. Ahmed.

All building plans were digitised and re-drawn by the author based on the sources credited in the individual figures.

Satellite imagery has been reproduced from Google Earth, with the necessary attribution provided in each image.

All maps were produced by the author using ArcGIS® software by Esri. ArcGIS® and ArcMap™ are the intellectual property of Esri and are used herein under license. Copyright © Esri. All rights reserved. For more information about Esri® software, please visit www.esri.com.

ACKNOWLEDGMENTS

This book is the publication of my DPhil thesis, which I wrote at the University of Oxford between 2010 and 2016. That first version of this book would never have been written without the support and guidance of my supervisor, Andrew Wilson, to whom I am immensely grateful. At the other end of this road, the version you are reading now would never have been finished or published without the infinite patience and kindness of the Publications Manager for the Society for Libyan Studies, Victoria Leitch, who I cannot thank enough.

I am very grateful to the Society for Libyan Studies for agreeing to and supporting the publication of this book. I must also thank the Society, along with David Mattingly, for allowing me to consult and reproduce several original photographs from the archive of the *UNESCO Libyan Valleys Survey*, as well as the School of Archaeology and Ancient History at the University of Leicester where it is currently housed.

I am deeply indebted to Janet DeLaine, David Mattingly, Josephine Quinn, Judith McKenzie, Bruce Hitchner and Martin Sterry, all of whom, at some point, read all or part of this book, offering many helpful comments and criticisms. I also owe a debt of thanks to all the administrators and staff in the School of Archaeology, the Faculty of Classics and Corpus Christi College at the University of Oxford, where I was based when the majority of the research and writing for this book was completed. I would also like to thank all the members of the EAMENA project for being exemplary colleagues, and especially Robert Bewley, for being so supportive and flexible while I completed my research and studies.

How does one properly thank so many people, scattered all over the world, for their friendship? All the countless conversations, coffees, adventures, drinks, laughs and occasional tears over the last ten years and more that have led to this book have made my life infinitely better and I am grateful for every one of those experiences and people. Special thanks must go to Amanda Sharp, Erica Rowan, Julia Nikolaus, Roberta Ferritto, Tyler Franconi, Candace Rice, Maxine Anastasi, Andy Dufton, Ben Russell, Nick Ray, Louise Rayne, Lisa Fentress, Julia Stoskopf, Lisa Brownie, Jessica Foy, Amy Abbott, Erika Woods, Paul Scheding, Nicolas Lamare, Christoph Lehnert, Jeremy Rossiter, Pascal Flohr, Mike Fisher and Michael Fradley for all those things and more.

The final, but most important, acknowledgments must go to my family. My sister, Christine Sheldrick, has gone above and beyond as a constant source of love and support and advice, in the best and worst times. She and my wonderful brother-in-law, Daniel Tersigni, never fail to make me feel loved and welcome and at home whenever I visit, for which I am profoundly grateful.

And at last, to my parents, Barry and Joan Sheldrick, I simply owe everything. I can honestly say that anything and everything I have ever achieved has been made possible by their endless support and unwavering love. This book is for them.

A BRIEF NOTE ON ARABIC PLACE NAMES AND WORDS

Many of the place names used in this book are Arabic names, since in many instances we do not know their ancient names (if they had one). There is no single system of transliteration that is universally accepted, though historically, as a result of their respective colonial histories (see Chapter 2), French conventions are more often used in Tunisia and Italian in Libya. Where possible, I have tried to avoid using Arabic terminology, though I have retained a few common words, for example landforms such as wadi, *gebel*, etc., and have used standardised forms for these throughout. For specific place names, in the interest of consistency with previous publications and for ease of cross-reference, I have adopted the spellings of places as they are rendered in the primary and/or most well-known publications which refer to them and thus with which most readers are more likely to be familiar rather than conforming to a single system of transliteration.

chapter one

Introduction

The region of Tripolitania is well-known for its spectacular Roman-period architecture in both city and country. The enormous and elaborate temples, baths, *basilicae* and other public buildings of the coastal cities of *Lepcis Magna*, *Sabratha* and others, have, not undeservedly, captured the attention and imagination of travellers and scholars alike for centuries and are evidence of the rich culture and great wealth of these ancient cities.[1] The architecture and settlement of the countryside are different from that of the cities in many ways, but no less important. Although not on a scale to rival the size or richness of the architecture of the urban centres, the buildings of the countryside, including lavish coastal villas, towering *gsur*, forts and monumental mausolea are striking evidence of large numbers of people not only surviving, but thriving, in an often harsh, marginal environment, on the southern-most edges of the Roman Empire. However, a far larger proportion of rural buildings are not nearly so impressive, being of far simpler construction and with little extant decoration, making them very difficult or impossible to date without other forms of evidence. For these reasons and others, rural farm buildings, particularly the small, unremarkable ones, have not received the same attention as the larger, more impressive structures. Nevertheless, large or small, lavish or plain, like all material culture, architecture is the outcome of a series of deliberate choices shaped by the context in which it was constructed. The activities that take place within buildings and the uses that people assign to them, give them meaning.[2]

In this book, data on the architecture and construction of over 2,400 rural structures, primarily farm buildings, from across Tripolitania and dating between the first century BC and the seventh century AD are brought together for the first time and analysed on a regional scale. The main aims of this study are two. The first is to present an updated synthesis of existing architectural data collected from both previously published material and new surveys conducted using satellite imagery in a standardised catalogue, in order to facilitate region-wide comparisons and analyses of these buildings, both quantitative and qualitative. While Mattingly's 1995 monograph *Tripolitania* remains the most thorough overview of the region as a whole during the Roman period, it has been 25 years since its initial publication, and several new surveys have been undertaken since that time, particularly in Syrtica, in the immediate hinterlands of *Lepcis Magna*, and in southern Tunisia, which have now been incorporated into the present analyses. In addition, the increasing availability of free, high-resolution satellite imagery has made it possible to conduct new, remote surveys specifically for this study, adding hundreds of new sites to the catalogue, and demonstrating the enormous usefulness of satellite survey in North Africa.

[1] It is only possible here to indicate a few of the key publications of the last century which reflect the relative attention that has been paid to the major urban sites of the region: *Lepcis Magna*: Romanelli 1925; Bartoccini 1927a; 1929a; 1931; 1958; 1961; Townsend 1938; Aurigemma 1940; Degrassi 1951; Ward-Perkins 1951; Bianchi Bandinelli, Vergara Caffarelli, & Caputo 1966; Floriani Squarciapino 1966; 1974; Bakir 1968b; Humphrey, Sear, & Vickers 1973; 1974; Caputo 1987; Laronde 1988; 1994; Bacchielli 1991; Ward-Perkins *et al.* 1993; Pensabene 2003; De Miro & Polito 2005; Di Vita & Liviadotti 2005; Tomasello 2005; 2011; Musso 2008. *Sabratha*: Bartoccini 1927b; Caputo 1939; Pesce 1953; Caputo & Ghedini 1984; Joly & Tomasello 1984; Kenrick 1986; Tomasello 1992; Bonacasa & Bonacasa Carra 2003. *Oea*: Boni & Mariani 1915; Marelli 1933; Micacchi 1934; Caputo 1940; Aurigemma 1967; 1970; Arata 1996. *Gigthis*: Constans 1916; Ferchiou 1984; 1988. *Meninx*: Morton 2006; Fentress, Drine, & Holod 2009; Ritter & Ben Tahar 2020. *General*: Aurigemma 1915; Bartoccini 1926; Guidi 1931; 1935; Haynes 1946; 1955; Di Vita 1966; 1983; 1990; 1992; Ward-Perkins 1968; Pensabene 1988; 1990; 2001; Bullo 2002; Masturzo 2003; Sears 2007; 2011; Kenrick 2009.

[2] On meaningful architecture, material culture, and identity: Preziosi 1979; Hillier & Hanson 1984; Trigger 1990: 126–129; Kent 1994; Locock 1994; Graves-Brown 1996: 90–91; Graves-Brown, Jones, & Gamble 1996; Holtorf 1997: 55; Bradley 1998: 71; Dobres & Robb 2000; Fentress 2000; Mattingly 2004: 22; Díaz-Andreu *et al.* 2005; Gosden 2005: 196–197; Hingley 2005: 74; Whyte 2006; Peña 2007: 1; Roth 2007: 59–61; Roth & Keller 2007; Wallace-Hadrill 2008: 9; Dietler 2010: 55–57; Hales & Hodos 2010; Mattingly 2011; Moore 2012.

The second aim of this book is to use the collected data to assess the development and significance of the main types of rural buildings which were constructed and used in Tripolitania during the period under study. Previous investigations in Tripolitania's countryside have typically focussed on either the impact of the Roman army on rural settlement and the development of the *limes*[3] or on settlement patterns and economic activities, particularly the production of olive oil and wine.[4] While many surveys have recorded and discussed to a greater or lesser extent the buildings of which these sites and settlements were composed, few have specifically focussed on them as meaningful in their own right[5] and many important questions about the construction, development, use and socio-cultural significance of rural buildings in this region remain insufficiently addressed or completely unanswered. How and why were buildings in different parts of rural Tripolitania similar or different? When and why were certain architectural forms and technologies adopted in different parts of the region? To what extent can these forms be explained by socio-cultural, functional, economic or environmental factors? By placing the focus on the structures themselves, this book will add a new dimension to our understanding of the role of farm buildings and other structures in the rural landscape and perhaps even the lives of the people who built and inhabited them.

To these ends, in this book, brief introductions to the geographical and historical context are followed in Chapter 2 by a summary of previous work that has been undertaken in rural Tripolitania, as well as the role that satellite imagery has now begun to play in rural investigations. Indigenous forms of architecture which were important before, during, and probably also after the main period under study are discussed in Chapter 3, followed by a summary of the state of our knowledge around the chronological development of rural settlement in Tripolitania, and a critical discussion of some of the issues associated with relying on survey data and ceramics to date buildings and settlement. Chapter 4 provides an overview of the evidence for Roman military buildings in Tripolitania and offers a new typology for them. Chapters 5 and 6 focus on the evidence for unfortified and fortified farm buildings, respectively, presenting quantitative analyses of the form, size and other aspects of the buildings for nine different geographical regions of rural Tripolitania, followed by discussions of the patterns observed. Further analyses of the interrelationships between the individual farm buildings in terms of patterns of settlement, as well as briefly introducing and discussing how other types of rural buildings which were often associated with the farms, such as tombs, temples, churches, enclosures, wadi walls, etc., fit into this picture are also offered. Finally, Chapter 7 offers a summary of the main findings of the preceding chapters and how this study fits into our wider understanding of Tripolitania, North Africa, and the Mediterranean during the Roman and Late Antique periods.

1.1 Regional Boundaries

Geographically speaking, ancient Tripolitania can be defined as the region of North Africa which lies between the gulfs of the Greater and Lesser Syrtes. Today, the larger part of the region falls within the boundaries of modern Libya, comprising the nine northwestern districts, which together are still known as Tripolitania. The remaining western portion of the region comprises the four southernmost governorates of modern Tunisia.

It would be misleading to speak of strict regional borders in the modern sense for ancient Tripolitania, but geographical, historical and archaeological evidence provides us with reasonable limits (Figure 1.1). In the west, Tripolitania is largely bounded by natural, geographical features. The Chotts Djerid and Fedjedj (large seasonal lakes/salt flats) along with the high hills of the Gebels Tebaga and Cherb, between Gabès (*Tacape*) and Telmine (*Turris Tamalleni*) create a natural barrier in the northwest part of the region which would have restricted movement between Tripolitania and the rest of western North Africa in ancient times.[6] From here, the western edge of the region runs more or less directly southwards, along the eastern boundary of the Great Eastern Erg, a vast sand sea, as far as the oasis of Ghadames (*Cidamus*), which marks the southwestern corner of my study area.

In the east, there are no obvious natural barriers, but various ancient sources explicitly identify the site of *Arae Philaenorum* as either the eastern limit of Roman Africa or the western limit of Cyrenaica.[7] According to Sallust and later writers, its name refers to the story of the two Carthaginian brothers who sacrificed their lives to secure the border between Carthaginian and Cyrenaean territories, though the origins of this story

[3] For example, Goodchild & Ward-Perkins 1949; Goodchild 1950b; 1951c; Rebuffat, Deneauve & Hallier 1967; Rebuffat *et al.* 1969; Rebuffat 1970b; 1975a; 1977a; 1989; Euzennat 1972; 1973; 1977; 1985; Trousset 1974; Mackensen 2008; 2009; 2010b; 2010a; 2011b; 2011a; 2012. See also Sections 2.1–2.2.

[4] For example, Oates 1953; Reddé 1985; 1988; Rebuffat 1985; 1988; Mattingly 1985b; 1988c; 1988a; 1995; 1996b; Barker 1996c; Longerstay 1999; 2003; Ahmed 2010; LeQuesne, Basell, & Sheibani 2010; Hobson 2012. See also Sections 2.1–2.2.

[5] A few exceptions include: Brogan & Smith 1984; Brouquier-Reddé 1992; Welsby 1992; Cività 1994.

[6] Trousset 1982; Mattingly 1995: 6–7.

[7] Polybius, *Histories*, 10.40.7; Pomponius Mela, *de Chorographia*, 1.33, 38; *Itinerarium Antonini* 65.6; Ptolemy, *Geography*, 4.3.14, 4.4.3; *Stadiasmus Maris Magni* 84; *Tabula Peutingeria* 7.2 (Bosio 1983: 115–116). Though cf. Pliny (*Natural History* 5.28–29), who placed the western border of Cyrenaica further northeast at *Borion* (modern Ras Taiunes, 23.5 km south of Benghazi) (Goodchild 1951a: 11).

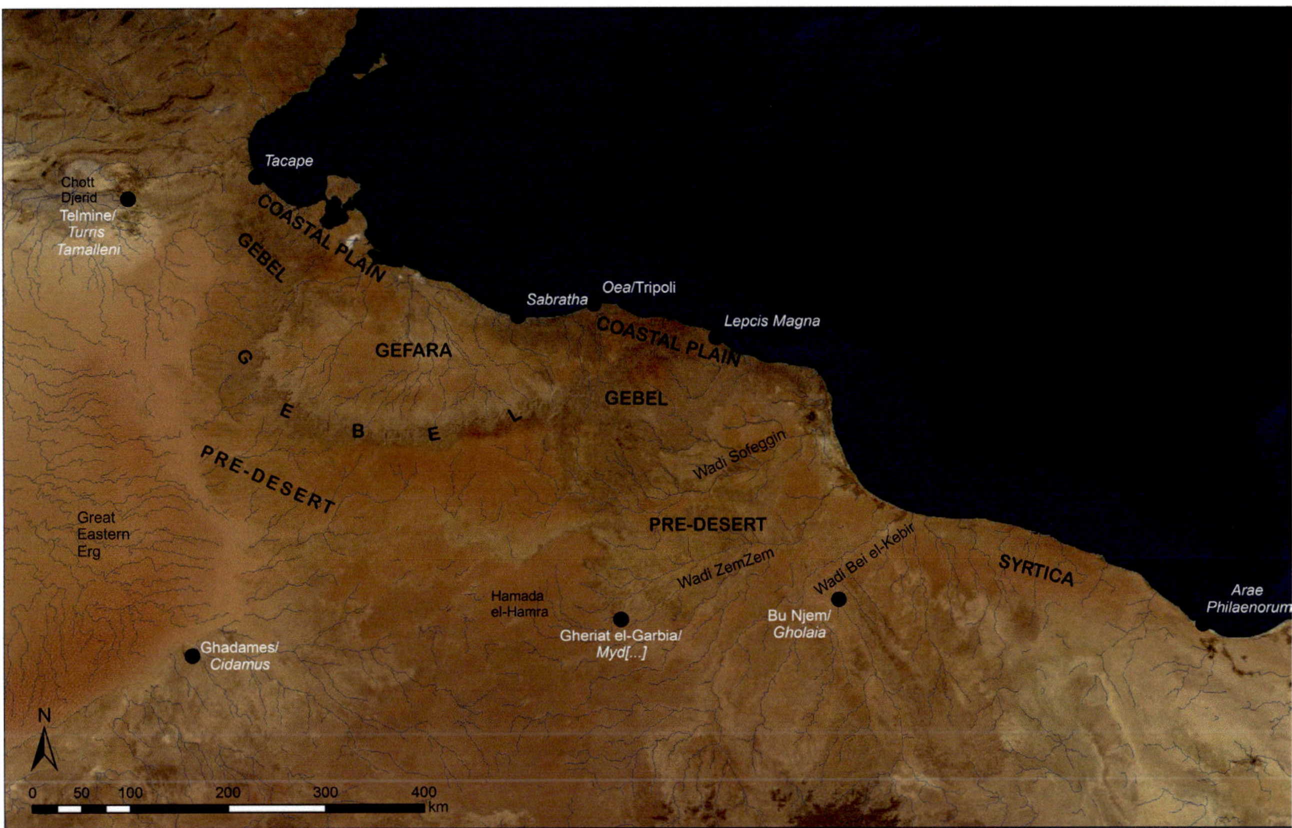

Basemap: Esri, DigitalGlobe, GeoEye, i-cubed, USDA, USGS, AEX, Getmapping, Aerogrid, IGN, IGP, swisstopo, and the GIS User Community
Drainage: Lehner, B., Verdin, K., Jarvis, A. (2008): New global hydrography derived from spaceborne elevation data. Eos, Transactions, AGU, 89(10): 93-94. Retrieved from http://hydrosheds.cr.usgs.gov (15 sec Flow Accumulation)

Figure 1.1: *Approximate limits and main geographic features of ancient Tripolitania.*

and how it came to be attached to this particular site are slightly obscure.[8] *Arae Philaenorum* was identified by Goodchild in the 1950s with modern Graret Gser et-Trab, approximately 6 km inland from Ras el-Aáli.[9] The remains of four columns which originally supported statues, and bearing two fragmentary inscriptions, one of which included the name of Diocletian, have been interpreted by Goodchild as a monument to the tetrarchs marking the eastern boundary of the Roman province.[10]

The southern limits of my project can therefore be drawn as a more or less straight line from the oasis of Ghadames (*Cidamus*) to *Arae Philaenorum*, running just south of the Severan oasis forts at Gheriat el-Garbia/*Myd[...]* and Bu Njem/*Gholaia*. However, not insignificantly, between these two areas lies the Hamada el-Hamra, a high, inhospitable rock desert whose north edge is marked by a number of steep cliffs. This natural feature projects well northwards into Tripolitania, effectively making permanent settlement impossible in this part of the region.

1.2 Climate and Environment

Within the boundaries described above, Tripolitania was, and is, a geographically and environmentally diverse region, which can be divided into several different zones. The Mediterranean coast of Tripolitania stretches around 1,000 km between the Greater and Lesser Syrtes. Much of the coastal plain is basically desert, especially in the eastern part of the region, but there are a number of fertile coastal oases, in particular around *Lepcis Magna* and Tripoli (*Oea*). The *gebel*, a series of mountain ranges, forms a broad arc from *Lepcis Magna* towards *Tacape*, surrounding a wide, semi-circular area of the coastal plain, known as the Gefara Plain. Much of the eastern part of the *gebel*, particularly in the Tarhuna region south and west of *Lepcis* was, and still is, agriculturally productive and, besides the oases which support large stands of date palms, this is the only area which seems to have had significant tree cover in the Roman period (though it has been largely deforested since). South of the *gebel*,

[8]Sallust, *Bellum Iugurthinum*, 79.1–10; Valerius Maximus, 5.6; Pomponius Mela, *de Chorographia*, 1.38–39. Cf. Quinn (2014), who argues that the story had Carthaginian origins, with earlier assertions of Malkin (1990) and Ribichini (1991) that the myth was Greek.

[9]Goodchild 1951a: 16; Goodchild 1952. See also Abitino 1979.

[10]Goodchild 1952: 101–102.

the pre-desert begins and gradually transitions into the Sahara Desert proper. While the transition to desert is relatively swift in the southwest, the region southeast of the *gebel* is largely characterised by broad, relatively flat plateaux (hamadas) which are cut by extensive wadi systems (seasonal watercourses), the most substantial of which are the Wadis Sofeggin, ZemZem and Bei el-Kebir. The main channels of the wadis are fed by numerous tributaries and drain north or northeastwards, sometimes collecting in large sebkhas (salt flats) near the coast, before flowing out to sea. Finally, to the east, the region of Syrtica is mostly desert, except for a narrow, fertile strip along the coast and the smaller wadi systems which drain northwards out to sea. South of Tripolitania is the true Sahara and the region of Fazzan, inhabitable only in a few clusters of oases.[11]

Though as noted, there were a number of important agriculturally-productive areas near the coast and in the eastern *gebel*, on the whole, much of Tripolitania is pre-desert or desert. The limit for dry-farming (i.e. without the aid of irrigation) is around 200 mm of rain per year. While the southern limits of the African provinces to the northwest of Tripolitania rarely fall below the 400 mm line, only a few small areas of the northern edge of Tripolitania in the region of *Lepcis Magna* and *Oea* and in the *gebel* receive over 300 mm of rain per year and the amount decreases rapidly as one moves southwards (though it should be borne in mind that the averages disguise very wide and erratic variations).[12] Nevertheless, evidence for settlement and agricultural production, including olive presses, in Tripolitania during the Roman period, is found in areas with as little as 100 mm. However, while smaller fluctuations certainly occurred, studies undertaken by the *ULVS* showed that the climate of Tripolitania has been relatively constant for the last 4,000 years, effectively ruling out climate change as a determining factor in changing settlement and land use patterns during that time.[13]

1.3 Historical Context and Human Geography

My investigation focuses mainly on the period between the later first century BC and the mid-seventh century AD, but, of course, there was a long and complex history of settlement and occupation in Tripolitania before this time.[14] Lithic scatters, rock art and other archaeological evidence attest to the presence of people in what is now modern Libya for tens of thousands of years. These early peoples were probably hunter-fisher-gatherers, and after the fifth millennium BC, pastoralists.[15] By the early first millennium BC, archaeological evidence suggests that in addition to continuing to practise pastoralism, the *Garamantes* of Fazzan to the south were also beginning to adopt agriculture, centred around large hilltop settlements.[16] Similar hilltop settlements, potentially dating to the same period, are also known in Tripolitania,[17] but these have been less thoroughly investigated, and transhumant pastoralism seems to have remained the chief mode of life for most its rural inhabitants until the later first millennium BC.[18]

The three coastal cities for which Tripolitania was eventually named – *Lepcis Magna*, *Oea* and *Sabratha* – were settled by Phoenicians by the fifth century BC, and in the case of *Lepcis*, possibly as far as back as the seventh century BC.[19] These port settlements were almost certainly part of the territory controlled by Carthage around the Lesser Syrte, collectively known as the *emporia* and may have paid tribute to that city.[20] They later passed into the hands of the Numidian Kingdom,[21] but it is debatable how much direct influence either of these empires actually had on the lives of the majority of Tripolitania's inhabitants. The Libyan origins of the town names and the later descriptions of the peoples inhabiting them as *Libyphoenices*, not simply Phoenician or Punic, suggest that a strong indigenous component of the population was maintained on the coast and the immediate hinterlands of the cities.[22]

---

[11] *Handbook of Libya* 1920: 10–14; Hornby 1945; Haynes 1955: 13–17; Mattingly 1995: 5–11; Barker 1996c: 4–7.

[12] Mattingly 1995: 7–11.

[13] Gilbertson 1996.

[14] For more in depth historical accounts of the region: *Tripolitania*: Haynes 1955; Di Vita 1982; Sjöström 1993; Mattingly 1995. *North Africa*: Gsell 1921; Romanelli 1970; Fage 1978; Law 1978; MacKendrick 1980; Clark 1982; Raven 1984; Bullo 2002; Le Bohec 2005.

[15] *Prehistoric Libya*: McBurney 1960; 1967; Barker 1981; 1989; 1996c: 83–109; LeQuesne, Basell, & Sheibani 2010. *Rock Art*: Graziosi 1942; Mori 1965; Barker 1986; Muzzolini 1986; Le Quellec 1987; Barnett 2002; 2005; 2006; 2009. See also di Lernia 2013; Mitchell & Lane 2013.

[16] Mattingly 1995: 34–37; Mattingly 2003b.

[17] See Section 3.1.2.

[18] Gilman 1974: 281; Barker 1981: 137; 1989: 39–41; 1996b: 103–109; Lemak 2006: 31–47.

[19] *Lepcis*: Howard Carter 1965; De Miro & Polito 2005: 121–127. *Sabratha*: Kenrick 1986: 125, 137, 312. *Oea*: Bakir 1968a: 199–200.

[20] Herodotus, *Histories*, 5.42; Pseudo-Skylax, *Periplous*, 110.1; Polybius, *Histories*, 3.22–24; Livy, *History of Rome*, 34.62.3; Di Vita 1968: 11–15; Rebuffat 1990b; Ganci 1995; Lancel 1995: 91–94.

[21] Polybius, *Histories*, 31.21; Livy, *History of Rome*, 29.33.8–9, 34.62.1–18; Kotula 1974.

[22] Mattingly 1995: 50. *Libyphoenices*: Diodorus Siculus, *Bibliotheca Historica*, 20.55.4; Livy, *History of Rome*, 21.22; Strabo, *Geography*, 17.3.19; Pliny, *Natural History*, 5.24; Ptolemy, *Geography*, 4.3.6.

After the fall of Carthage in 146 BC, Rome's involvement and influence in North Africa was growing.[23] During the Jugurthine War of the late second century BC, *Lepcis* formed an alliance with Rome but the cities themselves and the region as a whole seem to have been more or less independent.[24] Sometime between 40 and 36 BC, following Caesar's victory in the Civil Wars and his imposition of a fine on *Lepcis Magna* for having supported Pompey,[25] the province of *Africa Proconsularis* was formed, uniting and extending the former provinces of *Africa Vetus* and *Africa Nova*.[26] While the coastal centres maintained a degree of independence and it is unclear when Tripolitania was officially incorporated into the province, the cities were effectively subject to Rome after this time.[27] This was not entirely the case, however, beyond the coast and the now-settled immediate hinterlands around the cities; in many parts of Tripolitania's interior, there still appears to have been considerable unrest throughout the Augustan and Julio-Claudian periods.[28]

Unlike other parts of North Africa, which began to see the arrival of immigrant settlers in the Roman period, there is no evidence to support the idea of substantial numbers of settlers immigrating to Tripolitania during this time.[29] The main population of both the coast and the interior of Tripolitania were almost certainly the same Libyphoenician and indigenous Libyan peoples as had already been living there for centuries. The names of a number of the indigenous peoples of North Africa and Tripolitania have come down to us from various ancient sources.[30] However, modern attempts to untangle these often problematic and contradictory accounts and map the territories of the various groups have made it clear that we cannot rely on the accuracy of the geographical descriptions,[31] and their value often lies more in revealing the outside prejudices and opinions of the region and its peoples, rather than factual descriptions.

Ethnographic comparison with the society of the modern descendants of ancient North African peoples, suggests that by the first century BC, indigenous Libyan societies probably operated on a hierarchical 'segmented structure', in which larger tribes or even tribal confederations were broken down into increasingly smaller units such as sub-tribes, clans and families. All of these could have different names, which has only further complicated the confusing and conflicting accounts of the sources above.[32] Nevertheless, repeated references to certain groups combined with archaeological evidence, including references to some of these tribes in epigraphic sources,[33] make it clear that neither can we entirely dismiss these accounts.

Keeping these issues in mind, the major groups active in Tripolitania in the early to mid-Roman periods and the period immediately preceding, seem to have been the *Gaetuli*, *Macae* and *Nasamones*. The *Gaetuli* were, according to Strabo, the largest of the Libyan tribes, though as Mattingly points out, they were probably never united as a single kingdom or confederation. Rather, the term probably referred to a relatively disparate and widespread group of communities, with people who were called *Gaetuli* located in various places across the North African interior from Tripolitania westwards to *Mauretania* (modern western Algeria and Morocco); to what extent they were all related is unclear. Confirming their presence in Tripolitania is the fact that the *Gaetuli* peoples were placed specifically in the region of the Syrtes by various authors.[34]

The *Macae* (or *Maces*) occupied a large territory in the central and eastern parts of Tripolitania, probably covering much of the eastern *gebel*, pre-desert and Syrtica.[35] If Herodotus is to be believed, the *Macae* were already established and exerted a certain amount of influence in central Tripolitania in the sixth century BC, having aided in the eviction of a Greek attempt at settlement in the area of the River *Cinyps* (Wadi Caam),

[23] Though it is now doubtful whether this involved the immediate and formal creation of an African province (Quinn 2004).

[24] Sallust, *Bellum Iugurthinum*, 77.2; Di Vita 1982: 520–529.

[25] Caesar, *Bellum Africum*, 97.3; Plutarch, *Life of Caesar*, 55.

[26] *Res Gestae* 25; Strabo, *Geography*, 17.3.25; Suetonius, *Augustus*, 47; Dio, *Roman History*, 53.12. Fishwick & Shaw 1977; Fishwick 1993; 1994. Though cf. Gascou (1984, 1987) who places the creation of *Proconsularis* in 27 BC.

[27] Pliny, *Natural History*, 5.29.

[28] *Cornelius Balbus against the Garamantes* (19 BC): Pliny, *Natural History*, 5.35–37. *Murder of proconsul by Nasamones* (3 BC): Desanges 1969. *Gaetulian War* (AD 3–6): *IRT* 301; Florus, *Epitome*, 2.31, Dio, *Roman History*, 55.28.3–4. *Tacfarinan War* (AD 17-24): Tacitus, *Annals*, 2.52, 3.20–21, 3.32, 3.73–74, 4.23–25. *Campaigns against the Garamantes and Nasamones* (c. AD 69–92): Pliny, *Natural History*, 5.35–38, Tacitus, *Histories*, 4.50; Ptolemy, *Geography*, 1.8, 1.10, 1.19; Dio, *Roman History*, 77.3.5. See also Mattingly 1995: 68–77; 2003b: 76–86; Wilson 2017.

[29] Thompson 1968; Rebuffat 1982: 196–199; Mattingly 1987; 1995: 160–170; Mattingly 1996a.

[30] For example, Herodotus (*Histories*, 4.168–199), Pseudo-Skylax (*Periplous*, 107–111), Diodorus Siculus (*Bibliotheca Historica*, 3.49–55), Strabo (*Geography*, 17.3.1–23), Pliny the Elder (*Natural History*, 5.1.1–8.46), Ptolemy of Alexandria (*Geography*, 4.3–6), and Corippus (*Iohannes*). See also Mattingly 1995: 26–28, Table 2:3 and fn. 31, below.

[31] See in particular: Bates 1914: esp. 39–72; Desanges 1962; Brogan 1975a; Mattingly 1995: 17–49; Rebuffat 2006.

[32] Mattingly 1992: esp. 32–35; 1995: 17–49.

[33] For example, the inscription found near modern Sirte recording the establishment of a formal boundary between the lands of the *Muducivvi* and the *Zamucii* (AD 87; *IRT* 854) or the Greek inscription found in Cyrenaica which records the dedication of five Cyrenaean *strategoi* for a victory over the *Macae* and the *Nasamones* (4th–3rd c. BC; Oliverio 1936: 160 no. 141; *SEG* 9.77, 26.1831, 29.1673, 38.1892; Laronde 1987: 52–53, 199).

[34] Strabo, *Geography*, 17.3.2, 17.3.19; Florus, *Epitome*, 2.31; Virgil, *Aeneid*, 5.192; Mattingly 1995: 29–32; Trousset 2002; Callegarin 2009; Moreau 2009.

[35] Rebuffat 1988; 2006; Mattingly 1995: 32–33.

not far from *Lepcis Magna*.[36] The *Macae* were also later associated with this feature, located just to the east of *Lepcis Magna*, as well as with the shores of the Greater Syrte.[37] To the east of the *Macae* was the territory of the *Nasamones*, who were chiefly located in Cyrenaica with an important centre at the oasis of Augila, but whose territory also overlapped westwards into Syrtica, with ancient authors also associating them with the Greater Syrte, like their neighbours to the west.[38]

To the south lay another important group, the *Garamantes*, whose independent kingdom was based in a series of oases in the region of Fazzan. Although this area is beyond the limits of ancient Tripolitania as defined for this study, the *Garamantes* were also certainly an active presence in the region until at least the first century AD and beyond.[39] While their power and sphere of influence in Tripolitania was probably reduced during the Roman period, communication and trade almost certainly continued between the *Garamantes* and the areas to the north and the routes by which this occurred must have cut directly through the eastern pre-desert and Syrtica.[40]

It was only after a series of campaigns during the late first century BC and first century AD against many of these peoples, that a comparative peace was achieved in the interior of the region, the last of which were major actions against the *Garamantes* and *Nasamones* in the wake of the civil war between *Lepcis* and *Oea*.[41] While the evidence suggests that sedentary, agricultural settlement had already been established in the immediate hinterlands of the coastal cities by the first century BC, it is not until the later first century AD that evidence begins to appear for substantial change in the settlement and subsistence strategies of the peoples living further inland, in the pre-desert and Syrtica, which would continue into the following centuries.[42]

During the second century AD, the urban coastal settlements of Tripolitania were prospering, with *Lepcis Magna*, *Oea*, *Sabratha* and *Tacape* all certainly or probably being promoted to the rank of colonia, and the tradition of monumental building which had begun in the previous century continuing to thrive.[43] This period also appears to have been relatively peaceful, but nevertheless, a permanent military presence was being established on the frontiers to monitor and guard major routes from the coast into the interior. The major fort at Remada/*Tillibari* is thought to date to the mid-second century AD in its earliest phase, and a number of other sites have yielded probable evidence for military occupation in this period and possibly even earlier.[44]

Monumental building activity in the coastal cities, particularly *Lepcis Magna*, reached its pinnacle in the late second and early third century AD, when Septimius Severus, a native of *Lepcis*, became emperor.[45] It was also during this time that the major forts at Bu Njem/*Gholaia* and Gheriat el-Garbia/*Myd[...]*, as well as a number of smaller military installations, were constructed.[46] These projects are often seen as having been part of a reorganisation of the frontier under Severus, perhaps connected to renewed trouble from local tribes, who were described in the *Life of Severus* as very war-like (*bellicosissimus*).[47] It is also around this time that the distinctive fortified farm buildings (*gsur*) of the pre-desert begin to emerge, and while the timing and their appearance suggests that there is a connection between the two, the nature of the relationship remains one of the important questions still open for debate.[48]

In the late third or early fourth century AD, Diocletian's reorganisation of the provinces resulted in the creation of the *provinicia Tripolitana*, with its capital at *Lepcis Magna*.[49] While the cities continued to be occupied and a certain number of building projects were undertaken during these periods, including fortification walls at some of the cities, they were not on the scale of the previous centuries. In addition, a major earthquake in the 360s, and possibly another some 50 years earlier

---

[36] Herodotus, *Histories*, 5.42.

[37] Silius Italicus, *Punica*, 2.60, 3.275; Diodorus Siculus, *Bibliotheca Historica*, 3.49; Herodotus, *Histories*, 4.175.

[38] Herodotus, *Histories*, 4.172–173; Lucan, *Bellum Civile*, 339–341; Mattingly 1995: 33.

[39] See for example, the *Garamantes*' involvement in the conflict between *Lepcis* and *Oea* in AD 69: Tacitus, *Histories*, 4.50; Mattingly 1995: 71–72.

[40] Ayoub 1967: 1–11, 27–48; Fontana 1995; Mattingly 1995: 36–37; 2003b: 355–362; 2010: 526–530 *et passim*; 2013; Liverani 2005b; Wilson 2012b; 2017. See also Mattingly *et al.* 2017.

[41] See fn. 28.

[42] See Section 3.2, Chapter 5.

[43] See for example, the aqueduct and Hadrianic Baths at *Lepcis* (*IRT* 357–358, 361), the Arch of Marcus Aurelius and Lucius Verus at *Oea* (*IRT* 232–233), the Antonine Temple at *Sabratha* (*IRT* 21), etc.

[44] See Chapter 4. Remada/*Tillibari*: Euzennat 1973; Euzennat & Trousset 1978; Trousset 1974: 114–118; Mattingly 1995: 90–92. See also Mattingly 1989: 137–139; 1995: 77ff; Trousset 2002.

[45] See for example, the Severan forum, arch, and basilica at *Lepcis Magna*: Ward-Perkins *et al.* 1993

[46] See Chapter 4.

[47] *Historia Augusta, Life of Severus*, 18.3; Di Vita 1966: 107–111; Mattingly 1995: 80–82; Guédon 2018: 115ff.

[48] See Section 3.2, Chapter 6.

[49] Chastagnol 1967; Di Vita-Evrard 1984; Mattingly 1995: 171–173. Epigraphic evidence starting in the early 3rd c. AD, does attest to the existence of a *regio Tripolitana* before this time, though its political and administrative significance are less certain (Di Vita-Evrard 1985; Mattingly 1995: 54–55).

caused serious destruction, from which they were not able to fully recover.[50] Nevertheless, while the coastal urban settlements were experiencing a degree of economic, and probably physical, decline, along with their immediate hinterlands, survey evidence suggests that the fourth century AD was actually the peak of fortified settlement in some areas further from the coast and it is possible that the economic decline of the countryside was not quite so quick or dramatic in all places.[51]

Beginning in the fourth century AD are references to a group known as the *Arzuges*, based in the western part of Tripolitania.[52] The name appears on a boundary stone dated to the reign of Trajan found on the western *limes*, presumably referring to a specific group of people,[53] though by the fourth century AD its meaning seems to have expanded to include all of the peoples living in what is now southern Tunisia, both in the coastal urban centres and in the interior.[54] By this time, the region seems to have become a separate entity from *Tripolitana* known as the *regio Arzugum*, with Modéran arguing that it had actually now become part of the province of *Byzacena*.[55]

Around the same time, tribal unrest began anew across Tripolitania. Though an early uprising was perhaps initially subdued by the emperor Maximian in the last years of the third century AD, this marked the beginning of a serious threat to the peace.[56] A number of new groups, or, at least partially, the same peoples discussed above but organised into new confederations and with new names, begin to appear in the ancient sources. One such group, the *Austuriani*, made a number of serious incursions into Tripolitania, probably from the southern oases, ravaging the regions around *Lepcis Magna* and *Oea*, in the second half of the fourth and early fifth centuries AD.[57] References to a group known as the *Laguatan* (or sometimes *Ilaguas*, *Leuathae* or *Lawata*) also begin to appear frequently in later texts.[58] It now seems likely that the *Austuriani* were, in fact, in some way related to the *Laguatan*, and while they are clearly identified as a sub-group of the latter by Corippus in the sixth century AD, their relationship between the two is not entirely clear for earlier periods.[59]

By the mid-fifth century AD, the Vandals had gained control over much of Africa, with Tripolitania coming under their rule, at least nominally, in AD 455.[60] However, by this time, the peoples of the interior, now sometimes collectively referred to in contemporary sources as *Mauri* (Moors), were becoming more and more independent and less subject to control from the coast, particularly in the eastern part of the region, and the Vandals had to be content to let the situation stand.[61] Procopius relates an incident in which the *Laguatan* (who he identifies as Moors), had "overpowered the Vandals...and made Leptis Magna entirely empty of inhabitants".[62] After their re-conquest of North Africa in AD 533, the Byzantines continued this policy and kept the peace with the *Laguatan* in the east through diplomacy. However, after a series of problematic incidents, the peace was ultimately destroyed by the massacre of 79 *Laguatan* chiefs which sparked a massive revolt, quelled only with great difficulty.[63] Another century later, the Arab invasions had begun and by the mid-seventh century AD a new era of Tripolitania's history was underway.[64]

1.4 Urban Settlement

This book is concerned mainly with the buildings and settlement of the countryside, which I will define simply as those areas outside Tripolitania's cities and towns and their immediate periphery, though the value of attempting to create a strict dichotomy between urban and rural has rightly been questioned in recent scholarship.[65]

[50] Goodchild & Ward-Perkins 1953; Di Vita 1990; Mattingly 1995: 178–185; Sears 2007: 70–77, *et passim*; Leone 2007: 51, 119–120; 2013: 103–107.

[51] See Section 3.2, Chapter 6. Brogan 1977: 126; Mattingly 1995: 202–209, 214–215; Barker 1996: 328–331.

[52] For example, St Augustine, *Letters*, 46.

[53] *CIL* 8.22763; Modéran 2003: 364.

[54] Goodchild 1950: 30–31; Mattingly 1995: 175–176; Rushworth 2004; Felici, Munzi, & Tantillo 2006; Trousset 2011.

[55] Modéran 2003: 364–373, though cf. Orosius (*Historiae*, 1.2.90) who suggests that all the peoples along the African *limites* could be called *Arzuges*.

[56] Corippus, *Iohannes*, 1.480–482, 5.178–180, 7.530–533; Procopius, *de Bellis*, 4.21–22.

[57] Ammianus Marcellinus, *Res Gestae*, 26.4.5, 28.6.1–5, 10–14; *IRT* 480; Fentress & Wilson 2016.

[58] Corippus, *Iohannes*, 1.144, 1.478–480, 5.178–180, 7.530–533; Ammianus Marcellinus, *Res Gestae*, 26.4.5, 28.6.1–5, 10-14; Procopius, *de Bellis*, 4.21–22; Reynolds 1977; Mattingly 1983; Modéran 2003: 289–310, *et passim*; Felici, Munzi, & Tantillo 2006. In particular, compare Mattingly's (1983) argument for a wide *Laguatan* confederation which eventually incorporated most of the pre-desert peoples, with Modéran's (2003: 302–310) rejection of this idea; see also Fentress & Wilson 2016.

[59] Corippus, *Iohannes*, 2.345: *Austur... seu gentis Ilaguas*; Mattingly 1983; Modéran 2003: 165–172, *et passim*.

[60] Courtois 1955; Jones 1968; Pringle 1981: 1–44; Raven 1984: 207–243; Brogan & Smith 1984: 231–232; Trousset 1985; Sjöström 1993: 35–42; Leone & Mattingly 2004; Merrills 2004; Dossey 2010; Merrills & Miles 2010; Conant 2012.

[61] Mattingly 1983: 98; Modéran 2003: 541–554; Conant 2012: 252–305.

[62] Procopius, *On Buildings*, 6.4.6 (Translation H.B. Dewing, 1940, Loeb Classical Library 343).

[63] Procopius, *de Bellis*, 4.21.5–22; Mattingly 1983: 99; Modéran 2003: 565ff; Conant 2012: 298.

[64] Brett 1978; Christides 2000; Modéran 2003; Kaegi 2010; Conant 2012: 362–370.

[65] For example, Horden & Purcell 2001: 89–122; Goodman 2007; Morley 2011.

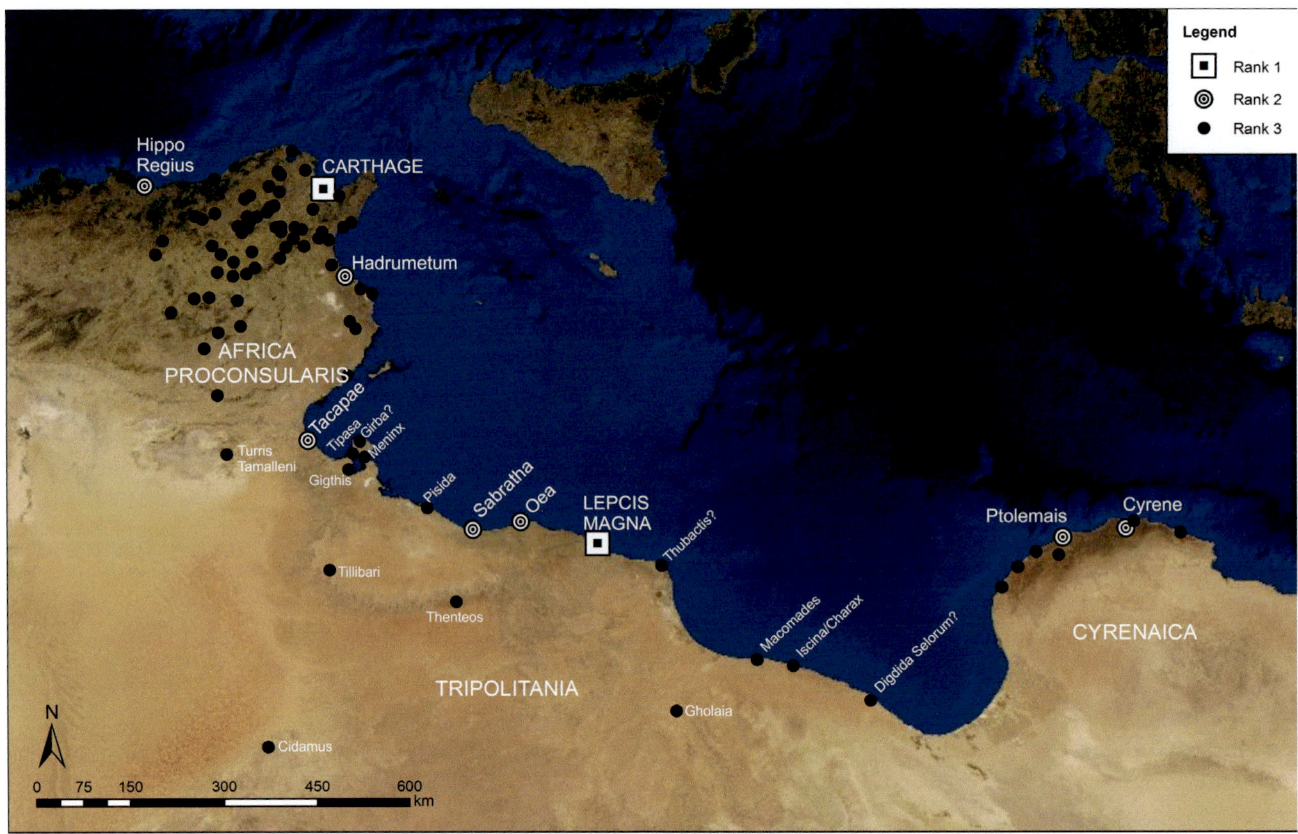

Figure 1.2: *Distribution and density of urban settlements in* Africa Proconsularis, *Tripolitania, and Cyrenaica, after the* Barrington Atlas *(Talbert 2000).*

Nevertheless, it will be useful to briefly discuss the distribution and density of the urban settlements in Tripolitania, which differed greatly from neighbouring areas.

A convenient place to start is the *Barrington Atlas of the Greek and Roman World*, which organises settlements into five size categories based on a combination of factors including population, size, rank and significance in terms of commercial, religious or other cultural features, the top three of which I will consider to have been 'urban'.[66] Although there is bound to be a degree of arbitrariness in such a system (a fact openly acknowledged by the creators), and the usefulness of these maps to assess chronological change is very limited,[67] we can use the *Barrington Atlas* as a base to establish broad trends in the distribution and density of urban settlement.

Only one site in Tripolitania, *Lepcis Magna*, achieves the highest settlement rank, while there are three of Rank 2 (*Oea*, *Sabratha* and *Tacape*). A further 15 sites can be called small to mid-sized towns or settlements (Rank 3). Of these 19 total urban sites, 14 (74%) are in coastal locations. If we compare these data to that of the rest of the province of *Africa Proconsularis* to the north and west and to *Cyrenaica* to the east, the differences in the range of small to mid-sized settlements are striking (Figure 1.2; Appendix Table 1).

There are 63 sites which fall into the small to mid-sized settlement category in the region of *Africa Proconsularis*. The disparity between Tripolitania and *Africa Proconsularis* in this regard is even more apparent when we consider that the land area of the former is more than twice that of the latter. Coincidentally, *Africa Proconsularis* has the same number of sites which can be considered coastal as Tripolitania (n=14), but in this case, this only accounts for 22% of the settlements, the rest being situated inland. The distribution and density of urban settlement in Cyrenaica is more similar to that of Tripolitania, with few mid-sized settlements and virtually none located much distance from the coast. However, the predominance of the fertile and forested Gebel Akhdar in the topography and the region's close relationship with the eastern,

[66] Talbert 2000: xxv. Cf. Hanson (2011: 236–237) who defines the Barrington Atlas sizes thus: "Rank 5 represents isolated villas, farms, baths, or hamlets, rank 4 small villages, ranks 2 and 3 towns and cities, and rank 1 extremely large cities".

[67] Talbert 2000: xxiii–xxvi. See also the following review which outlines a number of drawbacks and concerns of the data and presentation: Alcock, Dey, & Parker 2001.

Greek world made Cyrenaica a very different place from both Tripolitania and *Africa Proconsularis*. These general trends in urban settlement were also confirmed by Wilson in a study of population sizes in the Roman Empire. He identified 56 cities of North Africa which he estimated to have populations of over 5,000 people in the mid-second century AD. Five of these were located in Tripolitania and four in Cyrenaica, all located on (or near) the coast, while 30 were found in *Africa Proconsularis*, again distributed throughout the region.[68]

There are a number of factors which may have contributed to this low density of urban settlements in Tripolitania. As already discussed above, *Lepcis Magna*, *Oea* and *Sabratha* were all of Punic foundation, as was *Meninx* and perhaps also some of the other coastal settlements. Thus, one factor suggested by Mattingly was that the pre-Roman, Libyphoenician communities established on the coast were, if not already urban centres, of a type and organisation that had made the transition to that status relatively straightforward. Conversely, the contemporary social and economic systems of the indigenous peoples in the interior of Tripolitania were perhaps less compatible.[69] He also theorises that smaller settlements were prevented from becoming larger and more successful on account of the major cities wanting, and being allowed, to maintain a monopoly on their power over wide territories.[70] While this may have been the case, as Wilson has pointed out, it is equally possible to suggest that the major cities held such wide territories and gained so much power *because* there were so few other existing towns or cities to rival them in the first place, perhaps due to the fact that only limited areas of Tripolitania are really environmentally suited to support substantial nucleated settlement.[71] As previously mentioned, the interior of *Africa Proconsularis* benefits from consistently higher levels of rainfall than Tripolitania, increasing its potential for agricultural productivity, and making it better suited to supporting a higher density of settlement, larger populations and more attractive to settlers immigrating from other parts of the Empire.

One point that should be borne in mind, however, is that the picture presented above potentially underestimates the number and significance of indigenous settlements that could have existed before and during the Roman period, and there is reason to believe that a number of the sites listed in Appendix Table 1 originated as tribal centres. For example, the modern city of Telmine, ancient *Turris Tamalleni*, was almost certainly the ancient settlement also known as *civitas Nybgeniorum*, i.e. the centre of the *Nybgenii* people, who are attested on milestones in the area.[72] The settlement was awarded municipal status under Hadrian and the relative speed of this promotion has suggested to Mattingly that it must already have been a well-established settlement by the early first century AD, if not earlier.[73]

Cidamus is listed by Pliny as one of the settlements of the *Phazanii*, and Mattingly has suggested that the other two named, *Cilliba* and *Alele*, specifically described by Pliny as *urbes*, could perhaps be identified with *Tillibari* and *Talalati*, respectively.[74] Similarly, in the *Aeneid*, Virgil mentions the *urbes* of the *Gaetuli*, and two *oppida Gaetulorum* are referenced in the *Bellum Africum*.[75] The names of other known settlements can also be related to various peoples; the settlements of *Marcomades Selorum* and *Digdida Selorum* were probably related to the *Seli* or *Psylli*, with the former, also sometimes known simply as *Macomades*, potentially also referencing the *Maces*, of which the *Seli* may have been a sub-group.[76] Epigraphic evidence suggests that the *C(h)inithii* were associated with *Gigthis*.[77] Notably, all of the settlements of Tripolitania's interior identified as urban certainly or probably had a Roman military presence, potentially representing a deliberate effort to monitor the major indigenous centres.

Several other oases could also have been pre-Roman or Roman-period tribal centres, but unfortunately, we know little about them, especially since many have been continuously occupied since ancient times. In addition, as discussed further in Section 3.1, pre-Roman indigenous architectures may, more often, have been constructed of less permanent materials, making them difficult to trace. Nevertheless, Trousset found evidence for Roman-period settlement in the form of architectural elements and inscriptions in a number of villages in the oases at the northwest boundary of Tripolitania (e.g. Bechri, Rabta and Douz), but modern occupation has obscured most surface evidence of ancient settlement.[78] Rebuffat also recorded evidence of ancient

68 Wilson 2011: 183–185, Tables 7.8 and 7.9.

69 Mattingly 1995: 137.

70 Mattingly 1995: 60–61, 134.

71 Wilson 1997: 72.

72 *AE* 1910, 21–22.

73 Mattingly 1995: 31, 131–132; Mattingly *et al.* 2020c: 202–4.

74 Pliny, *Natural History*, 5.35; Mattingly 1995: 30.

75 Virgil, *Aeneid*, 4.40; Caesar, *Bellum Africum*, 25.2; Luisi 1992.

76 Mattingly 1995: 32–33.

77 *CIL* 8.22729.

78 Trousset 1974: 41–50. A recent re-evaluation of finds from these oases can be found in Mattingly *et al.* 2020c: 201–206.

settlement, again, probably of the Roman period, in the oases of Waddan, Zella and Sinawan, and more recent surveys by al-Haddad in Waddan and Hun have identified further material dating to the Roman period.[79] While these settlements were probably of a different character to the Punic and Roman towns and cities further north, we should not discount the possibility that at least some of these could have beensubstantial tribal centres, and could perhaps even have been considered to be urban, as recently argued by Mattingly and Sterry for sites such as Jarma and Qasr ash-Sharraba in Fazzan based on their complexity, size and other characteristics.[80]

[79] Rebuffat 1970c; 1972; Mattingly *et al.* 2020b: 130–137.

[80] Mattingly & Sterry 2013; Sterry & Mattingly 2020.

chapter two

Previous Work, Sources and Methodology

There is a large and ever-growing body of archaeological data from the Tripolitanian countryside, as major investigations and surveys have been carried out in the region for more than a century, though more recently hampered by the political unrest which has made Libya inaccessible to most foreigners since early 2011. In the first two sections of this chapter I will review some of the major projects which have been undertaken in rural Tripolitania, pre- and post-World War II, followed by a discussion of the important contribution that satellite imagery and remote sensing has also now begun to make to this picture. In the last section of this chapter, I will give an overview of the methodologies used to collect and analyse the data for the present study, combining the evidence described in the first three sections.

2.1 Before World War II

As early as the seventeenth century, reports began emerging from North Africa describing the archaeological remains of Tripolitania, particularly along the coast and in the region of *Lepcis Magna*.[81] It was not until the nineteenth century, however, that more detailed descriptions and accounts of the archaeology of Tripolitania's interior appeared, when European travellers such as Lyon, the Beechey brothers, Barth, Rae and Borsari began striking out more frequently beyond the coast and even into the Sahara.[82] While the purpose of these expeditions was not primarily archaeological, the detailed and valuable accounts which these explorers provided of the remains repeatedly speak to the interest that these monuments clearly aroused at the time. In addition, they are evidence of the early realisation that far from being the sparsely inhabited desert which it was at that time, the interior of Tripolitania was, in ancient times, home to a substantial, sedentary population.[83]

Towards the end of the nineteenth century, serious archaeological interest in Tripolitania was growing, but modern political borders began to cause a divergence in the character and focus of work being done in different parts of the region. Tunisia was officially occupied by the French in 1881, and while some archaeological expeditions and investigations had been carried out there before this time,[84] after the occupation, the rapid and systematic recording and mapping of the Roman remains of the country began in earnest.[85] The main Roman-period coastal settlements of Tripolitania which fall within the borders of modern Tunisia – *Gigthis*, *Zitha*, *Tacape* and *Meninx* – were given some attention;[86] however, there were no remains on the spectacular scale of *Lepcis Magna* or *Sabratha*. The focus of investigations in the Tunisian part of Tripolitania, from an early time, turned to the archaeology of the Roman army and its activities on the frontier, as well as other topics which served the colonial agenda, such as the use and control of water resources.[87] In particular, a major focus was placed on identifying the Roman roads and routes of the *limes Tripolitanus*, described in sources such as the *Antonine Itinerary* and the *Tabula Peutingeria*.

[81] In particular, reports by C. Lemaire, the French consul in Tripoli (1706, republished in Omont 1902) and M. Durand (1694, republished in Cagnat 1901).

[82] Lyon 1821; Beechey & Beechey 1828; Barth 1857; Rae 1877; Duveyrier 1864; Borsari 1888.

[83] Barth 1857: 63.

[84] For example, Guérin 1862.

[85] Tissot 1884; 1888; Reinach 1888; Babelon, Cagnat, & Reinach 1893; Gauckler 1896.

[86] *Gigthis*: Guérin 1862: 220ff; Reinach 1885; Constans 1916. *Zitha*: Reinach & Babelon 1886. *Tacapae*: Monlezun 1885; Hilaire 1900. *Meninx*: Gilbert 1885.

[87] For example, Carton 1888; Gauckler 1897.

A number of military forts and outposts were identified in this manner,[88] but there was a tendency to put too much emphasis on these routes as linear borders, which supposedly represented the geographical limits of Roman domination.[89] There was also a tendency to identify most of these structures as the work of the military or Roman colonists without question, whereas today it is becoming clear that some of these buildings were indigenous in origin.[90]

Meanwhile, in the later nineteenth and early twentieth centuries, the Turkish government was putting more and more restrictions on European travellers in Libya which it controlled at the time, until voyages and archaeological investigations into the interior were ultimately banned, with few exceptions.[91] One such, however, was Cowper's detailed investigations in the Gebels Gharian, Tarhuna and Msellata, and the eastern Gefara Plain, into what he and earlier explorers thought were megalithic, religious monuments (*senams*),[92] but were shown, less than two years later, to be Roman-period olive presses.[93]

It was not until 1910 that the first Italian expeditions began survey and reconnaissance in the region, mainly along the coast, but a few early forays into the interior were also made.[94] With the Italian invasion of Libya in 1911, followed closely by the commencement of World War I, archaeology became less of a priority. Most of the Italian archaeologists working in Libya moved to Tripoli, and work continued, but only in the immediate vicinity and relative safety of the city.[95] After the end of the World War I, there was increasing pressure on the archaeological superintendents to ensure that archaeology fitted with the colonialist goals and ideologies of the fascist state.[96] In order to maintain the support, both moral and financial, of the government and to attract tourists, the focus was increasingly on the rapid clearance and reconstruction of the large urban monuments of *Lepcis Magna* and *Sabratha*, a policy which unfortunately resulted in the unrecorded destruction of much of the earlier and later archaeological record.[97] Outside the cities, important investigations were undertaken at a number of coastal villas,[98] but until the subjugation of Fazzan in the 1930s, it still remained relatively unsafe to venture into the interior, and the amount of work undertaken there was nowhere on the scale of that in the urban coastal sites.[99]

When looking back at this early archaeological work, it is important to bear in mind the political agendas of the time.[100] It was in the interests of both the French and Italians to interpret any archaeological remains of the region as the work of Romano-Italian colonists, not of indigenous peoples, in order to justify their own occupation and colonisation.[101] Both countries drew explicit comparisons between their own colonial activities and those of the Romans, in order to reinforce the idea that modern European states were the heirs to the ancient empires, and as such, it was their duty, and right, to protect and control what they felt to be their own cultural heritage.[102] However, while this has meant that the discussions and interpretations in these early studies are often, at best, rather outdated (and, at worst, blatantly racist), many of their physical descriptions, maps and catalogues are still extremely useful, particularly in areas that have subsequently been disturbed or completely destroyed by later development.

2.2 After World War II

World War II marked a brief cessation in archaeological investigations in Tripolitania as both Tunisia and Libya saw intense military action. In 1943, the Allied Forces gained control of the region and two British Army officers stationed in Tripolitania, Mortimer Wheeler and John B. Ward-Perkins, recognised the significance of the ruins they encountered there and were instrumental in arranging for their protection. In the years after the war, British archaeologists set about organising and continuing the survey, excavation and restoration projects already underway thanks to the Italians, in particular

[88] For example, *Tisavar*: Gombeaud 1901; *CIL* 8.11048; *Bezereos*: Merlin 1921; *Talalati*: Renault 1901; Boizot 1913. Ksar-Tarcine/*Tibubuci*: Gauckler 1900; 1902. Benia Guedah Ceder: Donau 1904.

[89] For example, Toutain 1895; 1896, or Pericaud and Gauckler's (1905) assertion that *Turris Maniliorum Abelliorum* (RLT086-g) was the work of Roman colonists. Cf. Mattingly (1995: 167, 200) who asserts convincingly that it was the home of a Libyan family.

[90] See Section 4.1.

[91] Cowper 1897: ix–x; Méhier de Mathuisieulx 1903; Mattingly 1995: xv.

[92] Cowper 1897. See also Barth 1857: 58–63; Fergusson 1872: 410–414; von Bary 1883.

[93] Myres 1899: 280; Manetti 1914; Mattingly 1988a: 181.

[94] Aurigemma 1915; 1930; Munzi 2001: 28–34; Balice 2010: 25–29.

[95] Boni & Mariani 1915; Aurigemma 1915; 1916; Romanelli 1916; Altekamp 2004: 58–59; Munzi 2004: 77–78.

[96] Altekamp 2004: 59–62.

[97] Altekamp 2004: 65–70; Munzi 2004: 86. See fn. 1 for examples of the publications which appeared during this time.

[98] Bartoccini 1926: 88–90; Aurigemma 1926; 1960; 1962; Guidi 1933.

[99] Aurigemma 1915: 19–28; Bartoccini 1928; Corò 1928; Cerrata 1933; Bauer 1935; Caputo 1942.

[100] Munzi 2001; 2004; Altekamp 2004; Balice 2010.

[101] Munzi 2004: 74–77.

[102] Altekamp 2004: 56–57, 62; Munzi 2004: 79; Dyson 2006: 60–61; Díaz-Andreu 2007: 269.

at *Sabratha* and *Lepcis Magna*, and continued on after Libya and Tunisia gained their independence in 1951 and 1956 respectively. [103]

It was during this time that more British archaeologists began to take an active interest in rural Tripolitania. Richard Goodchild, who was appointed Antiquities Officer for the British Military Administration in Libya, was an early and influential contributor, writing on a variety of sites and topics in rural Tripolitania.[104] One particularly important area he addressed was the sites and olive farms of the Gebel Tarhuna.[105] Goodchild and David Oates, who had undertaken a similar study in another area of the *gebel*,[106] rightly identified and emphasised the important role that olive farming played in the wealth of the coastal cities and Tripolitania's economy, setting the foundations for many future investigations on the topic.[107] Another of Goodchild's major research interests was the archaeology of the frontier, and although some of his ideas concerning the role of the fortified farm buildings (*gsur*) on the frontier and the so-called *limitanei* 'soldier-farmers' that he believed occupied them, (based on the model described in the *Life of Severus Alexander* in which conquered lands were given back to local leaders on the condition that they defend the frontier) are no longer accepted, his re-thinking of the *limes* as a defensive frontier zone, rather than a linear border remains an important step in the region's archaeological history.[108]

Another British archaeologist who took a very keen interest in the archaeology of the Tripolitanian countryside was Olwen Brogan. Like Goodchild, Brogan's interest and contributions to the archaeology of Tripolitania were many and varied,[109] but two areas of her research are of particular significance here. The first was her discovery that, contrary to Goodchild's belief that the third-century *gsur* (fortified farm buildings) had represented the earliest settlement in the pre-desert areas and that their construction had been part of an official Roman initiative, there was clear evidence for unfortified farms which dated back to the first and second century AD. Furthermore, while the presence of imported pottery and Neo-Punic inscriptions showed sustained contact and exchange with the coast, the names recorded in the inscriptions of both the *gebel* and pre-desert clearly indicated that the peoples inhabiting these buildings were indigenous Libyans.[110]

Brogan, along with D.J. Smith, was also responsible for the first thorough survey and excavation of the site of Ghirza, one of the largest settlements known from the pre-desert and probably an important rural centre during its main occupation period from the third to sixth century AD. Located 200 km south of *Lepcis Magna*, the site consists of over 40 distinct buildings, including six very large *gsur*, extensive evidence for agriculture, and multiple cemeteries with at least 14 monumental mausolea which bear features of classical, Punic and indigenous Libyan traditions in their form, decoration and inscriptions.[111] Although acknowledging the 'essentially Libyan character' of Ghirza, Brogan and Smith believed that the inhabitants had descended from *Libyphoenices* who had migrated from the coast and *gebel*, rather than indigenous Libyans who had adopted aspects of Punic culture through contact with peoples to their north.[112]

Meanwhile, French archaeologists in both Tunisia and Libya were continuing their investigations into the military sites of the *limes*. Over three seasons in the late 1960s and early 1970s, Euzennat and Trousset led a survey of the Tunisian part of the *limes Tripolitanus*, incorporating into their investigations a combination of the reports made by previous explorers and aerial photography. This survey was published in 1974 as *Recherches sur le Limes Tripolitanus* (*RLT*) and presented a catalogue of more than 100 sites, both newly discovered and previously known from investigations in the late nineteenth and early twentieth century.[113] However, while this publication acknowledged the presence of settled indigenous farmers based on the agricultural remains and mausolea observed, the main focus was on the military and, like Goodchild, the conclusion reached was that the fortified farms had an 'official' purpose and their inhabitants were also responsible for defense of the frontier.[114]

The most extensive and influential survey of the Tripolitanian countryside in the last 50 years was the Anglo-Libyan *UNESCO Libyan Valleys Survey* (*ULVS*), which was carried out between 1979 and 1989 in the pre-desert area south of *Lepcis Magna* and *Oea*, and

[103] Goodchild 1949: 9–11. *Sabratha*: Bartoccini 1950; Caputo 1950; Kenrick 1986; Dore & Keay 1989; Fulford & Tomber 1994. *Lepcis Magna*: Degrassi 1951; Ward-Perkins *et al.* 1993.

[104] For example, Goodchild 1952; 1964; 1976b.

[105] Goodchild 1951c. See also Caputo 1942; Aurigemma 1954.

[106] Oates 1953.

[107] For example, Mattingly 1985b; 1988a; 1988c; 1994; Ahmed 2010.

[108] *SHA Severus Alexander* 58.2; Goodchild 1948; 1950b; 1954; 1968; Goodchild & Ward-Perkins 1949.

[109] Brogan 1954; 1964; 1965a; 1965b; 1968; 1975b; 1975a; 1977; 1978; 1980.

[110] Brogan 1964; 1968. See also Di Vita 1964: 65–79.

[111] Brogan & Smith 1984; Mattingly 1995: 197–200; 1999; 2003a; Purcaro 1996.

[112] Brogan & Smith 1984: 227, 230.

[113] Trousset 1974.

[114] Trousset 1974: 129–163. Cf. Rebuffat's (1980) concerns and criticisms, particularly on Trousset's typology and his criteria for inclusion in the study.

produced more than 30 articles and a final, two-volume monograph and gazetteer published in 1996.[115] This survey covered approximately 75,000 km^2 of the Wadis Sofeggin and ZemZem, and data were collected from well over 2,000 sites, ranging from prehistoric to modern times, though most date from the late first to mid-seventh century AD.[116] The *ULVS* project set out to systematically address and explain the long-known but little-understood fact that archaeological evidence quite clearly indicated that the pre-desert had been more densely populated and more intensively cultivated than it is today, and subsequently to try to determine whether it would be feasible to re-establish settlement there. The large set of data collected by the *ULVS* project enabled the researchers to expand and improve upon the settlement and building typologies which Goodchild and Brogan had begun to develop in their earlier works.[117] In addition, having largely disproven the suggestion that agriculture was possible in the Roman period because of a more favourable climate, the findings of the *ULVS* revealed a picture of cultural continuity in the pre-desert. While much of the evidence they found points to a significant degree of cultural contact and exchange, they also emphasised that the agricultural exploitation of the land was based on land-use techniques that were developed from pre-existing indigenous technologies.[118]

The Franco-Libyan *Prospection des Vallées du Nord de la Libye* (*PVNL*) project was also initiated by UNESCO as a complement to the *ULVS* project in the region of the Wadi Bei el-Kebir and Syrtica, and undertook two seasons between 1979 and 1980, identifying around 60 sites.[119] The analysis of this material was less comprehensive, but the results for the Wadi Bei el-Kebir were broadly similar to the findings of the *ULVS*, where *fermes à cour* (open farms) and *tours* (*gsur*) lined the wadi (though they only encountered four examples of the latter). Their investigations in Syrtica revealed a different settlement pattern, with fewer farms, consisting of multiple buildings, all clustered near the coast.[120] Between 1990 and 1996 another Franco-Libyan team undertook a survey in five wadis just to the east of the *PVNL* area, called the *Prospection archéologique dans cinq vallées de la region syrtique* (*PARS*).[121] The results of this survey were only published in one brief preliminary report and two other short articles, revealing similar patterns as seen by the *PVNL* team, but unfortunately, unlike the previous two surveys mentioned, did not include a gazetteer of sites.[122] All of these projects located and recorded sites almost exclusively through ground survey, though the methods and intensity with which this was carried out varied from area to area, ranging from intensive survey and surface collection on foot to recording the approximate location of standing buildings seen from moving vehicles.[123]

In 1995, David Mattingly published his monograph, *Tripolitania*, which was the first thorough account of the region as a whole during the Roman period and remains an influential and important synthesis of the archaeology of the region until that time. In the 1980s and '90s, Mattingly had taken part in the *ULVS* project and developed a strong interest in the production of olive oil and its role in Tripolitania's economy.[124] Both of these experiences played a strong role his book and he continued to emphasise the indigenous contribution to culture and identity in Tripolitania.[125] Since this time, Mattingly has also undertaken several major survey projects in Fazzan to Tripolitania's south, following on the work of Charles M. Daniels in the 1960s and '70s, including the Fazzan Project, the Desert Migrations Project, the Peopling the Desert Project, and the Trans-Sahara Project. All of these projects have aimed to explore and understand the ancient life and economy of the ancient Saharan peoples in Fazzan, particularly the *Garamantes*. These investigations have revealed significant economic exchange between Saharan oases and the Mediterranean during the Roman period, many of the routes for which cut directly through Tripolitania.[126]

Two other significant works published in the 1990s investigating aspects of the rural architecture of Tripolitania, Brouquier-Reddé's *Temples et Cultes de Tripolitaine* and Sjöström's *Tripolitania in Transition: Late Roman to Early Islamic Settlement* are worth mentioning here. A substantial and useful part of both of these works is a large catalogue of sites, but there is room for further discussion and analysis of the structures they recorded and their significance for the development and role of architecture in rural areas.[127]

[115] Barker 1996c; Mattingly 1996b.

[116] Barker 1996: 26.

[117] Barker 1996c: 111. Goodchild 1950b; Brogan 1964; 1968; 1977; Brogan & Smith 1984.

[118] Barker *et al.* 1996; Barker & Gilbertson 1996a; Mattingly 1996a.

[119] Reddé 1988. See also Rebuffat 1982; 1988; Reddé 1985.

[120] Reddé 1988; Rebuffat 1988.

[121] Longerstay 1999: 53–54.

[122] Longerstay 1999; 2000; 2003.

[123] Barker 1996a: 21–35; Reddé 1988: 11–17.

[124] Mattingly 1985b; 1988c; 1988a; 1988b; 1994.

[125] Mattingly 1995.

[126] Mattingly 2003b; 2007; 2010; Mattingly *et al.* 2007, plus multiple yearly reports and articles in *Libyan Studies*. See also Daniels 1968; 1970; 1975; 1989.

[127] Brouquier-Reddé 1992; Sjöström 1993.

Between the late 1980s and 1990s, a Franco-Tunisian team of archaeologists and geologists undertook an investigation of the coast of Tunisia, published in 2004 as *Le littoral de la Tunisie: Étude géoarchéologique et historique*.[128] The aim of the project was to examine the physical transformations which the coastal environment of the country had undergone since antiquity and the effects that these transformations had on ancient settlement and resource exploitation in coastal contexts. Only 37 of the sites recorded in this publication are in Tripolitania, but significantly, a number of the sites recorded were smaller scale rural settlements, rather than substantial port towns or luxury villas, which often tend to be the focus of coastal investigations.

Also beginning in the 1990s, the *Institut National du Patrimoine (INP)* of Tunisia began publishing the *Carte National des Sites Archéologiques et des Monuments Historiques*. Their intention is to provide coverage of archaeological, ethnographic and historic sites for the entire country and for all time periods, having divided it into 290 map sheets each covering 640 km^2. They were compiled using both the evidence from earlier maps and investigations, such as the *Atlas Archéologique de la Tunisie*, and new surveys conducted specifically for this project.[129] As of early 2020, only three sheets in Tripolitania have been fully published;[130] however, preliminary information, including geographical co-ordinates, for a further 15 of these sheets have so far been published online,[131] and work by the *INP* is ongoing.

Between 1996 and 2000, a survey of the island of Jerba directed by Elizabeth Fentress, Ali Drine and Renata Holod identified dozens of farms, villas, mausolea and two possible forts from throughout the Hellenistic and Roman periods, but unlike other areas of Tripolitania, there are very few standing remains left which has limited the usefulness of the material for this study.[132] Also beginning in the mid-1990s was the archaeological mission of the *Università Roma Tre*. Over the course of more than ten seasons, the Italo-Libyan team has undertaken survey and excavation in a number of areas in the hinterlands of *Lepcis Magna*, identifying nearly 500 sites and focussing in particular on illuminating the settlement and land-use patterns of that area from the pre-Roman to early Islamic periods.[133]

In 2007, a Libyan archaeologist, Mftah A. M. Ahmed conducted the *Tarhuna Archaeological Survey* (*TAS*), the first major survey in the region since the 1950s, which formed the basis of his PhD thesis, completed in 2010, and subsequent monograph published in 2019. Ahmed's findings have confirmed and even further emphasised the importance of the agricultural activities of the central *gebel* region in Tripolitania's economy, having recorded dozens of olive oil and wine pressing and amphora production sites and re-recording and updating our understanding of many sites originally identified by Cowper, Goodchild, and Oates. He was able to place his investigations in the context of the *ULVS* investigations and the Italo-Libyan surveys around *Lepcis Magna* mentioned above, and his analyses of the rural buildings he encountered have confirmed many of the findings of the *ULVS* in terms of typology and chronological development, while also helping to refine them for this particular region of Tripolitania.[134]

Between 2007 and 2009, a mitigation survey on behalf of Shell Libya was undertaken in the area of the Sirte Basin along the frontier of Tripolitania and Cyrenaica, though unfortunately, only two brief summary articles have so far been published.[135] Over the course of three seasons, the *Shell Sirte Basin* (*SSB*) survey was able to increase the number of known archaeological sites within the survey area from 30 to over 3,000 dating from the Palaeolithic to the present, and including approximately 200 previously unknown Romano-Libyan sites. This project has completely changed preconceptions about the archaeological potential of the region, which had hitherto often been neglected. The majority of sites which were identified as Romano-Libyan in date from the Tripolitanian side were located in Area 212, c.60 km northwest of the site of *Arae Philaenorum*. This project made extensive use of satellite imagery to locate sites, as well as observations made in the field during the environmental and seismic surveys carried out by (non-archaeologist) Shell Libya crews. A minority of sites was then located using GPS technology and visited in the field based on these data in order to make further observations and do limited surface collections for dating purposes. [136]

[128] Slim *et al.* 2004.

[129] Mrabet 1998: 9–10.

[130] Mrabet 1998; Mrabet 2000a; Mrabet 2000b.

[131] http://www.inp.rnrt.tn/Carte_archeo/html/index_fr.htm.

[132] Fentress, Drine, & Holod 2009.

[133] Fontana, Munzi, & Ricci 1996; Munzi & Pentiricci 1997; Munzi 1998; Munzi & Abd el-Aziz el-Nemsi 1998; Cifani *et al.* 2003; Munzi *et al* 2004; Munzi *et al.* 2004–2005; Munzi & Felici 2006; Munzi 2010; Munzi *et al.* 2010; Musso *et al.* 2010; Cirelli, Felici, & Munzi 2012; Schörle & Leitch 2012. Munzi *et al.* 2014; Munzi *et al.* 2016.

[134] Ahmed 2010; 2019.

[135] LeQuesne, Basell, & Sheibani 2010; LeQuesne 2011. This was in part due to the fact that Shell Libya was dissolved and the project halted due to the revolution which took place in Libya in early 2011. I am grateful to Charles LeQuesne for taking the time to discuss and clarify some of the details of the project with me.

[136] LeQuesne, Basell, & Sheibani 2010: 8–9.

In 2011, the *Ghadames Archaeological Survey* was begun to investigate the walled palmery and its immediate surroundings, but this was interrupted after only a few weeks by the Libyan Revolution.[137] Since then, as mentioned in the introduction to this chapter, field survey in Libya and parts of southern Tunisia has been made increasingly difficult due to the political instability in the region. At the time of writing, foreign missions to Libya are still all but impossible, and while Libyan archaeologists continue to conduct surveys and excavations, their work has often been hampered by the difficult and sometimes dangerous conditions. Nevertheless, archaeologists in both Libya and Tunisia have found ways to continue their work, and collaborations with foreign colleagues have continued, in part thanks to the increasing use of remote sensing techniques.[138] For example, the *Tunisian-Libyan mountain heritage documentation project* established in 2019 and led by Héla Mekki, has for the first time conducted a systematic survey of the El Dhaher/Nefoussa Mountain Range, recording nearly 4,000 sites, from all periods, in Tunisia and Libya, using a combination of satellite imagery, topographic maps, and field survey.[139]

2.3 Satellite Imagery and Remote Sensing

While the use of satellite imagery in archaeology is by no means a new phenomenon, thanks to the ease with which high-resolution satellite imagery can now be freely consulted via platforms such as Google Earth and Bing Maps, more and more archaeologists are incorporating satellite imagery into their work. There is a rapidly growing body of writing on its use for remote sensing in archaeology and heritage. In particular, many projects in North Africa and the Middle East have used satellite imagery to continue and even begin new work in regions where it is difficult to travel and work due to political restrictions or ongoing conflicts.[140] Tripolitania is well-suited for using satellite imagery to identify archaeological sites and buildings, particularly in the pre-desert areas, thanks to the excellent preservation of many sites, the relatively sparse vegetation in the region, and the almost complete lack of widespread modern development beyond the coast. In these areas, the remains of buildings are highly visible and it is often possible to make out building plans and measure the dimensions of sites and structures with a relatively high degree of accuracy. Furthermore, as archaeologists utilising aerial and kite photographs have known for decades, the view from above can often be extremely useful for interpreting and making sense of sites which, when standing on the ground, can appear as a confusing mass of rubble.

There are, however, a number of important limitations and caveats associated with data obtained through satellite imagery, especially in instances where it is not possible to verify the information collected from imagery on the ground. First, it should be noted that the resolution and quality of the satellite imagery which is publicly available is not consistent throughout the region and is constantly being updated, imposing arbitrary limits on where this type of survey can be applied. The resolution of the imagery varies from between c.0.5 m per pixel (e.g. Worldview-2, QuickBird, GeoEye-1), at which resolution one can make out walls and sometimes even individual large ashlar blocks, to 15 m (e.g NASA/USGS LandSat, ESA Copernicus) per pixel, or occasionally more.

Second, while comparisons of building and site dimensions which were measured accurately in the field (i.e. not paced or estimated) and those taken with the Ruler Tool in Google Earth suggest that the latter are relatively reliable, it should go without saying that they are not a substitute for proper architectural survey and should be treated as approximate only. On the other hand, these measurements are probably at least as good as many found in earlier publications or recorded during rapid surveys which were measured in paces or only estimated. Thirdly, the information that can be obtained through satellite imagery about individual buildings is restricted, in most cases, to their horizontal size and layout. Unless or until sites have been observed on the ground, we remain largely ignorant of other equally important attributes such as height, materials and construction techniques.

Finally, another limitation on the data obtained from satellite imagery is that it is rarely possible to determine dating and phasing from the imagery alone. It can and should be asked, therefore, how we can be sure that sites identified solely from satellite imagery actually date to the period under study. The simple answer is that without physically visiting the site, we cannot be completely sure. However, we can note that the *ULVS* project, for example, collected information on structures from all periods, and in general, most sites which could be classified by their plan and construction type as unfortified or fortified farm buildings were, in fact, datable by associated ceramic evidence to the Romano-Libyan period. Therefore, by using the appearance of sites which are already known from previous surveys and whose antiquity and archaeological

[137] A short summary of the findings of this survey are in Mattingly *et al.* 2020c: 195–198.

[138] See, for example, Nebbia *et al.* 2016; Rayne *et al.* 2020.

[139] "GHF/J.M. Kaplan Award Funds Documentation" 2019; Mekki 2021.

[140] For example, Allan & Richards 1983; Dorsett *et al.* 1984; De Meyer 2004; Sever & Parry 2006; Casana & Cothren 2008; Kennedy & Bishop 2011; Lodewijckx & Pelegrin 2011; Comer & Harrower 2013; Cunliffe 2013; Hanson & Oltean 2013; Rayne *et al.* 2017; Tapete 2017; 2019; Khalaf & Insoll 2019; Casana 2020.

significance have been confirmed on the ground as a guide, it is not unreasonable to suggest that sites identified with satellite imagery and which are of a similar form, location and character can, at least tentatively, be ascribed a similar date and interpretation.

2.4 Methodology

Due to the on-going conflicts and political unrest that disrupted Libya and Tunisia between early 2011 and 2015 when I conducted the bulk of the data collection and research for this study, it was unfortunately not possible for me to undertake fieldwork at any of the sites discussed in this book. Nevertheless, the sources described in the first three sections of this chapter have provided an enormous and varied set of data on structures and settlement in the Tripolitanian countryside for the period under investigation. However, despite this wealth of information, there are two major issues with these data which will be addressed by the present study. First, as previously mentioned, none of the published investigations discussed above have focussed their attention specifically on the architecture in the region. Second, due to the varied nature and goals of the different surveys and the various ways in which the data have been, and continue to be, collected, it has previously been very difficult to compare the results of these different surveys except in very broad terms.

The first major step in my research was therefore to compile and map the available material into a usable and uniform database in order to establish regional distributions and patterns for different types of sites and structures. I created a relational database which is presented in table form in Appendices A, B and C, which give the data for military, unfortified and fortified buildings, respectively. Wherever possible, I have retained published sites codes and numbers to ensure ease of cross-referencing. In cases where only numbers were used, to avoid confusion, I added a prefix referencing either the survey or author's name, e.g. Site 62 from Trousset's *Recherches sur le Limes Tripolitanus* = RLT62 and Site 4 in Cowper's *Hill of the Graces* = Cowper04.[141] For new sites identified using satellite imagery, I used a wadi or region code from previous surveys where possible or assigned a new one, plus my own initials (NS) and sequential numbers to create new site codes, e.g. a new site identified in the Wadi Khanafes in the *ULVS* survey area = Kn-NS01. Finally, I added a suffix to each site code identifying the building recorded there as unfortified (-f), fortified (-g), tower (-t), or villa (-v);[142] where there was more than one recorded building at a site, a number was also added, e.g. Gb024-f1 and Gb024-f2. A full key and explanation of the site codes used can be found accompanying the appendices.

Not all of the projects discussed above had published or otherwise made available full site catalogues at the point when I concluded my data collection in 2015. Hence it has obviously not been possible to incorporate all of the data published subsequently into my quantitative analyses, though general findings and results have been discussed and referenced where possible and relevant. However, it should be kept in mind that it was not my goal to provide a completely exhaustive catalogue of sites from the Tripolitanian countryside, but rather to collect enough information to make comparisons between the rural architectures of different areas of the region.

I began my data collection by recording the sites and information that were available in the published sources discussed in Sections 2.1 and 2.2, and where possible, I located the sites using open-access satellite imagery via Google Earth or Bing Maps. While some of the more recent surveys published co-ordinates which could be used to find the sites, many were conducted before GPS technology was widely available, and it was necessary to relocate sites using published sketch maps and descriptions, which were not always completely reliable. As a result, I have been able to create more accurate maps than have previously existed for much of this data. In addition, thanks to the high resolution of much of the imagery, I have also been able to add, confirm and correct where necessary, site dimensions and plans for a large number of sites, since for reasons of time and logistics in the original surveys, these types of measurements were often only estimated, paced off or not recorded at all.

It was during the course of identifying and mapping the previously published sites using satellite imagery, that the scale of the number of sites within and around the published survey areas that had not previously been recorded became clear. As a result, I decided to conduct a limited amount of new remote satellite survey to augment the existing data set; sites identified during these remote sensing activities account for approximately a third of the total number of sites in my catalogue.

My satellite imagery surveys were conducted in two main ways. In the eastern half of the region, surveys were specifically targeted along the wadi courses, looking for evidence of structures and settlement within a few hundred metres of their banks. The reason for this is related to the history of intensive survey in the rural areas of Tripolitania, which is heavily biased towards the eastern regions; as a result, we have a far better understanding of the settlement patterns and distribution there. What previous surveys, particularly the *ULVS* project, have

[141] Trousset 1974; Cowper 1897.

[142] It is important to note that in the case of the latter two especially, these codes were often assigned based on the interpretations given in the publications in which they were originally recorded, before I had finalised my own typologies and use of these terms, as discussed in later chapters.

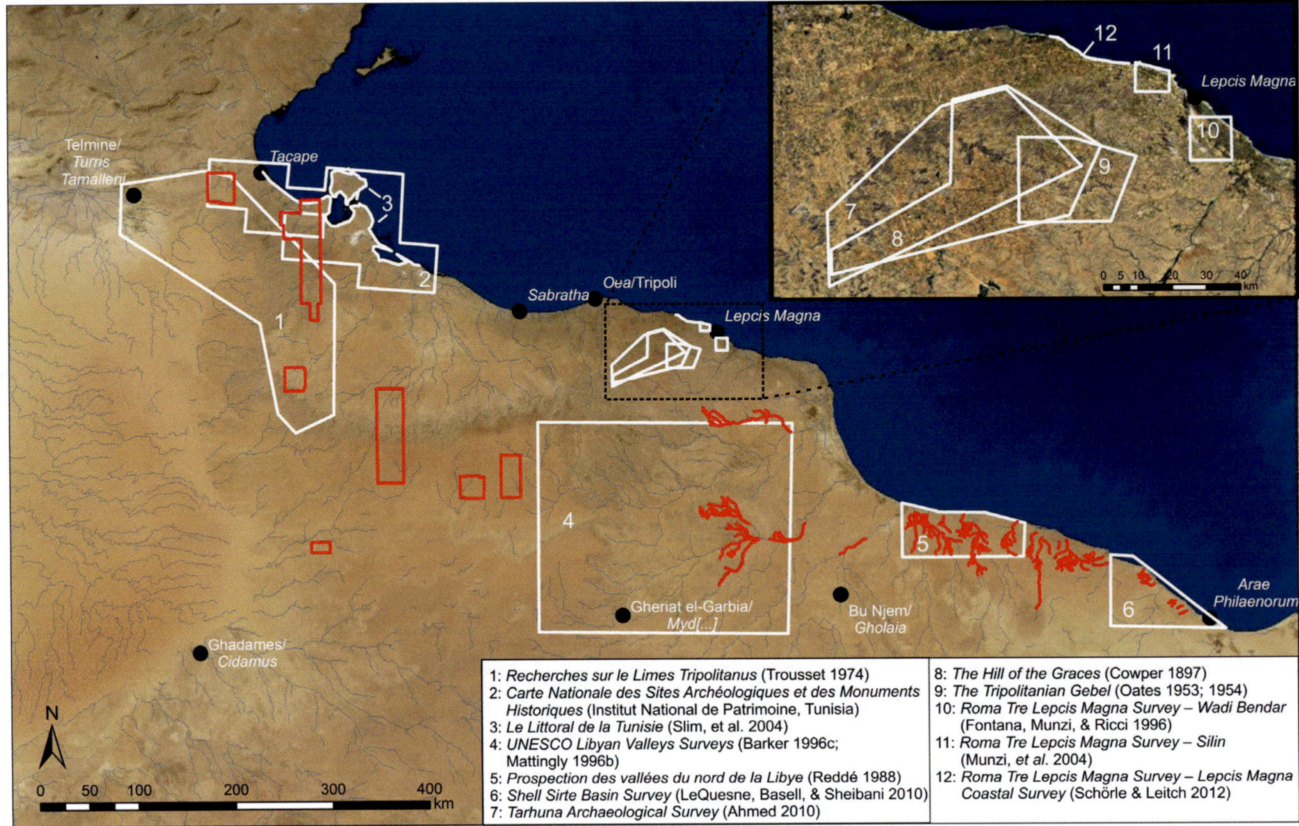

Figure 2.1: *Areas of published (white) and new satellite surveys (red).*

demonstrated is that during the period under study, settlement in the pre-desert areas and in Syrtica was closely related to the wadi-courses, being influenced by the availability of water and the fertile soil of the wadi-beds which was suitable for agriculture. While this is not to say that there was no activity during this period in the areas between the wadis, there is strong evidence to suggest that the majority of sedentary, agriculturally-based settlement cannot be found in these areas. In the western half of the region, I conducted full-coverage survey within seven defined blocks of area, to which I assigned area codes WT1 through WT7. The locations chosen were determined by two factors: the desire to target specific areas where limited or no archaeological work had previously been undertaken and the availability of high-resolution imagery in Google Earth at the time.

There are two important notes which should be kept in mind regarding these satellite imagery surveys. First, in both the cases of targeted wadi surveys and areas of full coverage, many areas overlapped with the regions of published surveys (Figure 2.1), as the boundaries indicated for the published surveys do not necessarily indicate that complete ground coverage was achieved in those areas. In addition, it was apparent that there were often unrecorded sites in close vicinity to previously recorded ones. This is in no way a reflection on the quality or thoroughness of previously published surveys, but rather a result of the advantages of satellite survey in terms of speed of survey and ability to view sites which may be inaccessible or obscured on the ground. Likewise, there are certainly many sites which it has only been possible to identify from ground survey and which are not visible on satellite imagery.

Second, there were a number of cases, particularly in Syrtica, where it is unclear whether the sites I have identified have been previously recorded or not. There is almost certainly some overlap with the *PARS* and *SSB* surveys in Syrtica,[143] but because detailed gazetteers or sufficiently high-resolution distribution maps have not been published for these surveys, it is not clear how much. I have marked all sites which I could not confidently match to previously published ones as 'new', but it may be that many of the sites have indeed already been identified by earlier surveys, and further research will be necessary to clarify the situation.

Having collected and catalogued these data, I divided the material into nine regions for analysis (Figure 2.2). These regions are based to a certain extent

[143] Longerstay 1999; LeQuesne, Basell, & Sheibani 2010.

on geographical zones and features such as the *gebel* and the extents of previous surveys, but also take into account patterns visible in the overall distribution of the recorded material. It should be kept in mind, therefore, that many of the blank areas on the maps provided are not necessarily indicative of a lack of archaeology, only that those areas have not been covered by my study for various reasons, such as time and availability of data.

On a similar note, since the main focus of this book is the analysis of buildings and architecture, the distribution maps should not be considered to be maps of known settlement in the region. While it goes without saying that architecture and settlement are strongly related, as discussed earlier, I have attempted to place a specific focus on the buildings themselves and with few exceptions, only recorded sites for which something could be said about architecture. An explanatory example is the situation on the island of Jerba. As summarised above, the survey published in 2009 by Fentress *et al.* found abundant evidence for rural settlement on the island; however, the vast majority of this evidence was in the form of artefact scatters. Due to environmental factors and the rate of modern settlement and agriculture there is very little architectural evidence remaining on the surface or visible from satellite imagery; this is also the case in many other areas of Tripolitania, particularly close to the coast and in the *gebel*. As a result, the distribution of known buildings on the island of Jerba from the period under study is not reflective of the distribution of known settlement and other human activity for the same period.

This was also, unfortunately, the case for a number of sites which were identified during the investigations of the *Carte Nationale des Sites Archéologiques et des Monuments Historiques* of Tunisia. In these cases, the published description of many sites was often either non-existent or too vague to identify what kind of site it was and/or what sort of building had been recorded (if there was one at all). If anything appeared in the satellite imagery, it was generally identifiable only as a low mound, about which very little could be said except its size. While I have little doubt that the mounds in question do represent ancient sites, their appearance is such that they could very easily have been defined or altered by modern activities such as ploughing. While these sites are important evidence of rural settlement, they add little to my discussion of buildings here, and as a result have not been included in my catalogues or main analyses.

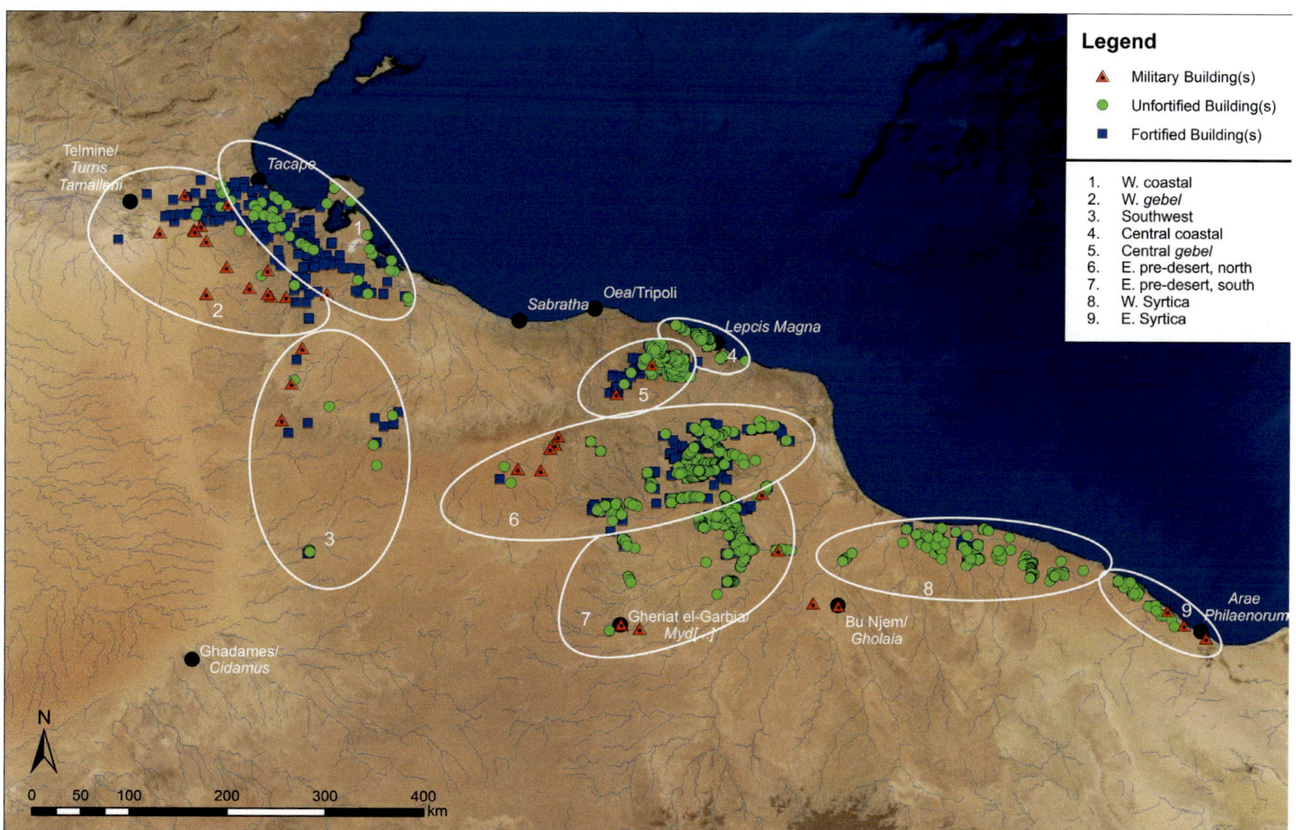

Basemap: Esri, DigitalGlobe, GeoEye, i-cubed, USDA, USGS, AEX, Getmapping, Aerogrid, IGN, IGP, swisstopo, and the GIS User Community
Drainage: Lehner, B., Verdin, K., Jarvis, A. (2008): New global hydrography derived from spaceborne elevation data. Eos, Transactions, AGU, 89(10): 93-94. Retrieved from http://hydrosheds.cr.usgs.gov (15 sec Flow Accumulation)
Roads (Barrington Atlas): Ancient World Mapping Center (2012)

Figure 2.2: *Distribution of all unfortified, fortified and military buildings recorded in the catalogue and regional divisions for analysis.*

Finally, it is worth acknowledging that due to the differences in data collection and site preservation that have been outlined in this chapter, the quantity and quality of data available across the nine main regions under study are in many ways imbalanced. This should always be kept in mind when gauging the significance of the analyses and results presented in the following chapters, particularly as this is often more likely the result of external factors than any reflection of reality, and where relevant I will highlight and address these imbalances in the text. For example, the starting sample size of recorded unfortified buildings in different regions varies between nine and 487, and it is clear that quantitative analyses and conclusions which are based on larger sample sizes will carry more weight. However, this does not necessarily invalidate the results of those areas with smaller sample sizes. Including these data provides a base from which to move our investigations forward, by drawing attention to and highlighting those areas where further evidence is clearly needed. New data may ultimately further support and confirm the trends suggested here, or might indicate that these data need to be revisited and new ideas formulated, either of which outcomes will be a useful step forward.

chapter three

Development and Chronology of Rural Settlement and Architecture

3.1 Pre-Roman and Indigenous Architecture and Settlement

As briefly outlined in Chapter 1, until the later first millennium BC, with the exception of a small number of urban (or proto-urban) settlements along the coast and in oases, the people living in Tripolitania were probably primarily nomadic or semi-nomadic pastoralists. There is some evidence that like in Fazzan and other parts of North Africa, fortified hilltop or promontory (*éperon barré*) settlements may have been common in the pre-Roman period,[144] but in general, what settlement existed in Tripolitania during this period was probably on a far smaller scale than developed in the first centuries AD.

It is likely that many earlier buildings and settlements also continued to be utilised and occupied into and throughout the Roman and later periods. Most are unfortunately still poorly understood in terms of their role in the landscape and relationship to other forms of settlement both before and during this time. Nevertheless, by looking at the general character of the architecture and rural landscape in the centuries leading up to the main period under investigation, we can better understand and appreciate the significance of the changes that later took place.

3.1.1 Stone Huts

Probably the earliest and most common stone structures known in Tripolitania are small, one-roomed buildings which are often referred to in publications simply as 'huts'.[145] This appellation is potentially confusing, however, since in common modern usage the term more often evokes buildings of more perishable materials (discussed in Section 3.1.3, below),[146] so to make the difference clear I will refer to these structures specifically as 'stone huts'.

In general, very little attention has been paid to these buildings and few surveys in any part of Tripolitania have recorded or even commented on them; whether this is because they never existed in other parts of Tripolitania, they have not been found because of poor preservation or biased survey techniques, or they have hitherto simply been disregarded as uninformative or uninteresting, is not always clear. Some were recorded in both the *UNESCO Libyan Valleys Survey* (*ULVS*) and *Shell Sirte Basin* (*SSB*) areas but the recording was not always systematic and not very detailed in architectural terms. In addition, in most cases it is not possible to know or distinguish between the different functions that structures of this type may have served, whether they were meant for temporary or permanent habitation, storage, animal pens or something else entirely. Furthermore, it can also be difficult to differentiate between structures which were originally completely stone built, only low foundations or bases for tents.

Around 430 sites were recorded by the *ULVS* as huts, hut settlements, tent bases or similar, which were not associated with larger buildings or settlements, and usually only in areas of relatively intensive survey. Only about a quarter of these had any sort of dimensions recorded and most survived only as low walls. In general, buildings identified as stone huts were less than c.8 x 8 m in size, consisted of only one room, and were built of locally available materials, using more or less roughly coursed drystone construction, sometimes with small uprights incorporated. The *SSB* survey also

144 Fentress 1979: 31; Ferchiou 1990a; 1990b; Mattingly 1995: 42–49; Barker 1996b: 105; Mattingly & Dore 1996: 116–118; Mattingly, Sterry, & Leitch 2013: 168–170.

145 For example, Barker 1996b: 105–106; Mattingly & Dore 1996: 140; LeQuesne, Basell, & Sheibani 2010: 16.

146 See, for example, the entry for 'huts' in the *Oxford English Dictionary*: "a dwelling of ruder and meaner construction and (usually) smaller size than a house, often of branches, turf, or mud…" (*OED* 2015).

Wadi Umm el-Agerem, E. pre-desert, south
(DigitalGlobe via Google Earth Pro, 3 Feb. 2010)

E. pre-desert (Barker 1996b: 107, fig. 4.16)

Figure 3.1: *Examples of stone huts in the eastern pre-desert and Syrtica.*

identified dozens of rectangular buildings which they identified as stone huts or tent bases, usually measuring c.5–6 m by 10–12 m in size.[147] Both surveys found that these stone huts were often found arranged in a line or clustered in groups (Figure 3.1).

The stone huts identified by the *ULVS* and *SSB* projects were sometimes associated with lithic material and very occasionally rough pottery, but in general, their simple, vernacular architecture makes them difficult to date. The evidence from surface collection in both the *ULVS* and *SSB* areas suggests that buildings of basically identical form and construction have been in use in the pre-desert from prehistoric until early modern times.[148] Satellite imagery has also revealed that the stone huts noted by the *ULVS* and *SSB* projects are only a very small fraction of the number that currently exist in the region.

[147] LeQuesne, Basell, & Sheibani 2010: 16.

[148] Barker 1996b: 105–106, 109, 140; LeQuesne, Basell, & Sheibani 2010: 15–17, 25.

However, the dating problems mean that it is impossible to know to what extent their current density and distribution might reflect ancient reality.

It is also worth briefly mentioning here a particular type of building which was noted during the *SSB* project in eastern Syrtica and which was differentiated from the types of stone huts already discussed above. LeQuesne *et al.* recorded c.40 sites composed largely of 'substantial rectangular buildings', which they named 'long huts', averaging c.5–6 m wide by c.9–12 m long (though occasionally even up to 25 m), taking the form of a single room or range of rooms, but which did not appear to fit into any previously known building typologies presented by the *ULVS* or *PVNL* projects. Some were found with Roman and Byzantine pottery, and occasionally both earlier and later pottery, as well as fragments of rotary querns. They could be isolated or occur in groups of 30 or more and anywhere in between, but while most of the Roman-period settlement of eastern Syrtica seems to have been located along the wadis not more than 10–12 km from the coast (see Chapter 5), the so-called long huts were often found far beyond these limits, sometimes more than 30 km inland. LeQuesne *et al.*'s conclusions about these buildings was that "it is difficult to interpret [them] as anything other than indigenous tribal settlement", continuing to connect them with the stone huts and tent footings of pre-Roman pastoralist camps.[149]

Until the first century AD, some stone huts were probably only occupied seasonally by transhumant pastoralists moving through the region with their herds.[150] As noted above, they were often arranged in lines, and sited on higher ground which looked out over wide stretches of land, an ideal situation for keeping an eye on large herds of animals.[151] Many stone huts probably maintained this function through the Romano-Libyan period, but we know very little about what relationship these types of buildings would have had to the unfortified and fortified farm buildings which began to appear. In particular, where they are contemporary, those within closer proximity to these larger buildings can probably be better interpreted as outbuildings and/or part of their surrounding settlements. Until closer investigations and excavations are undertaken in some of these buildings, however, we remain largely ignorant of the purposes they served and the relationships they may have had to larger farms and settlements.

Because we know so little about stone huts, I have not included them in my database and analysis; however, they potentially represent a rather significant proportion of the 'background' against which the later and larger stone buildings discussed in the following chapters were developed. It should additionally be borne in mind that the distinction between stone huts and small farm buildings is rather blurred and there are almost certainly examples that have been identified as stone huts which could reasonably have been identified as small farm buildings, and vice versa.

3.1.2 Fortified Hilltop Settlements

As briefly mentioned at the beginning of this section, Tripolitania was home to several sites that can be described as fortified hilltop settlements. There has, in previous investigations, sometimes been a lack of differentiation between these types of settlements and settlements that have one or more fortified buildings, which are the subject of Chapter 6. A fortified hilltop settlement, as opposed to a fortified building, is one in which the entire settlement is sited on a defensible hilltop, often completely surrounded by a defensive wall, and at which there was no individual or central building which could be singled out as the main focus of the settlement. While long known and frequently cited, when defined in this particular way, fortified hilltop settlements in Tripolitania have not often been the subject of focussed investigation and analysis. For this reason and the points below which differentiate these settlements from the buildings discussed in the rest of this book, both fortified and unfortified, I have discussed these settlements separately and more briefly here and they have not formed a part of my main analyses.

Only around a dozen sites identified as fortified hilltop settlements were recorded in the eastern pre-desert during the *ULVS* project and a single example reported by the *PVNL* survey;[152] a site known as Qasr Glul near Ghadames was also investigated by the *Ghadames Archaeological Survey*.[153] However, Mattingly's prediction that more would surely be found in the region if people started specifically looking for them has proven correct.[154] A large number of these types of settlements in the eastern pre-desert and in the *gebel* have now been identified via remote sensing and I also noted several more during my own satellite surveys, though unfortunately little work on these sites beyond their identification has yet been published.[155] These settlements could be quite extensive, but the buildings recorded in the eastern pre-desert at least were most often of relatively plain and rough, drystone construction, usually consisting of

[149] LeQuesne, Basell, & Sheibani 2010: 25–27; see also LeQuesne 2011: 27–28.

[150] See Section 1.3, fn. 18.

[151] LeQuesne, Basell, & Sheibani 2010: 16–17.

[152] Mattingly & Dore 1996: 116–118, 147–150; Mattingly & Flower 1996: 160–161; Rebuffat 1988: 52–53.

[153] Mattingly *et al.* 2020c: 196.

[154] Mattingly 1995: 47–48.

[155] Mattingly, Sterry, & Leitch 2013; M. Sterry, 2014, pers. comm.

Bir Zayden, W. Syrtica
(DigitalGlobe via Google Earth Pro, 24 Jun 2004)

Unnamed, Southwest (DigitalGlobe via Google Earth Pro, 20 Aug. 2010)

Zz001, Wadi ZemZem, E. pre-desert, south
(DigitalGlobe via Google Earth Pro, 6 Sept. 2012)

Unnamed, Southwest (DigitalGlobe via Google Earth Pro, 2 Sept. 2011)

Figure 3.2: *Examples of hillforts.*

clusters of small oval or rectangular rooms, often not much more than the stone huts which were discussed in Section 3.1.1, though sometimes there were larger complexes and buildings (Figure 3.2; see also Figure 4.14).[156]

Although in some ways their fortified character suggests that these settlements had more in common with the buildings and settlements discussed in Chapter 6, many seem to have been established much earlier; the dates of finewares recovered at a number of the *ULVS* examples suggest occupation from as early as the first century AD and continuing into the fifth century and beyond.[157] In addition, there is good reason to believe that many of these sites may actually have been established prior to this time. Mattingly has pointed out that the presence of these early imported finewares suggests that these sites were probably already relatively well-established by that period.[158] Furthermore, Sallust's accounts of the presence of established fortified hilltop settlements in Numidia, and archaeological research on similar settlements in what is now modern Tunisia and to the south in Fazzan have shown that hillforts were an important form of pre-Roman settlement to both the west and south of Tripolitania, supporting the idea that similar settlements would also have been present in Tripolitania at this time.[159]

It appears, then, that in the eastern pre-desert at least, there were a number of pre-existing fortified hilltop settlements (just as there were probably pre-existing oasis settlements) and these continued to be occupied when the unfortified farm buildings discussed in Chapter 5 began to appear, though the territories they were found within tended not to coincide. Later, however, the distinction between fortified hilltop settlements and the fortified buildings discussed in Chapter 6 began to be slightly more blurred; the territories occupied by these different types of sites began to overlap more, and more complex buildings similar to fortified towers and compounds begin to be found at hilltop sites.[160] However, unlike the farm buildings and settlements, the fortified hilltop settlements seem to have been less obviously associated with features which can be directly related to agricultural activities such as wadi walls. In addition, many of these fortified hilltops were actually quite a distance from the wadis (although the same might be said of many fortified farm buildings sited in similar locations), and indeed, some appear not to have had any convenient sources of water, suggesting that they were only seasonally occupied, and that the most important aspect of these settlements was their defensibility.[161] It has been suggested by Mattingly therefore that these settlements were occupied by a separate segment of society which retained the semi-pastoralist lifestyle of the pre-Roman period.[162]

3.1.3 Non-Stone Architectures

My investigation deals primarily with stone architecture, as unsurprisingly, stone is the material for which we have the most and best evidence in rural contexts during the period under study in Tripolitania. However, it is also important to acknowledge the existence of non-stone architectures and we should not underestimate their possible role in the landscape in both pre-Roman and Romano-Libyan times.

The topic of stone vs. non-stone materials in architecture has been an important theme in a number of articles that deal with the transition in different societies from perishable to permanent materials.[163] In particular, Büchsenschütz discusses the 'privileged' position that stone construction has often been given in studies of architecture, from Vitruvius (who associated wooden buildings with very early and primitive peoples) onwards, explicitly pointing out "*l'idée qu'une habitation digne de ce nom, une 'maison', n'existe qu'à partir du moment où elle est réalisée en pierres et couverte de tuiles, alors que la 'hutte' de bois et de terre n'est qu'un abri provisoire, archaïque, sans grand intérêt*".[164] It is not insignificant, however, that unlike many areas of the Roman Empire, stone was a commonly available resource in most of Tripolitania, whereas wood suitable for building may have been a scarcer commodity, especially in the pre-desert regions and Syrtica.

Buildings constructed of organic materials can be extremely difficult to trace except in particularly favourable circumstances; however, written and artistic evidence attest to their existence in both pre-Roman and Roman times. Ancient authors discussing North Africa mention buildings called *mapalia* (or *magalia*), a term which is usually translated as 'huts'.[165] The origins of the term are unclear and the exact descriptions tended

[156] Mattingly & Dore 1996: 118.

[157] Mattingly & Dore 1996: 147–150; Mattingly & Flower 1996: 160. Recent radiocarbon dates from a mortar sample from Gasr Glul gave a date of calAD 435–625 (Mattingly *et al.* 2020c: 196).

[158] Mattingly 1995: 47.

[159] Sallust, *Bellum Iugurthinum*, 37, 92–94; Ferchiou 1990a; 1990b; Ben Hassen & Maurin 1998: 185–188; Mattingly 2003b: 136–142; Liverani 2005b.

[160] Mattingly & Flower 1996: 160.

[161] Mattingly 1995: 42; Mattingly & Dore 1996: 116–118.

[162] Flower & Mattingly 1995: 56–58; Mattingly & Flower 1996: 160; Mattingly 1996a: 321.

[163] For example, Büchsenschütz 2001; Izzet 2001; Colantoni 2012.

[164] Vitruvius, *de Architectura*, 2.1; Büchsenschütz 2001: 223.

[165] For example, Herodotus, *Histories*, 4.190; Pliny, *Natural History*, 5.22; Sallust, *Bellum Iugurthinum*, 18; Virgil, *Georgics*, 3.340; Pomponius Mela, *de Chorographia*, 1.36–37. See also Lewis & Short 1879: 1112; Bates 1914: 168–170; Le Coeur 1937; Marcy 1942; Fentress 1979: 30–31.

to vary, but these *mapalia* seem to have been a type of structure constructed of lightweight wooden frames and reeds; two possible examples are illustrated in a pair of mosaics from El-Alia, Tunisia.[166] Isidore of Seville also uses the terms *casa* and *tugurium* for essentially similar types of structures while distinguishing *mapalia* as a specifically Numidian type of hut with rounded sides.[167]

Structures of organic materials need not necessarily have been temporary or only used by nomadic or semi-nomadic peoples. Pomponius Mela, writing in the first century AD, specifically contrasted the more 'civilised' people living closer to the coast in North Africa who lived in *mapalia*, with the less cultured peoples of the interior who followed their herds, bringing their *tuguria* with them.[168] Sallust also refers to both *tuguria* and *mapalia*, using the latter collectively to essentially mean village.[169] Marcy has speculated that some *mapalia* could have had low stone walls, on top of which a lighter, even portable, upper part could be placed, enabling people to return to the same spots over and over again.[170] A similar technique of using low stone foundations with upper walls and a roof of more perishable materials, though not portable in this case, is also known from later-first millennium BC sites in Fazzan.[171]

Similarly, structures such as tents of cloth or leather were almost certainly also used in the area before, during, and after the Romano-Libyan period, coexisting with stone-built structures. The locations of tents are sometimes indicated by areas that have been deliberately cleared of stone to create a flat surface or by circular or rectilinear arrangements of stones that were used as bases, though it can be difficult to differentiate between the latter and small stone huts or enclosures, particularly from satellite imagery.

There is little direct evidence for any of the types of buildings just described for Roman-period Tripolitania, but huts built primarily of palm fronds have been used in many parts of North Africa, including Tripolitania, until modern times. Travelling in the area of Tripoli in the 1890s, Myres photographed a number of huts of this type which were constructed and used by the Hausa people.[172] In Fazzan, until quite recently, huts known as *zaribas* were commonly constructed amongst dwellings of more permanent construction, generally as temporary shelters or for poorer labourers.[173] It seems very likely that buildings of a comparable form and construction would have been used in similar contexts and for similar reasons during the Roman-Libyan period.

Other less permanent materials which may have been used in both pre-Roman and Roman periods were mudbrick and/or *pisé*. There is evidence for the use of mudbrick for interior walls in *Sabratha*, so it was clearly in use, at least along the coast, in Tripolitania.[174] LeQuesne *et al.* also recorded the remains of mudbrick buildings east of Ajdabiyah, in the southwest part of Cyrenaica, just to the east of the current study area.[175] Buildings of mudbrick or similar techniques are also well-documented in Fazzan for the Garamantian (c.300 BC to AD 700), Islamic and modern periods (c.AD 700 until the twentieth century).[176] There is little direct evidence for the use of mudbrick in rural Tripolitania, again perhaps related to the abundance of natural stone which was readily available. Nevertheless, there is reasonable speculation that mudbrick or other similar techniques could still have been used in rural Tripolitania, especially for the upper storeys of buildings, but our evidence is simply lacking.[177]

3.2 Rural Settlement Chronology

3.2.1 Ceramics and Dating

Our current understanding of the chronological development of rural settlement in Tripolitania during the Hellenistic and Roman periods is largely based on the recovery and dating of ceramics, particularly finewares, found during surface surveys. For the earlier periods, this chiefly included imported black-glaze wares, *terra sigillata* imported from Italy and Gaul, and African Red Slip wares (ARS) imported from northern Tunisia. Later on, more locally-made versions and substitutions, such as Tripolitanian Red Slip wares (TRS) were more common,[178] though to date only one production site has been

[166] Bates 1914: 169; Picard 1990: 8, fig.3, 9, fig. 5.

[167] Isidore of Seville, *Etymologies*, 15.12.

[168] Pomponius Mela, *de Chorographia*, 1.36–37.

[169] Sallust, *Bellum Iugurthinum*, 46.

[170] Marcy 1942: 25.

[171] Mattingly 2003b: 162.

[172] Historic Environment Image Resource (HEIR) Project, Institute of Archaeology, University of Oxford. http://heir.arch.ox.ac.uk, Resource ID: 34450.

[173] Mattingly 2003b: 156, 158–160, 173–176.

[174] Kenrick 1986: 127–128, 151–152.

[175] LeQuesne, Basell, & Sheibani 2010: 22.

[176] Mattingly 2003b: 136–176; Mattingly *et al.* 2013a; 2013b; 2020a.

[177] Mattingly & Dore 1996: 124.

[178] Hayes 1972; 1980; Dore 1985; 1988; 1996; Bonifay 2004.

identified.[179] Other types of ceramic vessels including amphorae, coarsewares and handmade pottery, are also important indicators of date.[180]

In general, the presence of ceramics is a reasonable indicator that people were at a site during a particular time period; however, we cannot assume that this information necessarily corresponds directly to the timing of the construction, occupation or abandonment of individual buildings or settlements. It can be argued that the earliest date indicated by finewares only reflects the stage at which pottery began to be imported to a site, and as Mattingly has previously noted, it seems likely that such importation of goods would only have started once a settlement had already been established.[181] In addition, as Lund has pointed out, when dealing with dated finewares, it is not always clear to what point in a vessel's life the dates might refer, whether its manufacture, acquisition or purchase, period of use, discard or deposition.[182]

Similarly, the date of the latest ceramics recovered from a site is no guarantee that the buildings (or even the ceramics themselves) were not used for years, decades or perhaps even centuries afterwards. We must also consider the role of non-ceramic vessels, which could have been used before, concurrently, or after ceramics were utilised or imported at a site. Pomponius Mela attests that the peoples of Africa used vessels of wood or bark/skin (*vasa ligno...aut cortice*) and Lucian described how the *Garamantes* and the tribes of the Greater Syrte region used ostrich eggs for vessels (as they supposedly had no pottery).[183] Brogan and Smith also reported finding fragments of decorated gourd vessels in middens at the site of Ghirza, probably dating to the late Roman period.[184] Furthermore, it is clear that nomadic or semi-nomadic peoples used ceramic vessels, and we cannot necessarily assume that the presence of pottery implies sedentarism. It is therefore more appropriate to say that the physical and chronological distribution of ceramic evidence testifies to potential patterns in the trade, supply and use of various types of finewares.

Nevertheless, due to the scarcity of excavated buildings in rural Tripolitania, surface ceramic data is often all that we have to go on in terms of dating sites and it is, of course, not my intention to suggest that we cannot or should not make use of this valuable material. However, it is important to emphasise that the chronological picture that is suggested by the survey evidence presented below is really one of imported fineware use and distribution, and to a lesser extent, that of other types of ceramic vessels such as amphorae and cooking wares. The degree to which fineware and other ceramic data (particularly that collected from surface survey) can be used as a proxy for the chronological development of rural settlement and the construction of buildings is still up for debate.[185]

3.2.2 Survey Evidence

Detailed quantitative data on dated ceramics which allowed analyses on the chronological development of rural settlement were available in six areas covered by four major survey projects (Figure 3.3). Unfortunately, not all of the surveys for which detailed ceramic data were available were the same as those for which architectural data were available, and there were many areas for which no ceramic data was available at all. As a result, it was unfortunately not possible to include that type of data for individual sites in my catalogue or factor it directly into the analyses in Chapters 5 and 6. However, we can still use these data to gain an idea of general trends in the chronology of rural settlement in a few different parts of Tripolitania.

The available ceramic survey data are summarised in Figure 3.4 and Appendix Table 2, divided by 50-year periods. It should be noted that with the exception of the *ULVS* data, which includes only unfortified and fortified farm sites, these data also sometimes include various other types of rural sites, including mausolea or quarries, but due to the way the data were presented, it was unfortunately not possible to extract these types of sites.

The earliest recorded material among these areas comes from Jerba, with a total of six sites which produced material from between 500 and 325 BC and increasing to 19 sites between 325 and 250 BC. Fourteen sites dating to the third century BC and one possibly as early as the fourth century BC were also identified in the immediate vicinity of *Lepcis Magna* and two areas of the coast to the east and west (around Silin) of *Lepcis*, suggesting that there was at least a limited amount of rural settlement in the immediate hinterlands of the larger coastal cities during this century.[186] It is worth noting that the *Lepcis Magna Coastal Survey* recovered no identifiable ceramics from sites along a 20 km stretch of the

[179] Felici & Pentiricci 2002; Munzi *et al.* 2004–2005: 458–460.

[180] Arthur 1982; Dore 1996: 352–355; Ahmed 2010: 248–287; Leitch 2010.

[181] Mattingly 1995: 47. He makes this note with regard to the dating of hillfort settlements in the pre-desert, but the point is generally applicable.

[182] Lund 2009.

[183] Pomponius Mela, *de Chorographia*, 1.36; Lucian, *Dipsades*, 6–7; Dossey 2010: 40.

[184] Brogan & Smith 1984: 93–94. Similar wooden and gourd vessels are also common in Garamantian graves (Mattingly, Sterry, & Ray 2019).

[185] Millett 1991; Frankovich, Patterson, & Barker 2000; Dossey 2010: 38–39; Schörner 2012.

[186] The leap in Jerba from 19 to 79 sites between the first and second halves of the 3rd c. BC seems quite drastic, but the total of 79 applies to the period between 250 to 50 BC, and it is possible that not all of them should be dated to as early as the second half of the 3rd c. BC.

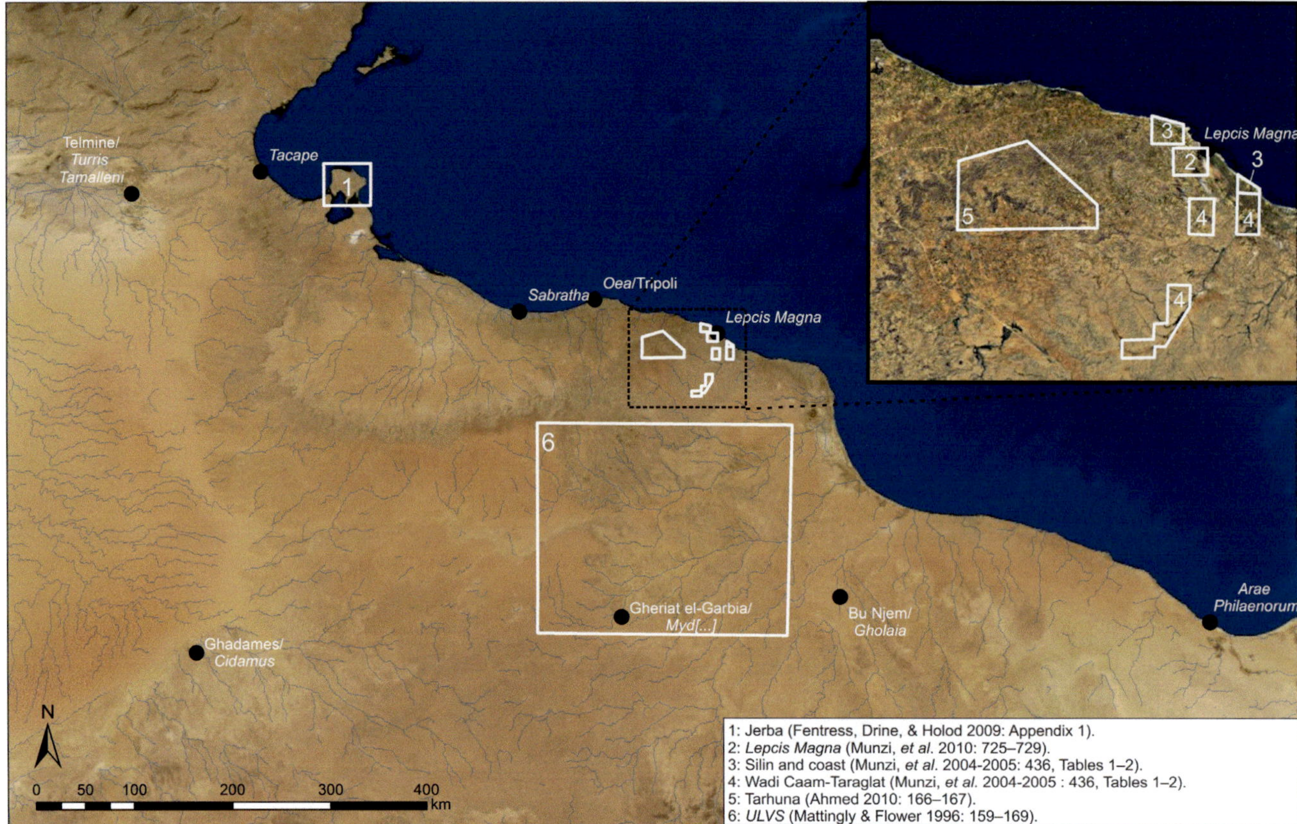

Basemap: Esri, DigitalGlobe, GeoEye, i-cubed, USDA, USGS, AEX, Getmapping, Aerogrid, IGN, IGP, swisstopo, and the GIS User Community
Drainage: Lehner, B., Verdin, K., Jarvis, A. (2008): New global hydrography derived from spaceborne elevation data. Eos, Transactions, AGU, 89(10): 93-94. Retrieved from http://hydrosheds.cr.usgs.gov (15 sec Flow Accumulation)

Figure 3.3: *Approximate locations of six survey areas for which detailed chronological survey data were available.*

coast west of Lepcis which could be dated before the first century BC.[187]

It is not until the second to first centuries BC that we see a noteworthy increase in the number of rural sites with finewares around the coast and the hinterlands of *Lepcis Magna*. Only one site was found in each of the Wadi Caam-Taraglat and Gebel Tarhuna areas with material which can be dated to the second century BC, increasing to three and seven respectively in the first century BC; however, the fact that even a few of these vessels were now starting to move greater distances inland is significant.

No rural surveys from the mainland of western Tripolitania have, as yet, specifically recorded the presence of second- to first-century BC ceramics. However, the ceramic evidence for the surveys conducted by the Tunisian *Institut National de Patrimoine* in that region has not been published in full and the accounts of the ceramics in what publications have been released so far are limited to very general descriptions for the Roman period, e.g. '*la céramique antique – commune, sigillée*'.[188] It might not be surprising to find a similar pattern of evidence of some limited rural settlement in the second and first centuries BC in the coastal areas and hinterlands around *Tacape*, *Gigthis* and *Zitha* (not to mention *Sabratha* and *Oea*, where no large rural surveys have yet been published).

An analysis by Guéry of some of the pottery from sites surveyed by Trousset in the interior of western Tripolitania concluded that none could be dated to earlier than the first century AD.[189] In the east, almost no material from Syrtica has been dated to earlier than the late first century BC (and this seems to have been fairly rare),[190] with the possible exception of two sites identified in the *Shell Sirte Basin* (*SSB*) survey which produced pottery that was generically described as 'Hellenistic'.[191] No material collected from the *ULVS* area was dated to before the first century AD.

There is little question that the evidence just discussed attests to the existence of rural settlement along the Tripolitanian coast and in the hinterlands of the main urban centres in the two centuries and more before Tripolitania was incorporated into the Roman Empire.

[187] Schörle & Leitch 2012: 151.

[188] Mrabet 2000b: 34 (158.035).

[189] Guéry 1986; Mattingly 1987: 85 fn.76.

[190] Longerstay 1999: 64.

[191] LeQuesne, Basell, & Sheibani 2010: 19 (SSB877 and SSB899).

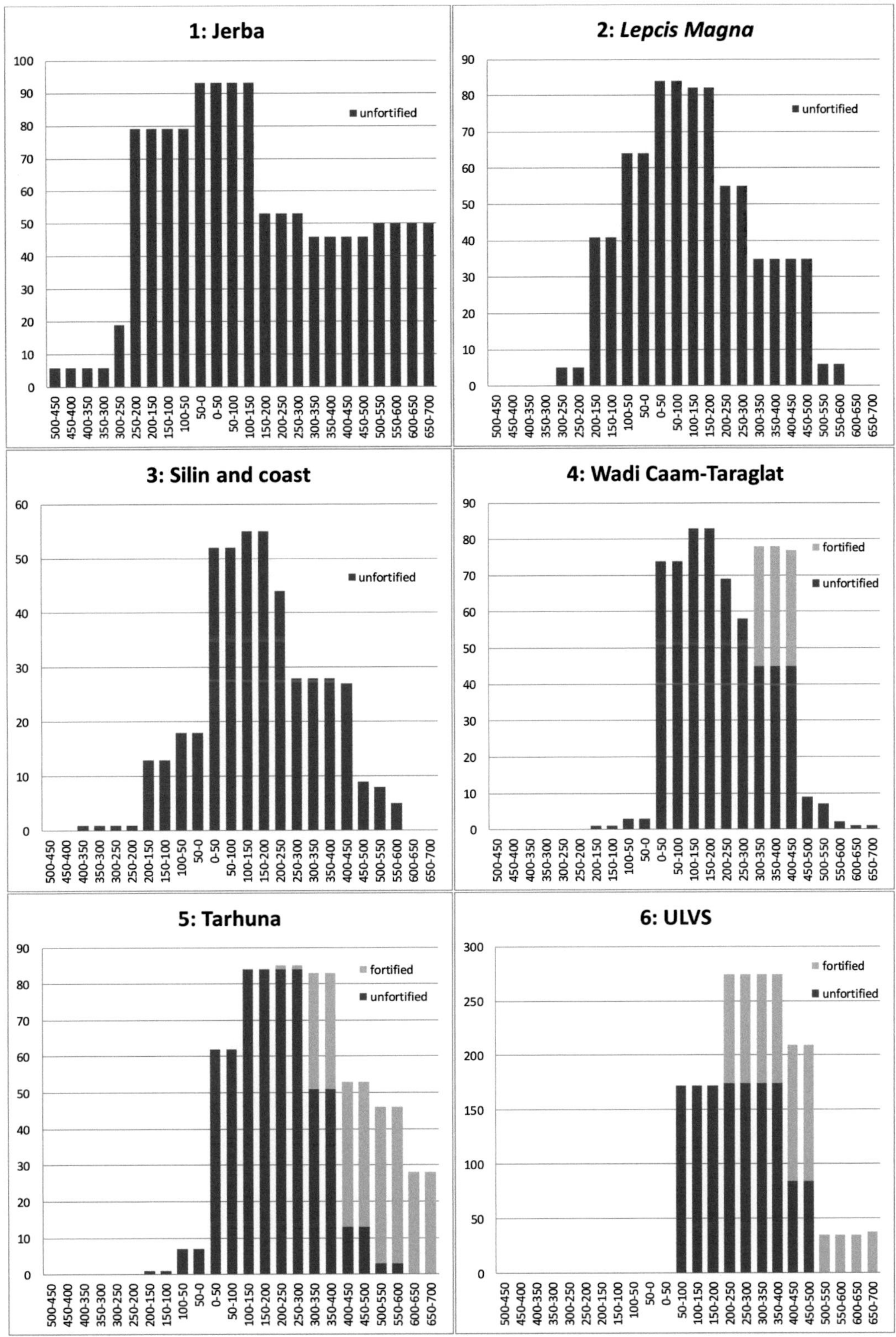

Figure 3.4: *Chronological distribution of ceramic evidence collected in six survey areas.*

The late first millennium BC increase of rural settlement which is implied by the ceramic evidence has been convincingly connected to the major political events of the late third and second centuries BC, i.e. the Second and Third Punic Wars, followed by the Jugurthine War. The ultimate outcome of these events was that Tripolitania and its cities gained a degree of independence which they had not experienced before. With the destruction of the region's main economic rival, Carthage, agricultural exploitation and permanent settlement was able to expand beyond just those areas within the immediate vicinity of the cities.[192]

[192] Cifani *et al.* 2003: 396–397; Munzi *et al.* 2004: 19–21; Ahmed 2010: 169.

However, the picture painted by the distribution of finewares in the centuries leading up to the first century AD potentially underestimates the density of activity and settlement in rural Tripolitania. As discussed in Section 3.1, there is still a great deal of uncertainty concerning the physical forms that pre-Roman settlements may have taken and we should not underestimate the importance of both buildings and vessels made of perishable materials, either or both of which may have been in use at various sites. In addition, surface materials on their own are essentially useless for dating the construction of individual buildings, stone or otherwise. Many of the sites identified above with ceramics dating to the second or first century BC have evidence for continuous occupation into at least the second century AD or later, and without excavation, we cannot know to what extent the last phases of building visible may or may not have differed from the first.

If the evidence of the finewares suggests that the second to first centuries BC saw a notable increase of rural sites over the previous period, the first century AD bore witness to a veritable explosion. In the areas already discussed along the coast and into the Gebel Tarhuna, the density of material datable to the first century AD increases significantly over earlier periods. For example, in the areas surveyed in the coastal regions east and west of *Lepcis Magna*, the number of sites with material dating to the first century AD increases from the preceding century from 18 to 52. In the areas further south, the growth is even more dramatic, increasing from 3 to 74 sites in the Wadi Caam-Taraglat, and 6 to 58 sites in the Gebel Tarhuna. In the west, on Jerba, although not apparently so drastic, the number of sites for the period from 50 BC to AD 150 increases to 93 from 79 in the period before. Unfortunately, as already mentioned, we have no specific data for the coastal mainland of western Tripolitania, but it does not seem inappropriate to use the evidence of Jerba as at least a broad guideline for what may have been happening in the immediate hinterlands of cities like *Tacape*, *Gigthis* and *Zitha*.

It is also not until the late first century AD that any significant amount of datable material begins to appear in the eastern pre-desert and Syrtica, with large amounts of imported fineware starting to occur in the *ULVS* area beginning in the second half of that century.[193] None of the published surveys in Syrtica provided specific numbers of sites by period but Reddé has suggested that the ceramic evidence for the *Prospection des Vallées du Nord de la Libye* (*PVNL*) area shows a peak of activity in the later first to second century AD and that the lack of later forms of ARS indicates that settlement in the wadis ceased in the late third or early fourth century AD.[194] Unfortunately, however, TRS sherds from this area were not specifically analysed, with the investigators simply making the observation that around 20% of the ceramics were probably of this type.[195] This potentially limits our understanding about later occupation of farms in that area, as different forms of TRS have been variously dated from the mid to late third century AD until the sixth or seventh century AD. Ceramics recovered during the *Prospection Archéologique dans cinq vallées de la Région Syrtique* (*PARS*) were dated as a group from the first century BC to the sixth century AD, though Longerstay concluded that the main period of activity represented was from the first to third centuries AD.[196] Only a few sites were actually visited in the *SSB* area, but most of the ceramics there were dated from approximately the first to fourth centuries AD.[197]

This apparent delay in the spread of finewares to the pre-desert and Syrtica was almost certainly related to the fact that it was not until the first century AD that a relative peace with the indigenous peoples of these areas was reached, as outlined in Section 1.3. Only then, it seems, did the peoples who came to settle these areas begin to truly take part in the trade and economic activities through which they could acquire these types of goods.[198] Interestingly, this is in contrast to the fact that there is evidence for imported finewares from the fourth century BC onwards in Fazzan, far to the south of Tripolitania. Even if this trade was not as abundant as in later periods, the routes by which these goods arrived must have traversed the pre-desert areas just mentioned.[199]

Into the second century AD, the situation in the region of *Lepcis Magna* and the surrounding areas seems to have remained stable in terms of numbers of sites, but these numbers begin to decline as early as the third century AD, falling steadily through the following centuries so that there were only 21 sites recorded by the early sixth century AD, and only two at which late seventh to eighth century AD coinage was found.[200] In contrast, while settlement on Jerba peaks at the same time or slightly earlier than the sites around *Lepcis Magna* and the coastal plain in the period between 50 BC and AD 150, after a certain amount of decline in the third century AD, based on the evidence of the ceramic material, rural settlement appears to have remained

[193] Dore 1996; Reddé 1988: 78–79.

[194] Reddé 1988: 79.

[195] Reddé 1988: 79–80; Dossey 2010: 67.

[196] Longerstay 1999: 64.

[197] LeQuesne, Basell, & Sheibani 2010: 23–24.

[198] Mattingly 1995: 50–53; 1996a: 319–324; Mattingly *et al.* 2017. One wonders if similar factors could have been at work in the western pre-desert.

[199] Mattingly 2013: 187; Leitch *et al.* 2017.

[200] Munzi *et al.* 2016: 72–73.

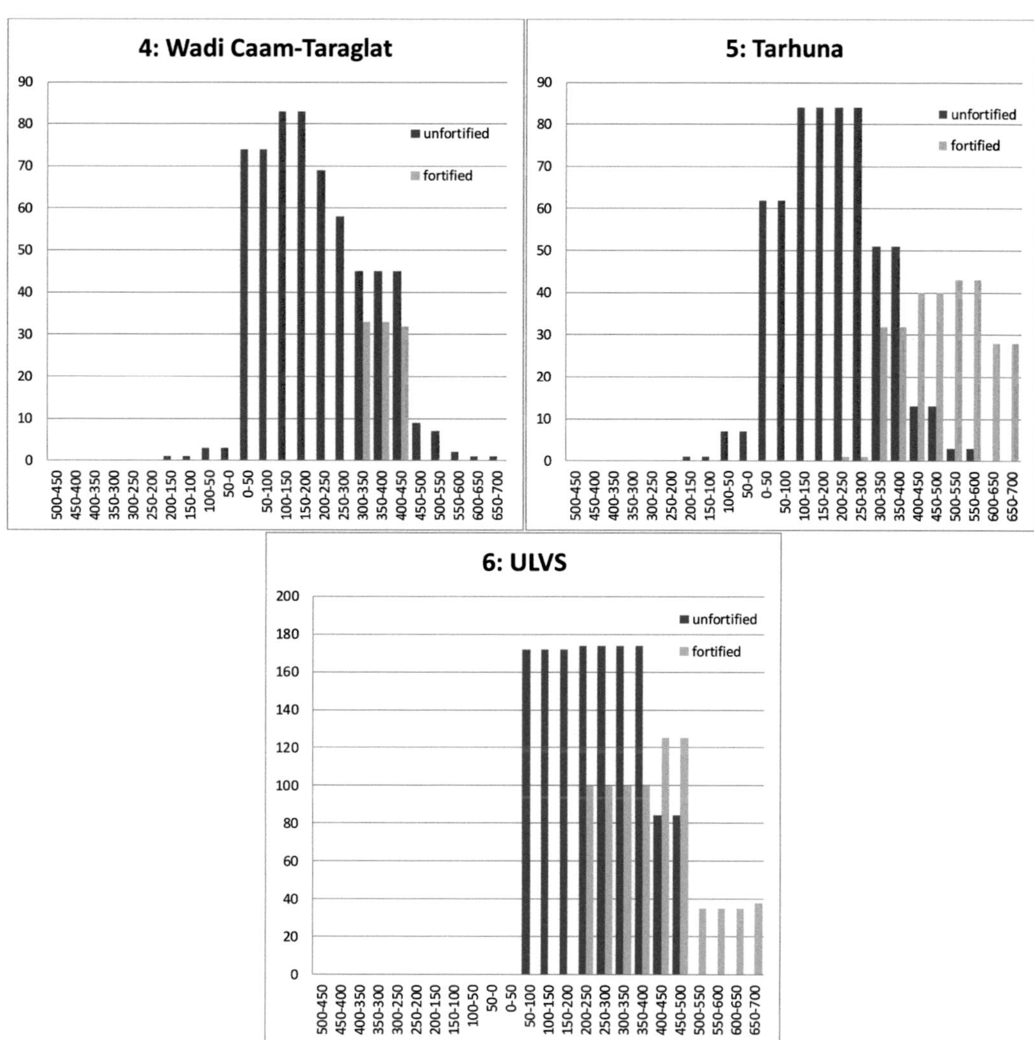

Figure 3.5: *Chronological distribution of ceramic evidence collected in three survey areas with unfortified and fortified buildings separated.*

relatively stable into the seventh century AD. An interesting question is whether this stability extended to other areas of western Tripolitania or was a situation unique to Jerba, but unfortunately we do not yet have the data to speak in detail about this.

Like the coastal areas, the number of sites in the Wadi Caam-Taraglat area slightly further inland peaked in the second century AD followed by some decline in the third century AD. However, rather than continuing steadily, this was followed by a small resurgence in sites in the fourth century AD, with the region only suffering a massive drop from 77 to 9 sites between the first and second halves of the fifth century AD. Having maintained a degree of stability through the second to fourth centuries AD, the Gebel Tarhuna also saw a certain amount of decline beginning early in the fifth century AD but seems not to have suffered as badly or as rapidly as the immediate hinterlands of *Lepcis Magna*. In the pre-desert region covered by the *ULVS*, the number of rural sites with datable material clearly peaks in the third to fourth centuries AD, falling off only slightly in the fifth century and then more drastically in the sixth to seventh centuries AD.

There appear to be two main reasons for the divergence between the more coastal regions and those further inland. The first is that the fates of the farms in *Lepcis'* immediate territories were probably more connected to the city itself which suffered greatly in the fourth and fifth centuries AD due to earthquakes and raids, with large parts of it already abandoned by that period.[201] The second reason, which contributed to the resilience in the numbers of rural sites in the interior, appears to have been the emergence of the fortified farm buildings in the third to fourth centuries AD in those areas.

If we refer back to Figure 3.4, it becomes clear how the inclusion of the fortified sites in the overall data for the areas of the Wadi Caam-Taraglat, Gebel Tarhuna and the *ULVS* region contributed to the patterns just discussed. In Figure 3.5 we see the same data presented

[201] Munzi *et al.* 2016: 72–73. See also Section 1.3.

in Figure 3.4 above for the three survey areas with fortified sites, but with the proportion between sites with unfortified and fortified buildings split apart in order to show the different patterns of development. In the Wadi Caam-Taraglat, removing the fortified sites from the fourth century AD data changes the number from 78 to 45 sites. While this is still a significant number, we can see that it is now a decrease in the number of unfortified building sites from the previous period, rather than an increase. A similar trend is seen in the Gebel Tarhuna data, so that in the fourth century AD, instead of maintaining almost the same number of sites from the third century, the number of unfortified sites with datable material falls from 84 to 51, and then to 13 in the fifth century AD. Interestingly, in the *ULVS* region, the number of unfortified farms with datable material remains relatively constant from the late first century AD until the end of the fourth century AD and actually increases by two sites (from 172 to 174 sites) between the first to second centuries AD and the third to fourth centuries AD. It is only in the fifth century AD that this number apparently falls by more than half to 84 sites; very few sherds which were securely datable to the fifth century and later (i.e. late TRS wares) were found associated with unfortified farms in the *ULVS* area.[202]

In the case of the fortified sites, we see a different pattern. In the Wadi Caam-Taraglat area, based on the fineware evidence, fortified sites would seem to appear rather suddenly in the fourth century AD and disappear just as suddenly a century and a half later, never outnumbering the unfortified sites. In the Gebel Tarhuna, we can see an increase in fortified sites beginning as early as the first half of the third century AD and a firmer establishment of the form in the fourth century AD. In the next century, the fortified sites move ahead of unfortified ones in frequency, and while the latter decrease drastically, the fortified sites remain fairly popular, even into the seventh century AD. A similar pattern is seen in the *ULVS* region, where fortified sites appear rather suddenly in the third to fourth centuries AD, but it is not until the fifth century AD that they appear to overtake the unfortified sites in numbers. Their presence continues, but in much reduced numbers through the sixth and seventh centuries AD. Whether this is indicative of population decline, a change in settlement patterns, or only reduction in the import or use of datable ceramics, is harder to say.[203]

The transitional period between unfortified and fortified sites is particularly problematic since many fortified sites were built quite closely to or directly on top of unfortified ones, and without excavation it is impossible to determine which ceramics date to which phase.[204] In the Tarhuna region, at least, evidence relating to the third century AD and earlier was counted as belonging to the unfortified part of the site, and evidence from the fourth century AD and later were counted as belonging to the fortified element. While this is obviously problematic and the transition at some sites was probably earlier or later, this should hopefully provide a reasonable 'average' and does not significantly affect the overall patterns of the increase and decrease of unfortified and fortified settlement. If we simply remove those examples which had both unfortified and fortified phases (11 of 122), the shape of the chronological distribution stays basically the same.

In addition, the timing of this transition is not entirely certain because later wares have, until recently, been more poorly dated and understood. For example, in the *ULVS*, for the purposes of their Gazetteer, the presence of any TRS on a site would generally place it in the Late Romano-Libyan period, which was defined as the fourth to fifth centuries AD onwards.[205] However, some early forms of TRS, when they can be identified, can potentially be dated to the mid to late third century AD.[206] In addition, Bonifay has more recently argued that the production of locally-made wares such as TRS which replaced imported vessels may have started earlier than previously supposed, particularly in inland contexts, where the cost of importing vessels over land would have been much higher than for areas closer to the coast.[207] Therefore, while we might be able to say that the volume of overall trade and consumption of imported finewares in the pre-desert was in decline by the third century AD, considering the number of possible problems with the data, I think we must be wary of assuming that this corresponds to a decline in unfortified settlement at this early period.

Nevertheless, in the *ULVS* area at least, in general it seems to be true that fewer examples of early ceramics are found at isolated fortified buildings compared to unfortified buildings in the same wadi. The converse is also true – later forms that commonly occur in association with fortified buildings are less common at unfortified ones.[208] So again, while of course we must allow for exceptions, this does support the idea that overall, sometime

[202] Mattingly & Dore 1996: 150–155; Mattingly & Flower 1996: 159–164.

[203] Mattingly & Dore 1996: 157–158; Mattingly, Sterry, & Leitch 2013: 185–187. According to Mattingly, Sterry, and Leitch, the amphorae and coarsewares indicate a similar pattern of decline in and after the 5th–6th c. AD.

[204] Mattingly & Dore 1996: 155. See also fn. 206.

[205] Mattingly & Flower 1996: 159–160; Scott, Dore, & Mattingly 1996: 14.

[206] Dore provided four different models for the chronological distribution of TRS forms and concludes that a model which distributes early TRS forms between the 3rd and 4th c. AD at a ratio of about 1:3 in probably most reasonable (Dore 1996: 322).

[207] Bonifay 2013; 2017.

[208] Dore 1988: 63.

in the third to fourth centuries AD, there was a general move from unfortified to fortified settlement types in the Gebel Tarhuna and pre-desert. This seems to parallel a general shift from ARS to TRS, i.e. from wares imported from other parts of North Africa to those manufactured in Tripolitania itself; Dore also noted this general trend with the casseroles assemblage from the *ULVS*, where by the fifth century AD, Tripolitanian products had completely replaced imported ones.[209] That this trend seems to be echoed at certain sites in Fazzan as well, where there is abundant evidence for imported finewares dating to between the first and third centuries AD but which drops off during the fourth century AD (though did not halt completely), could be indicative of some disruption in the trade networks which were supplying the ARS.[210]

Fortified buildings also certainly continued to be inhabited and constructed beyond the chronological limits of my study of the seventh century AD into the Islamic period, though the fineware evidence would seem to suggest that by this point settlement was on a severely reduced scale.[211] However, as with the evidence for the beginning of the period, we should not assume that the decline of certain finewares towards the end of the Romano-Libyan period necessarily meant a decline in population and settlement. More recent studies suggest that there are serious problems with the tendency to view the seventh to eighth centuries AD as the decline and end of so-called Roman North Africa, rather than a period of change and transition to an early medieval Islamic North Africa.[212] A decline in the import and consumption of finewares is a significant trend, and the development of local industries to replace them is certainly worthy of discussion in terms of supply and trade, but it does not necessarily correlate directly to patterns in settlement, population, or architecture.[213] Chronologies are beginning to show that certain ARS forms may have had a longer life than has previously been supposed, continuing to be produced before, during, and after the Arab conquest of North Africa.[214] Additionally coarsewares and handmade vessels which have traditionally been much more difficult to date with precision, and indeed vessels made of perishable materials, could easily have filled whatever void might have been left by a decline in the import of finewares.

It is also in the *ULVS* data in particular that we can see some of the major problems with relying on ceramic data from surface surveys to discuss the chronology and development of sites. The analyses and discussion above are based on the number of sites at which pottery that can be dated to specific centuries or periods was found, regardless of the quantity or ratio of different kinds of pottery found at those individual sites. As we have just seen, based on the figures cited above, the evidence would suggest that the number of unfortified sites occupied in the *ULVS* region did not begin to decline until the late fourth or fifth century AD. However, this is not the conclusion that is reached by the authors of the *ULVS* publications based on the *overall* chronological and typological distribution of ceramics recovered from all unfortified sites and analysed together as a single assemblage. According to the overall analysis which was based on the frequency of typological groups of ceramics present, the *ULVS* investigators concluded that activity on the unfortified farms was very high in the late first century AD, peaked in the second, and began to fall off again already in the third century AD (Figure 3.6a).[215] Conversely, although the peak of activity at fortified sites matches that given above in the fourth to fifth centuries, the overall ceramic data suggests that fortified sites were already being occupied by the second century AD, as opposed to the rather sudden third century appearance suggested above (Figure 3.6b). There is in this latter case, however, a relatively high probability that some of the earlier ceramics actually belong to unfortified sites which were replaced by the later fortified ones.[216]

The authors of the *ULVS* were aware of the limitations of the survey data and were careful both in their attempts to mitigate the problem and in warning against putting too much faith in specific dates of the chronological phases they identified.[217] However, they were not as concerned with analysing the lives of the buildings themselves, and so this particular discrepancy between the two different chronological distributions deserves some review and discussion. The main problem appears to be in what the *ULVS* authors termed the Mid Romano-Libyan period, dating between the third to fourth centuries AD and defined by the presence of ARS Hayes Forms 31 and higher.[218] The chart

[209] Dore 1996: 352–354. Though this does not appear to be the case with the amphorae, where Tunisian imports continued to play an important role in later periods.

[210] Mattingly 2013: 175–179; V. Leitch, 2014, pers. comm.; Leitch *et al.* 2017.

[211] Mattingly & Flower 1996: 166–167.

[212] King 1989; Sjöström 1993; Fenwick 2013.

[213] Fentress & Perkins 1988; Millett 1991; Fentress *et al.* 2004; Bonifay 2013; 2017.

[214] Bonifay 2004.

[215] Mattingly & Dore 1996: 150–155. It is worth noting that a very substantial proportion of the finewares included in this distribution come from a single site, Lm004, but removing them does not affect the overall shape of the distribution.

[216] Mattingly & Dore 1996: 155.

[217] Barker & Gilbertson 1996b: 43–45; Mattingly & Flower 1996: 159–160; Dore 1988: 61–63.

[218] Mattingly & Flower 1996: 159–160; Scott, Dore, & Mattingly 1996: 14.

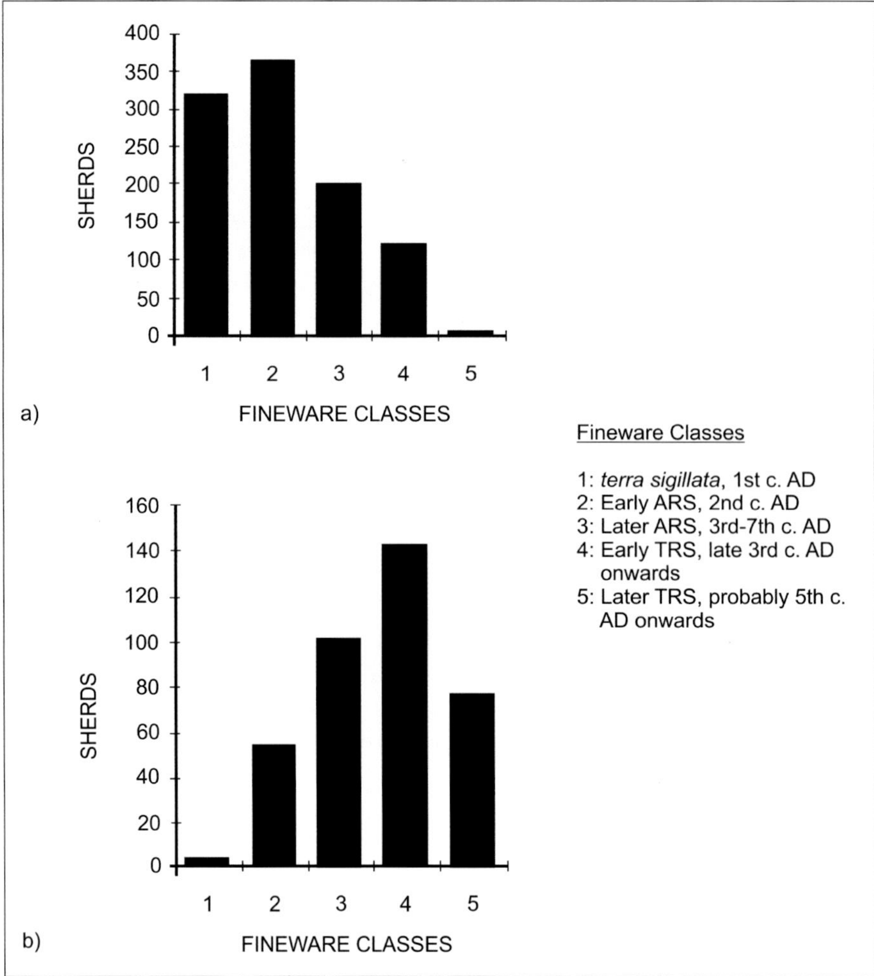

Figure 3.6: *Chronological distribution of ceramics recovered for all a) unfortified and b) fortified farm buildings in the* ULVS *area (after Mattingly & Dore 1996: 150, fig. 5.38 and 156, fig. 5.43a).*

shown in Figure 3.6a shows without question that in total, for all unfortified sites, there were fewer sherds of these types collected in the *ULVS* area than earlier forms of ARS and t*erra sigillata* which could be dated to the first to second centuries AD (defined as the Early Romano-Libyan period). However, according to the published distribution maps, even though there were fewer Mid Romano-Libyan sherds in total, it appears that they were spread over essentially the same number of unfortified sites as the earlier forms.[219]

What the issue comes down to therefore, is the relative importance of the total number of sherds found within the survey area and the number of sites at which sherds of those types were found. While the survey recovered more than c.55,500 sherds altogether, the average number of sherds collected at each site was apparently only 49, of which, on average, finewares only accounted for five.[220] At sites with this low rate of recovery, in my opinion, even a single sherd which can be securely dated must be considered as potentially significant.

In summary, the ceramic data just discussed have illuminated some very broad chronological trends in the settlement and occupation of different areas of Tripolitania. However, while these kinds of data can tell us that a site was probably occupied, or at the very least was the site of some human activity during a particular period, they cannot tell us anything with certainty about the establishment, construction, or abandonment of the physical settlement or associated buildings. As a result, chronologically speaking, my analyses of the physical forms and construction of both unfortified and fortified sites presented in Chapters 5 and 6 will treat the buildings within each sub-region of Tripolitania as a single group dated extremely broadly to the periods of main activity discussed above. It should go without saying that this does not mean that sites of one type or the other were not constructed or occupied outside of these periods, only that the material that we have seems to point to these periods as the most active in terms of their occupants' participation in the wider economy and trade of these particular goods.

[219] Mattingly & Flower 1996: 160–167, figs. 6.2–6.8.

[220] Dore 1996: 319.

chapter four

Military Architecture and Settlement

The arrival and continued presence of the Roman military in rural Tripolitania had a profound effect on the development of civilian settlement. As established in previous chapters, beyond the immediate hinterlands of the coastal cities, it was not until after a number of military actions in the first century AD that sedentary farming seems to have become more widespread as a way of life, and with it, the construction of permanent stone farm buildings. In addition, the establishment of the *limes* and the frontier zones created new routes of communication, while simultaneously restricting access through and monitoring older ones, resulting in new and different opportunities for the interaction and exchange of ideas, technology and goods.

For the purposes of this chapter, by military architecture I mean buildings which were constructed by and for the Roman army to serve a strategic or defensive purpose.[221] As briefly discussed in Sections 2.1 and 2.2, far more buildings in rural Tripolitania were previously identified by earlier scholars as military, or, as Goodchild suggested, that fortified buildings were occupied by *limitanei* (soldier-farmers). In his view, the tower-like *gsur* in particular, were deliberate copies of military buildings, the earliest examples of which "were clearly designed and constructed by Roman military architects", while later ones were "the work of indigenous hands following the approved model".[222] While this interpretation is no longer widely accepted, the strong physical similarities between certain types of military buildings and those which are now strongly believed to be civilian in origin are undeniable, and differentiating between military and civilian buildings remains problematic. There has been a certain amount of inconsistency in the criteria traditionally used to identify military structures, particularly in early studies along the *limes*, and without epigraphic or other explicit forms of identifying evidence, it can be very difficult to differentiate between military and civilian buildings with confidence. In the first part of this chapter, therefore, I will discuss and evaluate some of the more widely utilised criteria in which we can identify military sites and structures and differentiate them from (primarily fortified) civilian ones. In the second part of the chapter, I will propose a revised typology for the known military buildings and settlements of Tripolitania, listed in Appendix A, followed by a brief discussion of their place in the architectural and settlement landscape of the region.

4.1 Identifying Military Buildings

4.1.1 Epigraphy and Terminology

Epigraphic evidence which explicitly records the construction and/or function of a building is probably the easiest way to identify structures as military. So, for example, an inscription discovered just outside the north gate of Ras el-Aïn/*Talalati* (RLT109) explicitly records the construction of the *castra...opportuno loco a solo* in AD 263.[223] Similarly, an inscription from a small round watchtower located c.1 km northeast of Gheriat el-Garbia/*Myd[...]* describes the construction of a *burgus*, also *a solo*, sometime between AD 222 and 235.[224] There is no known dedicatory inscription for the building at Bir Rhezene/*Bezereos* (RLT072), but an inscription found inside the fortlet which clearly mentions the presence of a *vexillatio leg(ionis) III Aug(ustae)* and contains a list of around 300 names of soldiers is compelling evidence for

[221] For other types of buildings associated with military sites and settlements see Section 4.3, below.

[222] Goodchild & Ward-Perkins 1949: 94. See also fn. 108.

[223] *CIL* 8.22765.

[224] *IRT* 895; Mattingly 1985a.

its identification as a military structure.[225] In addition, at least two other fragmentary inscriptions from the vicinity of the fortlet, one of which was an altar, also mention the legion.[226] Unfortunately, building inscriptions, military or otherwise, which are this explicit and can be confidently attributed to a specific structure are rare in the Tripolitanian countryside.

Furthermore, even epigraphic evidence can sometimes be misleading. For example, changing ideas about the origins of the term *centenarium* have necessitated a reinterpretation of the buildings on which it is attested. There are currently four known epigraphic instances of the term *centenarium* in Tripolitania, two Latin and two Latino-Punic: Gasr Duib (Db001),[227] Ksar Tarcine/*Tibubuci* (RLT098),[228] Gasr Sidi Ali ben Zaid/Henchir el-Aftah (Oates 101-g)[229] and at a fortified building near Bir Scemech in the Wadi Sofeggin.[230] It has traditionally been interpreted as a military term, indicating a structure under the command of an officer called a *centenarius*, or garrisoned by a military detachment or unit known as a *centuria*.[231] However, as Mattingly has pointed out, neither of these interpretations is particularly satisfactory, as the vast difference in size and form between, for example, the relatively small Gasr Duib (Db001) at 15.5 x 15.5 m (240 m^2) and *centenarium Aqua Viva* in Numidia, at c. 88 x 87 m (7,656 m^2), makes it unlikely that we can assume they held the same size of garrison or were commanded by the same rank of officer.[232]

In addition, the latter two Tripolitanian attestations listed above are Latino-Punic texts with no reference to the military or any other particularly compelling reasons to suggest such an identification.[233] Goodchild interpreted this as support for his argument that these buildings were built by indigenous soldier-farmers or *limitanei*, and that "in the mind of its Libyan constructor, the 'gasr' was no less a part of the *Limes Tripolitanus* than…the official *centenarium* at Gasr Duib".[234] However, more recently Adams has proposed an alternative etymology and meaning for *centenarium*, arguing that from a linguistic standpoint, it makes more sense for the word to have been derived not from *centenarius*, but *centenum*, which was a type of wheat (probably rye, barley, or something similar). Therefore, a centenarium was a fortified granary and the term could easily have been expanded to mean more generally fortified food-store.[235] In light of the Latino-Punic examples, this interpretation is very attractive; however, if this was the case, its significance for military buildings, as Gasr Duib (Db001) and Ksar Tarcine /*Tibubuci* (RLT098) almost certainly were, remains unexplained.

In our earliest attestation of the term at Gasr Duib (Db001), dated to AD 244–247, the inscription seems to suggest that 'barbarian incursions' into the region were curtailed through the construction of the *nouum centenarium*.[236] While the safe-guarding of food and other supplies was surely an important task, it seems slightly curious to emphasise that particular aspect of its function when the rest of the inscription seems to refer to the overall defense of the *limes* zone. In this case, if we accept Adams' interpretation of the term, perhaps we can assume that already by this date the meaning of the term had expanded to more generally indicate a fortification.

There are also a certain number of sites for which epigraphic evidence suggests the presence of a military detachment, but where little or no evidence for a military structure has yet been found. The oasis of Ghadames (*Cidamus*), for example, almost certainly had a military presence, as inscriptions found at the site attest and based on the importance of its location on one of the routes leading inland from the coast (Figure 4.4, A).[237] Similarly, the site of Aïn el-Auenia (*Auru?*, Figure 4.4, B) has produced inscriptions attesting to the presence of a legionary vexillation and soldiers of the *cohors I Syrorum Sagittariorum*. Legionary tile-stamps suggest that it was probably a significant site, but again, as we currently have no physical architectural evidence, we cannot be certain about its status.[238] A fragment of a Severan inscription found at Bir Tarsin has also led Mattingly to propose

[225] *ILAf* 27.

[226] *ILAf* 26, 28.

[227] *IRT* 880.

[228] *CIL* 8.22763.

[229] IRT 877.

[230] *IRT* 889. This inscription was photographed *in situ* above the doorway of a fortified farm building near Bir Scemech in the lower Sofeggin and published in the 1920s by Petragnani (1928: 80); however, it was removed and built into an Italian fort at some point after this, and later taken by Goodchild to the museum at *Lepcis Magna*, and its exact original location is no longer known (Goodchild 1950a: 137). It is very likely that it belonged to one of the fortified farm buildings which were later recorded by the *ULVS* in that area, but it is now unclear exactly which one.

[231] Goodchild & Ward-Perkins 1949: 92; Smith 1968; Trousset 1974: 136.

[232] Mattingly 1995: 103; Leschi 1941: 170.

[233] Kerr 2005; Jongeling & Kerr 2005: 62–64.

[234] Goodchild & Ward-Perkins 1949: 94.

[235] Adams 2007: 550–554. See also Munzi, Schirru, & Tantillo 2014.

[236] *IRT* 880: *regionem limi[tis Ten] / theitani partitam et e[ius] uiam incursib(us) barba[ro] / rum constituto nouo centenario […] / […] s prae[cl]userunt.*

[237] *IRT* 907–909; Mattingly 1995: 97; Mattingly *et al.* 2020c: 195.

[238] Brogan & Reynolds 1960: 51, nos 1–2; Reynolds & Simpson 1967.

the existence of an outpost there (Figure 4.4, C).[239] The reference to the *limes [Ten]theitanus* in the Gasr Duib inscription suggests that the site of T(h)enteos, which is mentioned in both the *Antonine Itinerary* (75.1) and the *Notitia Dignitatum* (*Occidentis*, 31.19) was nearby, probably at or near Zintan (Figure 4.4, D); a series of Roman ruins have been reported just to the west of the city at Edref, though nothing that would certainly indicate a military identification.[240]

Further complicating matters are a series of place names known from the *ostraca* of Bu Njem for which we do not have secure locations. Two of these are more certainly military sites, based on the contexts in which they are mentioned: *Galin..i[*, and *Secedi*.[241] The location of the former is essentially a mystery, though *Secedi* seems to have been within three days' (at most) journey of Bu Njem.[242] A further four named places (*Arnum*, *Boinag*, *Esuba* and *Hyeruzerian*) have been proposed as outposts. Each of these appears in one or more *ostraca* as a location to which at least one soldier has been dispatched, but there is little other information about the location or types of sites these may have been.[243]

On the basis of the epigraphic and other evidence therefore we can speculate with reasonable certainty that some type of military building once stood at many of these locations, and they are certainly relevant to discussions about the nature and development of the frontier. However, in the absence of physical evidence, we can say little with confidence about these hypothetical buildings.

4.1.2 Appearance and Construction

The presence of certain physical features on buildings is sometimes used to make a case for military identification. However, these vary widely in their reliability and exceptions can be found for almost all of them. Therefore, while some of these features may indeed be commonly found in military buildings, none can be cited as infallible indicators of military identification.

One reasonably reliable indicator of military status is the so-called 'playing card' shape, i.e. rectangular or square enceintes with wide, rounded corners. This form was commonly used for military structures throughout the empire and Tripolitania was no different. It has been suggested that rounded corners were better than squared ones at withstanding battering (based on the same principle of distribution of weight which lay behind the strength of arches), a fact which was already known and exploited in ancient times.[244] Buildings of very large size (c. 0.5 ha or more) which take this particular 'playing card' form can usually be interpreted as military with some confidence. However, we must be more cautious with smaller structures, as many civilian, fortified buildings also employed rounded corners, though usually not as pronounced.[245]

Another feature which is often associated specifically with late Roman military buildings was the addition of projecting towers at the external corners and sometimes also along the exterior walls. Buildings with this feature (sometimes also known as *quadriburgi*) are known to have occurred both in Tripolitania and in many parts of the empire (Figure 4.1).[246] However, it has now become apparent that in Tripolitania (and also in Fazzan to the south) this feature was not restricted to military architecture (Figure 4.2). As a result, structures which have long been identified as military buildings on this basis are now being reconsidered. For example, Mattingly, Sterry and Leitch have recently argued for the reclassification of at least one Tripolitanian building which has previously been identified as military (Gasr Bularkan/Mselletin, Md002-g) and also note the doubts raised by Lenoir about another (Benia Guedah Ceder, RLT059-g), based on its asymmetricality and lack of gate-towers.[247] Based on this argument we might also question Henchir Temassine (RLT025) which is often considered to be military (Figure 4.3).[248]

Certain construction techniques are sometimes used to support military identification. For example, the similarity of the very high quality ashlar masonry and rounded, rebated corners observed at both Gheriat esh-Shergia (GS001) and Gasr Isawi/Banat (Nf037) has been cited as evidence that both are military constructions.[249] The general rarity of civilian buildings constructed in ashlar masonry, particularly in the more remote regions of Tripolitania makes this argument not entirely unreasonable;[250] however, again, the existence

239 *IRT* 887; Mattingly 1995: 80–81.

240 Hammond 1964: 10; 1967: 13; Mattingly 1995: 97.

241 Marichal 1992: 106, 192–193 no. 85 (*Galin..i[*), 200–203 nos 94–95 (*Secedi*).

242 Marichal 1992: 106–108, 200–204 (nos 94, 95); Mattingly 1995: 87–88. According to recent calculations concerning the speed of travel, this probably works out to a maximum of c.200 km, and more likely substantially less than that (Scheidel 2014: 14 fn.24).

243 Le Bohec 1989: 443; Marichal 1992: 106; Mattingly 1995: 105.

244 Vitruvius, *De Architectura*, I.5.5; Von Petrikovits 1971: 198. Though cf. Gregory's skepticism of this theory (Gregory 1989; 1997: 51).

245 See Section 6.2.1

246 Goodchild 1950b: 33–34; Trousset 1974: 133–135; Mattingly 1995: 191–194. See also Euzennat 1986; Kennedy & Riley 1990: 167–212; Reddé 1995; Băjenaru 2010: 58–60, 169–179; Mattingly, Sterry, & Leitch 2013: 174.

247 Mattingly, Sterry, & Leitch 2013: 174, fn. 45 & 46; Lenoir 2011: 280–281.

248 Trousset 1974: 53, 133–134; Mattingly 1995: 193; Mattingly, Sterry, & Leitch 2013: 175, fig 3.

249 Mattingly 1995: 104–105; Mattingly & Dore 1996: 115. For illustration, see Goodchild 1954: Plate XIII, c; Di Vita 1964: Tav. XXXV.

250 See Sections 5.2.4 and 6.2.4.

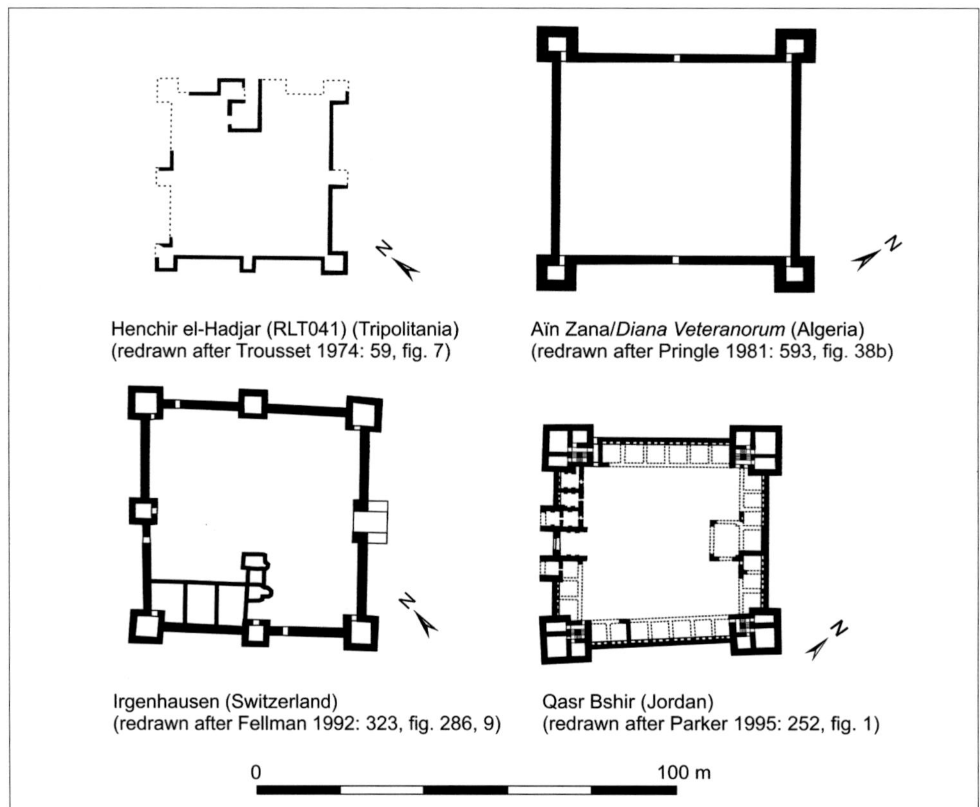

Figure 4.1: *Military buildings with projecting towers from around the Roman Empire.*

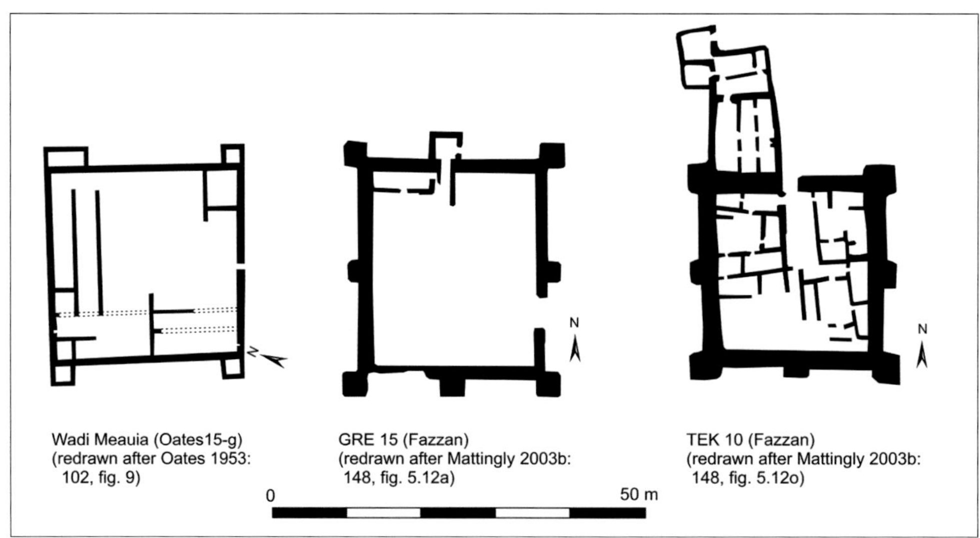

Figure 4.2: *Civilian buildings in Tripolitania and Fazzan with projecting towers.*

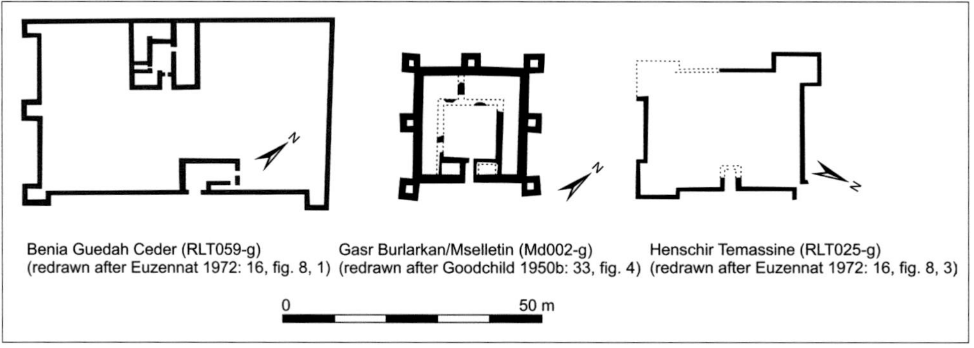

Figure 4.3: *Buildings in Tripolitania with projecting towers previously identified as military but now thought to be (potentially) civilian.*

of probable exceptions, such as the partial construction of a farm building in ashlar in the southern part of the eastern pre-desert (Lm004-f1), mean that neither can it be relied upon by itself as a consistent method for identification.[251]

4.1.3 Date

As already discussed in Section 3.2.2, the distribution of finewares suggests that generally speaking, civilian fortified farm buildings were not commonplace in Tripolitania until the third to fourth centuries AD. If we accept this as true, it is possible to suggest that fortified structures which can be dated to earlier than this time are more likely to be military in origin, though we must be cautious as this is a very broad generalisation and obviously unhelpful for military structures of a later date. Mattingly put forth this argument for the site of El Medina Ragda (HH004), where a number of first- and second-century AD finewares were collected.[252] While ultimately I have also identified this site as military, it is important to note that the ceramics in question were obtained through surface collection; without excavation we cannot be sure that they are not associated with an earlier building or site that is no longer visible on the surface.

In addition, we must also bear in mind the long lifespans of these buildings and the potential for re-use. The fact that so many fortified buildings are still standing to multiple storeys, particularly in the pre-desert, suggests that they could have been in regular use for very long periods of time, potentially centuries. The poor state of our knowledge concerning the dating of both military and civilian structures in the absence of well-excavated sites means that with only a few exceptions, we have very little detailed information about site phasing and how their function may have changed over long periods of time.

4.1.4 Location

Fortified buildings found at strategically important locations, such as oases, springs or the intersection of known trade routes (which often coincide and in many cases were likely tribal centres) are often identified as military establishments. A suspected Roman military presence has also been proposed for many of these nodal points, even in cases where there is little material evidence for it. Archaeological evidence has shown that the oasis of Mizda (Figure 4.4, E) was certainly settled in the Roman period and it has long been suspected to have had a military presence, but there is as yet no epigraphic or architectural evidence to support this theory.[253] Similar arguments have also been made for El-Hamma (*Aquae Tacapitanae*) and Telmine (*Turris Tamalleni*) (Figure 4.4, F, G), where, again, there is definite evidence for Roman occupation of the sites, but, as yet, no direct evidence for a military presence.[254]

Rebuffat has also argued for the existence of military detachments at several oases in southern Tripolitania. At the oases of Materes and Tfelfel, east of Ghadames in the southwestern pre-desert, he observed a scatter of second- and third-century AD ceramic and amphorae sherds, in association with two '*endroits des fortins*'. Slightly further north at Chawan, he also identified two rectilinear '*fortins*', one possibly with projecting towers on the enceinte, suggesting that perhaps they were occupied by allies of *Cidamus* (Ghadames), tribes allied to Rome or auxiliary soldiers.[255] Further east, he recorded two tower-like structures at the oasis of Zella with third-century ceramics which he identified as possible outposts attached to Bu Njem. Rebuffat also makes reference to a military presence at Waddan, though it is worth noting that while a recent survey by al-Haddad at the oasis has identified sites of Roman date, so far no evidence of a military presence has been found.[256] While a military presence would not necessarily be out of the question at some of these oases, given what we now know about civilian fortified settlement and trade and without further investigation, it is equally plausible that they were indigenous and civilian in nature.

Finally, proximity to and visibility with other military sites can also be a useful indicator of military status, particularly in cases of smaller outposts and watchtowers in the vicinity of larger sites. So, for example, the small tower known as Mergueb ed Diab (RLT074) located on a hilltop c.1 km southeast of Bir Rhezene (*Bezereos*, RLT072) can be reasonably interpreted as an observation or signalling post for the latter. Equally, towers in positions with good visibility found in close proximity to the linear features known as *clausurae*[257] are also good candidates.

4.1.5 Summary

As the discussion above demonstrates, in the absence of explicit epigraphic evidence, there is no simple or completely reliable way to identify military architecture. While certain physical features may be more common in military structures, many have also been observed in civilian structures, and it is therefore not possible to

[251] Lm004: Barker & Jones 1984.

[252] Mattingly 1995: 102; Scott, Dore, & Mattingly 1996: 127.

[253] Goodchild & Ward-Perkins 1949: 92; Mattingly 1995: 97; Schimmer 2012.

[254] Hammond 1964: 8–9; Mattingly 1995: 97.

[255] Rebuffat 1972: 323–324.

[256] Rebuffat 1970c: 183–185; Rebuffat 1977b: 405; Mattingly *et al.* 2020b: 132–136.

[257] See Section 4.2.6.

make generalisations based on the evidence of any one of these features alone. However, the presence of several of these features together can form a reasonably strong case for military identification. So, for example, we can argue for the military identification of the building at a site such as Gheriat esh-Shergia (GS001), based on its location at an important oasis on a main route to the interior, its construction of fine ashlar masonry with rounded corners, and the fact that the small watchtower associated with the main fort at Gheriat el-Garbia (GG007) is visible from this location.

Nevertheless, the evidence for each case must be weighed individually, taking into account as many factors as possible and even then, we cannot always be certain in our identification. Undoubtedly, therefore, some of the examples I have included in my analysis have potentially been misidentified and there are certainly other sites for which some argument for a military identification could theoretically be made; however, until further investigations at individual sites can be undertaken, the issue will remain unresolved.

4.2 Typology and Analysis

Using the criteria discussed above, I have catalogued 38 individual structures from across Tripolitania which can certainly or probably be identified as military in nature (Appendix A; Figure 4.4).[258] In the following sections I propose a revised typology for these structures which divides them into six groups: major forts, marching camps, minor forts, fortlets, outposts, and observation posts (watchtowers and *clausurae*), each of which will be discussed below in turn. We can question the validity and subjectivity of architectural typologies; however, based on the amount and type of evidence that is currently available for these structures, I believe that this system usefully divides the evidence into broad groups based on observable architectural differences and is an improvement on typologies that have been proposed before.

Many of the military buildings identified here were already known in the late nineteenth and early twentieth centuries and recorded during investigations along the *limes Tripolitanus* by French scholars and explorers, particularly in southern Tunisia. Although it was evident that there were a wide variety of different buildings, there were few explicit attempts at the time to organise the buildings they observed into a detailed architectural typology, with many structures simply identified by the generic term *fortin*.[259] Cagnat noted the wide variation in the size, proportions, and features of what he called *castella* or *burgi*, giving examples in three approximate size groups; however, it was only the smallest, usually round *turres*, that he explicitly separated as a different category.[260] Slightly later in Libya, other scholars, such as Goodchild, Ward-Perkins and Di Vita, sometimes distinguished different categories of military sites, identifying various sites as forts, road-stations, or outposts, but still stopped short of an explicitly defined typology.[261]

In the early 1970s, Euzennat proposed a more formal typology for the Roman military structures of southern Tunisia, followed shortly afterwards by Trousset's *Recherches sur le limes Tripolitanus*.[262] Both scholars based their systems on the same investigations and material, primarily using size and plan to make distinctions between types (the latter even re-using the illustrations from the former) and both using the same terminology for the categories they established, from largest to smallest: *castra/camps*,[263] *castella* and *centenaria*, with Trousset also adding the category of *tours de guets* (watchtowers). A more recent attempt by Krimi to re-evaluate the same material resulted in a similar typology to those proposed by Euzennat and Trousset, consisting of *camps* (*castra*), *fortins* (*castella*), *centenaria*, *praesidia* and *tours*.[264] However, in a clear example of the subjective nature of typologies, their distribution of the evidence into these categories in all three cases was not exactly the same.

In particular, Trousset's wider definition of *castra*, as opposed to Euzennat's more restricted definition, was problematic. While Euzennat grouped Remada/*Tillibari* (RLT129) and Ras el-Aïn/*Talalati* (RLT109) together as *castra* based on their size of around 1 ha or more, Trousset also included three more examples: Bir Rhezene/*Bezereos* (RLT072), and less certainly, Henchir Medeina/*Thebelami(?)* (RLT125) and Henchir Mgarine/*Agarlabas(?)* (RLT023); the latter and largest of these was only c. 0.45 ha, and Bir Rhezene/*Bezereos* only c. 0.28 ha (see Figure 4.6 and Figure 4.7 below). Trousset argued that *Bezereos*, at least, must have been a major post based on its appearance in the *Notitita Dignitatum* as well as the epigraphic evidence mentioned earlier for a large detachment of

[258] I have marked (with a *) a further 19 'possible' military sites in Appendices B and C, but for which we have less convincing evidence, and these have generally not been included in the following discussions.

[259] For example, Guérin 1862; Toutain 1903; Toussaint 1905; 1906; Cagnat 1913: 524–568; Cagnat & Merlin 1920.

[260] Cagnat 1913: 682–683.

[261] Goodchild & Ward-Perkins 1949; Goodchild 1950b; 1954; Di Vita 1964.

[262] Euzennat 1972: 13–18; Trousset 1974: 129–142.

[263] N.B. that by *camps* most French publications mean permanent forts, rather than temporary ones, which is the meaning usually intended by the term 'camp' in a military context in English.

[264] Krimi 2007.

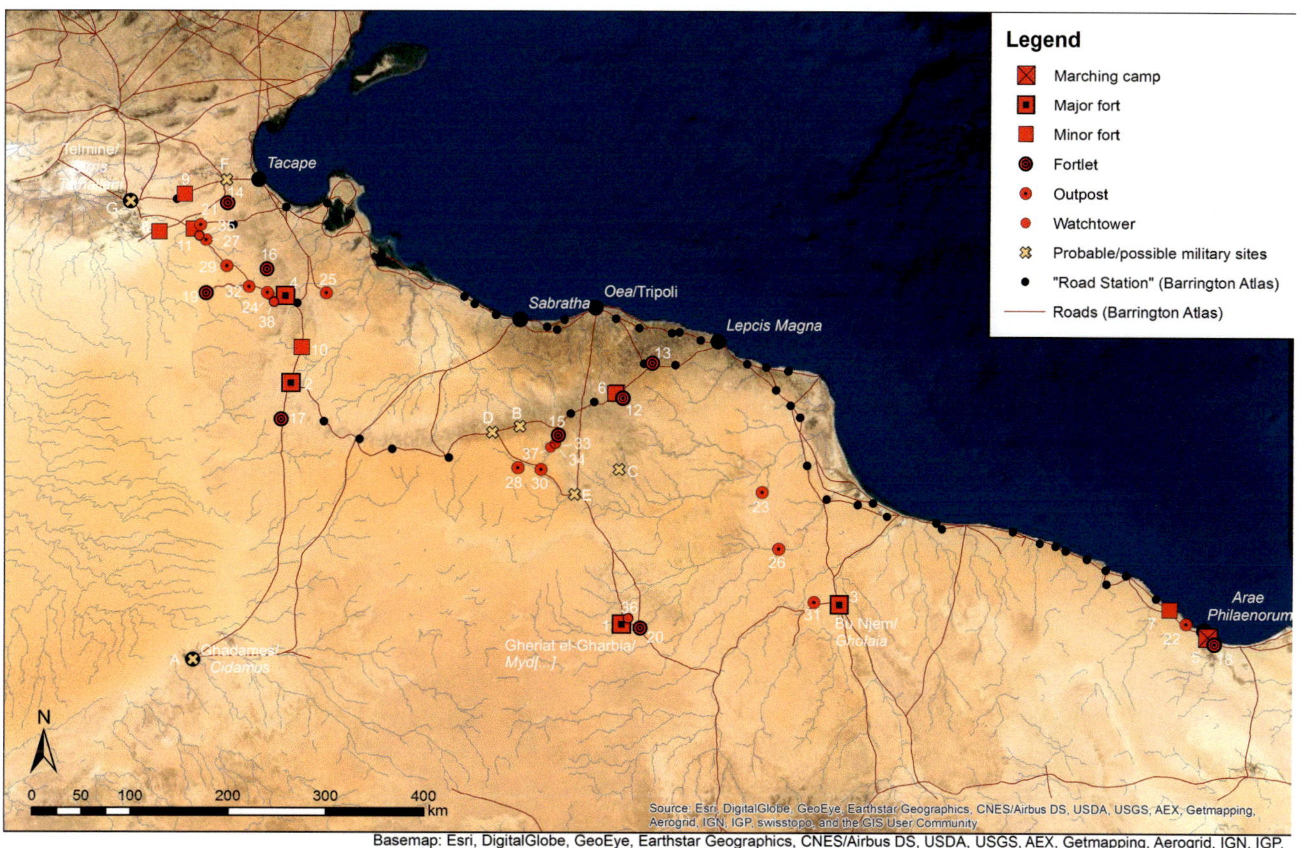

Basemap: Esri, DigitalGlobe, GeoEye, Earthstar Geographics, CNES/Airbus DS, USDA, USGS, AEX, Getmapping, Aerogrid, IGN, IGP, swisstopo, and the GIS User Community
Drainage: Lehner, B., Verdin, K., Jarvis, A. (2008): New global hydrography derived from spaceborne elevation data. Eos, Transactions, AGU, 89(10): 93-94. Retrieved from http://hydrosheds.cr.usgs.gov (15 sec Flow Accumulation)
Roads (Barrington Atlas): Ancient World Mapping Center (2012)

Figure 4.4: *Distribution of known and suspected military buildings and roads in Tripolitania. Numbers correspond to those used in Appendix A.*

c. 300 soldiers from the *Legio III Augusta*;[265] the other two were included because of their larger size. However, as Mattingly has pointed out, given its comparatively small size, *Bezereos* probably could not actually have housed that many men. He suggests rather that a large portion of these men would likely have been stationed at smaller outposts under the command of an officer located at *Bezereos*, or perhaps even that there was a larger, as yet undiscovered building somewhere nearby.[266]

In addition, while the larger two examples were equipped with towered gates on each of their four sides, to the best of our knowledge, the smaller three had only single entrances; because our knowledge of their form is unfortunately lacking, we cannot say whether they had gate towers, and if so, what form they may have taken. While this is not to say that the smaller sites were not also strategically important ones, as is indeed suggested by the inclusion of *Bezereos* in the *Notitia Dignitatum*, architecturally speaking, it is clear that we are dealing with two separate groups of buildings.

Another issue with the systems proposed by Euzennat, Trousset and others, is the attempt to relate the building categories they defined to Latin terms known from inscriptions and historical sources. As already discussed in Section 4.1.1, inscriptions which can be securely attached to rural buildings, military or otherwise, are uncommon in Tripolitania, and the appearance of the types of Latin terms used above even more so. The term *castrum* is attested in inscriptions at both Bu Njem/*Gholaia*[267] and Ras el-Aïn/*Talalati* (RLT109)[268], so is not particularly problematic. Terms such as *burgus*[269] and *praesidium*[270], on the other hand, are each only attested once in the epigraphic record of Tripolitania, and *castellum* not at all. In addition, as the discussion

[265] *Notitia Dignitatum, Occidentis*, 31.20; *ILAf* 27. Trousset 1974: 131–133.

[266] Mattingly 1995: 84, 100.

[267] *IRT* 918; Rebuffat 1973a: 122; Rebuffat 1977a: 57; Rebuffat 1995: 82. This does not include instances of title *mater castrorum*, which was given to Julia Domna (e.g. in *IRT* 868, from Ain Wif/*Thenadassa*), and later Julia Mamaea, since it was not a reference to the building which may have stood on the location.

[268] *CIL* 8.22765.

[269] *IRT* 895.

[270] *IIAf* 9.

above concerning the term *centenarium* illustrated, we do not always have a good idea what these terms mean, let alone whether they referred to specific types of buildings. There is reason to believe that some of these terms could have had little to do with the size or appearance of a building, but rather with its function, making attempts to apply them to other buildings simply on the basis that they looked similar, extremely problematic. So, for example, we might imagine that it could be appropriate to refer to a multi-storeyed structure which was intended for the storage of grain both as a *centenarium* and a *turris*; which of these appeared in a dedicatory inscription would have been determined by other factors.

This is not to say that some, or even all, of these terms were not used for the military buildings of Tripolitania, as they certainly were in other parts of the empire. However, just as the terms we use in English, such as fort, fortlet and tower, etc. can be, to a certain degree, interchangeable and flexible in their application, the contradictory nature of the ancient written and epigraphic sources suggests that the same was probably true of the Latin.

In a review of Trousset's book, Rebuffat proposed as an alternative the use of descriptive phrases such as *fort à bastions rectangulaires* or *fort à casernements périphériques*.[271] A very similar system was utilised by Lenoir in his study of Roman military camps of North Africa and the Near East,[272] though he limited his discussion to buildings which were over c.1,000 m^2 and for which he felt there was sufficiently detailed architectural information available (which in Tripolitania gave him a sample of only 11 buildings).[273] By using descriptive categories of this type, Rebuffat and Lenoir avoided much of the baggage that is associated with both ancient and modern terminology, making the differentiation between form and function more explicit. While there was almost certainly some relationship between the type and size of military post and form of building which appeared at a site, they were able to address the problematic assumption that this relationship was always a straightforward and consistent correlation.

Mattingly also rejected the use of Latin terminology, opting instead to use English terms, identifying five categories of military buildings from across the region: forts, fortlets (and road stations), outposts, (watch)towers and late Roman fortlets with projecting towers. His system was based mainly on size of building (i.e. ground area), and in the case of the last category, the presence of square projecting towers. He was careful to note that the identification and classification of military structures based solely on any single feature is problematic and endeavoured to take other features into account such as date, similarity of plan, and distance/relationship to other known military sites, and to judge examples on an individual basis.[274]

My own typology which is presented below most closely resembles Mattingly's in that it uses modern English terms and is based mainly on size, as this is, in general, a useful place to start, in that it can give us an idea of the potential importance of the site and the number of troops that might have been stationed there. Having compared the ground areas of the 35 military structures for which we have dimensions, we can observe some distinct groupings visible in the data (Figure 4.5). The first two groups, comprising the five structures which far outstrip the rest of the examples, are unsurprising and do not differ much from the systems described above: the four major forts of Ras el-Aïn/*Talalati*, Bu Njem/*Gholaia*, Remada/*Tillibari* and Gheriat el-Garbia/*Myd[...]*, and the single largest structure in a category on its own, the possible marching camp at Bir Umm Garanigh (SSB527-mc).

The major departure of my typology from those above is the grouping of six buildings measuring between approximately 2,700 and 5,700 m^2 into their own category which I have called 'minor forts', rather than including them with the larger or smaller buildings which has usually been the case in previous typologies. One potentially useful point which may support this grouping and can help to refine a system based on size is Frere and St Joseph's suggestion that forts and fortlets should be differentiated by the presence or absence of a *principia*. They argued that "a military site, however small, which was occupied by an independent unit with its own administration is a fort; the garrison of a fortlet lacked its own administrative apparatus, because the troops comprised a detachment from a unit whose head-quarters were elsewhere".[275] In his 2007 study of fortlets in the northwestern provinces, Symonds demonstrated that in that region at least, this system was viable, commenting that while "in practice, size is generally a good indicator of whether a site is a fort or a fortlet…in those grey areas where dimensions converge, a functional difference such as that denoted by the absence of a *principia* must be preferred to an arbitrary maximum size".[276]

Symonds' argument for the use of this system is convincing; however, there is a major problem with the application of this premise to the Tripolitanian material, namely the identification of the *principia*. Too

[271] Rebuffat 1980.

[272] Lenoir 2011.

[273] Lenoir 2011: 363 fn. 26.

[274] Mattingly 1995: 90–115; 193–194.

[275] Frere & St Joseph 1983: 135.

[276] Symonds 2007: 261

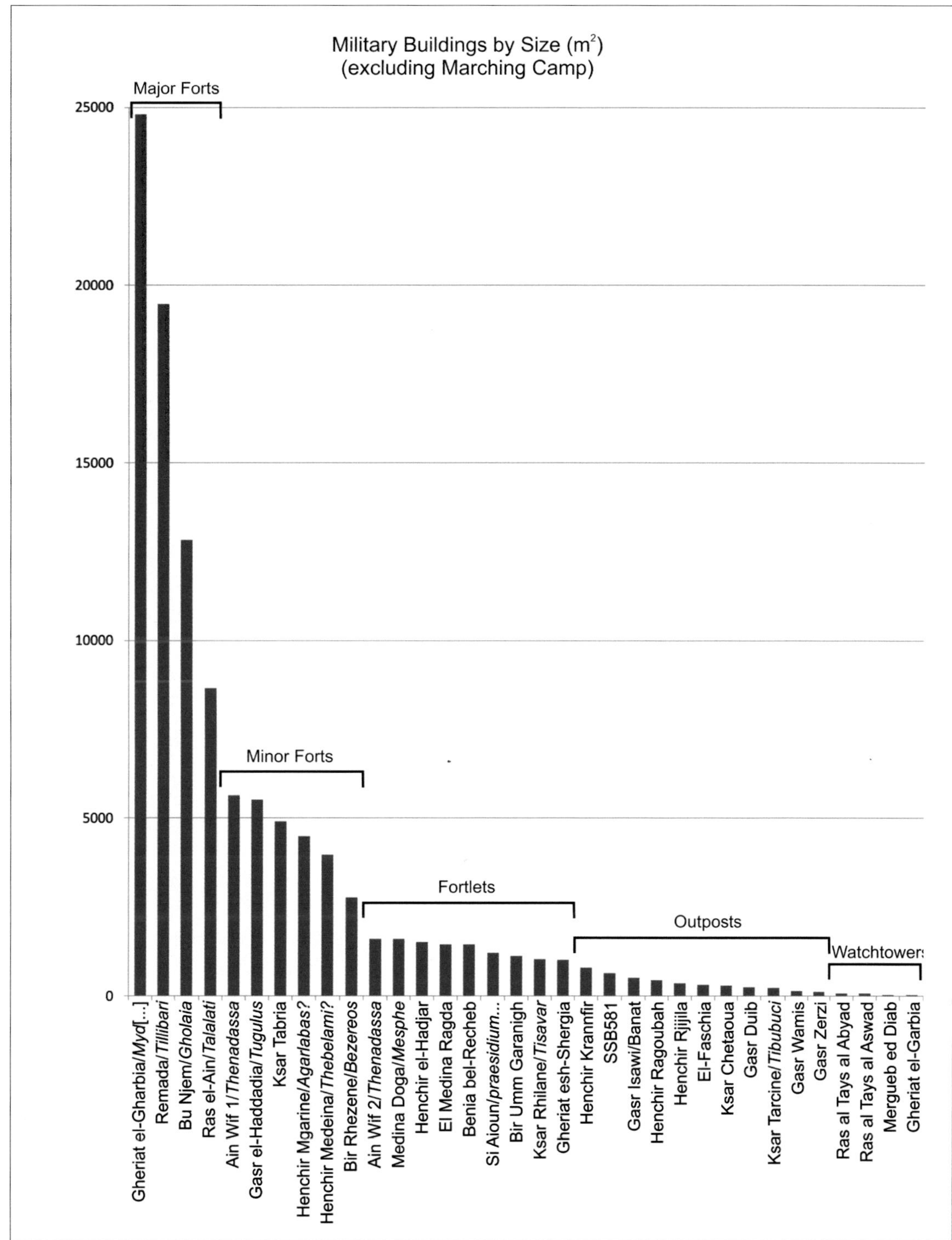

Figure 4.5: *Ground area (m²) of known military buildings in Tripolitania.*

few military structures in Tripolitania have been excavated or surveyed in detail, so in most cases we have only the basic, external outlines of buildings with no understanding of the internal arrangements. As discussed in more detail further below, three of these six 'minor forts' do appear to have 'central' buildings; we are unfortunately ignorant of the interior arrangements of the other three. However, without more detailed investigations, we cannot necessarily assume that any centrally placed structure was a *principia* or that the absence of a centrally placed building meant that one did not exist in another form. In addition, at least one building which is classified below as a 'fortlet' based on its small size (Ksar Rhilane/*Tisavar*), also has a central building which could potentially be identified as a *principia*.

The remainder of the buildings measuring 1,600 m² and below, comprises the fortlets, outposts and observation posts. The sizes of the buildings in these three groups were less distinctly clustered and divisions were established between them using a combination of plan type, size, and in the case of the latter, location.

4.2.1 Major Forts

Four structures in Tripolitania can be identified as major forts (Appendix A: 1–4; Figure 4.6). They varied in their size, proportions and dates of construction, but all shared characteristics commonly found in forts across the empire, including the wide rounded corners already discussed above in Section 4.1.2, and the presence of gates, each guarded by a pair of towers, on all four sides. In addition to their size, the latter feature is one of the main characteristics which distinguishes major forts from minor forts and fortlets, which usually have only one main entrance.

With the exception of the first phase at Remada/*Tillibari* (2), which had rectangular, internal towers, all of the gate-towers on these buildings projected externally and most were rectangular or semi-circular. The exceptions were the distinctive pentagonal shape of the main, eastern gates (*portae praetoriae*) at Gheriat el-Garbia/*Myd[...]* (1) and Bu Njem/*Gholaia* (3), a form which is also repeated at the legionary fort of *Lambaesis* (Algeria). At Gheriat el-Garbia, the interior of the defensive wall was further equipped with small, rectangular towers spaced at regular intervals between the gates.

The defensive walls of the three largest examples were all between 2.4 and 2.5 m thick, consisting of a sand and rubble core, faced on both sides with mortared blocks of roughly-shaped masonry, in more or less regular courses. The walls of the smaller and later Ras el-Aïn/*Talalati* (4) were constructed using a similar technique, but employing smaller, irregular facing blocks and were only around 1.5 m thick. All of the gate-towers of Gheriat el-Garbia and Bu Njem were faced with ashlar blocks, save one pair of D-shaped towers at Gheriat el-Garbia.[277] At both the earlier Remada/*Tillibari* and the later Ras el-Ain/*Talalati*, the towers were constructed in much the same fashion as the rest of the walls, though at the latter, the arched gates were still constructed using ashlar blocks.

The only major fort for which we have a detailed knowledge of the interior plan is Bu Njem/*Gholaia*, though recent excavations at Gheriat el-Garbia/*Myd[...]* are revealing new information about that site as well.[278] Given their size, major forts were more akin to walled settlements, and would have housed several buildings of various function, including a *principia*, a *praetorium*, *horreae*, barracks, stables, etc., all arranged on a rectilinear grid plan. They could also house baths and temples, though sometimes these facilities were located outside the bounds of the fort.[279]

The earliest of these major forts is thought to be Remada/*Tillibari*, which was probably established sometime in the mid-second century AD. No modern excavations have been undertaken at the site, but an inscription from AD 197 records repairs to an *aedes* which was apparently old enough to have already fallen into disrepair by this period.[280] Almost nothing remains of the ancient building today, so its chronology is unclear, but in a later phase, projecting gate-towers were added, and it seems to have been still occupied at least in some form as late as the fifth century AD, as attested by the appearance of a *limitis Tillibarensis* in the *Notitia Dignitatum* (though whether this occupation was continuous, we do not know).[281]

Bu Njem/*Gholaia* was constructed in the early third century AD and Gheriat el-Garbia/*Myd[...]* is thought to be more or less contemporary, both being related to the reorganisation of the *limes* under the Severans. However, while Bu Njem appears to have been abandoned around AD 263, recent research suggests that Gheriat el-Garbia was occupied until c.AD 275/80, and then reoccupied around 60 years later for another century or so, probably into the mid-fifth century AD.[282] If the inscription found at Ras el-Aïn/*Talalati* does indeed record the foundation of the site, it was constructed in AD 263, just around the time that Bu Njem/*Gholaia* was abandoned, and occupied into the late fourth century AD, repairs having been recorded in AD 355–360.[283]

As Figure 4.4 shows, all of these major forts were strategically located at the intersections of main routes leading inland and through the *gebel*, often at oases, and were the main military bases of the region. However, while in terms of their size, the major forts of Tripolitania far outstripped any other rural structures in the region, military or civilian, it can be easy to overlook the fact that considering the geographical size of the region, when compared to military buildings from the rest of North Africa and the Empire, they were relatively small. None of the known military structures of Tripolitania was legionary-sized and there is nothing to suggest that any of the sites for which we do not have architectural

[277] Mattingly and Welsby argued that this deviation in shape, along with the small masonry rather than large ashlar-faced construction used indicated that this gate had been reconstructed at some later period (Welsby 1983: 62; Mattingly 1995: 92–93). However, recent excavations by Mackensen have established that the remaining tower is, in fact, keyed in and therefore, contemporary, arguing that the difference in masonry was to accommodate the rounded shape (Mackensen 2011b: 288–293; 2012: 50–51).

[278] Bu Njem: Rebuffat, Deneauve, & Hallier 1967; Rebuffat *et al.* 1969; Rebuffat 1970b; 1970a; 1975a; 1977a; 1989. Gheriat el-Garbia: Mackensen 2010b; 2011b; 2012.

[279] See Section 4.3

[280] Euzennat & Trousset 1978: 134–135.

[281] *Notitia Dignitatum, Occidentis*, 31.6; Trousset 1974: 114–118; Euzennat & Trousset 1978: 135–140.

[282] Bu Njem: *IRT* 914–916; Gheriat el-Garbia: Di Vita 1966: 107–111; Mackensen 2012: 55–58.

[283] Dedication: *CIL* 8.22765 (=*ILT* 3). Repairs: *CIL* 8.22766–22768. Trousset 1974: 98–102. Mattingly points out that ceramic evidence from the early 3rd c. AD from the site and the fact that *Talalati* appears in the *Antonine Itinerary* suggests that the site could therefore have started as a smaller military site dating to the Severan period, or that there could have been a civilian settlement on the site (1995: 98).

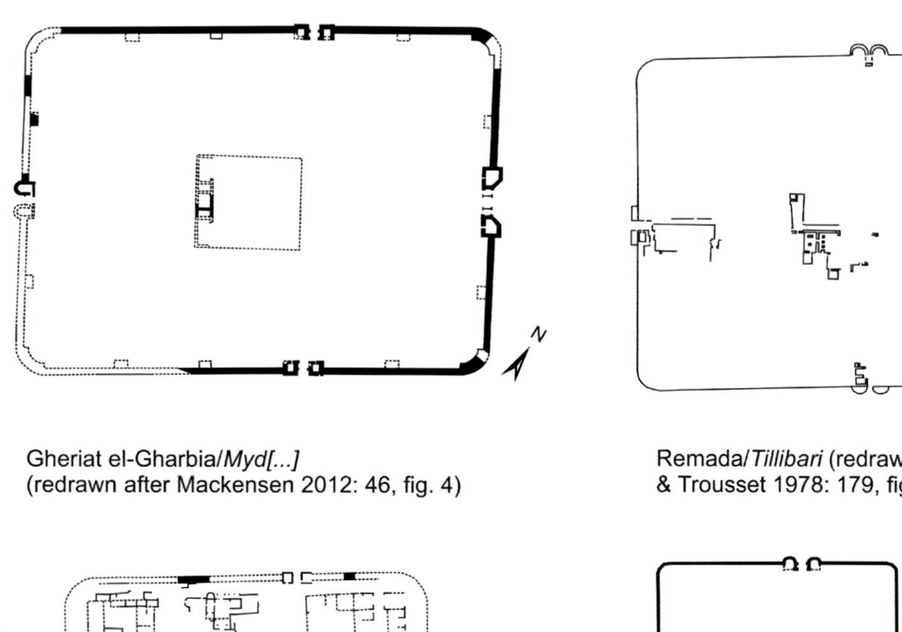

Gheriat el-Gharbia/*Myd[...]*
(redrawn after Mackensen 2012: 46, fig. 4)

Remada/*Tillibari* (redrawn after Euzennat & Trousset 1978: 179, fig. 4, after Donau)

Bu Njem/*Gholaia* (redrawn after Rebuffat 1989: 157, fig. 1)

Ras el-Aïn/*Talalati* (redrawn after Mattingly 1995: 98, fig. 5:7)

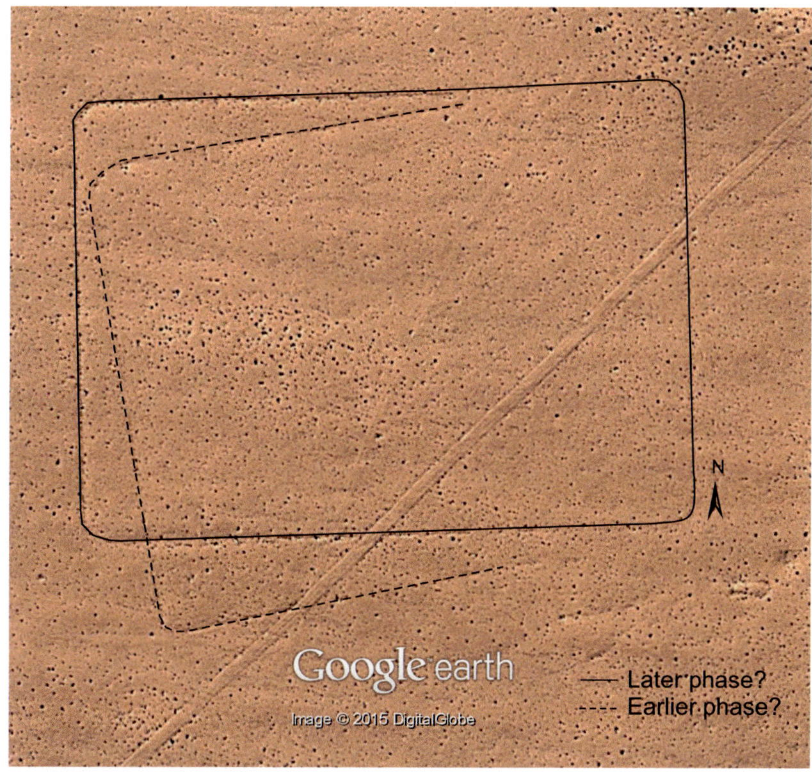

SSB527-mc, Bir Umm Garanigh
(Digital Globe via Google Earth Pro, 26 Dec. 2011)

Figure 4.6: *Major forts and marching camp.*

evidence were any larger. Compare, for example, the legionary fort at *Lambaesis* which was c.22.5 ha in area, to Gheriat el-Garbia, which was only just over a tenth of that size.

The epigraphic evidence suggests that the major forts of Tripolitania served as bases for vexillations of the *Legio III Augusta*, or auxiliary cohorts such as the *Cohors II Flavia Afrorum* and others.[284] Kennedy and Riley estimated that a cohort of around 500 men would need around 1.5 ha of space, which is consistent with the sizes of the forts identified here, and Gheriat el-Garbia, at 2.5 ha might even have been able to accommodate up to 1,000.[285] It is probable that in this region there was never any expectation of attack from a large, organised force, so smaller units actually made more sense. In addition, limited availability of water and other resources was potentially also a factor in the decision to garrison the region with smaller units.[286]

4.2.2 Marching Camp(?)

The identification of the possible marching camp at Bir Umm Garanigh (SSB527-mc) (Appendix A: 5; Figure 4.6) is uncertain, but its large size, playing-card shape and location along the coast road lends support to this identification, as does the presence of a much smaller, but more substantially constructed and permanent structure less than 200 m to its northeast, which is identified below as a fortlet (SSB527-g). At over 4 ha in size, it is larger than any of the other known military structures in Tripolitania. Its visibility on satellite imagery potentially suggests a ditch and bank construction and there is no trace visible on the satellite imagery of internal structures, both of which features have contributed to its identification as a marching camp, i.e. an enclosure which would have been constructed for short-term occupation by a force on the march. It overlies what looks like an earlier phase on a slightly different alignment, suggesting that this site was utilised more than once, perhaps even for the outward and return journeys of a single campaign. Its date is unknown, but Goodchild reported the presence of first century AD ceramics at the smaller fortlet mentioned above, which could suggest that the marching camp was similarly early, or perhaps even pre-dated the more permanent fortlet.[287]

I know of no other certain examples of marching camps in North Africa; however, a larger number are known in Britain with which we can make some preliminary comparisons.[288] Jones estimated that at the lower end, the temporary camps of Britain could probably have housed around 480–690 men per hectare, though she stressed that there were a number of variables that could affect this number and that these calculations are still highly speculative.[289] If we assume that during the early Empire, on average, a Roman legion comprised around 5,000 men, this means that a single legion on the march would require a camp between 7 and 10 ha in size; this accords with Frere and St. Joseph's estimate that a single legion would need a camp of around 7.3–8.1 ha.[290] A couple of possible examples have also been identified in the slightly more comparable environment of Jordan by Kennedy and Bewley, for which a capacity of more than 1,000 men per hectare was estimated.[291] Using Jones' calculations therefore, we can suggest that at the lower end, the c.4 ha marching camp at Bir Umm Garanigh could have accommodated between 1,920 and 2,760 men, i.e. approximately half of a legion, or if we accept Kennedy and Bewley's higher estimate, perhaps even a full one.

4.2.3 Minor Forts

Six structures ranging in size from c.2,700 to 5,700 m^2 are identified here as minor forts (Appendix A: 6–11; Figure 4.7).[292] Like the major forts, all were rectilinear, with rounded corners, and with the possible exception of Ain Wif 1/*Thenadassa* (6), were square or nearly so. To the best of our knowledge, unlike their larger counterparts, each had only a single main entrance and only one of these, Ksar Tabria (RLT070) (8), appears to have had any externally projecting towers, with a pair of D-shaped towers protecting its entrance and round towers on each of its external corners. Trousset suggested that this feature was potentially indicative of a late Roman date, drawing comparisons with Constantinian fortifications from the north-western empire; however, as Mattingly has pointed out, beyond the towers, the appearance of the fort is consistent with other third-century AD examples in the region, and it could be that the towers were later additions.[293]

---

284 For example, *IRT* 895, *IRT* 913; Euzennat 1973.

285 Kennedy & Riley 1990: 139; Mattingly 1995: 77–89.

286 Gichon 1990: 203.

287 Goodchild 1952: 97–98; LeQuesne, Basell, & Sheibani 2010: 19–21.

288 Wilson 1974; Frere & St Joseph 1983: 19–31; Welfare & Swan 1995; Jones 2012.

289 Jones 2012: 47–58. Cf. also Richardson 2000; 2002; 2003.

290 Frere & St Joseph 1983: 20.

291 Kennedy & Bewley 2004: 175.

292 It should be noted satellite imagery has revealed that the site of Gasr el-Haddadia/*Tugulus* is rather larger (5,520 m^2/80 x 69 m) than originally estimated by Goodchild (3,600 m2/60 x 60 m) on the basis of an oblique aerial photograph (Goodchild 1976b: 157–158; Mattingly 1995: 120).

293 Trousset 1974: 74; Mattingly 1995: 101.

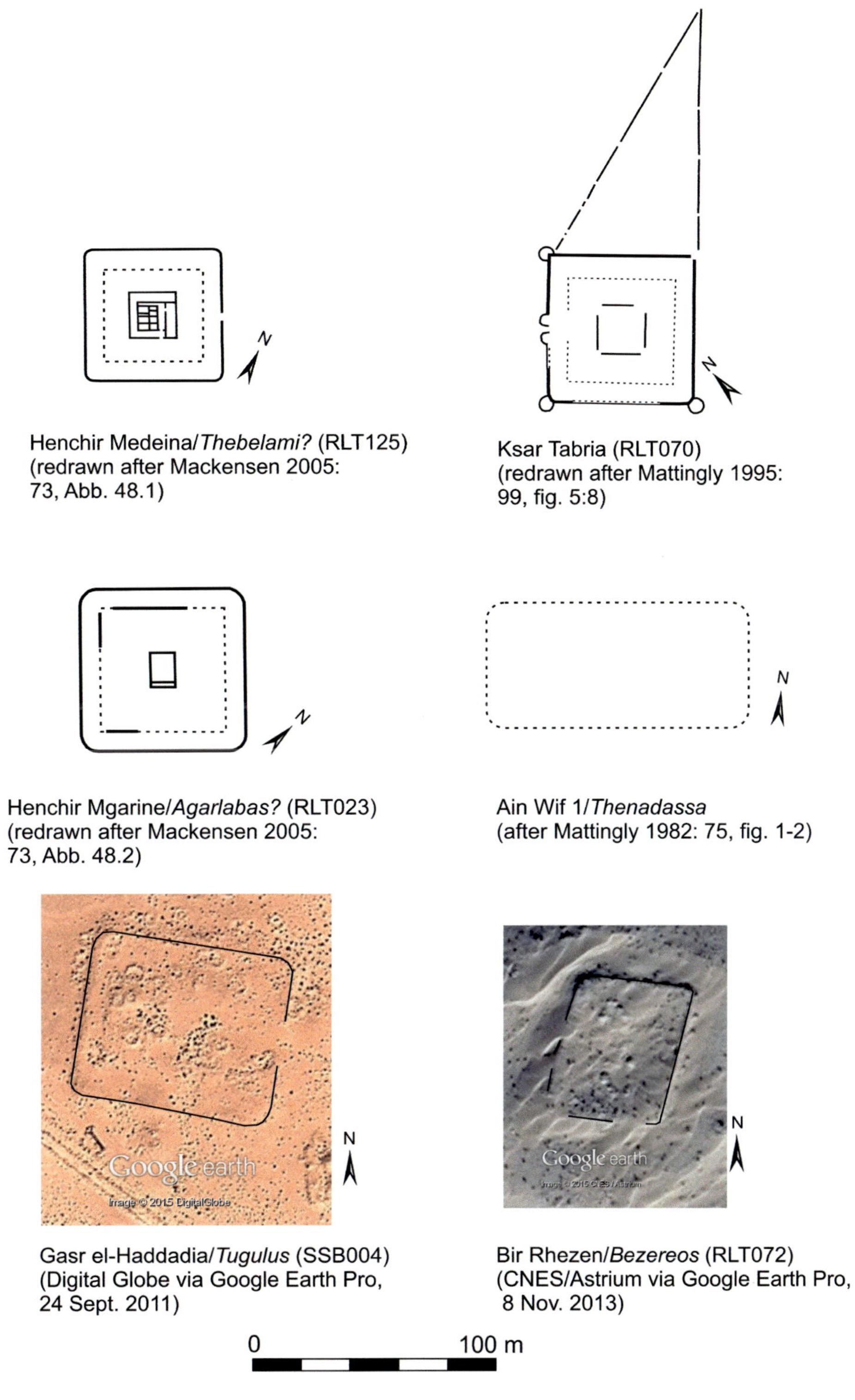

Figure 4.7: *Minor forts.*

The exterior defensive walls of this group of minor forts are mostly recorded as being constructed of irregular or roughly shaped masonry and/or rubble, sometimes without a central core, though the specific materials and construction techniques used in the largest – Ain Wif 1/*Thenadassa* – remain unknown. None appear to have utilised the very fine ashlar blocks which were employed for the gates of the major forts, but a brief report in the 1960s of a survey around Gasr el-Haddadia/*Tugulus* (7), does mention walls of ashlar masonry.[294] In addition, Bir Rhezene/*Bezereos* (11) may also have incorporated ashlar masonry into its construction; although obscured

[294] Bakir 1967: 251. Two photos published by Cerrata (1933: 225), labelled as Gasr Haddadia/*Tagulus* [sic], show irregularly sized, but cut masonry; however, I strongly suspect that these actually show the nearby and better-preserved early Islamic structure which was probably constructed with materials robbed from the earlier minor fort discussed here (Goodchild 1952: 97).

now by later building and sand dunes, the building is described by Trousset as being constructed *en moellons*, and a photograph of the site appears to show a number of ashlar blocks in the background, which could suggest the use of *opus africanum* construction.[295]

Internally, three of these minor forts – Henchir Medeina/*Thebelami(?)* (10), Henchir Mgarine/*Agarlabas(?)* (9) and Ksar Tabria – seemingly had similar plans: rooms ranged along all four sides of the exterior enceinte with a separate building placed in the centre. There is evidence for the former two that at least some of the interior structures utilised *opus africanum*. As discussed above, we might interpret these central structures as *principia*, though without further investigation we cannot be certain that that was their function. The interior layouts of the others are unclear and while it is tempting to see them as having had similar arrangements, we should be wary of making assumptions. Indeed, as Gichon has pointed out in the context of the eastern frontier in the Negev region in modern Israel, fortified courtyard buildings with large, open spaces in the centre were well-suited for desert frontiers where possible threats were usually not from large, organised groups or armies, but rather from smaller tribal bands. The large enclosed space of courtyard buildings meant that various everyday activities and training could take place within the protected confines of the fort itself, and so they were not at risk from sudden or surprise attacks. In addition, this space could be used to accommodate temporary guests such as military or civilian travelers, performing the function of 'rest-stops', sometimes known as caravanserais.[296] Since these military structures were usually sited along the only viable routes through these harsh environments and they often controlled the rare water sources, this was probably a necessary and important additional function of these buildings, along with the smaller fortlets and outposts.

Like the major forts, all seem to have been located at strategically significant points along the major routes of the region. Three (Ksar Tabria, Henchir Mgarine/*Agarlabas(?)* and Bir Rhezene/*Bezereos*), are clustered in the northwest part of the region along the roads leading to and from the group of oases around the Chott Djerid and *Turris Tamalleni* (where, as mentioned in Section 4.1.4, there was potentially another military site). Two (Henchir Medeina/*Thebelami(?)* and Ain Wif 1/*Thenadassa*) are found along the *gebel* route between *Tacape* and *Lepcis Magna*, and the last (Gasr el-Haddadia/*Tugulus*), along the coast road, near the eastern edge of the province.

The dating evidence for the minor forts is poorer than for the major forts, but as a group, they all appear to have been occupied during the same broad period, in the second to third centuries AD, and in the case of Gasr el-Haddadia/*Tugulus*, potentially as early as the first century BC.[297] Only the site of Bir Rhezene/*Bezereos* offers any direct epigraphic evidence (as already discussed above in Section 4.1.1), confirming the presence of a *vexillatio leg(ionis) III Aug(ustae)* during the early third century AD.[298] Dates for the others have been estimated largely on the basis of surface pottery, and to a lesser extent, appearance. In the case of Ain Wif 1/*Thenadassa*, the second century AD date evident by the ceramic evidence is supported by an inscription recording major repairs to a military bath-house, which Mattingly has convincingly dated to the Severan period, suggesting that there was a major military occupation on the site during the second century AD, before a Severan reoccupation (as fortlet Ain Wif 2).[299] In any case, using the same occupation estimates as for the major forts, these minor forts could probably have housed around 100, or maybe up to 200 men in the larger cases, though if there were cavalry, it would be far fewer.[300]

4.2.4 Fortlets

I have identified nine buildings which can be classified as fortlets (Appendix A: 12–20; Figure 4.8). While the size difference between minor forts and fortlets is relatively clear, discriminating between small fortlets and large outposts is more problematic, as the difference between these two classes of site is arguably as much or more related to the function of the military post as to the size and appearance of the structure itself. I have drawn a relatively arbitrary line between fortlets and outposts at 1,000 m², a decision which is based in large part on the appearance of Ksar Rhilane/*Tisavar* (RLT100) (19), as its form with a possible central *principia*, seems to belong in the category of fortlets. However, some of the smaller examples from this category could also conceivably be interpreted as outposts, particularly the smallest example included in this section (Gheriat esh-Shergia), and vice versa.

All nine of the fortlets fit into a narrow size range between 1,000 and 1,600 m² and can be divided into two basic groups – those with projecting corner towers and those without. All of the structures in the latter group

[295] Trousset 1974: 75–76, fig. 26a.

[296] Gichon 1990.

[297] Dating: Ain Wif/*Thenadassa*, Mattingly 1982: 78–79; Gasr el-Haddadia/*Tugulus*, Goodchild 1952: 97; Bakir 1967: 251; Ksar Tabria, Trousset 1974: 73–75; Henchir Mgarine/*Agarlabas(?)*, Hammond 1964: 8; Guéry 1986: 602; Mattingly 1995: 100; Henchir Medeina/*Thebelami(?)*, Trousset 1974: 109–110.

[298] *ILAf* 26, 27, 28.

[299] *IRT* 869; Mattingly 1982.

[300] Kennedy & Riley 1990: 139; Mattingly 1995: 99, Table 5:2.

were rectilinear structures, the exterior enceintes of which were constructed using a variety of techniques, from the drystone rubble walls of Bir Umm Garanigh (18) to the fine ashlar of Gheriat esh-Shergia (20). Four of the seven in this group have some evidence for central, interior structures and two of those utilised *opus africanum*. Unfortunately, with the exception of Ksar Rhilane/ *Tisavar*, this group of buildings is poorly known, particularly their interior arrangements and construction; nevertheless, the points already discussed with regards to the minor forts as to the presence of a possible central *principia* versus the advantages of having a large, central courtyard are equally applicable here.

We know a good deal more about Ksar Rhilane/ *Tisavar* because it was almost fully excavated in the early twentieth century. Except for its small size, it seems to have more in common architecturally with the minor forts discussed above, in that it has the classic playing-card shape, with ranges of rooms placed around the interior of the enceinte and a centrally placed building which is generally interpreted as a *principia*. Its similarity of form to the larger structures in this respect can perhaps be taken as an indication of its importance, but it is difficult to say with certainty. The enceinte was constructed of large, cut stones (*pierres de taille*) in the lower courses, and smaller, more irregular blocks in the upper

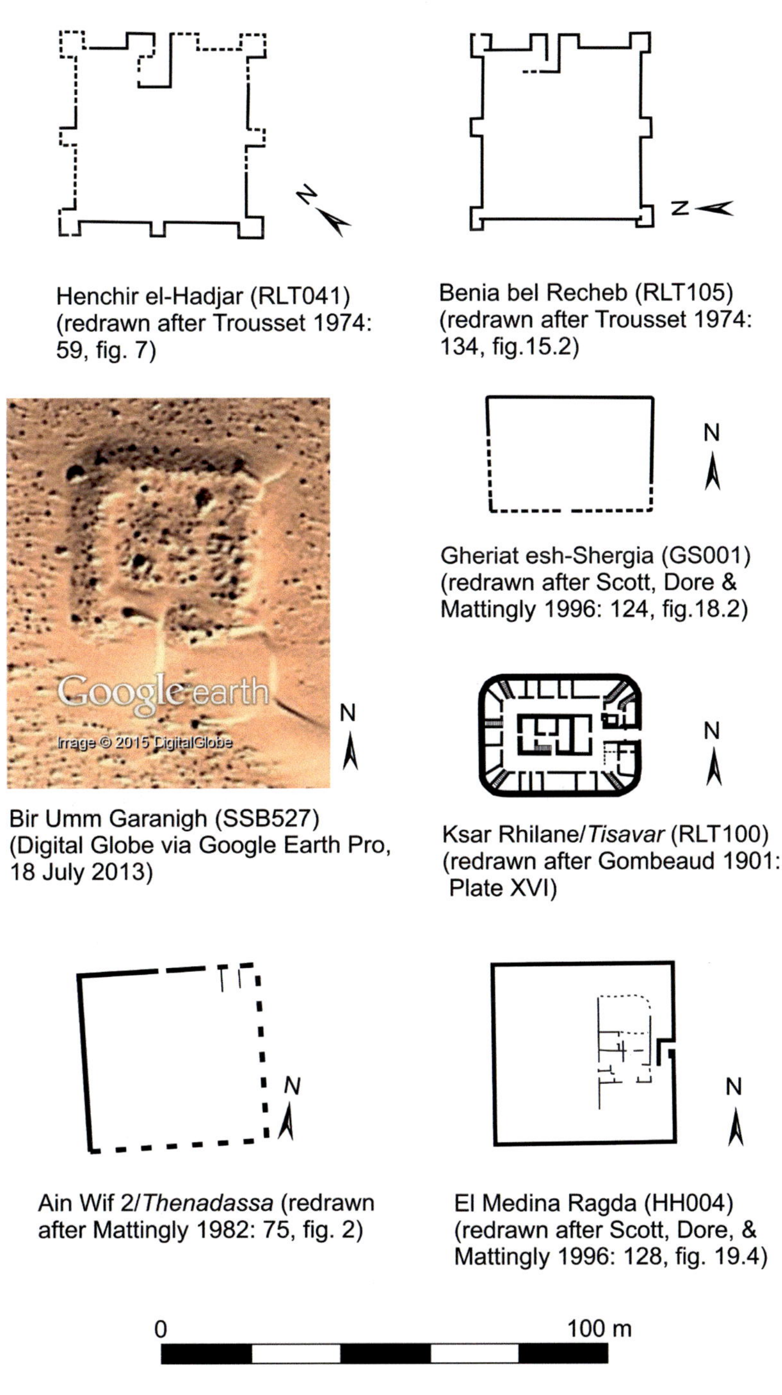

Figure 4.8: *Fortlets.*

ones. The interior building was probably *opus africanum*, as the corners of the building formed of ashlar blocks still remain, but the intervening walls, probably of smaller stone and therefore more susceptible to robbing, do not.[301]

The earliest of these buildings appears to be that at Bir Umm Garanigh, at the eastern edge of the province, which produced pottery dated to the first century AD.[302] Both El Medina Ragda (15) and Medina Doga/*Mesphe* (13) can be broadly ascribed to the first to fourth centuries AD,[303] though in the case of the latter, the surrounding settlement was almost certainly established by the early first century AD, and probably earlier, as it was a strategically important location, at the junction of several roads and tracks, including the *gebel* road leading to *Lepcis Magna*, and near to the border between the territories of *Lepcis* and *Oea*.[304] Ksar Rhilane/*Tisavar*[305], Si Aioun/*praesidium* (17)[306], Ain Wif 2 (12)[307] and Gheriat esh-Shergia[308] have all been dated to the second to third centuries or early fourth century AD, on the basis of surface pottery as inscriptions and excavations have been rare at these sites.

The second group of fortlets consists of two very similar structures with projecting towers: Henchir el-Hadjar (RLT041) (14) and Benia bel Recheb (RLT105) (16). Each had rectangular corner towers and an additional tower in the centre of each side (with the exception of the west wall of Benia bel Recheb). No internal buildings are known at the former, but some traces of buildings constructed of small, rough masonry were observed at Benia bel Recheb.[309] Both structures are largely constructed using well-cut, large or ashlar masonry; the walls of Benia bel Recheb in particular appear to have been constructed of a single layer of ashlar blocks, rather than being composed of an interior core of rubble and earth faced with masonry, as seems to be more common in the larger military buildings of the region.[310]

The similarity in form of Henchir el-Hadjar and Benia bel-Recheb suggests that they were probably closely contemporary. They are usually dated to the late third or fourth century AD on the basis of their distinctive form, which is paralleled in later Roman military structures in many areas of the Empire,[311] though unfortunately, there is little other secure dating evidence available for either site. Guéry identified only one type of fineware, two fragments of Hayes 197; this type was placed in the late second to mid-third century AD by Hayes, though more recently, Bonifay has identified variants dating to the fourth and early fifth centuries AD. A fragment of a Christian lamp which was also found at the site would seem to support a slightly later date.[312] It is tempting to see their location to the northeast of the main *limes* road (Figure 4.4, nos 14, 16) as part of an overall contraction of the western *limes* into the *gebel*, potentially coinciding with the construction of the *clausurae*.[313]

If we continue to follow the estimates used above of around 1.5 ha for 500 soldiers, each of the fortlets could probably have housed between 30 and 60 men; Mattingly estimated that Ksar Rhilane had a garrison of around 80 men in the Severan period.[314] It is possible that many of these fortlets had a small command centre so that they could act independently when necessary, but some were probably also directly related to one of the major or minor forts in their vicinity.

It is in this category and those that follow that differentiating between military and civilian structures, as discussed above, becomes more difficult, and it is worth mentioning here a few examples which have sometimes been identified as fortlets, but for which there is less secure evidence to support a military interpretation. One relatively well-known example is Benia Guedah Ceder (RLT059-g), already mentioned above (Section 4.1.2, Figure 4.3), which has often been identified as military in nature in the past on the basis of its projecting corner towers.[315] The sites of Sc001-g (Gasr el-Aswad) and Nf083-g (S'dada) in the central pre-desert have also sometimes been suggested as possible fortlets, based on their large size (1,350 and 2,365 m^2 respectively) and relatively regular internal arrangements (Figure 4.9);[316] however, their irregular external plans (determined in

[301] Gombeaud 1901; Trousset 1974: 92–94; Mackensen 2010a.

[302] Goodchild 1952: 97–98.

[303] Scott, Dore, & Mattingly 1996: 127; Mattingly 1995: 99, Table 5:2.

[304] Goodchild 1951c: 48–51; Mattingly 1995: 102, 133; Bigi *et al.* 2009: 25–27.

[305] *CIL* 8.11048; Gombeaud 1901; Trousset 1974: 94.

[306] *ILAf* 9; Trousset 1974: 120.

[307] *IRT* 868, 869; Mattingly 1982.

[308] Mattingly 1995: 103–105, though in this case dating has been further complicated by the structure's incorporation into more recent military structures.

[309] Hammond 1964: 16.

[310] Trousset 1974: 96, fig. 28.

[311] For example, Mattingly 1995: 193–194; Kennedy & Riley 1990: 167–212; Reddé 1995. See also Section 4.1.2.

[312] Guéry 1986: 602–603. Hayes 1972: 209; Bonifay 2004: 225.

[313] See Section 4.2.6

[314] Mattingly 1995: 101.

[315] Military: Trousset 1974: 67–68; Mattingly 1995: 193. Civilian: Lenoir 2011: 280–281.

[316] Nf083-g: Mattingly 1995: 194; Scott, Dore, & Mattingly 1996: 267. Sc001-g: Scott, Dore, & Mattingly 1996: 273.

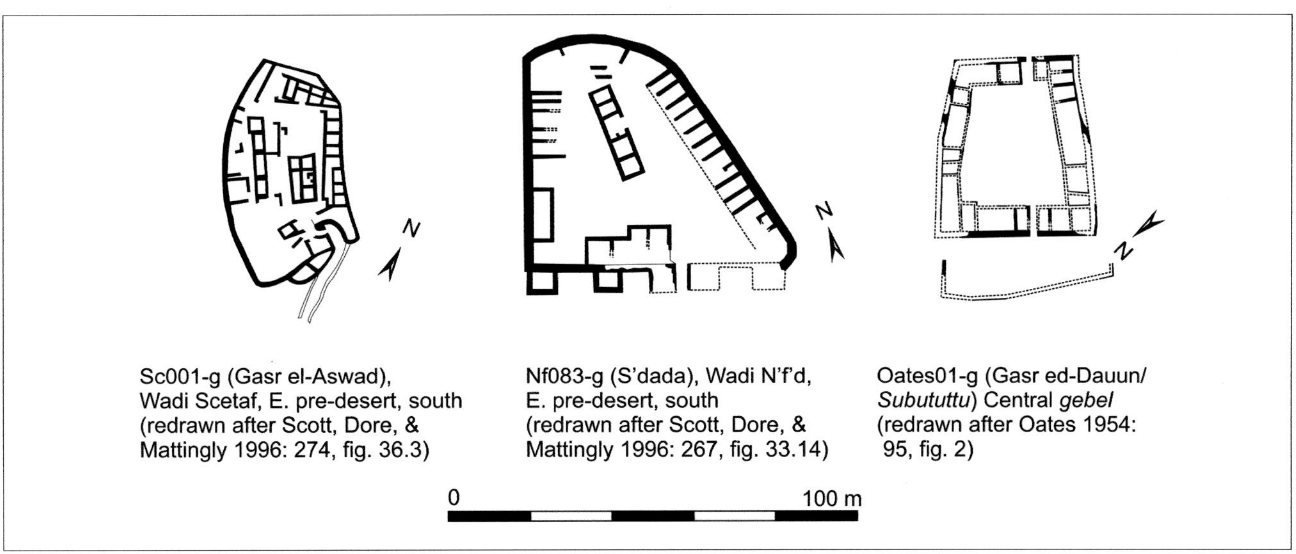

Figure 4.9: *Possible but unconfirmed fortlets.*

both cases by location on an irregularly shaped hilltop), and a lack of any other specific evidence make a military identification less secure.[317] Similarly, at Gasr ed-Dauun (Oates01-g, *Subututtu*), a large fortified building of irregular shape could potentially have been military in nature, but there is little beyond its size to explicitly support this identification.[318] Finally, it is also possible to suggest that SP43a-g, a large, fortified courtyard compound (1,258 m^2), located in western Syrtica might be a good candidate to have been a fortlet. Although there is nothing specific to suggest that it was military in nature, the general scarcity of other large fortified buildings in this region and its proximity to the coast road are potentially supportive of such an identification.

4.2.5 Outposts

In the category of outposts can be included 12 probable examples, ranging between 100 and 800 m^2 in size (Appendix A: 21–32; Figure 4.10). Most of these appear to have been rectilinear in plan, often with rooms ranged around a central courtyard or lightwell, with a single entrance. Gasr Duib (Db001) (28), Gasr Wamis (Wm001) (30), Kasr Tarcine/*Tibubuci* (RLT098) (29) and probably also Gasr Isawi/Banat (Nf037) (23) were multi-storeyed towers, and others probably also incorporated multiple storeys, in whole or in part, but poor preservation makes it difficult to be sure. In at least one case, Ksar Tarcine/*Tibubuci*, the central courtyard on the ground floor was surrounded not by separate rooms but troughs, which has prompted the suggestion that this floor served as a stable, while the soldiers lived on the upper floors.[319]

At least two of these outposts, Ksar Tarcine (RLT098) and Ksar Chetaoua (RLT096) (27), also had additional, and in both cases irregular, enceintes surrounding them (the areas of which are indicated in brackets in Appendix A). At Ksar Tarcine, this enceinte was an irregular pentagonal shape while that at Ksar Chetaoua was trapezoidal, with irregularly shaped corner towers. It is difficult without more investigation to suggest with certainty what the function of this extra, enclosed area would have been, but it is not difficult to imagine that it could have been useful for various military training activities or for keeping animals. Bir Mahalla (RLT101) (32) was described by Blanchet as being similar in form to Ksar Tarcine/*Tibubuci*, in that it consisted of a central tower-like structure surrounded by an enceinte,[320] and Henchir Ragoubah (RLT108) (24) possibly also falls into this group, comprising a central building with an irregular enceinte; unfortunately, we know very little about either of these sites and I was unable to relocate them using satellite imagery to confirm their forms.

Henchir Krannfir (RLT076) (21), Gasr Isawi/Banat (Nf037) and El-Faschia (ZZ004) (26) all employed ashlar masonry. The other structures for which we can identify a construction technique utilised smaller, coursed masonry, though varying in the regularity of the individual blocks from unshaped or roughly shaped rubble to more regularly cut blocks. Unfortunately, our dating evidence for this group is very poor; while a Roman date can generally be inferred for those that employed ashlar masonry, the

[317] Indeed, in a more recent article Mattingly no longer appears to identify these two examples as military in nature (Mattingly, Sterry, & Leitch 2013: 176, fig. 4).

[318] Oates 1953: 89–92; 1954: 94–96.

[319] Trousset 1974: 90.

[320] Gauckler 1899: 204.

SSB581 (Digital Globe via Google Earth Pro, 18 Dec. 2011)

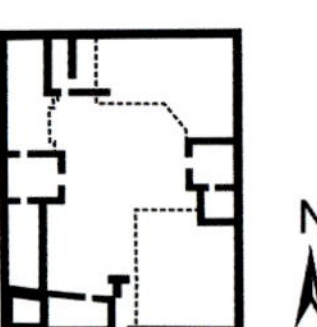

Henchir Krannfir (RLT076) (redrawn after Toutain 1903: 326, fig. 5)

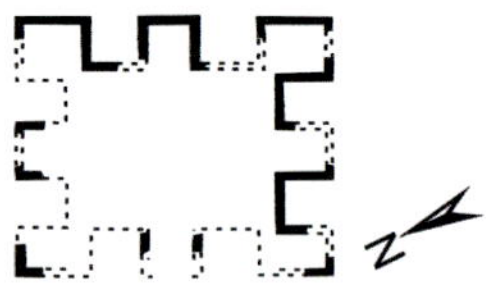

Henchir Rjijila (RLT119) (redrawn after Trousset 1974: 134, fig. 15.4)

Ksar Chetaoua (RLT096) (Digital Globe via Google Earth Pro, 16 Mar. 2012)

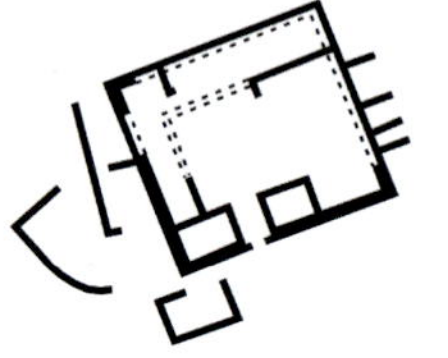

Gasr Isawi/Banat (Nf037) (redrawn after Barker & Jones 1981: 28, fig.9)

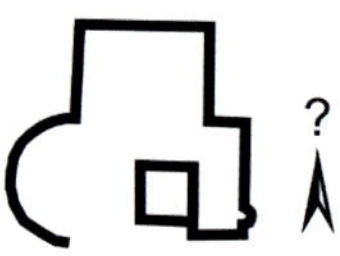

Henchir Ragoubah (RLT108) (redrawn after Blanchet 1899: 140, fig. 17)

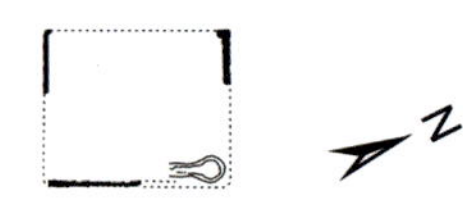

El-Faschia (ZZ004) (redrawn after Scott, Dore, & Mattingly 1996: 315, fig. 44.11)

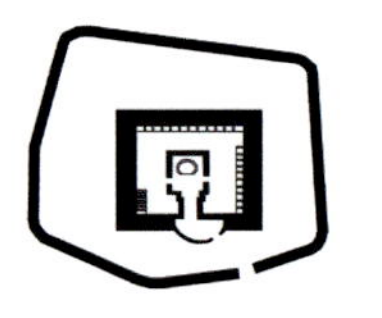

Ksar Tarcine/*Tibubuci* (RLT098) (redrawn after Gauckler 1902: 327)

Gasr Zerzi (redrawn after Rebuffat 1970b: fig. 6)

Gasr Duib, ground floor (Db001) (redrawn after Goodchild & Ward-Perkins 1949: 89, fig. 17)

Gasr Wamis (Wm001) (redrawn after Scott, Dore, & Mattingly 1996: 308, fig. 42.1)

Figure 4.10: *Outposts.*

only one for which we have dating evidence is Gasr Isawi/Banat, which produced ceramic material dating between the first and fifth centuries AD.[321] Gasr Zerzi (31) and Gasr Duib (Db001) have been dated to the third century AD, and Kasr Tarcine/*Tibubuci* (RLT098) to the fourth century AD, on the basis of epigraphic evidence.

Worthy of its own description, with its distinctive projecting corner and side towers, is Henchir Rjijila (RLT119) (25). Its form can be compared to the fortlets of Henchir el-Hadjar (RLT041) and Benia bel-Recheb (RLT105), though it was smaller, with different proportions, and was constructed using the *opus africanum* technique rather than ashlar. Ceramic evidence from Henchir Rjijilia (RLT119) also suggests a fourth-century AD date. In terms of its location north and east of the original *limes* route (Figure 4.4, no. 25), this might again support the suggestion, that along with the two fortlets just mentioned, it was part of a northwards contraction of the frontier.

In general, these buildings most likely acted as checkpoints along the main routes between the larger military posts, and as the name suggests, as outposts through which the main bases could extend their monitoring of the surrounding area. They almost certainly would have been manned with detachments from the larger installations and reported directly to them. Some of these outposts were very small (though multiple storeys could make up for some of the loss in overall ground space) and were probably occupied by as few as ten men, and perhaps up to around 30 in the larger cases.

4.2.6 Observation Posts: Watchtowers and Clausurae

I have recorded six probable free-standing military watchtowers, three of which were in close proximity to and almost certainly associated with *clausurae* (Appendix A: 33–38; Figure 4.11). The very small number of recorded examples is probably more related to preservation and survey techniques than the ancient reality. Because of their small size, even those that were built in stone are more likely to be missed during survey both on the ground and via satellite imagery, particularly if they have not survived to a very great height.

Most of the recorded watchtowers were constructed of coursed rubble or masonry. One example, Henchir Ragoubah (RLT108-t) (38), is recorded as having employed ashlar masonry; however, no size was recorded for this site and it is generally poorly known. I have included it in this category on the basis of Trousset's description of it as a *tour de guet*, but the

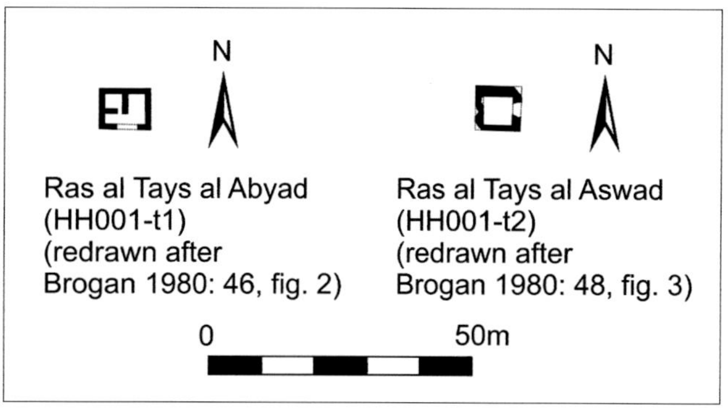

Figure 4.11: *Watchtowers.*

reliability of this interpretation is unclear. Watchtowers were either rectilinear or round in shape, usually with only a single internal room and sometimes with a staircase leading to upper storeys. The only tower for which we have any type of secure dating is the small round tower GG007-t (36), located c. 1 km northeast of the major fort at Gheriat el-Garbia/*Myd[...]*, with which it was quite clearly contemporary, and can be dated to the first half of the third century AD on the basis of an inscription found there (*IRT* 895).[322]

The function of watchtowers could be varied, but as the name implied, most were probably related in some way to monitoring certain routes or areas. Some were located on high crests to act as signalling towers, while others lined routes of communication, both marking the way and providing posts from which activity along them could be observed. The few examples that we have in Tripolitania were usually closely associated with larger military installations, but could be slightly further out and used to keep watch over areas of settlement and water sources, by just a few soldiers.[323]

In some cases, the watchtowers functioned in conjunction with the linear constructions commonly known in Roman contexts as *clausurae*. These long walls sometimes incorporated towers and gates into their construction, and served as ways to observe, direct and control the movement of people and livestock through the landscape.[324] They could be several metres tall, taking the form of earthen banks or walls of coursed rubble or masonry, and sometimes with accompanying ditches. These types of constructions have not been individually catalogued here, but there are several known in Tripolitania. The most well-known within my study area is probably the Tebaga *clausura* located in the western *gebel* which stretched for more than 17 km and had a number of towers attached to it (Figure 4.12), but others including that at Hadd Hajar in the eastern pre-desert, and also Bir Oum Ali (just beyond

[321] Scott, Dore, & Mattingly 1996: 263.

[322] Mattingly 1985a; Mackensen 2012: 44.

[323] Trousset 1990.

[324] Trousset 1974: 139–141; Brogan 1980; Trousset 1984; Mattingly & Jones 1986; Mattingly 1995: 106–115; Napoli 1997: 99–100; Krimi 2007: 142–145.

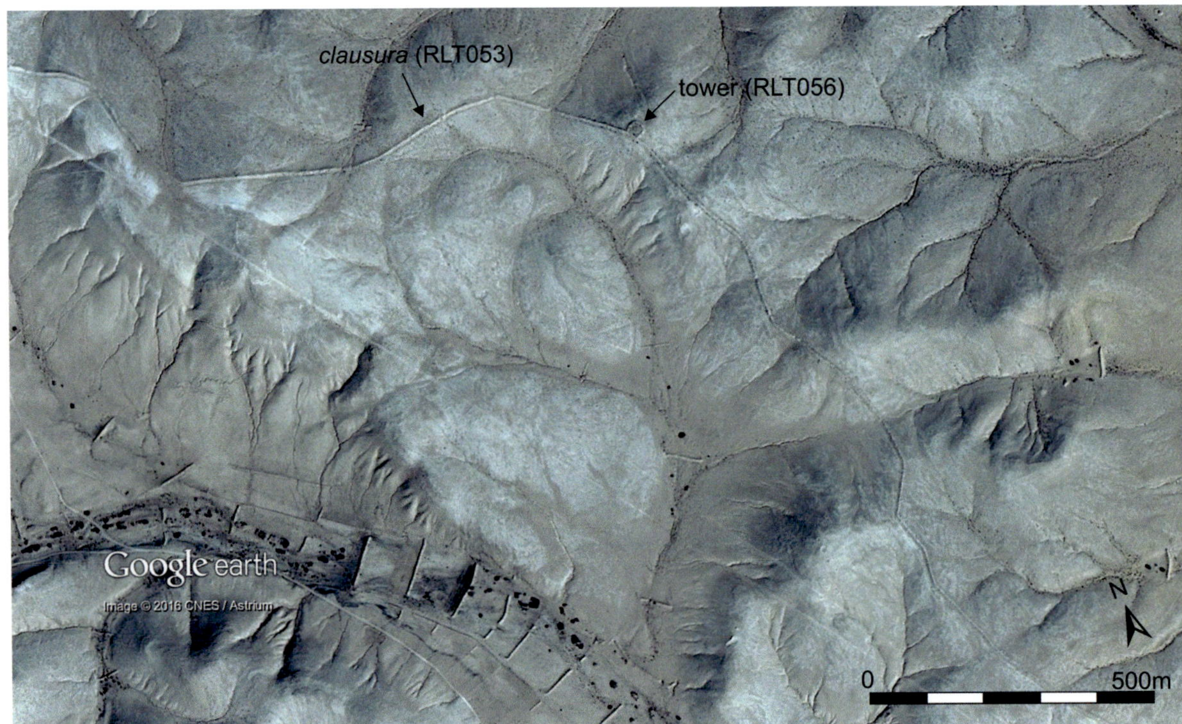

Tebaga *clausura* (RLT053) and tower (RLT056) (CNES/Astrium via Google Earth Pro, 5 Feb. 2016)

Figure 4.12: *The Tebaga* clausura *(western* gebel*).*

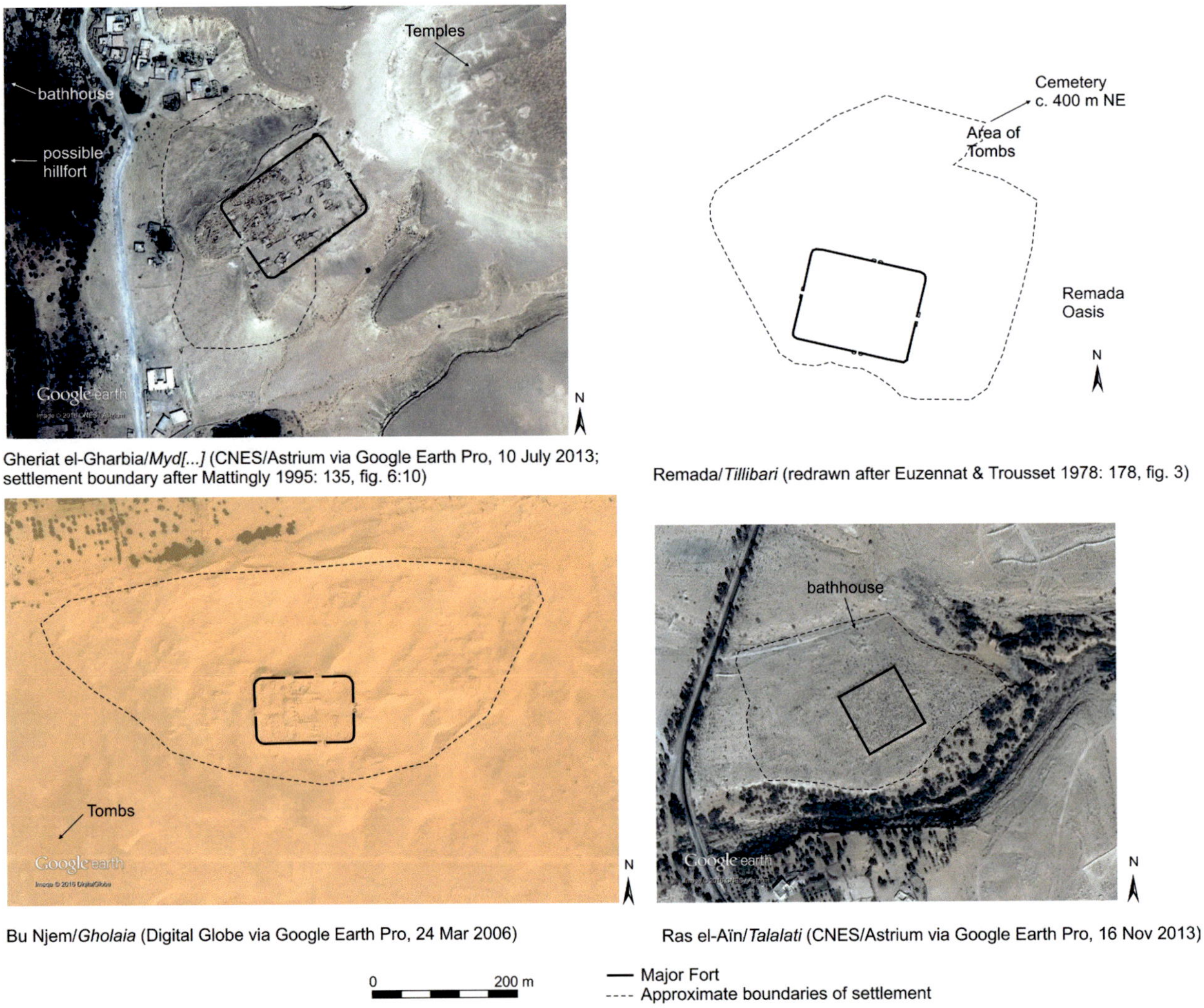

Gheriat el-Gharbia/*Myd[...]* (CNES/Astrium via Google Earth Pro, 10 July 2013; settlement boundary after Mattingly 1995: 135, fig. 6:10)

Remada/*Tillibari* (redrawn after Euzennat & Trousset 1978: 178, fig. 3)

Bu Njem/*Gholaia* (Digital Globe via Google Earth Pro, 24 Mar 2006)

Ras el-Aïn/*Talalati* (CNES/Astrium via Google Earth Pro, 16 Nov 2013)

0 200 m

— Major Fort
---- Approximate boundaries of settlement

Figure 4.13: *Major forts with approximate settlement extents.*

the western bounds of my study area) are also significant. Most of these have been dated very broadly to the third century AD, though more work is needed to confirm these dates.[325] Recent investigations by Sterry and Mattingly have also identified several previously unknown examples in the western *gebel* region bringing the known total to more than 20.[326]

4.3 Military Settlements

In addition to the buildings described above, other buildings or even substantial settlements were also sometimes found at military sites. Some of the outbuildings, like baths and temples, may have been constructed to serve the personal and social needs of the soldiers, and in that sense, are also military architecture. However, the distinction between military and civilian becomes rather more blurred with these types of structures and the settlements of which they were a part.[327] The issue is also complicated further by the fact that some of these settlements likely developed from pre-existing indigenous centres, at which military bases were deliberately established for the purposes of monitoring them and creating a visible presence, as previously mentioned in Chapter 1.

All four of the major forts discussed above had extramural settlements (*vici*) several hectares in size (Figure 4.13). At Bu Njem/*Gholaia*, an extensive settlement with a surrounding wall, constructed of poorly mortared rubble, can clearly be seen on aerial photography and in satellite imagery spreading to the northeast and northwest of the fort.[328] The excavation of one of the buildings of the settlement, *Le Bâtiment aux niches*, revealed several rooms attached to a courtyard, constructed in irregular masonry, with niches sunk into the interior walls, which were covered in plaster, and vaulted.[329] Temples dedicated to Jupiter Hammon, Mars Canapphar, Vanammon and others have also been identified in the area surrounding the fort, and there was also a necropolis to the southwest, which had both military and civilian tombs.[330]

The settlements associated with the other major forts are less well investigated and little can be said definitely about their architecture or form. The remains of a possible settlement can be seen on the slopes below the major fort of Gheriat el-Garbia on an aerial photograph first published by Goodchild, though more recent satellite imagery visible in the figure above seems to indicate that they are now in very poor condition.[331] Just to the northeast of the fort, however, are the remains of a number of probable temples, and to the west of the fort in the oasis itself, a bathhouse sits below a possible pre-existing hillfort.[332] Ras el-Aïn/*Talalati* appears to have been surrounded on all sides by structures, including a bath building to the north which was investigated in the early twentieth century, all bounded by a wall on the west side.[333] At Remada/*Tillibari*, the settlement, like the fort itself, seems to have been completely overbuilt, but Donau recorded at least three mausolea located c. 200 m north of the fort itself and traces of a probable settlement between, enclosed by a stone and earth wall.[334]

Settlements also grew up around and in association with smaller military posts, but again, little detailed work on the architecture or phasing of these sites has yet been carried out. The minor forts of Bir Rhezene/*Bezereos*, Henchir Mgarine/*Agarlabas(?)*, Henchir Medeina/*Thebelami* and Ain Wif 1/*Thenadassa*, are also all described as having had associated settlements, with the latter also having remains of a bath-house.[335] Evidence for settlements has also been recorded at the fortlets of Ksar Rhilane/*Tisavar* and Medina Doga/*Mesphe*.[336] The outpost of Gheriat esh-Shergia was strategically located in an oasis where it is not unlikely that an indigenous settlement already existed, and Gasr Isawi (Nf037) was established beside a hilltop settlement that probably pre-dated the military building and its accompanying settlement (Figure 4.14). The outpost of Henchir Rjijila (RLT119) also had a group of buildings surrounding it, clearly visible on satellite imagery, and was located at the base of a high hill with an enclosure, of unknown date.[337]

These types of settlements were probably mutually beneficial to both the soldiers and the often-local civilians who occupied and utilised them, in that the military was provided with goods and services, while the soldiers provided customers and protection for local

[325] Napoli 1997: 69–72

[326] Mattingly *et al.* 2013c: 80, fig. 117.

[327] Fentress 1979: 124.

[328] Rebuffat, Deneauve, & Hallier 1967; Rebuffat *et al.* 1969; Rebuffat 1970b; 1970a; 1975a; 1977a.

[329] Rebuffat *et al.* 1969: 21–31; Rebuffat 1970b: 133–135.

[330] Rebuffat 1990a; Brouquier-Reddé 1992: 148–160.

[331] Goodchild 1954: 60–66, Plate X, b.

[332] Jones & Barker 1983: 64–67; Scott, Dore, & Mattingly 1996: 98–105; Mackensen 2012: 53–54.

[333] Lecoy de la Marche 1894: 399–402; Boizot 1913; Trousset 1974: 98–102; Mattingly 1995: 137–138.

[334] Trousset 1974: 114–118; Euzennat & Trousset 1978: 125–126.

[335] Hilaire 1901: 97; Trousset 1974: 52, 109; Mattingly 1982; 1995: 137.

[336] Gombeaud 1901: 89–92; Goodchild 1951c: 48–51; Mattingly 1995: 137.

[337] Trousset 1974: 106.

Gasr Isawi (Nf037) (Digital Globe via Google Earth, 27 Aug 2012)

Henchir Rjijila (RLT119) (Digital Globe via Bing Maps)

0 200 m

— Outpost
---- Approximate boundaries of settlement

Figure 4.14: *Outposts with settlements.*

farmers, merchants and craftsmen.[338] Furthermore, studies about Roman military settlements in other parts of the empire have begun to emphasise the cultural complexity of these communities and to rethink traditional ideas about how different spaces were used and the people who were using them, including not only soldiers, but women, children, slaves, etc.[339] Some of these settlements continued on for a time after the forts themselves fell into disuse, though most remained on a relatively small scale. [340]

4.4 Discussion

The overall distribution of the known military structures of the region can be divided into three rough groups: west, central and eastern. This is probably partially to do with the history of work being concentrated in these regions, and in particular, the relatively high number of military buildings known from the western region may be related to the specific attention that the *limes* have traditionally been paid in southern Tunisia by French scholars. This western group consisted of the routes leading from *Tacape* and the oases along the eastern side of the Chott Djerid towards Ghadames. All of the military buildings which have projecting towers are found in this group, a fact which is made more interesting because, while none of the certainly military structures of the central group is known to have incorporated projecting corner towers, a small number of structures in that area now believed to be civilian do. While the use of projecting towers on military buildings was probably part of the same pattern which saw this feature become common in other parts of the empire, the use of this same feature in civilian fortified buildings in the east, may have been part of the trend identified above in which buildings as far south as Fazzan also had projecting towers.[341]

Like the western group, the military buildings of the central part of Tripolitania appear to be focused on the route through the *gebel* which connected *Lepcis Magna* and *Oea* to *Tacape*, and the two routes south into the pre-desert and beyond via Gheriat el-Garbia/*Myd[...]* and Bu Njem/*Gholaia*. The eastern group consists of only a few examples in Syrtica, clustered relatively closely together along the coast road at the eastern edge of the region; beyond these examples, we do not have much evidence for a military presence in Syrtica. There is also a relatively large gap in the central *gebel* and southwestern areas between Remada/*Tillibari* and the probable post at Zintan, and southwards towards Ghadames past Si Aioun/*praesidium*.

It is unclear whether these gaps are a reflection of ancient reality, preservation, modern survey factors or some combination of the three. Some sites which appear in itineraries and are sometimes referred to using the vague term of 'road stations' (as in the *Barrington Atlas*), dotting the coast and *gebel* roads, could potentially be candidates for military sites, but since in most cases we know very little about these potential settlements, many of which may not have been related to the military at all, we must be cautious in how we interpret them. Additionally, modern development and agriculture along the coast and in the *gebel* may have destroyed evidence for buildings in these areas, and the shifting sand dunes of the southwestern pre-desert may have obscured any remaining evidence.

If we refer back to Figure 2.2, we can begin to see the geographic relationship between the known military and civilian buildings of the region. In the northwest part of the region, the line formed by the location of the known military buildings does seem to form an approximate geographic limit to the settlement of the region, with many of the military sites set well behind the area which was agriculturally viable. Mattingly *et al.* have also observed that the distribution of *clausurae*, mainly recorded in the west, appears to suggest "a strong correlation of the linear barriers with the limits of intensive sedentary farming".[342] Similarly, Gheriat el-Garbia/*Myd[...]* and Bu Njem/*Gholaia* also seem to coincide with the approximate limits of known settlement, although at least two possible settlements have also been recorded south of these limits at Umm el-Gueloub, approximately halfway between the two major forts and a small building in the Wadi Neina, c. 90 km south of Bu Njem.[343] It is especially significant that these posts were constructed after most of that settlement was established, suggesting that the military buildings were not meant to create boundaries, but were placed at those points because that is where the natural limit of densest settlement was already to be found.

The distribution of military buildings in the central *gebel* and the eastern pre-desert, further emphasises that the *limes* did not act as a defensive border. Rather, the Roman military's role was clearly one of controlling and monitoring the people who were already there, and

[338] Hanel 2007: 410–413.

[339] Mattingly 1995: 134–137; Goldsworthy & Haynes 1999; James 2001; Allison 2013.

[340] For example, Bu Njem/*Gholaia*: Rebuffat 1989: 156, 165; Gheriat el-Garbia/*Myd[...]*: Mackensen 2012: 55–58; Ras el-Aïn/*Talalati*: Mattingly 1995: 137.

[341] See Section 4.1.2, above, and Section 6.2.1.

[342] Mattingly *et al.* 2013c: 80.

[343] Umm el-Gueloub: Rebuffat 1982; Wadi Neina: Brogan 1965b.

those who were moving between Tripolitania and the areas to the south for purposes of trade or otherwise. While before the fourth century AD defense against outside incursions was probably occasionally necessary, the Roman military in Tripolitania is probably better understood as an 'army of occupation', as described by Isaac in relation to the role of the military in the eastern empire.[344] Unless we are missing a very large part of the evidence, the idea that the relatively sparse and small military installations, particularly in the eastern part of Tripolitania, would have been able to defend the frontier from any concerted, large-scale invasions is simply not believable.

It is fairly clear, therefore, that the expansion of rural settlement and the penetration of military installations further into the pre-desert during the later first and second centuries AD were related and occurred in tandem. On the one hand, a military presence was necessary in these regions to maintain the peace and keep watch over the groups who, although now peaceful, had not that long previously been rather troublesome. At the same time, the presence of the military might have offered not only a level of order and security to the inhabitants of the region, but could also have helped rural settlement to thrive and expand. The extension of the military routes southwards would have meant better roads and trade routes, which would enable rural peoples to obtain goods and ideas from further away and to trade their own wares more easily and along further distances. From an architectural standpoint in particular, this could have meant access to tools, resources and specialists to build the types of structures which had not previously been seen in the region, at least not beyond the coast, for example those with ashlar masonry and detailed sculptural decoration. In addition, although we would no longer suggest that the military was directly involved in or responsible for the construction of the fortified buildings of the region, we might suggest that the monumental nature of these imposing military structures potentially made an impact on local leaders, who sought to make statements of wealth, power or prestige through the imitation or adoption of certain aspects of these buildings in their own homes, as explored further in Chapter 6.

[344] Trousset 1974; Mattingly 1995: 68–69; Isaac 2000.

chapter five

Unfortified Architecture and Settlement

The unfortified buildings and settlements of Tripolitania took many different forms, but commonly comprised varying combinations of single-storeyed structures and open spaces bounded by low walls or ranges of rooms. In addition to quantitative and qualitative analyses of several different aspects of these unfortified buildings, in this chapter I will show that the two main unfortified building types observed in the region, farmyard and courtyard buildings, differed significantly. Not only was this in their physical forms, but also in their development, distribution and uses for reasons related to both economic conditions and socio-cultural traditions.

Importantly, unfortified buildings are also, as their name implies, in many ways defined by the characteristics which they did not have, that is, features that have traditionally been interpreted as defensive, such as surrounding ditches, high, substantially constructed walls or single, defensible entrances. I, therefore, explicitly identify the buildings in this chapter as unfortified to differentiate them clearly from the significant number of buildings and settlements in Tripolitania which *can* be identified as fortified, as discussed in Chapter 6, particularly in the pre-desert region, but which otherwise had many of the same domestic, agricultural and/or pastoral functions.

On the other hand, we should not necessarily assume that unfortified sites were not defendable or their inhabitants not concerned with security; for example, we can point to buildings which on the whole can be classified as unfortified, but have possible watchtowers incorporated into their structures (e.g. BUN007-f6 or Lg003-f). And conversely, as discussed in the next chapter, it would be a mistake to assume that all of the apparently defensive features associated with fortified sites were solely the result of a (perceived) need for protection or security. Furthermore, this analysis is reliant on the reports and descriptions of others and what can be deduced from photographs and satellite images to differentiate between unfortified and fortified structures, so occasional miscategorisations are inevitable. Nevertheless, while we can point to certain problems with this dichotomy and it is important to remain cautious and flexible in its application, in general, it is possible to identify key differences in the morphology and development of so-called unfortified and fortified buildings which suggest that it remains not entirely inappropriate to maintain this distinction.

5.1 Farms and Farm Buildings: Terminology

One of the most common forms of settlement that survive archaeologically in rural Tripolitania, unfortified or otherwise, is the farm, broadly defined here as a rural area of land and its associated buildings, which together are primarily intended for agricultural and/or pastoral purposes. This includes, but is not necessarily limited to, the cultivation of plants, the rearing of animals and the processing of their associated products. There may be differences in scale, form of land tenure and the types of buildings which are present, but in socio-economic terms, any settlement which meets these criteria can theoretically be considered a farm.

A source of occasional confusion, however, is that the term farm is also commonly used in written sources to refer specifically to the buildings which are associated with this form of settlement. In the *ULVS* publications for example, the authors consistently use terms such as 'courtyard farms' and 'fortified farms' in contexts where they are clearly discussing buildings.[345] This usage is not limited to the English language – the

[345] For example, in Mattingly & Dore 1996; Mattingly & Flower 1996; Barker 1996c, *passim*.

same is seen, for example, in French publications with *fermes à cour* or *fermes à enclos*.[346] Context, of course, usually makes it clear whether an author is referring to the settlement as a whole or the building specifically, but for a study focussed specifically on architecture, this can sometimes be problematic when we consider sites with multiple structures in close proximity. For example, at the site of Lm004 in the southern part of the eastern pre-desert, five separate buildings have been identified. Detailed investigations have revealed that one was a dedicated press building while another has been interpreted as the primary habitation building and the site as a whole has, quite reasonably, been interpreted together as a single farm.[347]

Unfortunately, this kind of detailed investigation which allows us to understand the specific function of different buildings has generally been the exception in Tripolitania; we are far less informed about other sites with multiple buildings. For example, I identified and recorded Ag-NS12 as a single 'site' with two farm buildings, c.35 m apart. These buildings appear to be very similar in their size and plan, each consisting of a rectilinear enclosure with a few buildings or rooms attached to the interior and exterior walls. But how should we interpret their relationship? Is this a single farm with two buildings which serve different purposes or house different parts of the same family? Or does one building serve as habitation for the owners of the farm while the other is intended for labourers, slaves, or animals? Or do the two buildings represent two different farms, with separate lands and properties, whose owners have chosen to construct their homes near to each other perhaps because of familial or other social ties or reasons of security? If they are two different farms, are they equal in status, is one dependent on the other, or are both dependent on a separate and larger estate? Considering that this site was identified solely through satellite imagery, we must also consider the possibility that these buildings are not even contemporary. These questions will be explored further in Sections 5.3 and 5.4, below, but it is important to make it clear that based on the current state of the material evidence, in most cases we cannot be completely certain about how buildings in physical proximity to each other were related in a socio-economic sense.

In order to avoid any ambiguity, therefore, I will refer to the structures discussed in this chapter by the generic term 'unfortified (farm) buildings'. This includes both structures and spaces which were probably intended for human habitation and those primarily intended for productive activities, e.g. pressing facilities, storage, animal shelters, etc. This is partly because we know so little about the use and organisation of space in this context; a general lack of detailed plans and excavations means that in the majority of cases it is simply not possible to differentiate between these types of spaces.[348] However, I would also argue that a strict separation between domestic and productive spaces is not always appropriate, particularly in smaller examples, where different types of activities may have taken place in the same spaces or buildings.[349] Therefore, as already mentioned, even though Lm004 can probably be interpreted as a single farm, it has five farm buildings. The site of Ag-NS12 has two farm buildings, but it is not clear how many farms as socio-economic entities those buildings might actually represent. It is important, therefore, to emphasise that because in most cases we cannot make this distinction, the quantitative analyses below generally give equal weight and importance to all buildings, regardless of whether they are isolated or occur in small groups.

It is not clear what terms ancient peoples may have used for the farms and buildings that they constructed and in which they lived. It is possible that some people may have spoken Latin, especially in the areas closer to the coast, even if not as their native tongue, and there is some limited evidence for the use of Latin terminology. For example, an inscription found in the southern part of the eastern pre-desert in the Wadi el-Amud, uses the basic Latin term for building or structure, *aedificium*, to refer to a building which appears to have been replaced by a new one (which is referred to only as *hoc opus*).[350] An ostracon dated to the fourth century AD discovered at Henchir Bou Garnin/*Villa Magna* (LT05) in the western coastal region used the terms *fundus* and *villa*, both of which can variously be translated as farm or estate.[351]

The term *villa* in particular is somewhat problematic and its use is complicated by the varied and inconsistent application of the term in different parts of the empire and in both ancient and modern writings for both farms in general and specific types of buildings. It should be noted, therefore, that with only a few exceptions of very large coastal complexes with abundant evidence for leisure activities and luxury decoration, in terms of their plans, I do not distinguish villas as a separate type from other farm buildings and will therefore not normally use

[346] Rebuffat 1988: 47–48.

[347] Barker & Jones 1984.

[348] The main exception in this study is where we have evidence of presses in the form of *in situ* orthostats.

[349] In contrast to, for example, Columella's ideal differentiation in *villae* between the *partes urbana*, *rustica* and *fructuaria* (Columella, *de Re Rustica* 1.6).

[350] Brogan 1964: 52.

[351] '...*in f(un)d(o) villa magna*...'. Merlin 1915: cxcii; Drine 2002: 2008.

the term. The presence of luxury elements is sometimes used as the means of differentiating villas as distinct from farms;[352] however, as will be discussed in Section 5.2.5, while the presence of luxury features almost certainly correlates to differences in size or construction technique, in terms of two-dimensional plan, they can and do occur in buildings which are otherwise no different from other rural structures.

It is likely, however, that the majority of the rural peoples with whom we are concerned here would not have spoken Latin as a primary language. There are a few terms that are known from Neo-Punic that may have been relevant such as *MZR*ʿ ('sown land' or 'cultivated soil')[353] and *ŠD* ('field' or 'farmland').[354] Of other terms which might have been used in local, indigenous languages, we are essentially, and unfortunately, ignorant. However, just as in English, we can suspect that in everyday parlance, a variety of terms, of different languages and origins might have been used interchangeably by various peoples, the popularity of different terms probably varying in different places and times.

5.2 Physical Characteristics and Analyses

I have catalogued 1,653 individual structures which can certainly or probably be identified as rural, unfortified farm buildings (Appendix B; Figure 5.1). As already discussed in Section 2.4 and illustrated in Figure 2.2, the material has been divided into nine regions in order to make comparative analyses across the study area (Table 5.1). In the sections below I present quantitative and qualitative analyses and discussion of four major categories of physical characteristics of the unfortified buildings in each of these regions: plan, size, materials and construction techniques and decoration and luxury features, as well as considering the place of presses, and how space may have been utilised in these buildings.

It is clear that there is a significant imbalance in the number of buildings catalogued in each area, with more than 75% of the unfortified sites identified located in the eastern pre-desert and Syrtica. This is almost certainly, at least partially, due to the uneven nature and limitations of both the field and satellite imagery surveys that have been undertaken in various areas, as discussed in Chapter 2. Therefore, we must be particularly cautious when comparing areas with very small sample sizes with those where there is more data, but it is nonetheless useful to try to place what results we can into wider contexts.

5.2.1 Form and Plan

There is a wide array of unfortified farm buildings known from rural Tripolitania, ranging from small, one- or two-roomed structures to huge complexes with multiple rooms and yards or courtyards. It is probable that many of the buildings would have undergone various transformations in their size and layout over their period of use, with the addition or subtraction of rooms, entire buildings, enclosures, etc. In the majority of cases, the form of the building analysed is almost always only the latest phase of its development visible above ground and without more detailed investigations, we simply cannot know to what extent the latest phase differed from the earliest. Until more excavations are carried out which can refine our dating specifically for the construction, use, renovation and abandonment of particular buildings, we will remain ignorant of any finer chronological developments in the layout of buildings.

	All	Published	%	Satellite	%
1. W. coastal	50	32	64	18	36
2. W. *gebel*	9	9	100	–	–
3. Southwest	11	1	9	10	91
4. Central coastal	94	94	100	–	–
5. Central *gebel*	156	156	100	–	–
6. E. pre-desert, north	365	312	85	53	15
7. E. pre-desert, south	414	252	61	162	39
8. W. Syrtica	487	152	31	335	69
9. E. Syrtica	67	–	–	67	100
Total	*1,653*	*1,008*	*61*	*645*	*39*

Table 5.1: *Number of unfortified buildings identified in each sub-region of Tripolitania.*

[352] For discussions on the term *villa* and if/how *villae* differ from farms see: Varro *de Re Rustica* 3.2; *Digesta*, 50.16.211: Florus, *Inst.*, 8; Harmand 1951; Percival 1976; 13–15; Rossiter 1978: 1–3; Millett 1990:91–92; Scott 1993: 1–6; Purcell 1995; Smith 1997: 10–11; Terrenato 2001: 5–6; Leveau 2002; Marzano 2007: 2–4, 82–101, *et passim*; Ahmed 2010: 102–106. Cf. De Vos, who chooses not to use the term at all (2000: 9–11).

[353] Krahmalkov 2000: 274.

[354] Krahmalkov 2000: 456.

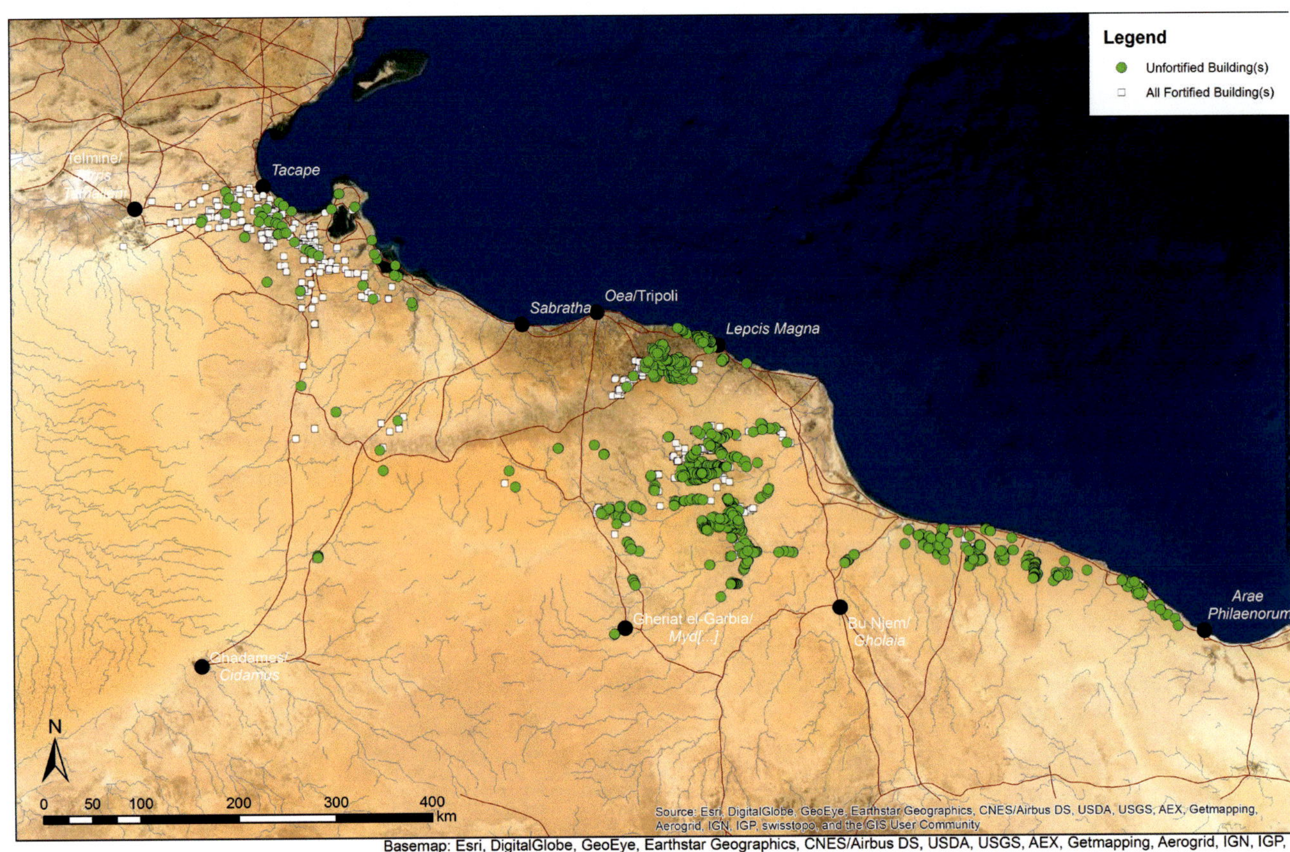

Figure 5.1: *Distribution of all catalogued unfortified buildings (n=1,653).*

Previous Typologies

Various typologies and terminologies have previously been employed to distinguish between different sorts of buildings. I have already made reference to some of these above: courtyard farms, *fermes à enclos*, etc. However, there has been little attempt at standardisation and as a result there has been a certain amount of inconsistency between (and sometimes even within) publications in the application of various terms and typologies.

In the surveys of the western regions, although evidence for structures was often found in abundance in the form of building materials and walls, the full plans of unfortified buildings seem to have been recorded relatively infrequently, often due to poor visibility and conservation, and in some cases, e.g. the *Recherches sur le Limes Tripolitanus* study, to a far greater interest in fortified and (presumed) military sites.[355] As a result, building plans were not typically used for determining a typology of unfortified buildings during the course of these surveys. Neither did the Italian surveys in the coastal plain around *Lepcis Magna* employ any particularly complex typology for unfortified buildings, probably for similar reasons as in the west: low overall conservation/visibility of complete building plans. A brief sentence describes the plans of *fattorie aperte* (open farms) as '*rettangolare o quadrata con cortile centrale*'.[356] In general, the extent of differentiation made between the unfortified sites was a distinction between farms (*fattorie*) and villas (*ville*) based on the presence of luxury elements (with the latter further divided into inland and coastal examples).[357]

In the *Tarhuna Archaeological Survey*, Ahmed developed a site typology based on the size of settlements, which he calculated based on the size of the spread of archaeological material and the types of remains that were visible at a site. However, while this is useful as a general indicator of the size of a site, it tells us little about the actual buildings themselves. The presence and number of presses was also an important factor in differentiating between what he termed oilery farms (5+ presses), large farms (3–4 presses) and small farms (1–2 presses). When luxury elements such as mosaics, wall-paintings, baths or porticoes were found associated with these sites, the word villa was also applied.[358] Using the number of

[355] Trousset 1974; Mrabet 1998; 2000a; 2000b; Fentress, Drine, & Holod 2009: 26–27, 87–89.

[356] Munzi *et al.* 2004–2005: 447.

[357] Fontana, Munzi, & Ricci 1996; Cifani *et al.* 2003; Munzi *et al.* 2004; Munzi 2010; Munzi *et al.* 2010; Musso *et al.* 2010.

[358] Ahmed 2010: 61–70.

presses as an indicator of farm size makes sense from an economic standpoint: the more presses at a site, the more olive orchards or vineyards a farm probably had in order to justify their presence.[359] However, from an architectural standpoint, it can only tell us so much. Ahmed makes the observation that "the architecture of [small farms] is similar to the larger farms, but on a reduced scale".[360] It would not be unreasonable to expect that a building with 17 presses would be larger than a building with only one, simply because they take up more physical space. Nevertheless, Ahmed provides no quantitative indication of the scale of size difference between these buildings that proves whether there is actually a strong relationship between number of presses and type or size of building.[361]

The existing typologies for the unfortified buildings of the eastern pre-desert and Syrtica are more complex than in other regions, but they are not without problems. In the final publication of the *ULVS*, unfortified farms were divided into three classes of building: 'farms employing ashlar masonry (*opus quadratum/opus africanum*)', 'open/courtyard farms' and 'gasr-type farms'.[362] The first and third categories were based on the type and quality of masonry used, while the second category was based on plan. This inconsistency is problematic, not least because according to their description, in plan 'farms employing ashlar masonry' often take the form of 'ranges around a courtyard'.[363]

The *ULVS* team also made a distinction between what they termed 'farms' and 'farmsteads' based on the number of rooms present, the latter being defined as having three or fewer rooms.[364] However, this rule was not applied consistently and we have no reason to believe that anyone in ancient times would have made a distinction between buildings based on this criterion. A more complex plan-based typology was devised for unfortified farms in the *ULVS* area in an unpublished MA thesis, in which the author concluded that the number of rooms made no real difference in the relative frequency of plan type; buildings identified as farmsteads were simply smaller versions of farms.[365] This is not to say there was not a perceived difference in smaller and larger farms and buildings, but the number of rooms does not seem to be the most appropriate way to divide them.

In eastern Syritca, the *Shell Sirte Basin* survey authors seem to have used broadly the same system as the *ULVS*.[366] In western Syrtica, Rebuffat identified four plan types for what he termed *fermes ordinaires* (as opposed to *fermes fortifiées*): '*fermes à cour*', '*fermes à enclos*', '*fermes modestes sans enclos*' and '*fermes élaborées sans enclos*'. In theory, the first two categories of farms were based on the same principle, with the *fermes à cour* being more regular in their plan, of better construction, and larger than the *fermes à enclos*. However, these differences seem not to have been based on any systematic measurements of these characteristics and, as Rebuffat admits, the distinction between the two is sometimes very vague.[367] In the *PVNL* publication, Reddé simplified this scheme further, dividing the unfortified farms into only two groups: '*fermes à bâtiments multiples de la plaine Syrtique*' and '*fermes à cour des vallées*'. As he explains, however, the main structures of the first group probably also had '*grandes cours*', but were more substantial and well-constructed than the buildings of the second group, and more often accompanied by smaller outbuildings.[368]

Revised Typology and Analyses

As the brief outline above has shown, there has clearly been a great deal of variation in previous descriptions and classifications of unfortified building types in Tripolitania. In order to conduct coherent and meaningful comparisons between the sites identified in these different surveys and regions, it was necessary to create a single, standardised typology. Of the 1,653 unfortified buildings in my catalogue, it was possible to distinguish a certain or probable plan from published material or satellite imagery for 1,200 (73%). I divided these plans into six types: farmyard, courtyard, open (undifferentiated), open complex, range (or block) and villa complex. The frequency of these types across the different regions of rural Tripolitania is presented in Table 5.2 and Figure 5.2.

Most of the unfortified buildings that I have identified fall into the broader category of 'open' farm buildings. In general, these open farm buildings incorporated one or more covered rooms, which are interpreted as having been intended for human and/or animal habitation, domestic activities or storage, and a large, open area, bounded by ranges of rooms, a wall or some other kind of fence, which could be used to corral animals as well as for any number of other domestic or productive activities.[369] I identify two main variations based on the

[359] For some calculations on the capacity of African olive presses see: Mattingly 1988a; 1993; Hitchner *et al.* 1990: 248–255.

[360] Ahmed 2010: 68.

[361] See Section 5.2.3

[362] Mattingly & Dore 1996: 118–122. See also Jones 1985: 264–266.

[363] Mattingly & Dore 1996: 118.

[364] Scott, Dore, & Mattingly 1996:12.

[365] Cività 1994: 72.

[366] LeQuesne, Basell, & Sheibani 2010: 23.

[367] Rebuffat 1988: 44–48.

[368] Reddé 1988: 69–71.

[369] See Section 5.2.3 below for further discussion of the use of space in open farm buildings.

	Farmyard	Courtyard	Open (undiff.)	Open complex	Range	Villa complex	*Total*
1. W. coastal	11	5	19	–	1	–	*36*
2. W. *gebel*	–	1	3	–	2	–	*6*
3. Southwest	–	1	9	–	–	–	*10*
4. Central coastal	–	5	3	–	–	4	*12*
5. Central *gebel*	–	33	14	–	–	–	*47*
6. E. pre-desert, north	114	31	49	38	11	–	*243*
7. E. pre-desert, south	233	33	43	11	31	–	*351*
8. W. Syrtica	354	12	29	24	9	–	*428*
9. E. Syrtica	44	–	13	7	3	–	*67*
Total	*756*	*121*	*182*	*80*	*57*	*4*	*1200*

Table 5.2: *Frequency of unfortified building types by region.*

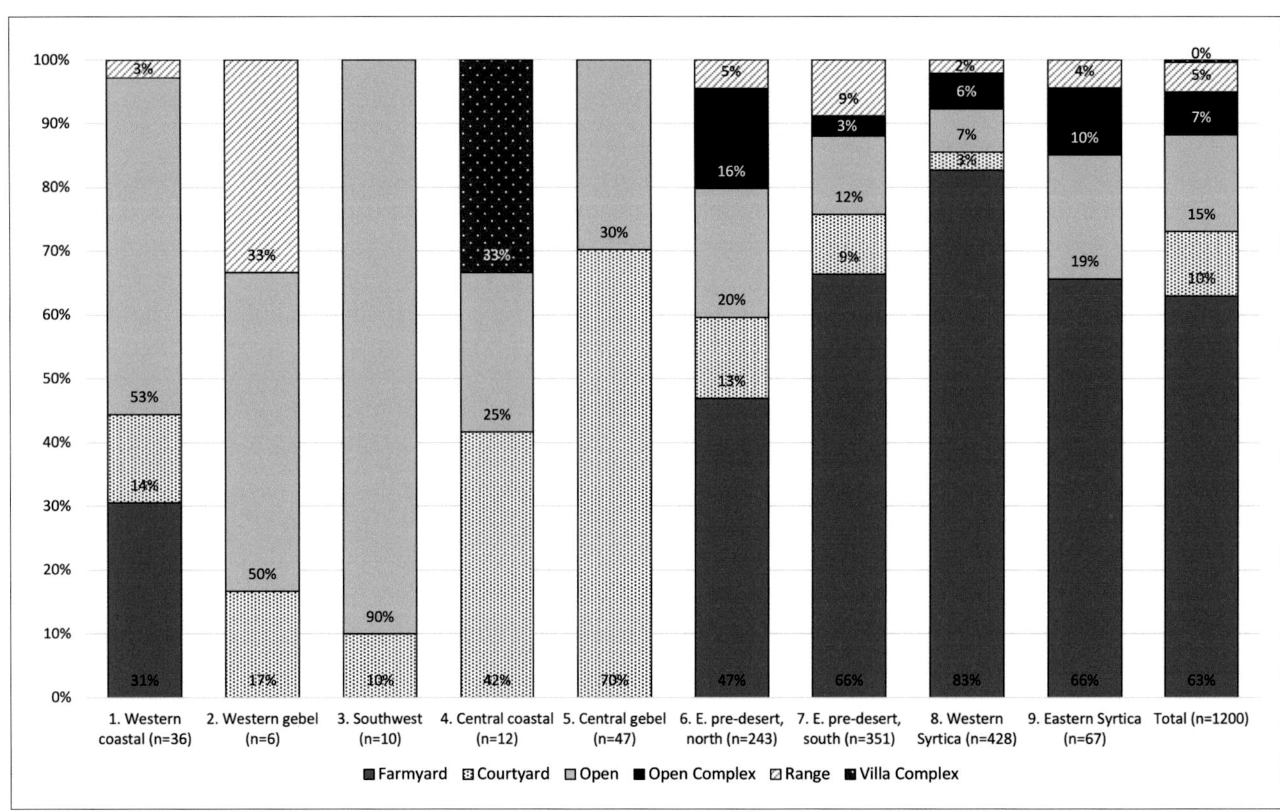

Figure 5.2: *Frequency of unfortified plan types, in total and divided by region.*

arrangement of the different components: farmyard and courtyard buildings.

The most commonly recorded type of open farm building in my study area overall is the farmyard type. In these structures, the number and arrangement of rooms can vary, but do not form a continuous range on more than one side of the attached open space (i.e. the farmyard), which could be rectilinear or irregular in shape (Figure 5.3). Courtyard buildings on the other hand are distinguished from farmyard buildings by the presence of continuous ranges of rooms on two or more sides of the defined open space (i.e. the courtyard), and are generally characterised by a greater degree of regularity and rectilinearity (Figure 5.4). While a definition requiring a continuous range of structures on two sides of a courtyard, rather than, say, three or four, is essentially arbitrary, it provides a more easily quantifiable way of identifying these structures than what in previous typologies seem to have been essentially subjective judgments of 'regularity' or 'substantiality'.[370] In addition, by

[370] As a result, it should be noted that a number of examples identified in the *ULVS* Gazetteer as 'courtyard farms' did not meet the requirements for my definition.

not using other physical characteristics such as size or construction in its definition, we can compare how these different characteristics intersect more objectively. Buildings which were identifiable as having covered rooms associated with a defined, open space, but for which the number and arrangement of rooms could not be ascertained were classified simply as open (undifferentiated).

Although they share basic physical similarities, the geographical distribution of farmyard and courtyard farms differs in some significant ways (Table 5.2, above; Figure 5.5 and Figure 5.6). Courtyard buildings were identified in all regions (though in very small numbers in many cases) except eastern Syrtica. On the other hand, no farmyard buildings were identified in the western *gebel*, the southwest, the central coastal region or central *gebel*; however, it should be noted that in all of these cases, there were undifferentiated open buildings, which could have been either farmyard or courtyard buildings.

In the regions where both farmyard and courtyard buildings were identified, their proportions also varied significantly (see Figure 5.2, above). In the western coastal area, farmyard and courtyard buildings accounted for 30% (n=11) and 14% (n=5) of the buildings of identified plan respectively. As we move

Gh046-f, Wadi Ghirza, E. pre-desert, south
(DigitalGlobe via Google Earth Pro, 7 Mar. 2012)

Ts-NS33-f, Wadi Tessa, E. pre-desert, south
(DigitalGlobe via Google Earth Pro, 28 Dec. 2014)

Jr-NS26-f, Wadi Jarif, W. Syrtica
(DigitalGlobe via Google Earth Pro, 10 Feb. 2013)

0 25m

Mm070-f, Wadi Mimoun, E. pre-desert, north
(DigitalGlobe via Google Earth Pro, 28 Dec. 2014)

Figure 5.3: *Examples of farmyard buildings.*

Oates08-f, Central *gebel* (Maxar Technologies via Google Earth Pro, 22 Jan. 2017)

DUN129-f, Central *gebel* (Maxar Technologies via Google Earth Pro, 22 Jan. 2017)

BUN007-f6, Beni Ulid North, E. pre-desert, south Reconstruction drawing, not to scale (Scott, Dore, & Mattingly 1996: 58, fig. 5.3, a)

Gh072-f, Wadi Ghirza, E. pre-desert, south (DigitalGlobe via Google Earth Pro, 28 Dec. 2014)

Figure 5.4: *Examples of courtyard buildings.*

south and eastwards, however, the pattern changes significantly. In the northern part of the eastern pre-desert, courtyard buildings accounted for 13% (n=31) of the unfortified buildings of identifiable plan, while farmyard buildings accounted for 47% (n=114). Further south in the eastern pre-desert, the proportions move to 10% (n=33) and 66% (n=233) for courtyard and farmyard buildings respectively, and in western Syrtica, courtyard buildings accounted for only 3% (n=12), while farmyards occupied the vast majority at 83% (n=354).

A single farmyard or courtyard farm building could have additional yards or rooms which extended or supplemented the 'main' construction. However, complicating matters somewhat, in the eastern pre-desert and Syrtica regions, is the fact that open farm buildings can

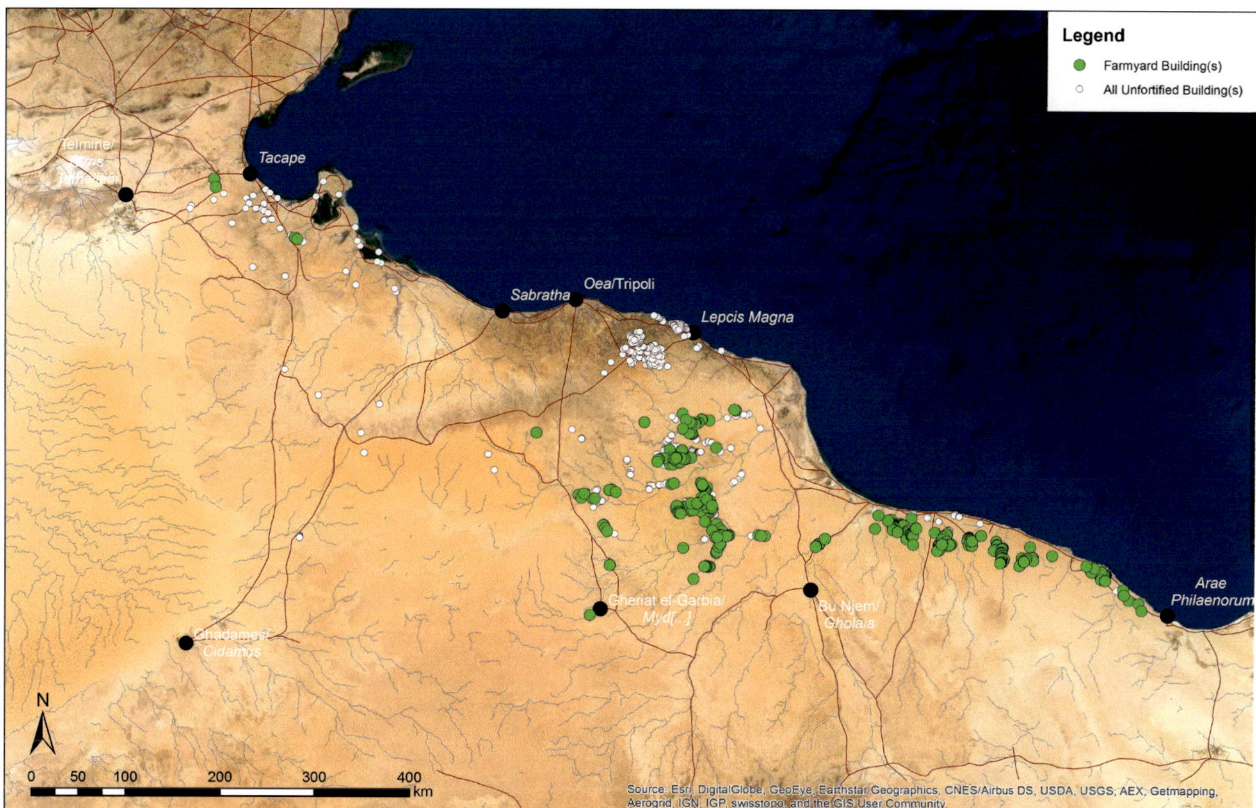

Basemap: Esri, DigitalGlobe, GeoEye, Earthstar Geographics, CNES/Airbus DS, USDA, USGS, AEX, Getmapping, Aerogrid, IGN, IGP, swisstopo, and the GIS User Community
Drainage: Lehner, B., Verdin, K., Jarvis, A. (2008): New global hydrography derived from spaceborne elevation data. Eos, Transactions, AGU, 89(10): 93-94. Retrieved from http://hydrosheds.cr.usgs.gov (15 sec Flow Accumulation)
Roads (Barrington Atlas): Ancient World Mapping Center (2012)

Figure 5.5: *Distribution of farmyard buildings.*

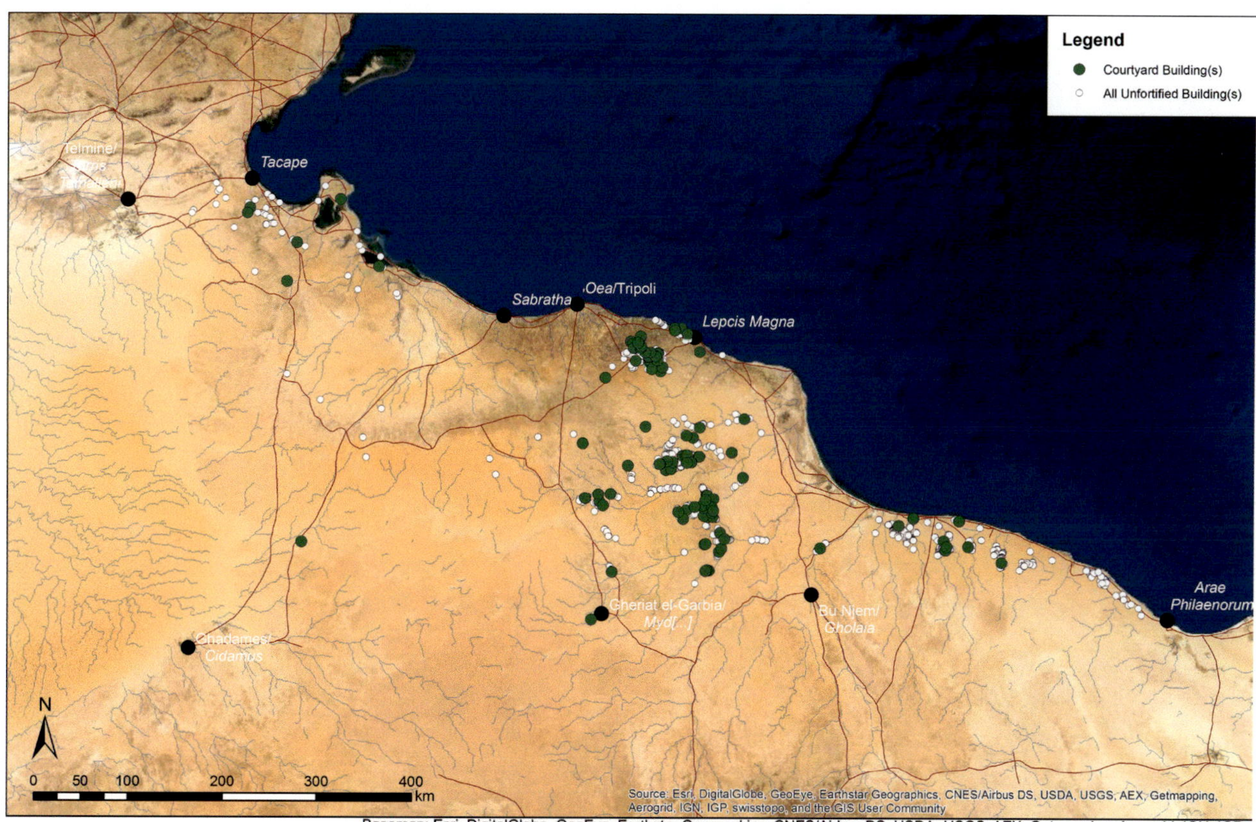

Basemap: Esri, DigitalGlobe, GeoEye, Earthstar Geographics, CNES/Airbus DS, USDA, USGS, AEX, Getmapping, Aerogrid, IGN, IGP, swisstopo, and the GIS User Community
Drainage: Lehner, B., Verdin, K., Jarvis, A. (2008): New global hydrography derived from spaceborne elevation data. Eos, Transactions, AGU, 89(10): 93-94. Retrieved from http://hydrosheds.cr.usgs.gov (15 sec Flow Accumulation)
Roads (Barrington Atlas): Ancient World Mapping Center (2012)

Figure 5.6: *Distribution of courtyard buildings.*

Ham-NS11-f, Wadi Hamra, W. Syrtica
(DigitalGlobe via Google Earth Pro, 21 Dec. 2011)

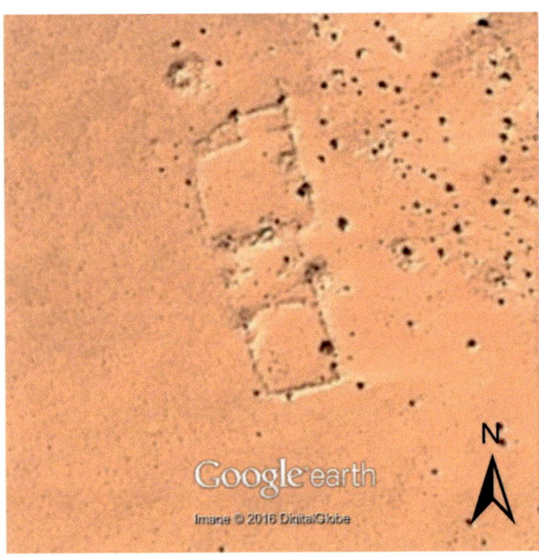

Jr-NS67-f, Wadi Jarif, W. Syrtica
(DigitalGlobe via Gogle Earth Pro, 10 Feb. 2013)

Bz050-f and/or Bz051-f(?), Wadi Buzra, E. pre-desert, north
(DigitalGlobe via Google Earth Pro, 28 Dec. 2014)

Mm215-f(?), Wadi Mimoun, E. pre-desert, north
(DigitalGlobe via Google Earth Pro, 27 Aug. 2012)

Figure 5.7: *Examples of open complexes.*

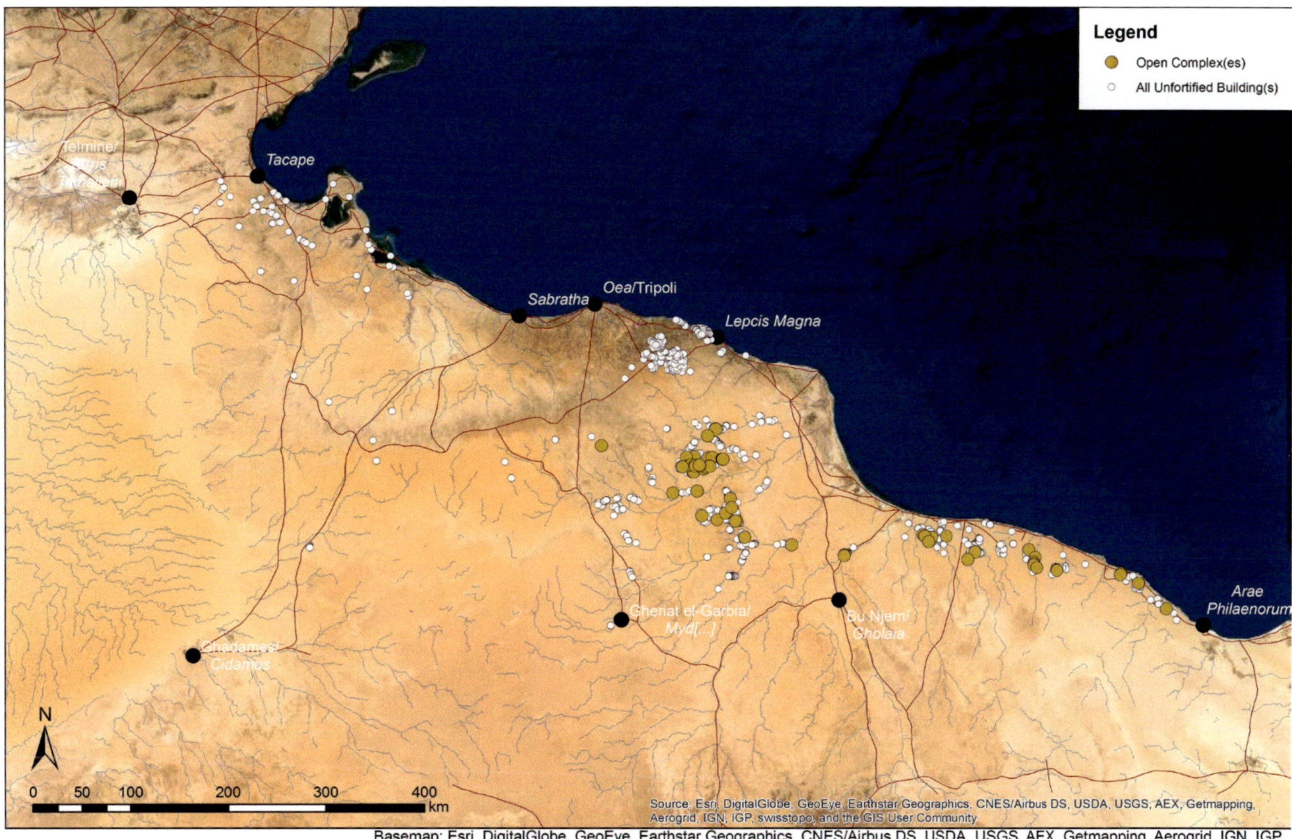

Basemap: Esri, DigitalGlobe, GeoEye, Earthstar Geographics, CNES/Airbus DS, USDA, USGS, AEX, Getmapping, Aerogrid, IGN, IGP, swisstopo, and the GIS User Community
Drainage: Lehner, B., Verdin, K., Jarvis, A. (2008): New global hydrography derived from spaceborne elevation data. Eos, Transactions, AGU, 89(10): 93-94. Retrieved from http://hydrosheds.cr.usgs.gov (15 sec Flow Accumulation)
Roads (Barrington Atlas): Ancient World Mapping Center (2012)

Figure 5.8: *Distribution of open complexes.*

and do occur in larger complexes consisting of several rooms and yards attached in varying and irregular combinations, sometimes extending over 100 m in length (Figure 5.7 and Figure 5.8). In general, if a structure could be divided into three or more separate units which could theoretically have stood on their own as farmyard or courtyard farms, it was catalogued as an 'open complex'. Unsurprisingly, the distinction between a large open farm building with multiple yards, multiple but physically separate farmyard or courtyard farm buildings, and open complexes is somewhat blurred. It is probable that in many cases multiple but physically separate open farms in close proximity and open complexes fulfilled a similar function in that they could be considered as very small hamlets or villages.

As already briefly mentioned in Section 5.1 above, there are a few examples of buildings which are characterised by the presence of very luxurious features and have complex plans which do not fit easily into any of the preceding categories, and I have termed 'villa complexes'. These were all located along the coast in the central coastal region near *Lepcis Magna* and include the well-known villas at Silin (SLN29-v) and Zliten (Zliten-v), as well as the Villa of the Odeon (LMCS01-v) and Villa of the Small Circus (LMCS02-v). There were certainly more of these types of buildings, a number of which are also known from around *Oea* and *Sabratha*.[371] However, these are frequently not completely excavated and made all the more difficult to understand due to the erosion which has more often than not taken its toll.

On the other end of the size scale, unfortified farm buildings consisting of one or more rooms set in a range or block formation without an enclosed farmyard or courtyard are also something of a problematic category. As already discussed in Section 3.1.1, buildings of this type have been constructed, used, and re-used from prehistoric until modern times and examples measuring less than c.8 x 8 m in size were categorised as stone huts and not included in my catalogue or analyses. An almost complete lack of systematic investigation into the construction, function, date or any other aspect of these small buildings means that we can say very little about them. Nevertheless, there seems little doubt that during the Roman period stone huts would have functioned both as outbuildings to larger buildings, for storage or animals, etc. and as temporary shelters for shepherds, and we should not discount the importance or significance of this building type in the landscape.

[371] Bartoccini 1929b: 95-103; Alcock 1950; Aurigemma 1960: 30–42; Di Vita 1966; Rossiter 1994.

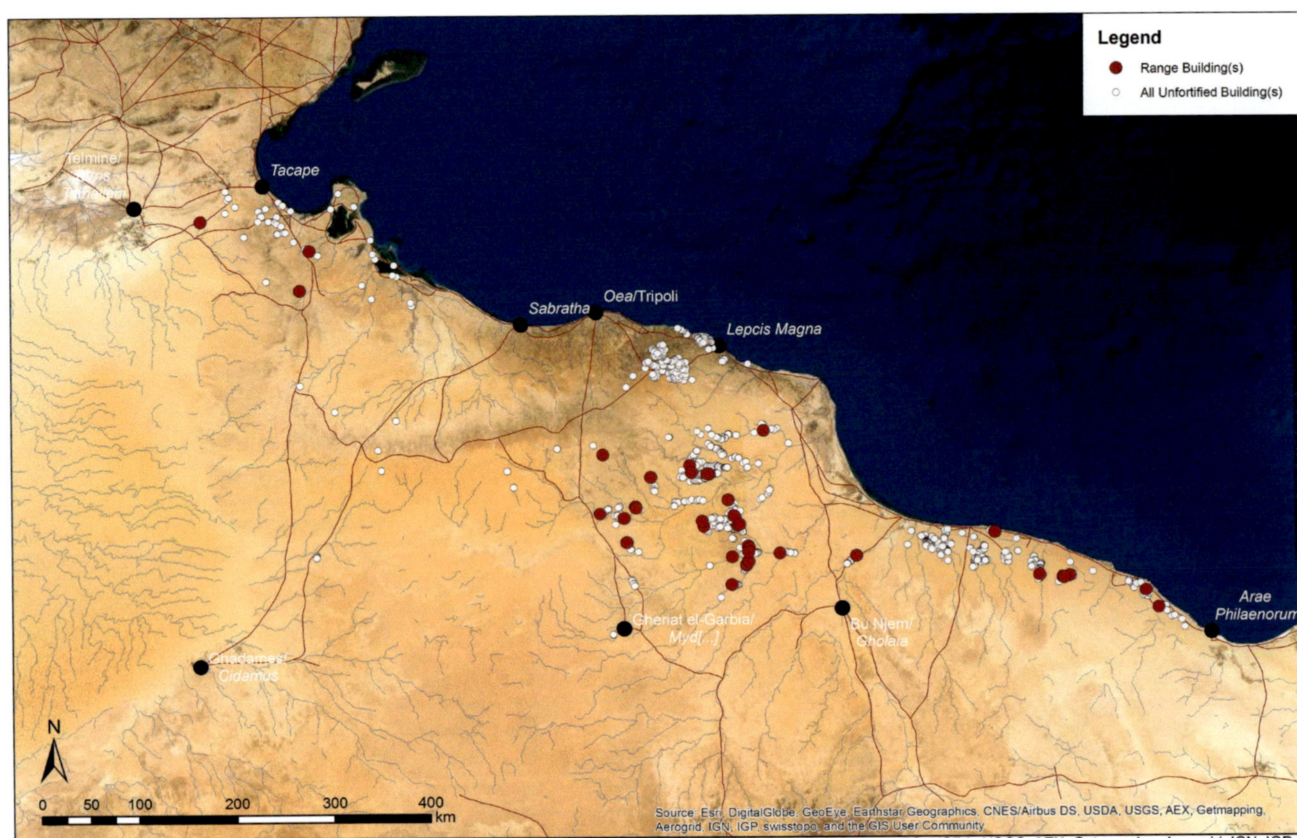

Basemap: Esri, DigitalGlobe, GeoEye, Earthstar Geographics, CNES/Airbus DS, USDA, USGS, AEX, Getmapping, Aerogrid, IGN, IGP, swisstopo, and the GIS User Community
Drainage: Lehner, B., Verdin, K., Jarvis, A. (2008): New global hydrography derived from spaceborne elevation data. Eos, Transactions, AGU, 89(10): 93-94. Retrieved from http://hydrosheds.cr.usgs.gov (15 sec Flow Accumulation)
Roads (Barrington Atlas): Ancient World Mapping Center (2012)

Figure 5.9: *Distribution of range type buildings.*

Free-standing, unfortified farm buildings over c.8 x 8 m in size occur relatively infrequently, but were included in my catalogue where possible (~5% of identifiable examples, n=57). Most of these were located in the eastern pre-desert or Syrtica where they occurred either on their own, in small groups or associated with larger structures (Figure 5.9). Their infrequency might suggest that they were a less important type of building in Tripolitania, but the situation is slightly more complicated than that. Buildings on the smaller end of the scale tend to be less visible and are more likely to be overlooked during both ground and satellite surveys. We might also note that examples identified as free-standing without yards could very well have had yards that are no longer visible, particularly if they were constructed of perishable materials (e.g. mudbrick, thorny branches, etc.). Alternatively, we might consider that some open farm buildings began their life as free-standing range structures, only to have yards or further structures added at a later date. Therefore, it is difficult to judge to what extent larger unfortified farm buildings without yards may have been an important part of the landscape in different areas. At least three of these buildings in the eastern pre-desert regions appear to have been free-standing press buildings (Lg002-f, Lm004-f5 and Mm141-f).

Finally, it is also worth considering the place of detached enclosures, i.e. open areas defined by a low wall or fence, with no covered building attached. Detached enclosures have not been included in this analysis for similar reasons as stone huts: their simple form makes them virtually impossible to date and few studies have paid them much attention as a structure type.[372] However, due to the ruined state of many sites and buildings, it can sometimes be hard to distinguish between detached enclosures and open farms, particularly in satellite imagery, and it is possible that some of the former have ended up classified as the latter and vice versa. Furthermore, it is worth asking whether there was much functional difference between an open farm building and a free-standing range-type building with a detached enclosure situated nearby; probably there was not.

The typology presented above is deliberately simple and as I hope I have made clear, there is significant overlap between these broad forms. In addition, as mentioned in the introduction to this section, we must remember that the plans of all of these buildings and complexes represent only the final phases of these structures. Additional rooms or yards could be, and probably were, attached to free-standing farm buildings, enclosures or existing open farm buildings in a piecemeal and sometimes

[372] The *ULVS* identified c.112 examples of detached enclosures (Mattingly & Flower 1996: 170).

disorganised fashion for any number of possible reasons, perhaps to accommodate an expanding family or production capacity. Without more detailed architectural investigations, we have no way of knowing at what point in a structure's life these types of modifications may have taken place, whether years, decades or even centuries after the first phase of construction. However, the system I have outlined above provides a useful base from which to make some broad regional comparisons.

Nevertheless, there are probably many different and equally reasonable ways of organising and dividing the material; typologies are subjective and not necessarily based in any true understanding of what criteria the people who originally built and inhabited these structures would have used to differentiate them, if they did so at all.[373] While ancient peoples would likely, of course, recognise a difference between a small, single-roomed farm building and a sprawling open complex with multiple ranges of rooms, consciously dividing them into discrete, well-defined categories may say more about our own ideas about buildings and architecture than ancient ones.

5.2.2 Size

Of the 1,653 individual unfortified buildings and complexes catalogued, I was able to record the total ground area for 1,139 (69%). The minimum, maximum, mean and median figures of these buildings, in total and divided by region, are presented in Table 5.3.

There are a few observations that we can make immediately about these data. In general, we have far more data for the size of buildings in the eastern pre-desert and Syrtica than in other areas, particularly the western *gebel* and southwest regions where the data are unfortunately poorer. Whereas the plans of unfortified farms are often clearly visible using satellite imagery in more arid regions, the *gebel* and coastal areas (both central and western) are much more densely populated and vegetated, obscuring the majority of ancient building remains. As a result, satellite imagery is of limited use in this area for the identification and measurement of individual unfortified farm buildings and we are generally reliant on measurements made during the course of ground surveys. However, even then, unfortunately, approximate building areas are not often recorded because large portions of these buildings are no longer above-ground.

In Table 5.3 below, the figures are for all building types together. While the largest individually recorded unfortified buildings were found in the eastern pre-desert and Syrtica, these regions actually had comparatively small sizes on average; the largest overall averages were found in the central regions, while the smallest were found in the western *gebel* and the eastern pre-desert (south). In all instances, we can note that the means were considerably larger than the medians. This indicates a significant skew in the data, more pronounced in the pre-desert regions and in Syrtica, which is caused by a lower proportion of examples of exceptionally large size.

If we divide the data further by building type, it is clear that the skew is partially accounted for by the inclusion of very small (range/block) and very large (open complexes and villa complexes) building types. Tables 5.4–5.6 and Figure 5.10 present the data in table and bar graph form respectively for all open farm buildings together (farmyard, courtyard and undifferentiated), and then farmyard and courtyard buildings individually.

As the tables and bar graph illustrate, there was a great deal of variation in the average size of open buildings between the different regions of Tripolitania. The trend most immediately visible in the bar graph is the comparatively large size of the buildings in the central regions, particularly the *gebel*, with average areas of over

	Total buildings	Minimum size (m²)	Maximum size (m²)	Mean (m²)	Median (m²)
1. W. coastal	38	96	5,330	1,188	900
2. W. *gebel*	7	60	1,017	435	240
3. Southwest	10	345	2,240	929	728
4. Central coastal	15	189	6,000	2,201	1,750
5. Central *gebel*	35	640	5,084	2,138	1,680
6. E. pre-desert, north	217	55	10,500	1,038	540
7. E. pre-desert, south	349	24	8,400	655	396
8. W. Syrtica	402	60	10,000	766	560
9. E. Syrtica	66	81	6,375	1,161	795
Total	*1,139*	*24*	*10,500*	*881*	*550*

Table 5.3: *Minimum, maximum, mean and median total areas for all unfortified buildings and complexes, divided by region.*

373 See Attema & Schörner (2012) concerning the problems with classifications of sites in rural landscapes of the Roman world, particularly Witcher (2012).

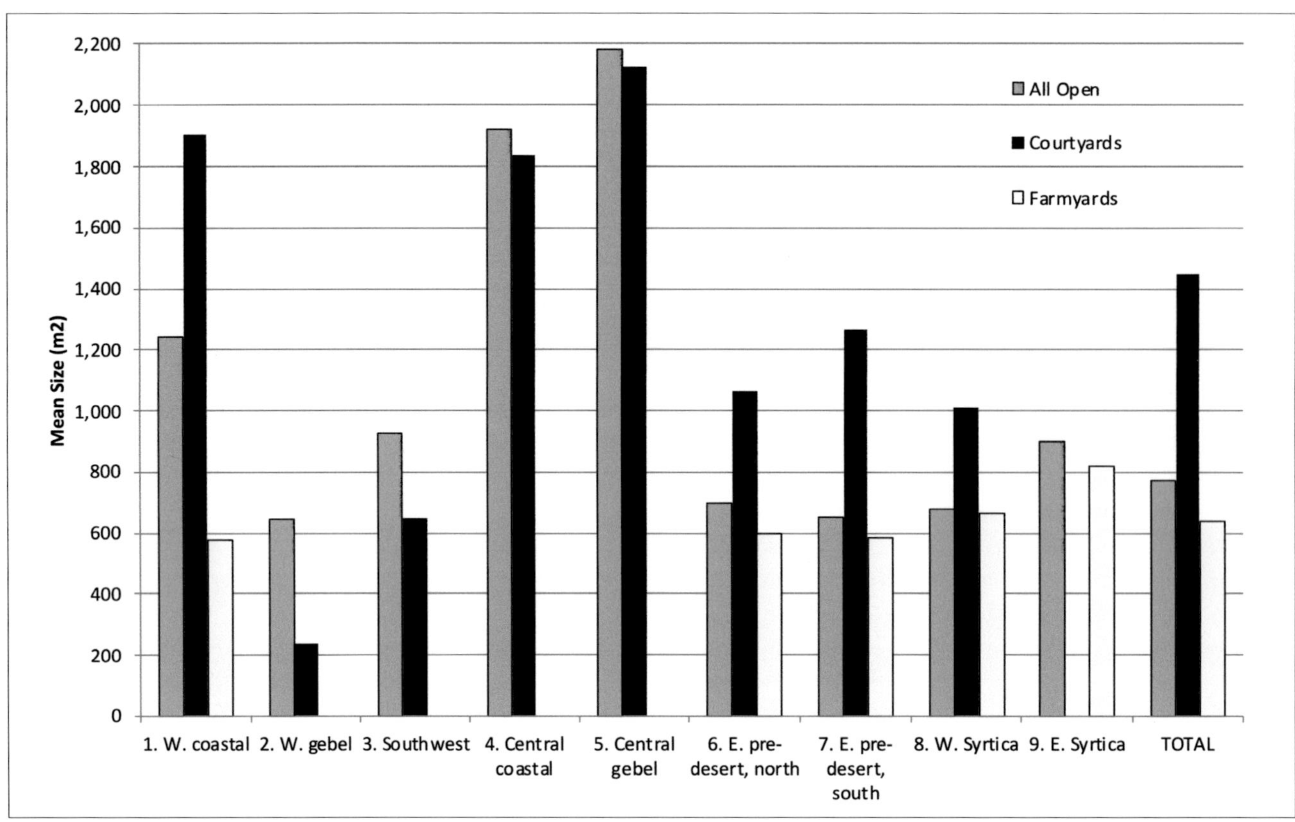

Figure 5.10: *Mean sizes (m²) of all open, courtyard and farmyard buildings, divided by region.*

	Total buildings	Minimum size (m²)	Maximum size (m²)	Mean (m²)	Median (m²)
1. W. coastal	34	156	5,330	1,241	914
2. W. *gebel*	4	240	1,017	645	662
3. Southwest	10	345	2,240	929	728
4. Central coastal	7	832	3,422	1,921	1,750
5. Central *gebel*	34	640	5,084	2,180	1,728
6. E. pre-desert, north	161	120	6,600	699	476
7. E. pre-desert, south	291	80	5,218	654	446
8. W. Syrtica	365	90	2,700	676	546
9. E. Syrtica	56	120	2,704	901	755
Total	*962*	*80*	*6,600*	*771*	*550*

Table 5.4: *Minimum, maximum, mean and median total areas for all open farm buildings (farmyard, courtyard and undifferentiated), divided by region.*

1,900 m². It is true that compared to other areas of Tripolitania, the sample size for this area is relatively small; however, it is not a coincidence that the central region is the area with the highest amount of annual rainfall and as a result, the area of highest agricultural potential and productivity in Tripolitania (as also evidenced by the high number of presses in the region discussed in Section 5.2.3). If we accept that the construction of larger buildings required more investment of time, effort and resources, we can conclude that the peoples who built these structures in this region must have been relatively wealthy, perhaps thanks to the success of their agricultural activities. In addition, these regions' closer proximity to the large urban centres of *Lepcis Magna* and *Oea* would have meant more access to markets and resources.

The area of the next largest group of open buildings is the western coastal region, with an average of 1,241 m² and it is probable that this larger size is due to a similar pattern to that around *Lepcis Magna* and *Oea*. Evidence of oil and/or wine production in the form of press elements attests to similar types of agricultural activity but due to the lower rainfall levels in this region, productivity was perhaps on a lesser scale, potentially reflected

	Total buildings	Minimum size (m²)	Maximum size (m²)	Mean (m²)	Median (m²)
1. W. coastal	5	550	5,330	1,903	1,196
2. W. *gebel*	1	240	240	240	240
3. Southwest	1	650	650	650	650
4. Central coastal	5	1,188	2,660	1,838	1,750
5. Central *gebel*	29	640	5,084	2,125	1,680
6. E. pre–desert, north	30	225	6,600	1,063	788
7. E. pre–desert, south	32	300	5,218	1,267	866
8. W. Syrtica	11	340	2,000	1,011	1,008
9. E. Syrtica	–	–	–	–	–
Total	*114*	*225*	*6,600*	*1,445*	*1,154*

Table 5.5: *Minimum, maximum, mean and median total areas for courtyard buildings, divided by region.*

	Total buildings	Minimum size (m²)	Maximum size (m²)	Mean (m²)	Median (m²)
1. W. coastal	11	160	3,025	580	280
2. W. *gebel*	–	–	–	–	–
3. Southwest	–	–	–	–	–
4. Central coastal	–	–	–	–	–
5. Central *gebel*	–	–	–	–	–
6. E. pre–desert, north	95	150	2,400	598	425
7. E. pre–desert, south	223	80	4,230	585	396
8. W. Syrtica	338	90	2,700	667	543
9. E. Syrtica	43	120	2,496	820	682
Total	*710*	*80*	*4,230*	*640*	*494*

Table 5.6: *Minimum, maximum, mean and median total areas for farmyard buildings, divided by region.*

also in the lesser importance and size of the urban centres in this area.[374]

The average sizes of the unfortified open buildings of the western *gebel* region, the eastern pre-desert and western Syrtica were similar, all falling between 645 and 699 m², though the low sample size of the western *gebel* (n=4) means that we must be wary of its significance. In general, however, lower levels of rainfall may have been a factor in these areas. Within this group, the open and farmyard buildings in the north wadis of the eastern pre-desert (the Sofeggin basin) were the largest, but not by enough of a margin to be particularly noteworthy. Potentially interesting, however, is the fact that the largest average size of courtyard buildings from these areas was found in the southern parts of the eastern pre-desert (ZemZem basin), rather than the northern. The margin of difference is not enormous, but nevertheless, this seems to be in contradiction to Jones' observations in the early stages of the *ULVS* project that courtyard farms in the Wadi Sofeggin were larger than those in the Wadi ZemZem, which is what one might reasonably expect, since the former is farther north and thus slightly better watered.[375]

The open farm buildings of the southwest region and eastern Syrtica had similar average sizes, 929 and 901 m², respectively, though in the case of the former, this high number is due to two large buildings of over 2,000 m² each, while the rest were all under 1,000 m². The relatively large average size of the buildings from eastern Syrtica, compared to western Syrtica and the adjacent eastern pre-desert however, is surprising considering the very low rainfall and the fact that until recently any amount of substantial Romano-Libyan settlement beyond the coast was almost completely unknown. Furthermore, while the averages for the open farm buildings of the eastern pre-desert and western Syrtica are boosted by the inclusion of the large courtyard farms (Table 5.5), no buildings of this type were identified in eastern Syrtica.

[374] It has more recently been argued that *Meninx*, on the island of Jerba, may have been a closer rival to *Sabratha*, *Oea* and even *Lepcis* in terms of wealth and importance than has previously been thought; however, its wealth was more likely derived from maritime products such as dyes and garum, than from agriculture (Morton 2003; 2006; Fentress, Drine, & Holod 2009: 133–174).

[375] Jones 1985: 274. This could also be a result of my redefinition of what constitutes a courtyard farm.

If we look only at the average sizes of the farmyard buildings (Table 5.6), it is evident that the average size actually seems to increase as one moves further east. If we divide the data for the farmyard buildings in the four regions of the eastern pre-desert and Syrtica into quartiles and compare the averages, we can get a clearer idea of where the difference lies (Table 5.7).[376]

What these data show is that the large overall mean for the open farms in eastern Syrtica is not necessarily due to the region having significantly larger buildings than anywhere else in the pre-desert or Syrtica. As the maximum figures in the fourth quartile show, the largest open farms in eastern Syrtica are considerably smaller than the largest example in the eastern pre-desert (south), and on par with the others. Rather, the large overall average in eastern Syrtica seems to be the result of the fact that it had fewer farms on the smaller end of the scale. The largest example in the first quartile from eastern Syrtica is already larger than everywhere else, resulting in a knock-on effect which increases the sizes and averages for each of the following quartiles.

While the lack of smaller buildings in eastern Syrtica would certainly be a significant trend, there is a potentially more mundane reason for this. In Syrtica, and the eastern half in particular, drifting sand obscuring sites is a much greater problem than in the eastern pre-desert region, making smaller buildings harder to identify both on the ground and using satellite imagery. We should also not discount the possibility that smaller buildings in this region were more often constructed in perishable materials. Finally, we must also use caution as the sample size from eastern Syrtica is much smaller compared to the rest of the eastern pre-desert and Syrtica.

Returning to Tables 5.5 and 5.6 and Figure 5.10, it is clear there were also significant differences in the size of farmyard and courtyard buildings. Where courtyard buildings occur, their averages were consistently larger than farmyard buildings. What this suggests is that in general, courtyard farm buildings were not simply open farm buildings which just happened to have ranges of rooms on two or more sides. Rather, it supports the notion that the courtyard farm building was a deliberately distinct type, constructed for specific reasons and only by those with the means to do so.

The data for open complexes were calculated separately because, as discussed above, they seem to be composed of several individual farm buildings which were joined together, and thus not comparable to single buildings. There were a total of 80 open complexes recorded, only in the eastern pre-desert and Syrtica regions, 77 of which had their sizes recorded (Table 5.8). Unsurprisingly, the average size of these buildings was very large, generally four to five times the average size of the individual farmyard buildings for the same regions. Like the farmyard buildings, however, the largest were again found in eastern Syrtica.

I also calculated the minimum, maximum, mean and median for the range type buildings, of which 52 had their sizes recorded, presented in Table 5.9. Because these buildings did not have yards, they are obviously far smaller on average than the open farm buildings and they are not directly comparable because of their different forms. Furthermore, most of the sample sizes are relatively small, making the statistical validity of these data more of an issue.

An interesting comparison could theoretically be made between the size of free-standing buildings and the sizes of the covered components of the open farm structures; however, in practice, this is a slightly problematic issue. In all of the size analyses so far presented, where applicable, the open areas of the farmyards and courtyards were included in the total ground areas of the buildings under discussion. Ideally, it would be helpful to analyse the ratio of covered to uncovered spaces; however, without a dedicated field survey, it has proved very difficult to obtain reliable, even approximate figures for these data. It was sometimes possible to make judgements about covered and uncovered spaces in the satellite imagery, but usually only in a small number of cases of relatively simple plan, which are not representative of the overall sample.

An analysis of this type was conducted in an unpublished MA dissertation for a small proportion (n=166)

	Q. size	Q. 1			Q. 2			Q. 3			Q. 4		
		Min	Max	Mean	Min	Max	Mean	Min	Max	Mean	Min	Max	Mean
6. E. pre-desert, north	23–24	150	322	*244*	323	425	*375*	432	750	*567*	751	2,400	*1,233*
7. E. pre-desert, south	55–56	80	225	*166*	228	496	*312*	400	713	*533*	714	4,230	*1,344*
8. W. Syrtica	84–85	90	357	*265*	360	546	*442*	550	812	*678*	814	2,700	*1,291*
9. E. Syrtica	10–11	120	483	*347*	500	682	*562*	700	1,122	*857*	1,125	2,496	*1,584*

Table 5.7: *Minimum, maximum and mean area for all open farm buildings in the pre-desert and Syrtica, divided by quartile.*

[376] Cf. for the use of this technique in houses at Pompeii and Herculaneum: Wallace-Hadrill 1994: 79–81.

	Total	Minimum size (m²)	Maximum size (m²)	Mean (m²)	Median (m²)
6. E. pre-desert, north	35	500	10,500	3,110	2,150
7. E. pre-desert, south	11	648	8,400	2,719	1,925
8. W. Syrtica	24	571	10,000	2,402	1,866
9. E. Syrtica	7	1,800	6,375	3,683	3,000
Total	*77*	*500*	*10,500*	*2,886*	*2,031*

Table 5.8: *Minimum, maximum, mean and median total areas for open complexes, divided by region.*

	Total	Minimum size (m²)	Maximum size (m²)	Mean (m²)	Median (m²)
1. W. coastal	1	96	96	96	96
2. W. *gebel*	2	60	195	128	128
3. Southwest	–	–	–	–	–
4. Central coastal	–	–	–	–	–
5. Central *gebel*	–	–	–	–	–
6. E. pre–desert, north	11	55	420	159	135
7. E. pre–desert, south	26	24	1,600	196	121
8. W. Syrtica	9	60	192	106	90
9. E. Syrtica	3	81	176	118	96
Total	*52*	*24*	*1,600*	*163*	*109*

Table 5.9: *Minimum, maximum, mean and median total areas for buildings without yards, divided by region.*

of the unfortified farms recorded in the *ULVS*, for which plans had been drawn (see Appendix Table 3). According to Cività, the mean total area of the farm buildings analysed was 779 m², the mean open area was 616 m², and the mean covered area was 292 m² (cf. Figure 5.3 and Figure 5.4).[377] While it should be emphasised that the means disguise a wide range of ratios, what it does illustrate, however, is that whether we include open spaces in our calculations does potentially make a very big difference to an analysis and discussion of building size. For example, I would suggest that in Syrtica, based on personal observations, we would probably find there was a far larger proportion of open space than covered space, which would go some way towards explaining the unexpectedly large averages observed in eastern Syrtica relative to the regions directly to its west.

More information about the relative sizes of covered and uncovered spaces could certainly be very illuminating and one can hope that future investigations will take this into account. If the ratios of covered to open space were substantially different in different areas, this might suggest that the relative function and significance of those spaces varied in different areas, which might in turn reflect differences in agricultural and socio-cultural organisation and traditions, as discussed in the next section. For the time being we simply do not have the data to support this kind of investigation, but as long as we allow for exceptional examples in which the ratio between these spaces was disproportionately large or small, I do not think that our lack of knowledge in this respect necessarily invalidates the analysis presented above which includes the spaces of yards and courtyards.

5.2.3 Use of Space: Presses, Crops and Animals

Given how little we know about the use of space in Romano-Libyan farm buildings, we should perhaps not make any assumptions about the relative importance of covered and uncovered spaces. In order to gain a better understanding of the possible relationship between them and whether we are justified in drawing this kind of distinction, we need a better understanding of what kinds of activities took place in indoor and outdoor spaces.

Interior space was almost certainly used for human, and probably to a certain extent, animal habitation, as well as specific production activities such as pressing. Outdoor areas were almost certainly used for keeping

[377] Cività 1994: 39–42. Unfortunately, Cività did not provide a full list of the buildings included in the analysis, so I was not able to divide the data any further or replicate her calculations. It has been noted in Appendix Table 3 that the open and covered area means do not add up to the total, which suggests that the exact same group of sites may not have been used for each calculation. In addition, many of the plans from which she was working were only paced or sketched and the measurements used are therefore approximate only. Nevertheless, despite these issues, I would maintain that the general pattern indicated is still valid.

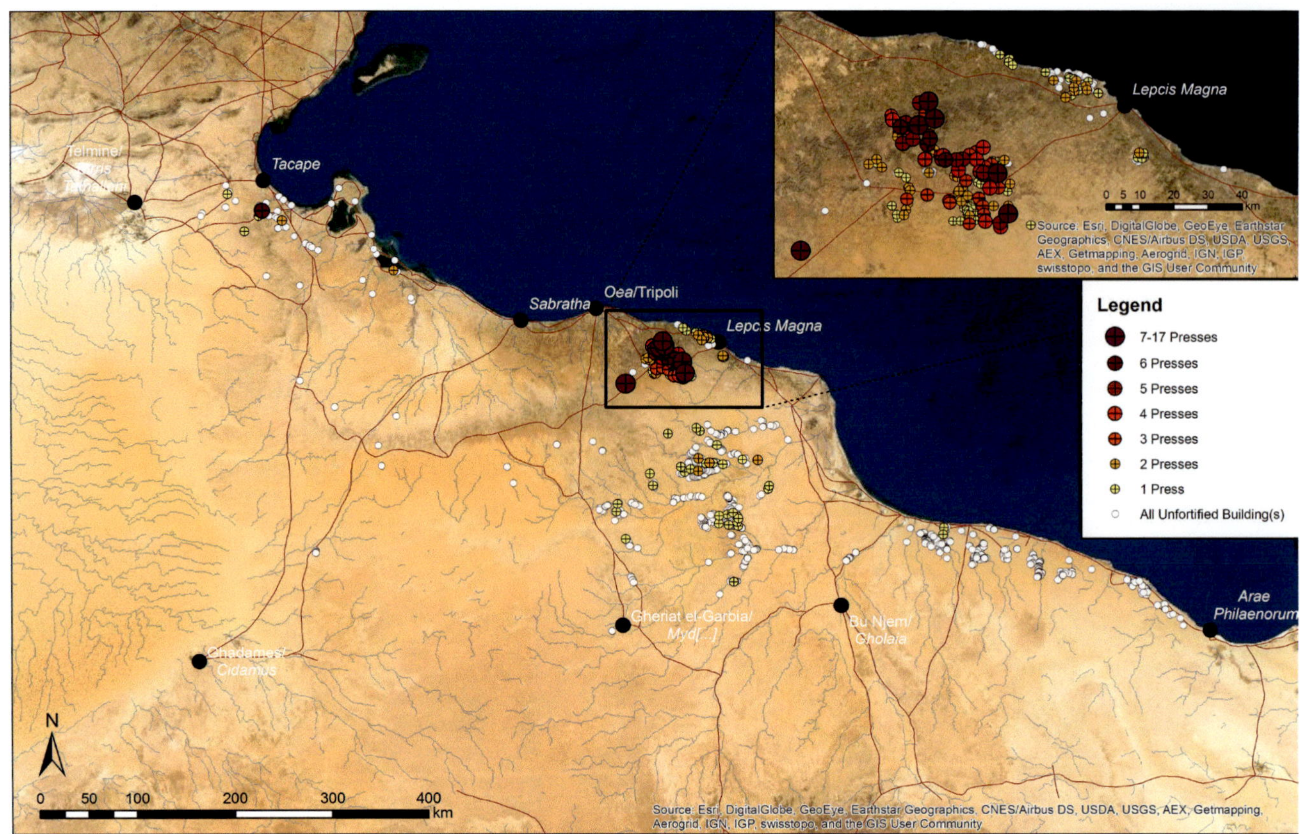

Figure 5.11: *Distribution of unfortified buildings with presses, divided by number of presses recorded.*

	Total buildings	Total buildings with presses		1	2	3	4	5	6	7–17
1. W. coastal	50	6	12%	2	2	–	1	–	1	–
2. W. *gebel*	9	1	11%	1	–	–	–	–	–	–
3. Southwest	11	–	–	–	–	–	–	–	–	–
4. Central coastal	94	28	30%	20	8	–	–	–	–	–
5. Central *gebel*	156	143	92%	47	37	26	13	10	4	6
6. E. pre-desert, north	365	22	6%	18	4	–	–	–	–	–
7. E. pre-desert, south	414	13	3%	13	–	–	–	–	–	–
8. W. Syrtica	487	2	0.4%	2	–	–	–	–	–	–
9. E. Syrtica	67	–	–	–	–	–	–	–	–	–
Total	*1,653*	*215*	*13 %*	*103*	*51*	*26*	*14*	*10*	*5*	*6*

Table 5.10: *Distribution of unfortified buildings with presses by region.*

animals (discussed further below) and probably provided additional space for various domestic activities and social interaction. It is unfortunately not possible to be much more specific about this, though at Ghirza, it was proposed that two hollows carved into the rock in the farmyard area of Gh127-30 were ovens, which might suggest that baking/cooking or other food preparation activities sometimes took place outdoors.[378] We can also imagine that any number of activities associated with the processing of other agricultural crops might occur outdoors in a farmyard or courtyard — threshing, winnowing, milling, drying, storage, etc. None of these activities necessarily requires a specifically delimited space, but it may not have been undesirable to have a more sheltered or private area, which could provide some level of protection against the elements or wild animals.

[378] Brogan & Smith 1984: 59.

The cultivation of olives and grapes and the subsequent production of oil and wine is well-attested in Tripolitania by the remains of presses and other oil and/or wine production equipment such as mills, press-beds, counterweights and tanks or basins lined with *opus signinum*. Evidence indicating the presence of one or more presses was recorded within or in close proximity to 215 of the 1,653 (13%) individual unfortified buildings in my catalogue (Figure 5.11). A summary of the distribution of the buildings with presses by region is presented in Table 5.10. Clearly, the overwhelming majority of sites with presses are found in the central *gebel* region, with the next highest numbers found in the areas immediately to the north and south, respectively.

The relationship between presses and the buildings under investigation here is slightly problematic because we cannot be certain in all cases whether or how presses were situated within them. Often, press elements are found *ex situ* and it is entirely possible in many cases that they were actually situated in dedicated press buildings outside of the main structure, as was the case in three examples noted from the eastern pre-desert (Lg002-f, Lm004-f5 and Mm141-f). However, the presence of one or more presses at a farm, whether or not they were incorporated into the main building, is significant because of the productive capabilities and potential wealth it theoretically represents. Of the 215 unfortified buildings with presses, 83 had an identifiable plan type (Appendix Table 4). Of these, all but the three, dedicated range-type press buildings already noted above were of the open type, and the majority were found in courtyard buildings (61%). This is especially striking in the eastern pre-desert regions, where overall, courtyard buildings are in the minority. Seven structures with presses were farmyard buildings (8%), 21 were unidentified open buildings (25%), and one was an open complex (none were found at villa complexes).

As mentioned above, although Ahmed previously used the number of presses to classify sites as small or large in the Tarhuna region, no quantitative comparison of the sizes of buildings with presses was attempted. Of these 215 buildings at which presses were found, 77 had their size recorded (Table 5.11).

Buildings with only one associated press varied the most widely, with sizes ranging from 77 to 8,000 m^2, though they had the smallest mean and median size. Between one and four presses, there is a clear trend of increase of mean size as the number of presses goes up; a decrease in mean size at five presses was followed by another increase at six presses (Figure 5.12). This pattern is disrupted for the examples which have eight, nine and 17 presses; however, each of these groups had only one example for which the size was recorded, so does not affect the overall interpretation. Indeed, if we take those three as a single group instead of individually, the average is 2,804 m^2, which fits the overall pattern well.

This is not to suggest that there is a direct causal relationship between number of presses and building size. However, the fact that there does seem to be some positive correlation between building size and number of presses, even if not overwhelmingly strong, might support the notion that the wealth generated through oil and/or wine production enabled the owners of those farms to construct larger buildings, or the promise of the wealth that it would generate, prompted owners to make a larger investment at the outset. The average size of all unfortified buildings was 881 m^2, while the average size of the 77 buildings with presses for which we had a size recorded was 1,661 m^2, a significant increase. If we divide this by region (Appendix Table 5), in most cases, the average size of buildings with presses was larger than the overall averages; the only exception to this trend was in the central coastal area, where the overall average is increased by the inclusion of the four large coastal villas, each over 3,000 m^2. This trend is partially explained by the fact that, as already established, courtyard buildings, which were already, on average, larger, were far more likely to have presses than other types of buildings.

Number of presses	Total buildings (with size recorded)	Minimum size (m²)	Maximum size (m²)	Mean (m²)	Median (m²)
1	40	77	8,000	1,148	783
2	12	300	5,330	1,576	1,232
3	4	1,280	4,875	2,311	1,545
4	7	1,085	5,084	2,634	2,442
5	6	800	4,480	2,242	2,160
6	5	952	3,750	2,706	3,024
8	1	1,775	1,775	1,775	1,775
9	1	3,882	3,882	3,882	3,882
17	1	2,754	2,754	2,754	2,754
Total	*77*	*77*	*8,000*	*1,661*	*1,275*

Table 5.11: *Minimum, maximum, mean and median sizes of buildings with different numbers of presses.*

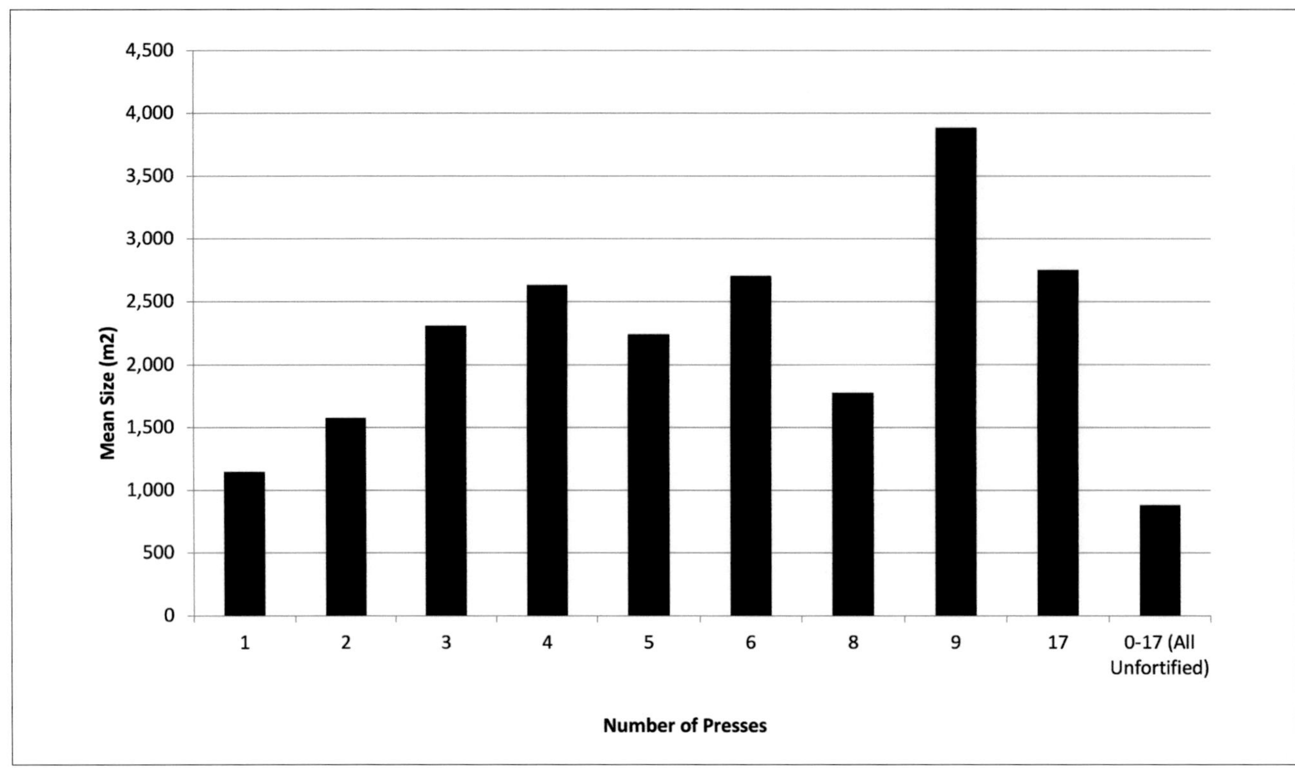

Figure 5.12: *Mean sizes of unfortified buildings, divided by number of presses.*

However, if we repeat the same analysis only for courtyard buildings, we can see that the same trend still holds true, where the average size of courtyard buildings with presses was 1,981 m^2, versus the overall average size of courtyard buildings of 1,445 m^2 (Appendix Table 6). Unfortunately, only six of the seven farmyard buildings with presses had their size recorded so we must be more cautious with the significance of the analyses, but here, the average size of farmyard buildings with presses (558 m^2) was actually smaller than the average size of all farmyard buildings (640 m^2) (Appendix Table 7).

On one hand, it is true that more presses simply need more room due to their size and the area needed for them to operate. However, as will be demonstrated in Section 5.2.5 below, sites with higher numbers of presses were also more likely to have luxury elements as well, suggesting that the need for space was not the only factor. On the other hand, we should ask ourselves to what extent looking for a correlation between the presence of presses and architectural characteristics might put undue emphasis on the importance of oil/wine production over other forms of production or completely separate factors. The problem here hinges on whether we believe that the presses were the actual *reason* for a building's existence, rather than simply one part. In the central *gebel* region, the vast majority of buildings identified had at least one press associated with them (92%), which might suggest that oil and wine production was an activity in which most farmers of the region were engaged (olive trees are still common on farms today). However, this was not the case in other regions. In the central coastal region, only 30% of the recorded buildings had an associated press and only 12% of the structures in the two western regions. Of the 1,333 farms in all regions of the eastern pre-desert and Syrtica combined, only 37 (< 3%) had presses. Again, some of this pattern can be accounted for by the fact that a certain proportion of the sites in the case of the latter regions are known only through satellite imagery. If we remove all of the buildings from these regions which were identified primarily through satellite imagery, we are left with only a slightly larger proportion of 37 of 716, or approximately 5%. Even if every single one of the buildings identified through satellite imagery turned out to have a press (which is extremely unlikely), we would only have a proportion of around 50%, still not near the rate in the *gebel*.

The fact that farm buildings with presses were consistently larger than those without might lend support to the idea that the production of oil and/or wine was one of the more lucrative businesses in most regions. However, the scarcity of presses overall in the regions of the pre-desert and Syrtica suggests that most people there were engaged in other activities, some of which may be less visible in the archaeological record: cereal agriculture, animal rearing, textile production, etc.

Botanical samples were analysed from four unfortified sites in the eastern pre-desert during the *ULVS* investigations (Nf082 (middens), BUN007 (middens), Mn006 and Lm004), though only one of these, Lm004 produced a large enough sample to draw any meaningful conclusions and comparisons. It is also important to note that the samples from Lm004 were apparently taken from post-primary-occupation layers, probably dating to the late third to fourth centuries AD.[379] These analyses suggested that a variety of crops were being cultivated and consumed in the region, including cereals such as barley and wheat (probably durum?), pulses such as peas and lentils, olives, grapes, figs, pomegranate, almonds, dates and other fruits and herbs such as purslane and dill.[380] The analyses suggested that the cereals were undergoing the earliest stages of processing on site (winnowing and coarse sieving), which implies that these products were, in fact, grown on site and not imported.[381]

Interestingly, the number of olive stones recorded from these samples was rather small, and in fact, none at all were found in the press building at Lm004.[382] Van der Veen suggests a number of explanations for this: that olives were not being consumed locally (i.e. only being used in the production of oil), that the stones were disposed of in as yet unexcavated areas of the site, or that the stones were not removed before the pressing. At least one millstone was recorded at the site of Md056, and a photograph in the *ULVS* archives shows another possible example from an unknown site in the Wadi Umm el-Agerem,[383] but there is little other recorded evidence for olive mills found in the *ULVS* study area. Nevertheless, the conclusions of the *ULVS* authors were that the presses found in the pre-desert region were for olive oil. They point out that millstones are frequently taken from sites and reused (though if that were the case, one might still expect to find them somewhere nearby, just *ex situ*) and that there are other methods of crushing olives. Also, in the case of Lm004, they point to the presence of multiple vats in a "classic arrangement for oil production and not typical of wine presses".[384]

Notably, however, Brun has more recently argued that at least some of the presses from the Tripolitanian pre-desert, including Lm004, were not for olive oil, but for wine.[385] Van der Veen's analyses show that grape pips were, in fact, found in large quantities at Lm004, which lends some support to Brun's interpretation. In either case, although the pressing itself required indoor space, the earlier stages of olive or grape processing could certainly have occurred outdoors. Unfortunately, to date, the *ULVS* is the only project in the region which has published archaeobotanical analyses; further investigations of this type are clearly needed to help us expand and refine our understanding of which plants were cultivated and consumed in other parts of Tripolitania.

A major function of farmyards and courtyards was almost certainly the penning and corralling of animals. We can imagine that many or even most farms throughout Tripolitania would have had lesser or greater number of animals for both consumption and labour: chickens, sheep, goats, and perhaps even a few draught animals such as camels, cattle, donkeys and horses, etc. Although it is probable that some farms would have had separate stables or pens for these animals, it is also very likely that farmyards and courtyards of the main farm buildings were used for this purpose.

Once again, the only detailed faunal analysis for Tripolitania comes from the *ULVS* project. Faunal evidence recovered from two unfortified farm sites from the eastern pre-desert (Lm004 and Nf082) indicates that the primary animals being kept at these farms were sheep and/or goats, with other animals such as gazelles, cattle, camels, equids, dogs and pigs playing a lesser role.[386] Herds of sheep and goats, valuable sources of meat, milk and wool, would probably have been pastured in uncultivated stretches of the wadis much of the time, watched over by shepherds as they are in modern times,[387] though it is not clear whether the herds would have remained in the pre-desert permanently, or were pastured further south in winter (which is the norm today).[388] Herds were probably not excessively large in size, since in the marginal area of the pre-desert, too many animals would potentially create competition for food and water resources.[389]

At certain times, it would probably be necessary to corral entire herds or parts thereof for various reasons – milking, slaughtering, shearing, etc. It has also been suggested by the *ULVS* investigators that if herds were kept in the pre-desert year-round, it would be necessary to pen them more frequently to ensure the protection of the crops growing in the wadis during the winter.[390] Bad weather and a desire from protection against thieving or wild animals could also have been factors in the decision to corral animals. The practice of using farmyards this

[379] Van der Veen, Grant, & Barker 1996: 259.

[380] Van der Veen 1985; van der Veen, Grant, & Barker 1996.

[381] Van der Veen, Grant, & Barker 1996: 254–256.

[382] Van der Veen, Grant, & Barker 1996: 245.

[383] The photo was unfortunately missing its film and negative number.

[384] Mattingly & Dore 1996: 135–140

[385] Brun 2004: 196.

[386] Clark 1986; van der Veen, Grant, & Barker 1996.

[387] Gilbertson & Hunt 1996: 222–223.

[388] Van der Veen, Grant, & Barker 1996: 257–258.

[389] Van der Veen, Grant, & Barker 1996: 258.

[390] Van der Veen, Grant, & Barker 1996: 257–258.

way was noted by the *ULVS* team at a modern farm in the Wadi Merdum.[391] They also noted that the walls of farmyards might be supplemented with branches or thorny bushes, which would help keep domestic animals from escaping and discourage wild animals or ill-intentioned people coming in over the walls.[392] Again, while it has not been possible to measure the exact ratios of indoor to outdoor space, the popularity of farmyard buildings in the eastern pre-desert and Syrtica and the dearth of presses, as opposed to the domination of courtyard buildings with presses in the central *gebel* and to a lesser extent, the central coastal and western regions, strongly suggests that in the former areas, the rearing of livestock and pastoralism remained far more important in the economic activities of the people living there.

It is clear, therefore, that outdoor space was an important part of many unfortified farm buildings. Whatever their exact purpose, it is not insignificant that while the walls of farmyards and courtyards were probably not as tall or as substantial as those of the covered buildings, they were still constructed of stone and therefore represent a considerable investment of time and energy. In addition, we can note that a large farmyard might indicate the ownership of large numbers of animals, which is typically an important measure of wealth and status in pastoralist societies,[393] or a need for more space in which labourers or slaves could go about their work. With this in mind, then, we can conclude that the overall size of open farm buildings may be as reasonable an indicator of relative wealth and access to resources as the size of the covered areas alone.

5.2.4 Materials and Construction Techniques

Materials

Virtually all of the farm buildings recorded in my catalogue, unfortified and fortified alike, were constructed primarily of local materials, either sandstone or limestone, which are readily available in most parts of Tripolitania. In particular, in the pre-desert and Syrtica there is very little soil above the limestone plateaux and in many places the bare rock is exposed.[394] Rocks and rubble of varying size litter the ground and so rough stone building materials are relatively abundant. However, depending on the size of the building desired this may not have been enough and it can only account for a certain size and regularity of blocks.

We know very little about stone-quarrying in Tripolitania, small-scale or otherwise. A recent collection of the known stone quarries in Tripolitania lists only six, four of which were found within a few kilometres of either *Lepcis Magna* or *Sabratha*;[395] the two others listed are located at Bu Njem and Ghirza. To these can be added several more small-scale quarrying sites distributed across the region, most of which appear to have been discovered and recorded 'incidentally', rather than through any particular interest in them in their own right. Several more examples were also observed in the hinterlands of *Lepcis Magna* by the *Università Roma Tre* surveys, which served the city, and along the coast during the *Lepcis Magna Coastal Survey*.[396] Unlike the larger-scale operations found near the coastal cities, these were much smaller and essentially opportunistic projects in which the natural erosion created by nearby wadis was exploited; in the case of Ghirza, this quarrying took place practically within the settlement.[397] What is less clear is who exactly was doing the quarrying and stone working/dressing, whether itinerant stone workers were sought out and hired to do this kind of work, or to what extent, having acquired the right tools, local peoples learned or were taught to do it themselves.

Other building materials appear to have been used less commonly in farm buildings, though in certain cases this is almost certainly related to preservation. As previously discussed in Section 3.1.3, one material which was probably used more frequently than the archaeological remains would suggest was mudbrick or similar techniques,[398] and we might speculate whether some of the sites in southwest Tunisia mentioned at the end of Section 2.4, which appear only as low mounds in satellite imagery, might be the remains of disintegrated mudbrick buildings rather than stone ones. In addition to being used for entire buildings, it has been suggested that this type of material may have been used for the upper walls of buildings, above stone foundations.[399]

In the western and central regions, there is some evidence for ceramic building materials such as brick and tiles.[400] These types of materials do not appear to have been a primary building material for most farm buildings but were probably used more frequently in the

[391] Scott, Dore, & Mattingly 1996: 182–183 (Md021).

[392] Mattingly & Dore 1996: 124.

[393] Cf. modern African pastoralist societies: Sutter 1987; Borgerhoff Mulder *et al.* 2010.

[394] Barker 1996a: 5.

[395] Russell 2013.

[396] Munzi *et al.* 2016: 76–78; Schörle & Leitch 2012: 151.

[397] Chiesa 1949: 28; Brogan & Smith 1984: 42 (fig. 3), 72.

[398] The use of mudbrick is better recorded and studied in Fazzan (Mattingly 2003b: 160, *et passim*).

[399] Mattingly & Dore 1996: 124.

[400] For example, western coastal: Mrabet 1998, Sites 147.011 (brick), 147.002, 147.012 (tile); Central *gebel*: Ahmed 2010, Sites TUT8, TUT38, TUT43, GUM87 (tile).

construction of bath buildings. There is no recorded evidence for the use of either of these materials in the construction of farm buildings in the eastern pre-desert or Syrtica. Excavations in the *ULVS* area suggested that the roofs of unfortified farm buildings were generally flat and constructed of timber and/or flat stones and covered in mud baked in the sun, as at Lm004.[401] Interestingly, imported marble, bricks and tiles were recovered from a probable bath building far to the south of the Tripolitanian pre-desert, at the *Garamantian* capital settlement of *Garama* in Fazzan in first- to fourth-century AD contexts, which make it clear that it was certainly logistically possible to import these kinds of materials into the region.[402]

Construction Techniques: Previous Investigations

As previously mentioned, virtually none of the survey projects from which I have gathered my data was specifically investigating architecture in itself and as a result, previous descriptions of masonry range from very detailed to frustratingly vague (or non-existent beyond the fact that a structure was built in stone) and are not supported by photographs or drawings as frequently as we might like. There has been a great deal of inconsistency in the style and frequency of recording of these characteristics, making it difficult to draw reliable conclusions from the published evidence. Additionally, while plans and sizes of buildings can be recorded with reasonable accuracy using remote sensing techniques, materials and construction techniques normally cannot. As a result, this is probably the area of my study that has suffered the most from my inability to visit the sites. Therefore, while I can provide a certain amount of insight into the frequency and use of some different types of construction techniques, further investigations into this aspect of Tripolitanian farm buildings are clearly necessary.

The typology of construction techniques that I will use below is loosely based on that used in the *ULVS* publications, as it is the largest group of material for which construction technique was recorded in a relatively systematic way, though this system is not without its problems. When they started their survey, the masonry classification system used by the *ULVS* team was based on the three-class system developed by Goodchild in the 1940s for the fortified *gsur*, and the observations of Brogan and Smith for the buildings of Ghirza.[403] It eventually became apparent that not only was Goodchild's system too simplistic with regards to the *gsur*, it was not appropriate for the unfortified farms, the numbers of which were far greater than had initially been anticipated. A new system of recording and classification was developed, but by this point it was too late to retroactively apply the new system to the work that had already been done.[404]

Another particular issue with the *ULVS* material is that if a building was still standing over a certain height, its masonry type was often classified only as 'standing structure' without an indication of the actual construction technique used. The result of this, unfortunately, is that we do not have specific details for what are probably the best examples of intact masonry in the region, though few unfortified buildings fall into this category. Furthermore, when multiple types of masonry were found on a site or within a single building, the *ULVS* team adopted a policy of only listing the highest quality type visible.[405] This choice was made with good reason given the parameters of the survey and sometimes further details were provided in the descriptions; however, as a result, it is unclear how many buildings in that region may actually have incorporated multiple standards of construction and masonry. Tellingly, a large proportion of unfortified farms in Syrtica were described in the *PVNL* survey as combining two separate construction techniques – one for the actual covered building and another for the walls of the yard. Similarly, a number of buildings in the Gebel Tarhuna were recorded as having used ashlar masonry (*opus quadratum*) for their main construction and *opus africanum* for internal partitions.[406]

Construction Techniques: Analyses

Although the walls of most unfortified farm buildings no longer stand very tall (in contrast to the many well-preserved fortified buildings) the size of the mounds and amount of fallen masonry at most sites suggests that these buildings were rarely more than one storey in height. I have identified ten different construction techniques which were used in the structures of Tripolitania. At the top of the construction hierarchy was ashlar masonry (sometimes called *opus quadratum* or *grand appareil*) (Figure 5.13). *Opus africanum* also employed ashlar blocks, but only as orthostats at more or less regular intervals along a wall, with panels of masonry which employed smaller blocks, such as *petit appareil* or coursed rubble (as described below) between them (Figure 5.14). Instances in which a combination of ashlar and *opus africanum* were utilised were also recorded.

Opus africanum has usually been ascribed a Phoenician or Punic origin,[407] though recently Camporeale has suggested that while the version of the technique

[401] Mattingly & Dore 1996: 122–124; Barker *et al.* 1996: 278.

[402] Mattingly 2003b: 165.

[403] Goodchild 1950b: 35–36; Brogan & Smith 1984: 47. See also Section 6.2.4.

[404] Mattingly & Dore 1996: 129; Scott, Dore, & Mattingly 1996: 8–11.

[405] Scott, Dore, & Mattingly 1996: 8–9.

[406] Ahmed 2010: 142–143.

[407] For example, Romanelli 1970: 56; Adam 1994: 120–121; Hanoune 2009.

Rm002-f, Wadi Umm el-Ramel, E. pre-desert, south
(*ULVS* Archive: F445/N5/30.10.1981)

Figure 5.13: *Ashlar masonry.*

Mn006-f, Wadi Mansur, E. pre-desert, north
(*ULVS* Archive: F120/N8/11.11.1980)

BUN007-f, Beni Ulid North, E. pre-desert, north
(Scott, Dore, & Mattingly 1996: 58, fig. 5.4b)

Oates09-f (Henschir Sidi Hamdan), Central *gebel*
(Oates 1953: Plate XXVII, a)

Figure 5.14: Opus africanum *masonry.*

Mm008-f, Wadi Mimoun, E. pre-desert, north (*ULVS* Archive: F169/N30/9.12.1980)

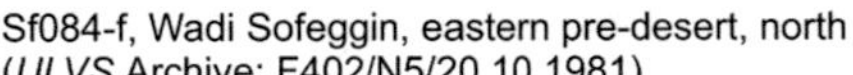

Sf084-f, Wadi Sofeggin, eastern pre-desert, north (*ULVS* Archive: F402/N5/20.10.1981)

Mm235-f, Wadi Mimoun, E. pre-desert, north (*ULVS* Archive: FB36/N30/1984)

Figure 5.15: *Regular masonry (top, lower left) and the remains of irregular masonry (lower right).*

which uses only vertical orthostats does have demonstrably Phoenician/Punic associations, the more well-known type of *opus africanum*, which utilises alternating vertical and horizontal orthostats (oft-cited examples of which are to be found in the Capitolium at Dougga, as well as at Pompeii) may have different origins.[408] *Opus africanum* walls in Tripolitania do not frequently survive above the level of the first course of orthostats, so it is difficult to know which version was typically employed, but a photo of Oates09-f (Henschir Sidi Hamdan) (Figure 5.13), does show what may be horizontally placed blocks in its standing piers. Indeed, there seems to be no practical advantage to the 'vertical orthostats only' type of opus africanum as it has been shown to be rather less structurally sound than its counterpart, since the piers are not in any way keyed into the intervening panels.[409]

Possible variations of the *opus africanum* building technique were also recorded, which involved the use of larger or smaller non-ashlar orthostats in a less regular manner, sometimes only to define doorways and corners. It is possible that some should, in fact, be classed as *opus africanum*, but in the absence of clear evidence either way, I have kept them as a separate category. Large or small orthostats were also sometimes employed only at the base of walls, with other types of masonry continuing between and above them,[410] but again, most walls have not survived high enough to confirm their appearance above the first courses.

The technique sometimes known as *petit appareil* was also commonly recorded in Tripolitania. In constructions of this type, a rubble and earth core was faced with varying sizes and qualities of more or less well-shaped and coursed stones.[411] This category is divided

[408] Camporeale 2013.

[409] Govoni, Custodi, & Sciortino 2002; Hanoune 2009: 30. This problem could also at least partially explain why (as we will see in the next chapter) *opus africanum* was not used as often for *gsur*, since the instability would have been compounded in taller walls.

[410] For example, Gh058-f, Sc006-f (Scott, Dore, & Mattingly 1996: 111, 276).

[411] Adam 1994: 136–139.

Gh118-f , Wadi Ghirza, E. pre-desert, south
(*ULVS* Archive, F-/N-/unknown)

Lg016-f, Wadi Legwais, E. pre-desert, north
(*ULVS* Archive: F481/N13/unknown)

Rm003-f, Wadi Umm el-Ramel, E. pre-desert, south
(*ULVS* Archive: F445/N33/30.10.1981)

Sf138-f, Wadi Sofeggin, E. pre-desert, north
(*ULVS* Archive: F419/N11/22.10.1981)

Figure 5.16: *Coursed rubble/drystone.*

into 'regular masonry' and 'irregular masonry', based on the regularity of the coursing and the quality of the stones used in the facing (Figure 5.15). Finally, a large proportion of buildings were constructed using coursed rubble or drystone, with or without an internal core (Figure 5.16). The difference between the coursed rubble/drystone category and the irregular and even regular masonry categories is unfortunately quite blurred and to a degree, subjective; it is based more on the quality of stones, with the former referring generally to unworked stone. Only a few examples of the last three categories were explicitly recorded as having used a bonding agent or mortar in their construction, all of which were in the coursed rubble category, and these were recorded as 'mortared rubble'. It is probable that more examples than these did use some kind of bonding agent in their construction, but unfortunately that information has not normally been recorded.

Finally, as already mentioned above, a particular group of buildings in Syrtica were recorded as employing a combination of construction techniques, in which the covered rooms of the unfortified farms were constructed in coursed drystone, of generally higher quality than the walls of the farmyards which consisted of two faces of irregular slabs or uprights containing a core of stone and/or earth.[412] Because the *PVNL* study was so specific about this, I have kept this group of buildings as a separate category. However, although this could be some kind of local trend, it is equally possible that combinations of this type were, in fact, more widespread but the published accounts are simply not specific enough in their descriptions.

Of the 1,653 individually catalogued unfortified structures, I was able to record the construction technique used for 641 (39%). The frequency of buildings using the types of masonry described in the last section across the study area is presented in Table 5.12 and Figure 5.17 and Figure 5.18. Unfortunately, no data on construction techniques were recorded for either the Southwest region or eastern Syrtica. In the case of the latter, however, it can be noted that Longerstay reported that the buildings identified in the *PARS* survey were generally constructed in either *moellons de petit appareil*, usually without a bonding agent, or the same technique

[412] Reddé 1988: 70.

	ashlar	ashlar & opus africanum	opus africanum	large orthostats	small orthostats	regular masonry	irregular masonry	coursed rubble/ drystone	mortared rubble	Syrtica group	*Total*
1. W. coastal	1	–	9	1	–	–	–	–	2	–	*13*
2. W. *gebel*	2	–	–	–	–	1	–	–	–	–	*3*
4. Central coastal	–	1	23	–	–	–	–	–	–	–	*24*
5. Central *gebel*	7	4	37	–	–	1	–	–	–	–	*49*
6. E. pre-desert, north	–	–	14	8	8	30	14	188	2	–	*264*
7. E. pre-desert, south	1	2	6	2	33	36	40	99	–	–	*219*
8. W. Syrtica	–	–	–	4	–	1	–	22	8	34	*69*
Total	*11*	*7*	*89*	*15*	*41*	*69*	*54*	*309*	*12*	*34*	*641*

Table 5.12: *Distribution of construction techniques employed in unfortified buildings, divided by region.*

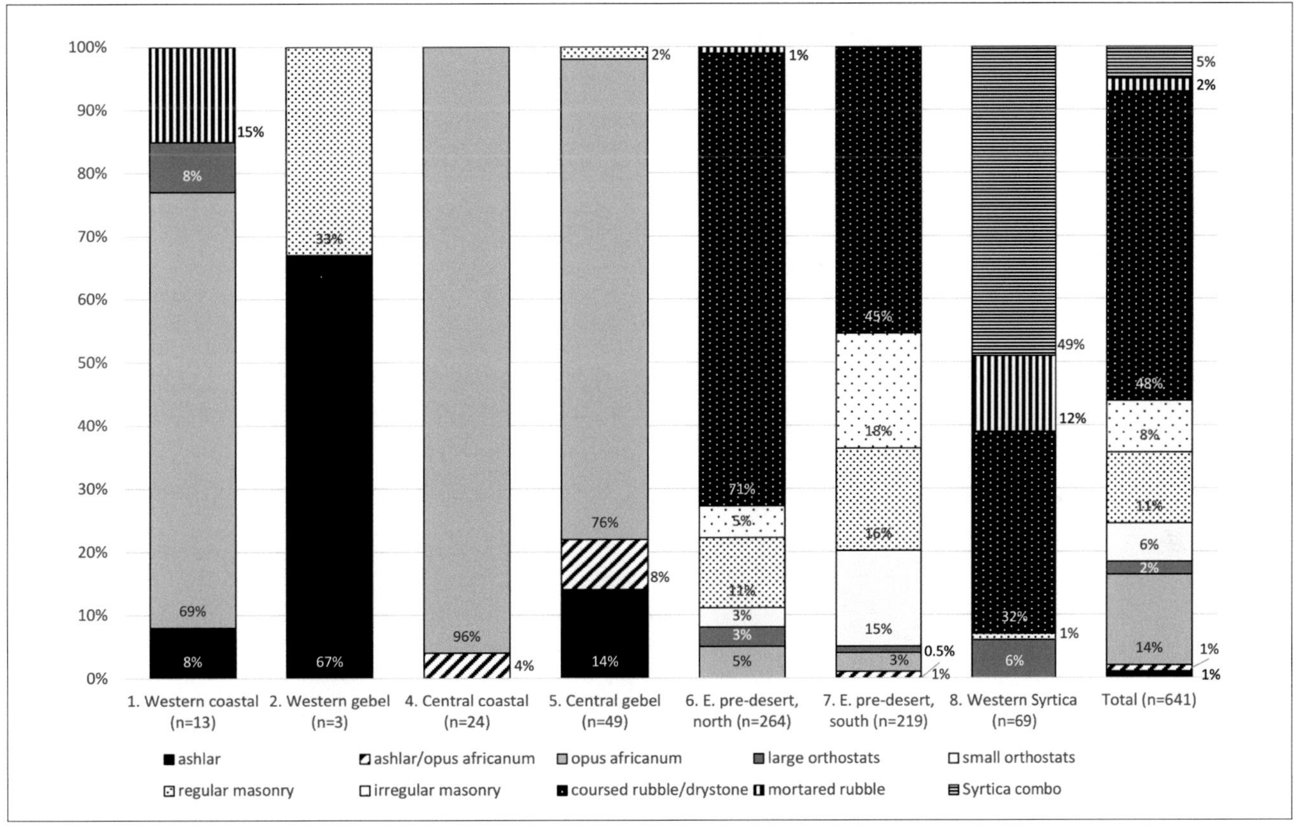

Figure 5.17: *Ratios of construction techniques employed in unfortified buildings in different regions of Tripolitania (excluding the Southwest and eastern Syrtica for which there were no data).*

of a rubble core faced on both sides by irregular orthostats sometimes used for yards in the *PVNL* region.[413]

By far the most popular building technique in both the western and central regions was *opus africanum*, followed by the use of full ashlar or a combination of the two, though yet again, we must be conscious of the low numbers of examples with this information recorded in the western regions, especially the *gebel*. The only other masonry type recorded in the central regions was one example of high-quality regular masonry in the *gebel*. In the west, where the sample was very small (n=16), only one example each of large orthostats (which could be *opus africanum*), regular masonry and mortared rubble were found.

It is worth noting, however, that the lack of excavations at sites in the coastal and *gebel* regions could severely

[413] Longerstay 1999: 60.

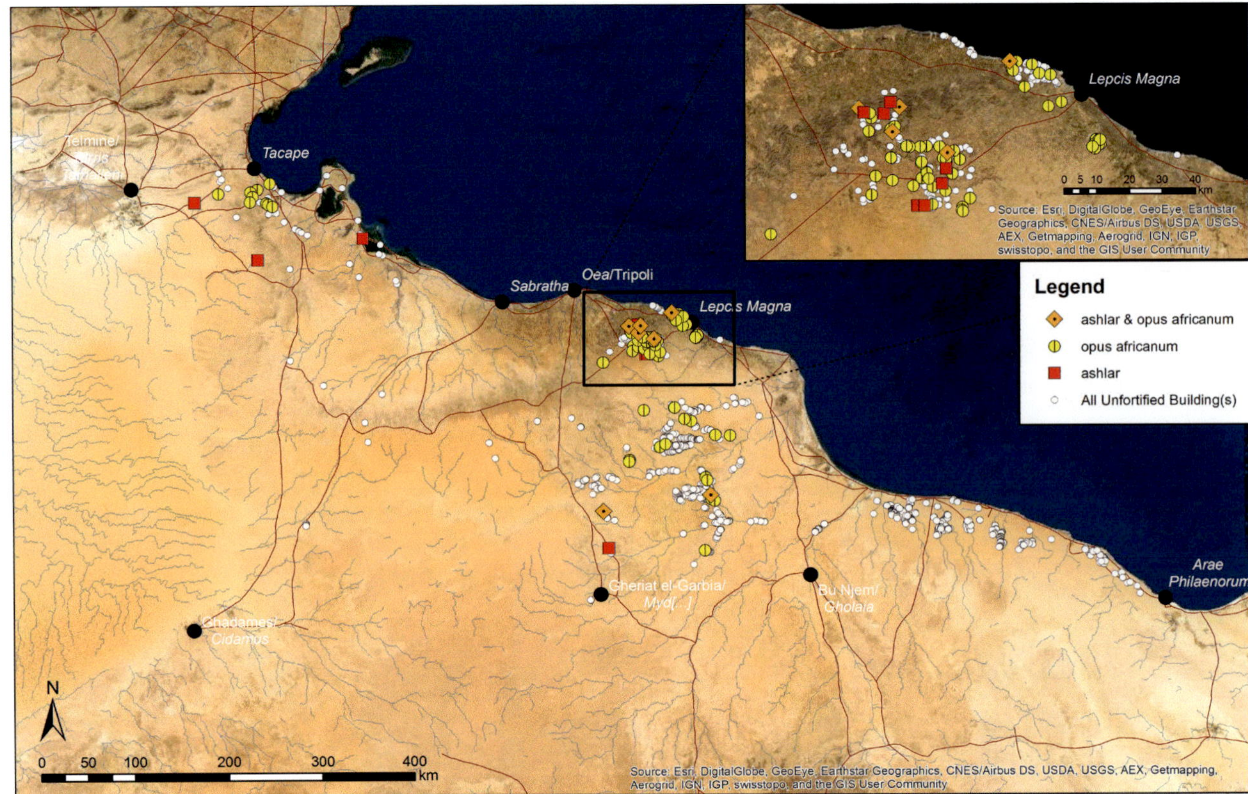

Basemap: Esri, DigitalGlobe, GeoEye, Earthstar Geographics, CNES/Airbus DS, USDA, USGS, AEX, Getmapping, Aerogrid, IGN, IGP, swisstopo, and the GIS User Community
Drainage: Lehner, B., Verdin, K., Jarvis, A. (2008): New global hydrography derived from spaceborne elevation data. Eos, Transactions, AGU, 89(10): 93-94. Retrieved from http://hydrosheds.cr.usgs.gov (15 sec Flow Accumulation)
Roads (Barrington Atlas): Ancient World Mapping Center (2012)

Figure 5.18a: *Geographical distribution of construction techniques used in unfortified buildings: ashlar and* opus africanum.

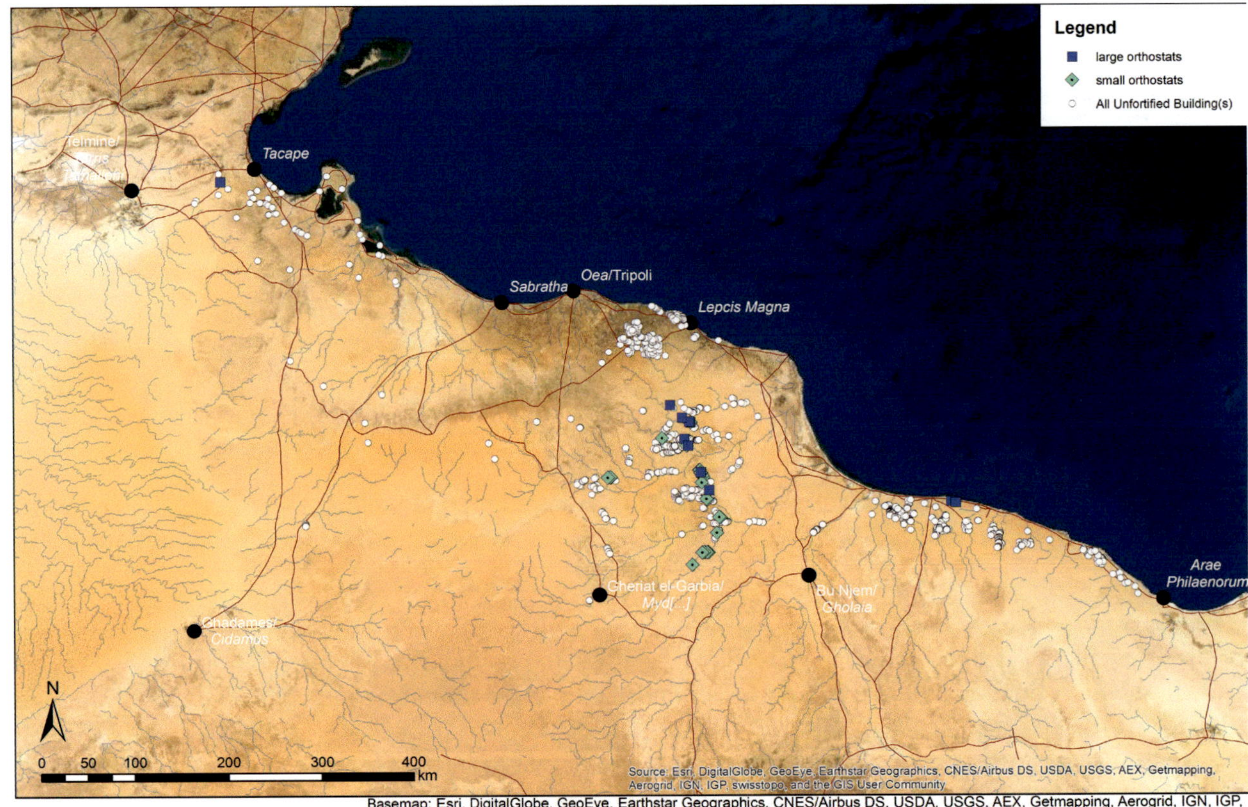

Basemap: Esri, DigitalGlobe, GeoEye, Earthstar Geographics, CNES/Airbus DS, USDA, USGS, AEX, Getmapping, Aerogrid, IGN, IGP, swisstopo, and the GIS User Community
Drainage: Lehner, B., Verdin, K., Jarvis, A. (2008): New global hydrography derived from spaceborne elevation data. Eos, Transactions, AGU, 89(10): 93-94. Retrieved from http://hydrosheds.cr.usgs.gov (15 sec Flow Accumulation)
Roads (Barrington Atlas): Ancient World Mapping Center (2012)

Figure 5.18b: *Geographical distribution of construction techniques used in unfortified buildings: large and small orthostats.*

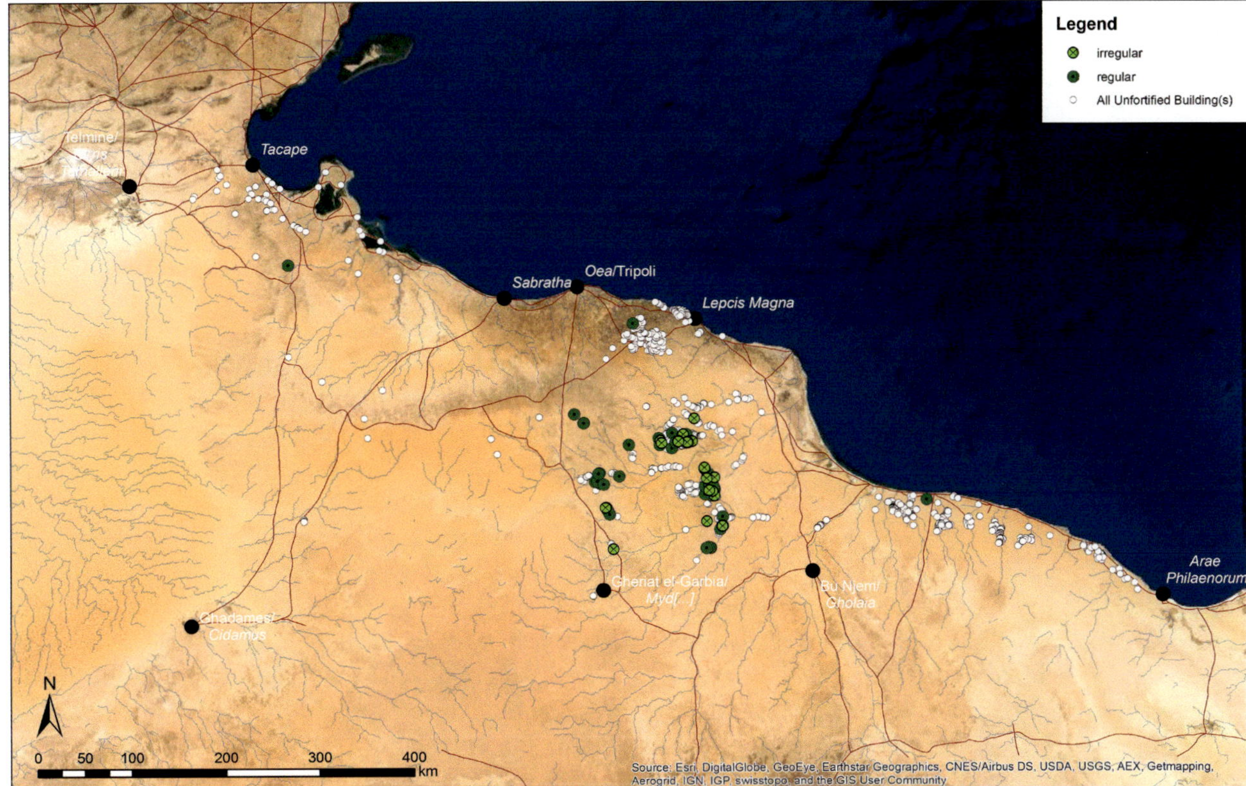

Basemap: Esri, DigitalGlobe, GeoEye, Earthstar Geographics, CNES/Airbus DS, USDA, USGS, AEX, Getmapping, Aerogrid, IGN, IGP, swisstopo, and the GIS User Community
Drainage: Lehner, B., Verdin, K., Jarvis, A. (2008): New global hydrography derived from spaceborne elevation data. Eos, Transactions, AGU, 89(10): 93-94. Retrieved from http://hydrosheds.cr.usgs.gov (15 sec Flow Accumulation)
Roads (Barrington Atlas): Ancient World Mapping Center (2012)

Figure 5.18c: *Geographical distribution of construction techniques used in unfortified buildings: regular and irregular masonry.*

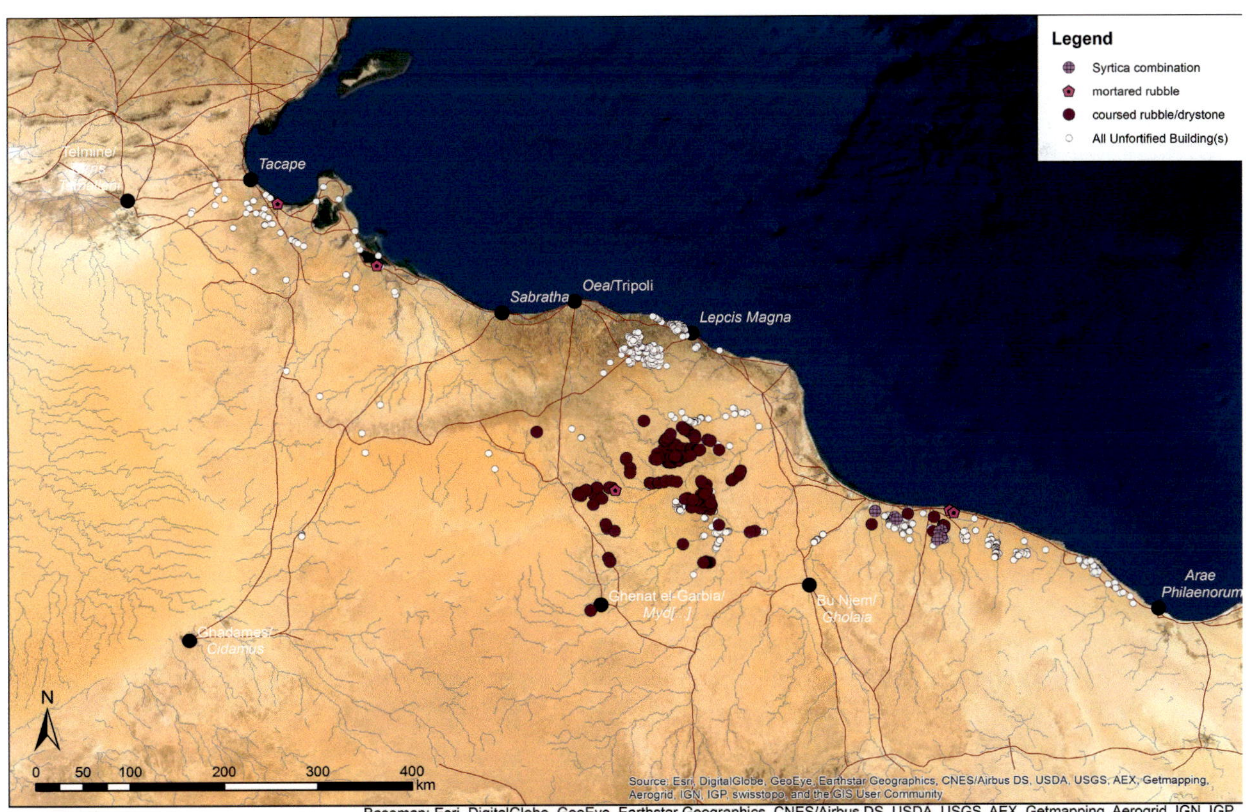

Basemap: Esri, DigitalGlobe, GeoEye, Earthstar Geographics, CNES/Airbus DS, USDA, USGS, AEX, Getmapping, Aerogrid, IGN, IGP, swisstopo, and the GIS User Community
Drainage: Lehner, B., Verdin, K., Jarvis, A. (2008): New global hydrography derived from spaceborne elevation data. Eos, Transactions, AGU, 89(10): 93-94. Retrieved from http://hydrosheds.cr.usgs.gov (15 sec Flow Accumulation)
Roads (Barrington Atlas): Ancient World Mapping Center (2012)

Figure 5.18d: *Geographical distribution of construction techniques used in unfortified buildings: Syrtica combination, mortared rubble and coursed rubble/drystone.*

bias our view in this regard. At many sites in which *opus africanum* construction was used, the ashlar orthostats are all that survive above ground. It is possible, therefore, that there were many other buildings which were constructed without employing ashlar blocks which have not left any trace above ground. This could be confirmed by actively testing sites at which large spreads of pottery were found during surveys but no masonry was identified (of which there are many examples). The use of ashlar techniques, predominantly *opus africanum*, was clearly a dominant construction technique in these regions, certainly far more common here than in the eastern pre-desert and Syrtica. However, with more intensive excavations, it might not be surprising to find a greater variety of construction techniques and materials in use than are currently represented in my catalogue.

In the eastern pre-desert and Syrtica, coursed rubble or drystone was the most commonly recorded construction technique (including the group of examples which employ a different construction for the yard in western Syrtica). Buildings employing ashlar masonry or *opus africanum* were rare in the eastern pre-desert; the technique appears to have been non-existent in Syrtica, though perhaps some of the buildings identified as employing large orthostats could be interpreted as *opus africanum*. It is also worth remembering that in an area where good quality building stone was rare to begin with, we may need to take into account a high incidence of stone robbing. There seems to have been a slight preference for the technique in the northern part of the eastern pre-desert over the southern part, which accords with a spatial analysis done by the *ULVS* team in which they showed that the average location for *opus africanum* farms was further north and east than the average for all farms of a similar date in their survey area.[414]

Regular and irregular masonry were the next most popular techniques used in the pre-desert, though it seems to have been rare in Syrtica. While the coursed rubble/drystone construction technique represented a clear majority in the north part of the eastern pre-desert, in the south, the two masonry techniques together almost equal that of coursed rubble and drystone. In addition, constructions employing small orthostats were also much more popular in the southern part of the eastern pre-desert than in the northern. The apparent lack of all of these types, including also *opus africanum* and ashlar, in the Syrtica area is potentially significant; we might interpret this as an indication that these types were not local developments. On the other hand, although the discrepancy between the northern and southern parts of the eastern pre-desert seems quite marked, it is not as clear whether this trend holds any real significance or whether it reflects trends in recording due to some of the inconsistencies discussed above.

[414] Mattingly & Flower 1996: 161.

In general, the use of bonding agents seems to have been recorded relatively rarely in all areas of Tripolitania, most frequently in western Syrtica. It is not always clear whether this is because bonding agents were not used or simply not recorded. The production of lime mortar required a lot of resources which was a potential deterrent in its use, though mud mortars may have been used more often.

Masonry Type and Plan

Of the 641 buildings for which the masonry was recorded, 434 also had an identified plan. The frequency with which different masonry techniques were used in different building types across the study area is presented in Table 5.13 and Figure 5.19 (excluding coastal villas complexes as there were only two examples).

The chart illustrates the strong relationship between courtyard buildings and the use of ashlar techniques, especially opus africanum. On the other hand, there was only one recorded instance of a farmyard building employing *opus africanum*, and none which employed ashlar masonry otherwise. Over half of the farmyard, undifferentiated open buildings and open complexes were recorded as employing the coursed rubble/drystone technique, with the remaining proportion divided by a wider variety of techniques. Interestingly, while the farmyard buildings and undifferentiated open buildings had similar proportions of coursed rubble/drystone, the latter had a much higher proportion of *opus africanum* recorded (19%); it is tempting to therefore see this as an indicator of the presence of courtyard buildings among this group, but it is difficult to be certain without further investigation. We can also point to a similarity between farmyard buildings and open complexes, and not with other building types with respect to construction techniques used.

If we further divide the data by region we can see that there is a clear relationship between the courtyard and open buildings of the central region and *opus africanum*, but courtyard buildings of the pre-desert were more often constructed of non-ashlar masonry types (Appendix Tables 8–12). It is difficult to compare, because no farmyard buildings were actually recorded in the central regions, but what this might indicate, is that while the use of *opus africanum* or other ashlar masonry techniques was an important defining feature of courtyard buildings in the central regions, this mattered less in the pre-desert where courtyard buildings were constructed using a variety of techniques.

Masonry Type and Building Size

A total of 384 buildings had both masonry type and building size recorded. It was therefore also possible to calculate the average sizes of unfortified farm buildings

	ashlar	ashlar & opus africanum	opus africanum	large orthostats	small orthostats	regular masonry	irregular masonry	coursed rubble/ drystone	mortared rubble	Syrtica group	*Total*
Courtyard	3	3	33	3	–	15	7	11	3	3	*81*
Farmyard	–	–	1	5	27	23	22	106	2	27	*213*
Open (undiff.)	–	1	16	2	1	13	2	44	3	3	*85*
Open complex	–	–	–	1	1	5	2	19	–	–	*28*
Range	1	1	2	1	1	7	7	4	1	–	*25*
Villa complex	–	1	1	–	–	–	–	–	–	–	*2*
Total	*4*	*6*	*53*	*12*	*30*	*63*	*40*	*184*	*9*	*33*	*434*

Table 5.13: *Frequency of construction techniques used in different building types across Tripolitania.*

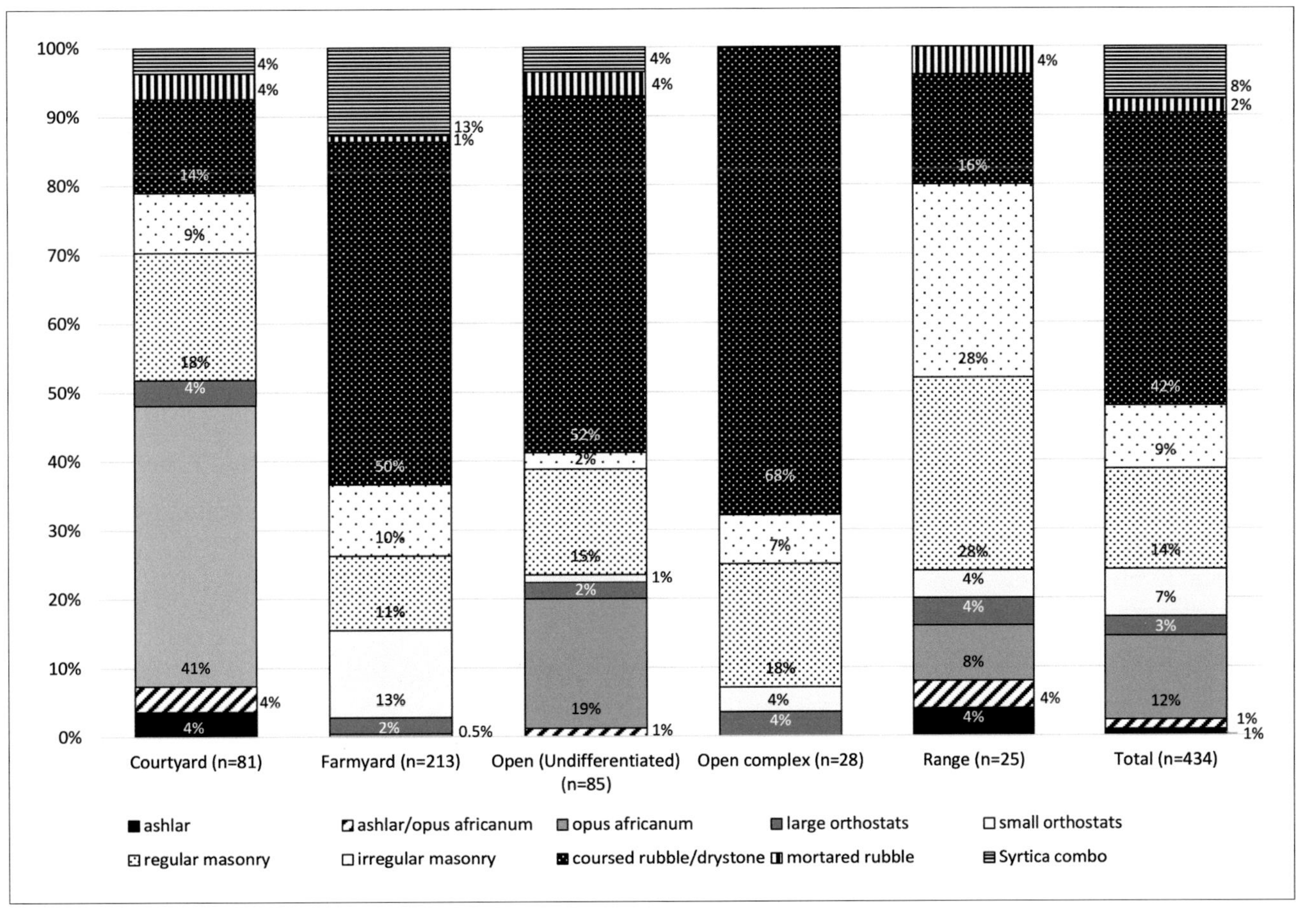

Figure 5.19: *Ratios of construction techniques used in different unfortified building types.*

broken down by both masonry technique used and region (Table 5.14), although there are gaps in the data as not all masonry types occur in all regions (or their sizes were not recorded).

The table illustrates that unfortified farm buildings constructed using techniques which employed ashlar blocks (i.e. ashlar and *opus africanum*) were, in general, larger than those which do not. There were only four buildings recorded as being constructed in ashlar which had their sizes recorded; three were located in the central *gebel* and identified as courtyard buildings (TUT12-f, TUT53-f, Cowper41-f) and the fourth was a very small probable range type building in the western *gebel* (RLT063-f). Another example, found in the southern pre-desert (Rm002-f, illustrated in Figure 5.13) was also constructed wholly in ashlar and was

	ashlar (n=4)	ashlar & opus africanum (n=5)	opus africanum (n=53)	large orthostats (n=12)	small orthostats (n=37)	regular masonry (n=63)	irregular masonry (n=39)	coursed rubble/ drystone (n=142)	mortared rubble (n=7)	Syrtica group (n=22)
1. W. coastal	–	–	1,325	850	–	–	–	–	5,330	–
2. W. *gebel*	60	–	–	–	–	504	–	–	–	–
4. Central coastal	–	3,969	1,733	–	–	–	–	–	–	–
5. Central *gebel*	1,622	3,025	2,082	–	–	700	–	–	–	–
6. E. pre–desert, north	–	–	1,275	1,229	1,342	537	921	1,340	–	–
7. E. pre–desert, south	–	919	1,335	416	512	596	425	725	–	–
8. W. Syrtica	–	–	–	187	–	–	–	281	595	510
All regions	1,231	2,371	1,713	956	691	572	578	1,033	1,271	510

Table 5.14: *Average size (m²) of unfortified farm buildings in different regions, divided by construction technique.*

also on the smaller end of the scale, but exact measurements were unfortunately not available.[415] However, it is worth noting that as we do not have full plans for the three larger examples, it is possible that they also employed *opus africanum* in other parts, since the resources needed to construct entire buildings of this size in ashlar masonry alone would have been massive. Five examples which were recorded as incorporating both ashlar and *opus africanum* were similarly large, with the exception of Lm004-f1 (88 m²) in the southern part of the eastern pre-desert, which like RLT063-f was of the range type.

This trend was previously observed by Cività and the authors of the *ULVS* for the eastern pre-desert region.[416] However, given that *opus africanum* was commonly used in courtyard buildings, which were previously demonstrated to be larger on average than farmyard buildings, this is of course, unsurprising. If we further break down these data by building type and compare the results for courtyard and farmyard buildings separately (Appendix Tables 13 & 14), the same pattern broadly seems to hold true; for example, courtyard buildings in the northern part of the pre-desert constructed of *opus africanum* were on average significantly larger than courtyard buildings constructed of other techniques. However, a significant exception is that in the southern eastern pre-desert, while buildings constructed in *opus africanum* were indeed usually of comparatively large size, what the overall averages disguise is that the reverse was not necessarily true, i.e. that the largest courtyard buildings were not necessarily always built of *opus africanum*. In fact, the largest courtyard buildings were constructed of coursed rubble/drystone. This would suggest, therefore, that there was no straightforward correlation specifically between construction technique and building size; different construction techniques could be utilised in buildings of any size. Rather, as demonstrated in previous sections, masonry technique was more closely linked to building type.

5.2.5 Decoration and Luxury

A number of unfortified rural buildings had decorative or 'luxury' features, such as baths, mosaics, marble, painted plaster or stucco, and architectural sculpture or decoration such as porticoes and capitals, etc.[417] All of these features were the result of a deliberate choice to incorporate them into buildings or sites and, notwithstanding differences in size and quality, all would have required a certain level of investment. It is not my intention to discuss here the artistic styles or merits of these features at any length; there are a number of studies on the design and significance of these features in rural Tripolitania to which one can refer.[418] Rather, I will explore here how the presence of one or more of these features relates to the type of physical characteristics already discussed above. The frequency and distribution of sites at which five different categories of decoration/luxury features were recorded is presented in Table 5.15 and Figure 5.20.

[415] Scott, Dore, & Mattingly 1996: 272.

[416] Cività 1994: 62; Mattingly & Dore 1996: 124.

[417] See, for example, Munzi *et al.* 2004–2005: 447 and Ahmed 2010: 102–106. See also fn. 358 above.

[418] For example, on mosaics: Aurigemma 1926; 1929; 1960; Di Vita 1966; Dunbabin 1978; al-Mahjub 1978–1979; Parrish 1985. On wall painting: Aurigemma 1962; Johnston 1982; Bianchi 2002.

	Total buildings	Total buildings with luxury elements		Baths	Mosaics	Marble	Plaster	Sculpture
1. W. coastal	50	5	10%	1	5	2	–	1
2. W. *gebel*	9	1	11%	–	–	–	–	1
3. Southwest	11	–	–	–	–	–	–	–
4. Central coastal	94	28	30%	4	13	19	14	7
5. Central *gebel*	156	30	19%	19	8	–	–	19
6. E. pre-desert, north	365	3	0.8%	–	1	–	–	3
7. E. pre-desert, south	414	4	1%	–	–	–	–	4
8. W. Syrtica	487	3	0.6%	1	–	–	2	–
9. E. Syrtica	67	–	–	–	–	–	–	–
Total	*1,653*	*74*	*4%*	*25*	*27*	*21*	*16*	*35*

Table 5.15: *Frequency of unfortified buildings at which luxury elements were observed.*[419]

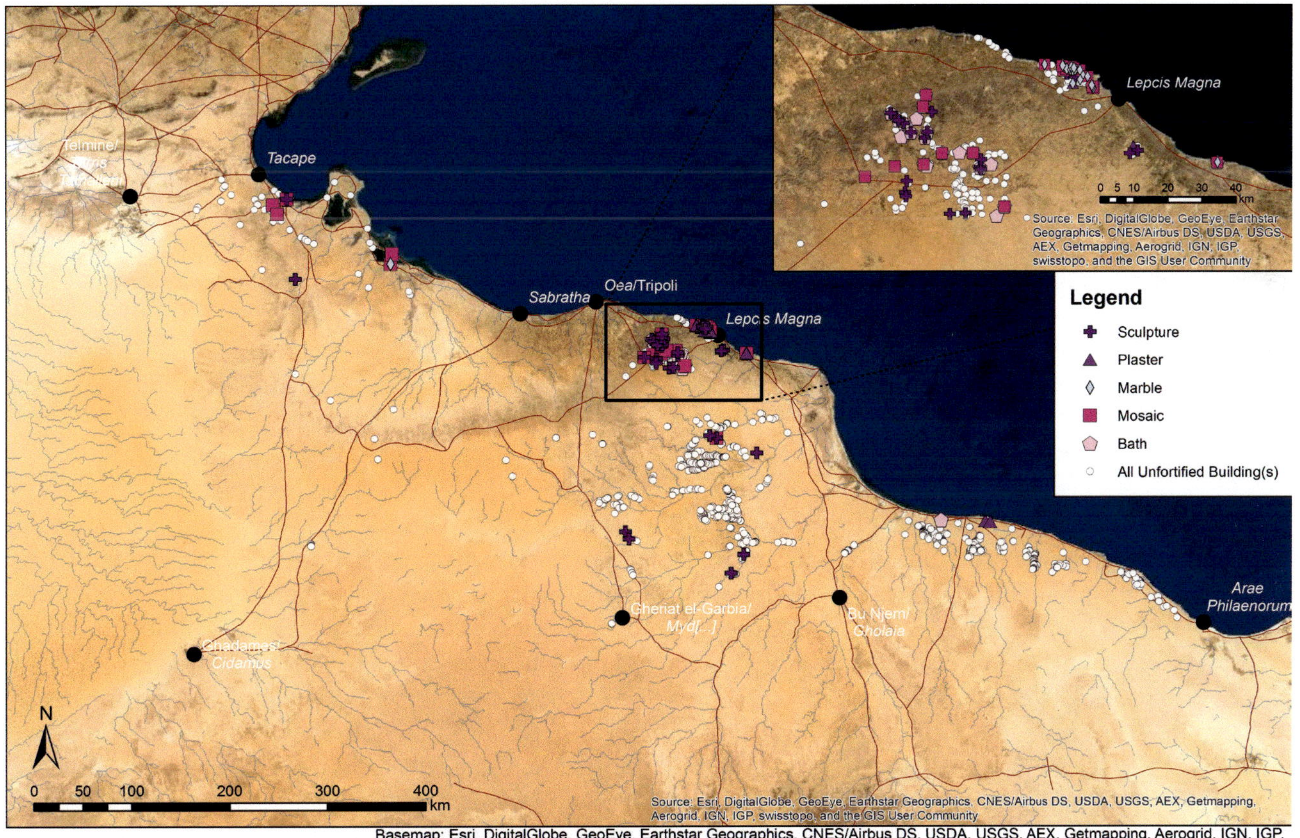

Figure 5.20: *Distribution of unfortified buildings with luxury elements.*

It is important to note first that while the indication given in the table that luxury features were found more frequently in the central and western regions near the coast and in the *gebel* is probably largely correct, we must be wary of reading too much into the exact numbers. A number of rural buildings in the regions of *Lepcis Magna* and *Oea*, particularly those located on the coast, are justifiably well-known for their high-quality décor (e.g. Zliten, Silin); however, the discovery of intact mosaics or *opus sectile* floors, particularly during surveys, is not a common occurrence. More often, a few slabs of marble or small amounts of *tesserae* are observed on the surface, and unless these are very highly concentrated, they are easily missed during surveys. Similarly,

[419] N.B. in many cases, more than one type of luxury feature occurred at the same site, e.g. site TUT20 in the central *gebel* had evidence for both a bathhouse and mosaics. While these are counted separately in the individual feature columns, in the 'Total' columns, TUT20 counts for only one.

the existence of bath facilities at a site are sometimes only indicated by the presence of a few hypocaust tiles. As a result, we rarely have any idea how extensive the use of these items may have been at a site or building, whether, for example, mosaics were used throughout or only in a few rooms. Neither do we have any idea of how reliable the figures in the chart above are, or the proportion of buildings which may actually have employed these materials, but of which there is no trace left on the surface or were not noted in the published records. Finally, of course, this type of evidence is not normally visible from satellite imagery, so we cannot know how many sites identified in that way may actually have had these features.[420]

Nevertheless, if we take the data with a proverbial grain of salt, a few interesting observations can be made. For example, it is probably unsurprising that we should find virtually no evidence for bathing facilities in the pre-desert, nor is it likely to be a coincidence that the one example that we do have from all of the eastern pre-desert and Syrtica (Qb09), was located not far from the coast road, where the supplies needed for the construction and maintenance of a bathhouse would have been more easily accessible.[421] Given the scarcity of water and wood for fuel in these regions, bathing was a luxury that may have been difficult to maintain beyond the coast and outside of the oases, even if one could afford to build the bathhouse itself.[422] However, it is equally possible that the people living in these regions simply had no interest in baths or bathing culture. Bathhouses were clearly more common at the sites of the *gebel* and coastal areas, which suggests a certain level of participation in that aspect of Roman culture; however, the subject of rural baths and bathing in Tripolitania is one on which very little work has been done to date.[423]

There are no marble sources in Tripolitania and its use in rural buildings therefore implies that the owners of these buildings were able to afford the high costs of importing this valuable material. The only evidence for marble use at rural farm sites is in the central coastal region, and one instance in the western coastal region; again, close to the coast, which may speak to the high cost of both obtaining and transporting marble overland. In the areas where it was recorded, the use of marble in a building is generally only indicated through the presence of a few slabs observed during surface survey and it is therefore not always clear how it was employed, whether as pavement, wall cladding, or some other type of furnishing. In addition, marble remains a high value item which is particularly susceptible to looting, so it is possible that it was, in fact, more widely utilised than the survey material would suggest.

Evidence for painted wall plaster or stucco was relatively rare, having been recorded in unfortified buildings only in the central coastal area and western Syrtica. Again, this is possibly a preservation issue, as painted plaster exposed on the surface will quickly degrade, and I suspect that this form of decoration was more common than the current record would suggest. At least one other example with painted wall plaster which is not in my catalogue was reported by Brogan in the Wadi Neina, c. 90 km south of Bu Njem.[424]

The majority of recorded examples of sculptural decoration consisted of the fragmentary columns and capitals, which in some cases probably formed parts of porticoes. Other types of sculptural decoration seem to have been rare at unfortified sites, though again, more examples might be discovered with more intensive investigations. Only four sites (one in the central coastal area and three in the eastern pre-desert, south) were reported as having some kind of decorative relief sculpture other than apotropaic phallic reliefs (discussed below).[425] However, in the case of most of the relief sculpture, and sometimes also with architectural elements such as columns and capitals, these elements were not found *in situ*, and so we do not know how, or even if, they were originally used in the farm buildings under discussion. There is often a good chance that a number of these could have come from funerary monuments, on which sculptural decoration was far more common.[426] Clearly, therefore, the resources to either make or commission sculptural decoration and inscriptions (of which none were found in association with unfortified buildings) were available, at least to some people, and so we might speculate that funerary monuments and domestic structures were felt to require different types of decoration for practical or socio-religious reasons.

There were also five sites at which reliefs in the form of phalli were noted (one in the central coastal region, two in the central *gebel*, and two in the eastern pre-desert;

[420] It is also worth noting that removing those sites which were identified using only satellite imagery increased the percentages of sites with luxury features only very slightly and did not affect the overall trends.

[421] Interestingly, Qb09 is also one of only two sites in Syrtica which have possible evidence for a press (see below).

[422] Rowan (2015) has also argued that olive oil pressing waste would have been an effective and logical source of fuel, which would make a great deal of sense in the *gebel* regions.

[423] Though see Ahmed's (2010: 148–153) brief summary discussion of the examples from his study area in the Gebel Tarhuna.

[424] Brogan 1965b: 57–59. This building appears to have been of the block/range type, c.6 x 22 m in size. It was constructed of 'roughly laid stones'. The interior of the south room had white plaster with a red painted stripe.

[425] Central coastal: BEN11-f, limestone relief with two-faced winged figure. Eastern pre-desert, south: Gh001a-f, rosette relief; Gh080-f, bull relief; Lm037-f, unspecified relief-decorated blocks.

[426] See Section 5.3.2

TUT09-f, Central *gebel*
(Ahmed 2010: 353, fig.13)

Mn006-f, Wadi Mansur, E. pre-desert, north
(*ULVS* Archive: F120/N2/11.11.1980)

Figure 5.21: *Examples of (apotropaic?) phallic reliefs.*

Figure 5.21).[427] These can almost certainly be interpreted as apotropaic images, and thus they are not strictly decorative, rather serving a particular socio-cultural function of protecting the household from the evil eye.[428]

Finally, we know extremely little about what other types of decoration these structures might have incorporated, beyond those discussed above. Particularly in the pre-desert and Syrtica, where we have little evidence for any decorative features, we can probably safely assume that in terms of luxuriousness they could not compete with the sumptuous coastal villas; however, I think it would be wrong to presume that other types of farms were necessarily drab and undecorated. While it seems not unlikely that more intensive survey and excavation might turn up more examples, it is also possible that integrated decoration of this type was simply not all that common in those regions. We could suggest that interior decoration may have been largely composed of perishable or portable materials – rugs, tapestries, wooden or metal fixtures, etc. Textiles recovered from Ghirza, in the eastern pre-desert, which have been dated to around the tenth century AD could give us a glimpse into the kinds of materials which we might imagine were used for interior décor, but this is only speculation.[429]

Luxury Elements and Building Plan, Size and Construction

The number of buildings at which luxury elements were recorded was relatively small (n=74) and the number of those which also had their plan, size and/or construction technique recorded was generally less than half that. Nevertheless, some cautious analyses can be attempted to try to determine what, if any, correlations existed between these characteristics and the presence of the luxury elements discussed above.

Only 33 of the 74 buildings with luxury features had a known building plan recorded (Appendix Table 15), but the majority of these were courtyard buildings (23/33, 70%). This further supports the idea that courtyard buildings were only constructed by people who had the means to do so. Unsurprisingly, three of the four villa complexes in my catalogue had the luxury features identified here recorded, and the fourth (Villa of the Small Circus, LMCS02-v) very likely had at least some as well, but these have not been mentioned in existing publications. There were no examples of farmyard buildings with luxury features, nor were there any reported in open complexes, emphasising that their large size was more due to the clustering of what were actually smaller units and a large amount of open space.

The average size of buildings that had one or more of the luxury elements discussed above (2,417 m^2) was far larger than the overall average (881 m^2) (Appendix Table 16), which can in turn probably be related to their correlation with courtyard buildings. A correlation between larger building sizes and the inclusion of luxury materials or facilities is again unsurprising if we relate both of those characteristics to greater wealth and/or status and the data for the central regions and for the northern part of the eastern pre-desert clearly support this idea. The numbers in the other regions are probably too small to be reliable at this point, but it is possible that we are seeing similar trends. In the western *gebel* region, there was only one building with luxury elements for which

[427] Central coastal: BEN01-f. Central *gebel*: Cowper67-f, TUT09-f. Eastern pre-desert, north: Md011-f, Mn006-f. The last of these, Mn006-f, was named the Farm of the Phalli because of it had at least four phallic relief carvings.

[428] Hunt *et al.* 1986: 17–19; Mattingly 1995: 162. See also Johns 1982: 60–75; Clarke 2007: 69–73.

[429] Brogan & Smith 1984: 291–308.

the size was recorded (RLT113-f1, fragments of columns and capitals) and it was of the range type, so it is unsurprising that it was much smaller than the average for all buildings in that region. In the western coastal area, again there was only a single building with luxury elements for which size was recorded (LT05), but in this case, it was of very large size (5,330 m^2).

The size difference between buildings with luxury elements and the overall average was very large in the north part of the eastern pre-desert (though it should be kept in mind that it was based on only three examples). Nevertheless, it is not insignificant that all three examples were from the same wadi system (the Wadi Merdum/Mansur) which is one of the northern-most of the eastern pre-desert region. In western Syrtica and the southern part of the eastern pre-desert, the average size of buildings with luxury elements was slightly smaller than the overall average for the region, but the averages disguise a very small sample with a wide variety of sizes, between 88 and 1,260 m^2.

As mentioned in Section 5.2.3, we can also measure the relationship between buildings with presses and those with luxury elements, and it is clear that there was a much higher likelihood that a building would have luxury elements if it also had one or more presses (Appendix Table 17). Of the 74 buildings where luxury elements were identified, just over half (40/74) also had presses. Conversely, 19% of the 215 identified buildings with presses had luxury features, whereas only 2% of buildings without presses (34/1,438) did.

Finally, we can also make a note of the possible relationship between luxury elements and construction technique. Of the buildings with their masonry type recorded, 35 had some type of luxury elements associated with them (Appendix Table 18). Again, the numbers involved here are far too small to make any firm conclusions. However, unsurprisingly, in the data that we do have, the unfortified buildings with luxury elements appear to trend towards the building techniques utilising ashlar masonry, with 83% (29/35) of structures with luxury elements employing ashlar, *opus africanum* or a combination of the two. Again, this can probably be related to fact that both ashlar construction techniques and luxury elements require a certain amount of wealth or resources, and especially in the case of the latter, what we might call disposable wealth.

5.3 Unfortified Settlements and Other Rural Structures

The previous sections have focussed primarily on the architecture and construction of individual buildings. However, as briefly discussed above in Section 5.1, it was sometimes the case that these buildings occurred in small groups, along with other types of rural and agricultural structures. In this section, therefore, I will present a basic analysis of the spatial relationships between unfortified farm buildings and what we can conclude about different types and sizes of unfortified settlements, followed by a brief discussion of how some other building types known from the region also fit into these settlements.

5.3.1 Settlements

In order to evaluate how the unfortified buildings related to each other spatially, I conducted analyses to determine into how many groups the recorded unfortified farm buildings could be clustered when different distances between buildings were allowed for, and then what the average number of buildings was within the groups. Each of these groups, whether composed of only a single farm building or multiple buildings has been called a 'settlement', in the very broad sense of indicating a place where people lived. There were, of course, also other types of rural settlements, as discussed, for example, in Section 3.1 which did not incorporate unfortified or fortified farm buildings and are not discussed here. All types of unfortified farm buildings from very small range-type buildings to open complexes were given equal weight for the purposes of this analysis, so we cannot make assumptions about the size or nature of these settlements. Furthermore, we should also remember that there were many other types of buildings and structures that may have formed part of these settlements, so even one-building settlements as presented here should be understood as settlements which had one unfortified farm building as defined in previous sections, but other buildings may also have formed part of these settlements, such as stone huts and non-stone buildings, as discussed in Section 3.1, and other types of structures as will be discussed in the next section.

Of the 1,653 individual unfortified farm buildings in my catalogue, I was able to record accurate co-ordinates for 1,210, either from published sources or by locating them on satellite imagery. To conduct this analysis, I generated multiple spatial buffers from the approximate centres of each building, to determine groups of buildings that fell within 50, 100, 200 or 500 m (Table 5.16) of each other; if the buffers of multiple buildings intersected, these were grouped into a single 'settlement'. This is not to say that there were not relationships between buildings which were further apart than this, but these arbitrary limits give us a point from which to begin discussing how buildings were grouped together and explore patterns in those groupings.

It is unsurprising that as the distance allowed between individual structures increases, the number of settlements falls, but it does confirm that a significant proportion of the unfortified buildings in most regions of Tripolitania could be found within half a kilometer

	Individual buildings	Number of 'settlement' groups			
		50 m	100 m	200 m	500 m
1. W. coastal	43	37	34	33	32
2. W. *gebel*	7	5	5	4	4
3. Southwest	10	10	8	7	7
4. Central coastal	15	15	15	15	15
5. Central *gebel*	82	82	82	79	71
6. E. pre-desert, north	262	219	178	152	107
7. E. pre-desert, south	336	252	205	178	134
8. W. Syrtica	388	315	226	176	121
9. E. Syrtica	67	63	54	44	32
Total	*1,210*	*998*	*807*	*688*	*523*

Table 5.16: *Number of 'settlements' into which unfortified buildings can be grouped based on different distances.*

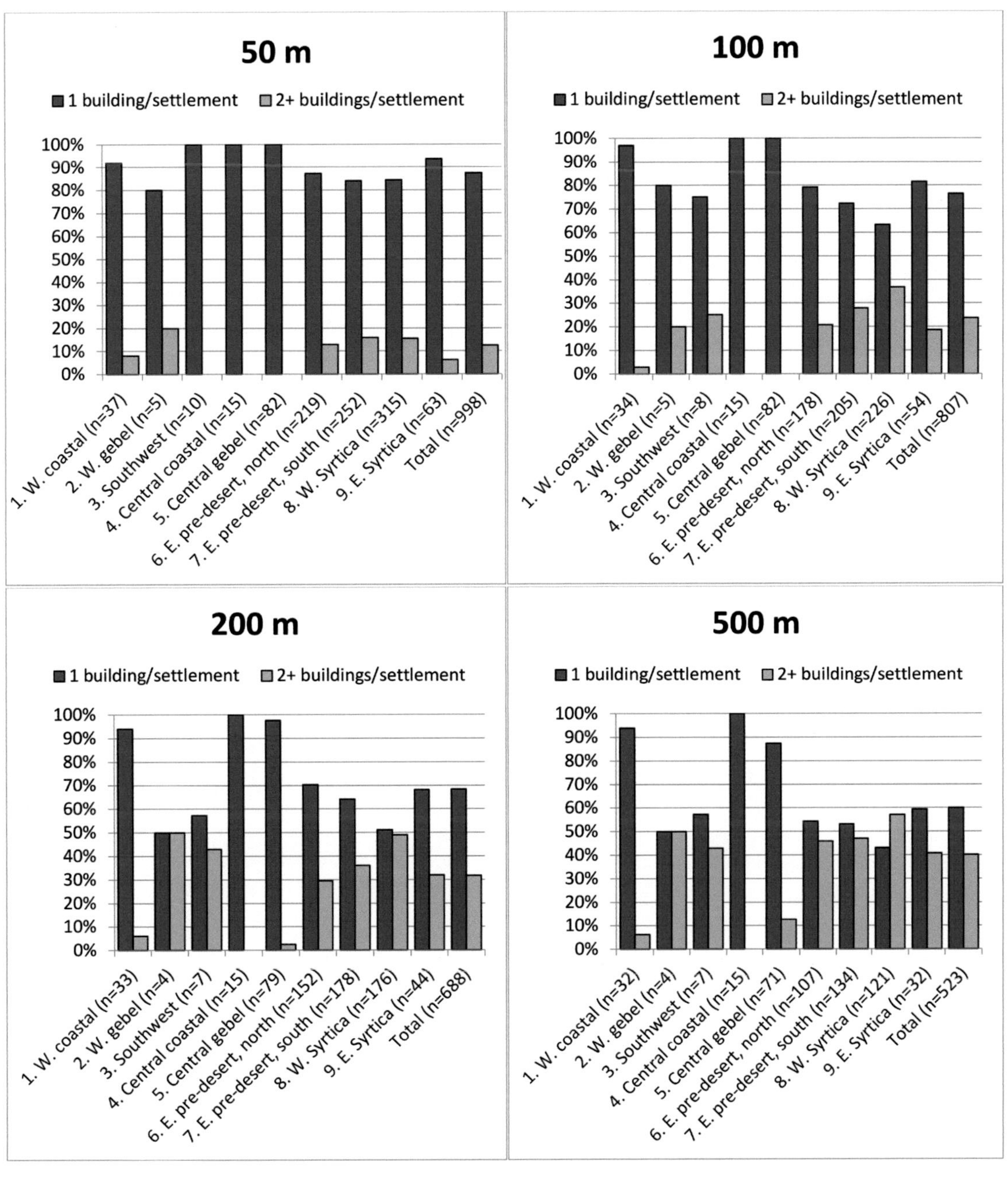

Figure 5.22: *Proportions of settlements with one vs. two or more individual unfortified buildings recorded.*

of one or more neighbours. Interestingly, however, the proportions of single-building settlements compared to those with more than one (ranging between two and more than 20) start to vary by region depending on the distance that is allowed for, as illustrated in Figure 5.22. In almost all cases, the greater number of unfortified settlements was composed of only one recorded building; nevertheless, it is notable that at 500 m distance, in six of the nine regions studied here, the proportion of multi-building settlements exceeded 40%, and in western Syrtica, settlements with multiple buildings actually outnumbered those comprising single buildings. Recorded instances of unfortified settlement in the west *gebel* and the southwest region are much rarer, so drawing conclusions about the density of settlement in these areas is more difficult. But when 500 m distance is allowed for, the proportion of single versus multi-building settlements much more closely matches that of the eastern pre-desert and Syrtica than the western coastal area and the central regions, which may be a factor of more similarity in environments.

In addition, the density of buildings within each of these settlements was not the same in all areas (Table 5.17). When a distance between the centres of buildings of only 50 m is allowed, there is not much variation in the size of settlements, with the average ranging from 1.00 building per settlement (i.e. no unfortified farm buildings were within 50 m of each other) in the southwest and central regions to a maximum of 1.40 in the west *gebel*. However, when we allow for a more dispersed settlement with up to 500 m between individual structures, the range increases to between 1.00 and 3.21 buildings per settlement.

In the central coastal and *gebel* regions few to no recorded unfortified farm buildings were within half a kilometre of each other, nor was this very common in the western regions; in none of these regions did the average settlement size rise above 1.75. However, in the eastern pre-desert and Syrtica, buildings were more often clustered in larger groups, with all the averages over 2.00, particularly in western Syrtica, which had by far the largest average, at 3.21. Furthermore, we can also recall that in the eastern pre-desert and Syrtica, a number of the structures that make up single-building settlements are open complexes, which could be very large structures made up of multiple units and indeed as large as, or larger than many other multi-building settlements.

Although true of all of the analyses above, it is especially important here to be cautious with how we interpret these results. First, all of these calculations measure the distance between buildings and settlements 'as the crow flies' and they do not take into account the terrain, which might include barriers to movement like wadis or cliffs. In addition, the measurements were taken from the centres of the buildings, rather than between the actual perimeters, so that two relatively large buildings that are '50 m apart' may in reality only have a few metres between their external walls.

Second, there is also an assumption in the cluster analysis that buildings of the same type within close proximity of each other were constructed and occupied at the same time. Particularly when it comes to the satellite imagery, it is impossible to know how two buildings relate chronologically, whether one was built later to serve as an addition and expansion to an existing farm or settlement, or was meant as a later replacement for an earlier one, which we know certainly happened when fortified buildings began to gain popularity. When we are dealing with two independent structures, ceramic assemblages may suggest different periods of occupation for each, but in addition to the overall problems with surface materials discussed in Section 3.2, depending on how close together the buildings are, the assemblages may not even be separable and we can only suggest a range of occupation for the site as a whole.

	Individual buildings	Average number of buildings per settlement at various distances			
		50 m	100 m	200 m	500 m
1. W. coastal	43	1.16	1.26	1.30	1.34
2. W. *gebel*	7	1.40	1.40	1.75	1.75
3. Southwest	10	1.00	1.25	1.43	1.43
4. Central coastal	15	1.00	1.00	1.00	1.00
5. Central *gebel*	82	1.00	1.00	1.04	1.15
6. E. pre-desert, north	262	1.20	1.47	1.72	2.45
7. E. pre-desert, south	336	1.33	1.64	1.89	2.51
8. W. Syrtica	388	1.23	1.72	2.20	3.21
9. E. Syrtica	67	1.06	1.24	1.52	2.09
Total	*1,210*	*1.21*	*1.50*	*1.76*	*2.31*

Table 5.17: *Average number of unfortified buildings in recorded settlements.*

Finally, the issue of preservation and recording techniques most clearly has an impact in these analyses. As stated in my methodology, my analyses recorded evidence for standing buildings only, not evidence for settlement in the form of artefact scatters and thus represents an absolute minimum density of known settlement. Furthermore, I can say with absolute certainty that neither my catalogue nor any other survey to date contains records for all of the known buildings in the region; since completing my catalogue I have noted hundreds, if not thousands, more sites using satellite imagery (and other projects doing similar things have reported the same). Thus, any analysis of buildings or settlement density is a starting point only.

Nevertheless, we can put forward some hypotheses as to why settlement distribution and density may have varied in different areas. Differing traditions and systems of land ownership and social organisation were probably an important aspect of this. In the central coastal and *gebel* regions, as well as in the western coastal area, many of the farms were probably owned by wealthy landowners who lived in the coastal cities.[430] Each farm with its surrounding lands was independently owned or leased and completely separate from its neighbours; some perhaps even had strictly defined boundaries. In this case, there was no need or desire for more than one main farm building within close proximity to others.[431]

Given the often-narrow stretches of wadi in which agriculture could be practised and in which herds could be pastured, one might expect buildings in the eastern pre-desert and Syrtica to be further apart than in other areas, but instead we find the opposite. Land was probably not delimited in the same ways in these areas as in the *gebel* and coastal regions and there are a number of reasons why in these areas, more closely clustered settlements may have been advantageous. People may have clustered around the rare water sources such as wells or larger, communal cisterns, and more closely clustered settlements would also have meant that it was easier to share resources in difficult times. Given the greater involvement in pastoralism implied by the large farmyard buildings, it might also have been advantageous to keep multiple herds together when they were not being pastured so that neighbours could help each other with processing activities or for reasons of security. Furthermore, familial, tribal or other social ties may have made it desirable or even necessary to create communities which were geographically closer together.

More complex analyses could be done in future to determine the spatial relationships between different types of buildings. For example, it would be interesting to know the ratio of courtyard to farmyard buildings in the settlements with more than one building or the relative sizes of buildings within each cluster to see whether buildings located closely together were normally of comparable sizes or if there were significant size variations which might suggest hierarchical or dependent relationships.

5.3.2 Other Structures

In addition to those already discussed in sections above and in passing, such as bath buildings and detached enclosures, several other types of buildings associated with the farm buildings and settlements discussed above are known from the Tripolitanian countryside. A common and important type of structure often recorded in association with farm buildings was 'wadi walls' which were constructed along and across wadi beds. The *ULVS* recorded hundreds of walls of varying size and shape, dividing them into different types based on their location, arrangement and form, and countless more are easily identifiable on satellite imagery across the region (Figure 5.23), dating between the early Romano-Libyan (or possibly earlier) and modern times.[432] Many echoed the construction techniques used in the farm buildings themselves, including rubble-filled walls with coursed facings, orthostats, coursed rubble or even just lines of boulders.[433] Most appear to have been built to help control and direct the flow of water and nutrient-rich sediments for agricultural purposes, or to collect the water into cisterns or natural basins for storage. The effort put into the construction and maintenance of structures and systems concerned with water is unsurprising given the relatively dry climate of much of Tripolitania and demonstrates a sophisticated knowledge of how to best exploit the local environment. Other functions which these walls probably played simultaneously included the delineation of field boundaries and perhaps in some cases, the control of stock, though in most instances the recorded walls seem to have been too low for such a function.[434]

Presses have already been discussed in earlier sections, but other structures associated with agricultural and other types of production have also been noted at various farm sites across the region, including threshing floors and storage pits.[435] In addition to the site where

[430] As, for example, appears to have been the case for the wealthy Pudentilla of *Oea*, whose *villa* is mentioned by Apuleius (*Apologia*, 87–88).

[431] Cf. Ahmed 2018: 50–52, on 'agricultural villages'.

[432] Gilbertson *et al.* 1984; Gilbertson & Hunt 1990; 1996; Gilbertson & Chisholm 1996.

[433] Gilbertson & Hunt 1996: 197.

[434] Gilbertson & Hunt 1996: 216–225.

[435] Mattingly & Dore 1996: 133–134.

Lg003-f, Wadi Legwais, E. pre-desert, north
(DigitalGlobe via Google Earth Pro, 14 Dec. 2014)

Unidentified Site, Wadi Meseuggi, E. pre-desert, north
(DigitalGlobe via Google Earth Pro, 14 Dec. 2014)

Figure 5.23: *Wadi walls.*

Kn005, Wadi Khanafes, E. pre-desert, south (*ULVS* Archive: F156/N28/1.12.1980)

An001a, Wadi Antar, E. pre-desert, north (*ULVS* Archive: F447/N6/14.10.1981)

Ghirza Tomb North C, E. pre-desert, south (Brogan & Smith 1984: Plate 74, a)

Ghirza Tomb South A, E. pre-desert, south (Brogan & Smith 1984: Plate 96, a; reproduced from Bauer 1935: fig. 14)

Figure 5.24: *Examples of mausolea.*

Tripolitanian Red Slip Ware appears to have been produced mentioned in Section 3.2.1,[436] a significant finding of the *Tarhuna Archaeological Survey* in the central *gebel* was several amphora kilns.[437] Temples, sanctuaries and other religious buildings and sites have been more rarely recorded in rural Tripolitania, and those that have been recorded tended to be relatively small, basic structures. Probably not many more than a dozen sites which can be identified as sanctuaries, temples or altars are currently known beyond the coastal centres, including those associated with the military sites as discussed in the last chapter, and of these, only a few can be associated with a known deity.[438]

Many cemeteries and tombs which were associated with farms and agricultural settlements have also been recorded in Tripolitania. Often these took the form of simple cairns, small cist tombs or hypogea, but at least 130 monumental mausolea have also been recorded in Tripolitania to date, the majority of which can most likely be dated to between the first and fourth centuries AD.[439] The majority of the known examples come from the central *gebel* and the eastern pre-desert, including the most well-known and most frequently cited from the settlement of Ghirza, though several are also known from the central coastal area and the western coastal and *gebel* regions.[440] In contrast to most of the farm buildings

[436] See fn. 179.

[437] Ahmed 2010: 246–285.

[438] Brogan & Smith 1984: 80–92; Rebuffat 1990a; Brouquier-Reddé 1992; Mattingly & Dore 1996: 141–142; Cadotte 2007: 431–452, *et passim*.

[439] Nikolaus 2016; 2017. I am very grateful to Julia Nikolaus for allowing me to read a draft of her article before publication and discussing her PhD thesis with me at length.

[440] For example, *Ghirza*: Bauer 1935; Brogan & Smith 1984; *Gasr Doga*: Aurigemma 1954; Bigi *et al.* 2009; *Various*: Brogan 1965a; Brogan 1978; Abdussaid 1996; Abdussaid 1998; Ben Rabha & Masturzo 1997; Faraj 1996; Matoug 1998, and many others.

in the eastern pre-desert, many of these often very large mausolea were constructed using ashlar masonry and frequently had elaborate sculptural decoration and/or inscriptions (Figure 5.24). The investment of resources into the construction and decoration of elaborate mausolea attests to the importance of these monuments and demonstrated the wealth and power of the rural elite who could afford to construct them. The inscriptions found on them as well as the fact that they were physically clustered together emphasised the importance of family lineage and groups, suggesting that a form of ancestor worship was an important aspect of Romano-Libyan culture,[441] and potentially supports the idea suggested above that farms tended to be clustered along family ties. There is also some evidence that monumental mausolea might have acted as landmarks and boundary markers.[442] In this light, then, it is perhaps not surprising that the conspicuous display of resources through the use of ashlar masonry and elaborate sculptural decoration was applied more frequently to funerary contexts than domestic ones.

5.4 Discussion

The analyses presented above have revealed a variety of trends in the frequency and distribution of different physical characteristics such as the plan, size and construction of unfortified farm buildings and settlements across nine different regions of the Tripolitanian countryside. In this section I will summarise the results of the analyses presented above and continue the discussion of the wider implications of the similarities and differences in the appearance and construction of these farms within and between these different regions, and some of the possible reasons behind them.

A large number of farm sites have been recorded by surveys in the central coastal and *gebel* regions, but the number for which we have specific data on their physical characteristics is unfortunately low, particularly with regards to size and plan. Based on the information that we do have, however, the unfortified farm buildings of these regions were largely characterised by the use of ashlar masonry types, particularly *opus africanum*, and the prevalence of the courtyard building type. On average, these buildings were more than twice the size of unfortified buildings in the other areas of rural Tripolitania. A notable percentage of the unfortified buildings had evidence for press facilities: 30% in the coastal area and 92% in the *gebel*. A significant proportion also had evidence of luxury features (30% in the coastal region and 19% in the *gebel*), such as baths, marble or mosaics, particularly in the large coastal examples. Similar findings were reported by surveys undertaken in the region of *Lepcis Magna* for which individual entries were not included in my catalogue and analyses.[443]

Although there were some differences between the eastern pre-desert regions and Syrtica, they seem to have had far more in common with each other than either did with the central regions. In these areas, the farmyard type building was far more prominent, though the buildings within this category ranged widely in size and complexity. Most construction did not employ ashlar blocks in any capacity, the most popular building techniques being coursed rubble or drystone, followed by forms of regular and irregular masonry. Courtyard farm buildings and ashlar building techniques did occur in these regions, but unlike in the central regions, they were a clear minority. Only 6% of the unfortified buildings in the northern part of the eastern pre-desert and 3% in the southern part had press elements reported and only two examples of possible presses are known from the 487 examples in western Syrtica and none at all from eastern Syrtica. Luxury materials or amenities were noted at less than 1% of the unfortified farm buildings in the eastern pre-desert or Syrtica.

The figures for the frequency of presses and luxury materials in the pre-desert and Syrtica reflect a minimum reality. A far greater percentage of the unfortified buildings in the eastern pre-desert and Syrtica (particularly the latter) were identified using satellite imagery than in other areas, and so it is of course possible that ground surveys will reveal that a number of these examples do, in fact, have presses or luxury materials. Nevertheless, the contrast in the frequency of these features between the central regions and the eastern pre-desert and Syrtica regions is wide enough to suggest that the trends are still likely to reflect some degree of reality.

Although comparatively poor when contrasted with the evidence from the east, we can still draw some tentative conclusions about the data for the western coastal and *gebel* regions. In many ways, the patterns visible in the unfortified building data seem to reflect a situation that was somewhere between those of the central *gebel*/coastal area and the eastern pre-desert/Syrtica. Courtyard buildings across these two regions were reported in higher proportions than in the eastern pre-desert and Syrtica, but were still fewer in number than farmyard buildings. However, it is important to note that the highest proportion were of undifferentiated open type, and more fieldwork will be required to get a better sense of what the true situation may be.

On average, the buildings of the west were smaller than those for the central *gebel* and coastal regions.

[441] Mattingly 2003a; Nikolaus 2016; Ray & Nikolaus 2019: 95–96.

[442] Jones & Barker 1983: 53; Mattingly & Flower 1996: 188–189; Fontana 1997.

[443] Munzi *et al.* 2016: 70–73.

Those in the western coastal zone were slightly larger or comparable to those in the eastern pre-desert and Syrtica, while the average size of the unfortified buildings in the western *gebel* was the smallest across all nine regions. The sample size of the latter was relatively small, with only seven buildings having their size recorded, but this points to the idea that the *gebel* region of the west may not have been the same type of productive and wealthy area as it was in the central region.

In the matter of construction, the west matches the situation in the central *gebel* and coastal regions more closely, with a clear preference for ashlar masonry techniques, particularly *opus africanum*. The proportion of sites at which presses and luxury elements were reported was 12 and 10%, respectively in the western coastal area, and 11% in both instances for the western *gebel* region (although in each case this was only one out of nine sites), again placing this group firmly between the results for the central *gebel*/coastal area and the eastern pre-desert/Syrtica. The proportion of presses is on the low side, and Mrabet suggests that this indicates that oleoculture was probably not the only or main occupation of the farmers in this region;[444] however, is it is notable that two of the six sites which had presses in the western coastal region had four and six presses respectively, more than any in the eastern pre-desert or Syrtica where the maximum number of presses known from any one site seems to have been two. In addition, the town of Limagues (not included in my catalogue because there was no specific architectural evidence) was recorded by Trousset as having '*nombreuses meules et de debris de pressoirs*' in its vicinity.[445]

The data for the southwestern region remains unfortunately poor and there are wide gaps in our knowledge of unfortified settlement in this region. The data from this region were based mainly on the evidence gathered from satellite surveys I conducted in four areas of the southwestern *gebel* and pre-desert (see Section 2.4), with a few pieces of evidence from elsewhere. I recorded ten possible unfortified buildings, spread over three areas (the last produced no unfortified sites), six of which were located in the vicinity of the oasis of Sinawan, and the reliability of their identification is questionable. We have no data concerning the construction techniques used or decoration of these structures, but all seem to have been of the open type and an average size comparable to that of the eastern pre-desert and Syrtica regions.

Much of the disparity in the size of buildings, the use of ashlar building techniques, and the distribution of luxury materials and facilities between the different regions can probably be connected to the relative success of the agricultural and pastoralist pursuits in those same regions, which were largely dependent on the environment. Simply put, larger buildings, ashlar masonry and luxury features required more resources and wealth, which could be generated through agricultural production, as evidenced by the high number of presses. The highest levels of rainfall in Tripolitania are to be found in the central *gebel* and coastal regions, followed by the western coastal area and *gebel*. The proximity of the coastal and *gebel* zones in both the central and west regions to the coastal urban centres would also have meant more access to material resources as well as more exposure to Mediterranean architectural trends and technologies and the specialists who designed and installed decorative features.

In the pre-desert and Syrtica (and probably also the southwest), where the evidence does not point to much that we would call luxury, we can remember, however, that in the earliest phases of sedentarisation the construction of stone buildings would have made a distinct mark in the landscape. Since there was very little pre-existing stone architecture, even if they were not especially huge or elaborate by the standards of the *gebel* or coastal regions, they may have been particularly impressive to those peoples who had not yet made the transition to sedentarism (and perhaps never would). The construction of courtyard and even farmyard buildings represented a significant investment of time, effort and resources and would therefore have been a very visible and meaningful declaration of participation in a new way of life and a new economic system based on settled agriculture. In addition, stone buildings served as permanent, immediately visible symbols of wealth and the control of resources, and therefore possibly also status, potentially making the adoption of this kind of architecture and settlement that much more appealing to an elite class.

The differences in the size and construction of the buildings between the regions of Tripolitania discussed above also raise some questions about the adoption and spread of architectural trends and technologies themselves. As discussed in Section 3.2, ceramic evidence suggests that the sedentarisation of the countryside probably started in the Hellenistic period in the immediate hinterlands of the urban coastal hinterlands in both east and west, spreading into the *gebel* regions by the second to first centuries BC, and probably not reaching the pre-desert regions and Syrtica until the mid to late first century AD.

The courtyard building was potentially present on farms in the immediate hinterlands of the coastal centres from early in this period of sedentarisation. The form had a long history throughout the Mediterranean,

[444] Mrabet 2011: 234–236. He suggests that this lower importance is reflected also in the quality of the construction of the presses themselves.

[445] Trousset 1974: 50, Site 18 (Limagues).

with courtyard buildings reported in Italy from as early as the sixth century BC,[446] and several examples of courtyard buildings have been identified in rural Punic settlements around the Mediterranean coast, including North Africa, from around the third century BC.[447] Their adoption in the coastal and *gebel* regions of Tripolitania therefore seems to have been part of a larger tradition of the form's use in the immediate hinterlands of Hellenistic-Punic coastal settlements around the Mediterranean. Its continued use in the coastal and *gebel* regions of Tripolitania into the Roman period is not at all surprising and courtyard buildings are also well attested throughout the rest of *Africa Proconsularis* during the Roman period.[448]

The fact that it is sometimes difficult to make a distinction between courtyard and farmyard buildings shows that there were clear similarities and overlap in their forms. However, the different patterns of distribution and trends in construction outlined in previous sections support the idea that there is much more to this distinction than simply the degree of regularity or fineness of construction that one could achieve. While courtyard buildings appear to have referenced the Hellenistic-Punic architectural traditions outlined above, I would argue that the farmyard type building developed separately in the eastern pre-desert and Syrtica in response to the changing settlement patterns and needs of the inhabitants of those regions, but also owed a significant debt to pre-existing traditions.

As discussed in previous chapters, before the first century AD, there are thought to have been few sedentary inhabitants in these regions. These areas were home to and utilised by various semi-nomadic pastoralist groups, chiefly the *Macae*, *Nasamones* and *Garamantes*. The earliest classes of imported ceramics known from these regions, dated to the first century AD, were found at farm sites in all of the areas surveyed in the pre-desert and Syrtica,[449] which implies that sedentarisation was a geographically widespread phenomenon from the beginning and occurred at more or less the same time throughout the region.[450] An important factor to consider, then, when thinking about the development of settlement and construction of buildings in the pre-desert and Syrtica is the extent to which we believe that the settlement of the indigenous peoples and the transition to a mixed agricultural-pastoral economy was or was not the result of 'official' encouragement or even pressure. The apparent rapidity and thoroughness with which sedentarisation occurred might suggest that there was some common incentive to do so. However, there is no evidence for any kind of deliberate settlement policy, and indeed, as long as their actions were properly controlled and supervised, semi-nomadic peoples could serve a useful role in the economy, providing avenues for trade and seasonal labour.[451]

Rather, Grahame has argued that pastoralist families or groups which were already successful recognised that there was much to be gained by increasing their emphasis on agricultural activities. As already mentioned in Section 5.2.3, in many pastoralist societies, wealth and status were often measured in livestock, but the unpredictability of the environment meant that increasing the size of one's flock could be very risky as it became more difficult to feed and water huge numbers of animals and the labour needed to tend them. As a result, there were frequent changes in the fortunes of different families and power dynamics quickly shifted. However, while there were also risks associated with agriculture, increasing investment in agriculture while continuing to undertake pastoral activities presented a way for those with large flocks to consolidate and provide more security for their wealth and position, ultimately leading to the emergence of an elite class. Grahame suggests that this development only occurred at this point in time due to the stability in the region that resulted from Roman imperialism, as it probably put an end to, or at least lessened, any major regional wars or feuds between different families or communities.[452] We can also suggest that local peoples must have perceived some benefit to taking part in the Roman economy through the production and trade of agricultural goods. In many ways, therefore, sedentarisation can be seen as a largely indigenous initiative, made possible, or in some cases maybe even necessary, by the changing political and economic environment. Even if it was not enforced, it is not hard to imagine that this kind of integration and participation of these peoples into the Roman economic system might have been encouraged and supported.[453]

[446] Colantoni 2012; Meyers 2012.

[447] Van Dommelen & Gómez Bellard 2008, especially chapters by Fentress & Docter, Gómez Bellard, López Castro, and van Dommelen & Finocchi. See also Fentress 2001. Cf. plans of buildings recorded at Can Sorà, Ibiza (Gómez Bellard 2008: 53, fig. 3.3), Daïat, Morocco (Ponsich 1970: fig. 57), and Sa Tanca 'e sa Mura, Sardinia (Madau 1997: 142).

[448] For example, Hitchner 1988; 1989; Hitchner *et al.* 1990; Carlsen & Tvarnø 1990; Dietz, Ladjimi Sebaï, & Ben Hassen 1995; de Vos 2000.

[449] Primarily Italian and Gaulish *terra sigillatas*: Reddé 1988: 78–80; Mattingly & Flower 1996: 160–163; Dore 1996: 321–331; LeQuesne, Basell, & Sheibani 2010: 24.

[450] Rather than, for example, being developed or imported into a few select areas and then spreading outwards (Mattingly 1998: 170–171).

[451] Garnsey 1978: 232–233.

[452] Grahame 1998.

[453] Mattingly 1995: 76, 144–147; 1996a: 319–325; 1998. See also Reddé 1985: 179–180. We should also bear in mind that given how difficult it is to trace transhumance archaeologically, we have very little idea what proportion of the total population was occupying these buildings, and what proportion continued to practise semi-nomadic pastoralism.

Another factor relevant to this change may have been the formal delimitation of tribal lands, which in turn may have prompted a change in ideas about land ownership, from communal lands to private estates;[454] the suggestion mentioned above that monumental mausolea may have acted as property boundaries is perhaps evidence of this. The ways in which this sedentarisation developed in the eastern pre-desert and Syrtica regions were probably driven by several factors that differentiated it from other parts of Tripolitania and North Africa. The first was basic environmental restraints: sedentary agriculture requires water, and so, that settlement developed along the wadi systems makes sense. Furthermore, using a GIS analysis of the *ULVS* material, Flower and Mattingly demonstrated that while the establishment of distinct 'estates' may have occurred early on, these were not determined by the division of lands into equal parcels, as was the case, for example, with the centuriation of other parts of *Africa Proconsularis.* Rather, the earliest farms seem to have been established at junctions and headwaters where the maximum water catchment could be achieved. The areas between these points were then infilled as settlement expanded. That infilling along the less desirable parts of the wadi occurred in this way, rather than people seeking out their own junctions or headwaters suggests that there was something keeping them within the vicinity of the earlier establishments, again, likely some kind of social-cultural ties or obligations.[455]

As emphasised in previous sections, we rarely have evidence which securely dates the construction of unfortified farm buildings in the eastern pre-desert or Syrtica, so technically it is impossible to say for certain whether the unfortified farm buildings which are the subject of this chapter were directly associated with or the result of the sedentarisation implied by the ceramic data. However, in the absence of evidence to the contrary, a correlation between the two seems likely. That the construction of stone farm buildings was connected in some way to sedentarisation is a reasonable enough notion – it would make little sense to invest the considerable energy and resources that must have gone into the construction of large stone buildings if they were not meant to be utilised regularly.

In any case, the botanical analyses discussed earlier provide fairly conclusive evidence for the cultivation of cereals and other foodstuffs in the wadis of the eastern pre-desert. That this was on a relatively large and organised scale is also evidenced by the many wadi walls found near many farm sites which would have been used to aid in irrigation. However, the long-term success of these ventures in the eastern pre-desert and Syrtica is up for some debate. Without the initial investment in and continual maintenance of irrigation installations, rainfall levels were simply not high enough to support much more than subsistence level farming. While the presence of any presses at all in the eastern pre-desert suggests a surplus production of wine or olive oil for distribution, in comparison to the *gebel* and coastal regions they were still relatively rare, and it seems unlikely that the farms of the eastern pre-desert and Syrtica would ever have been able to really compete with their neighbours to the north and west.

It is not a coincidence that the proportion of the buildings in which presses were found in the pre-desert and Syrtica which were of the courtyard type was much higher than the overall average. Wine or oil production might have been a relatively new occupation in those regions. Since there was little previous tradition of stone architecture in the region, it does not seem strange to think that those who decided to try their hand at this occupation, who must have been wealthy enough to acquire and install the necessary equipment and buildings and own enough trees or vines to make this worthwhile, would have borrowed the design for their farms from buildings in areas where that type of production was already well-established, i.e. the *gebel* and coastal area.[456]

It is probable, however, that most of the inhabitants of the pre-desert and Syrtica could not rely on agricultural production alone for their survival and income. And why would they? Considering the important role of pastoralism prior to the first century AD, taken together with the evidence of the faunal remains recovered during excavation, the notion that stock-keeping and pastoralism continued alongside agriculture as an extremely important occupation in those regions is an obvious and uncontroversial conclusion. However, by creating a sedentary base, larger work forces could be supported and agricultural activities made it easier to keep both people and larger flocks of animals fed.[457]

The farmyard form, therefore, was a product of the new mixed pastoral-agricultural economy being practised. I argued earlier that corralling and protecting animals was probably an important function of both courtyards and farmyards. In the case of the farmyards, I would take this one step further and suggest that in the pre-desert and Syrtica at least, the corralling and stabling of animals was, in fact, the primary function of the farmyard and the motivation behind the development of the building type. Before widespread sedentarisation took place, animals could be allowed to graze

[454] Brett & Fentress 1996: 53.

[455] Flower & Mattingly 1995: 65ff.; Mattingly 1997.

[456] Mattingly, Barker, & Jones 1996: 112.

[457] Grahame 1998: 103.

freely in whatever wild vegetation grew in the wadi beds. However, as sedentary agriculture began to increase in importance, it may have become more necessary to have places where one could corral herds of animals to keep them from running free in the now-extensively cultivated wadis. The ubiquity of the farmyard form and the clear effort that must have gone into their construction reflects the continued prominence and importance of stock-keeping in the lives of the peoples in the eastern pre-desert and Syrtica during the Romano-Libyan period.

Interestingly, it has been argued by some authors that farmyard buildings directly referenced pastoralist encampments in their construction.[458] The development and use of these buildings in these regions, therefore, would have had significant meaning to those who constructed, occupied and viewed them, particularly when they first began to be adopted. On one hand, they still referenced traditional forms of settlement, but on the other, were physical manifestations of a change in lifestyle and economic strategies, and also a reflection of the successes made possible by that change.

The interregional analyses summarised above give us a broad picture of the Tripolitanian countryside, but downplay the heterogeneity of size, form and construction which was also prevalent within each of these regions. In most regions, there is a visible hierarchy of forms, with farms of *opus africanum* and courtyard type buildings at the top and small, irregularly constructed farmyard buildings and huts at the bottom. However, the socio-economic significance of the differences between farms of smaller and larger size within the various regions is not always clear. It may have been that in some cases at least, smaller farms were occupied by tenants or even slaves, who were attached to or dependent on large elite estates. In theory, the owners of the estates would then have profited from the exploitation of labour and the collection of rents or dues.

We have little direct evidence for this kind of system in Tripolitania but comparisons have previously been drawn with the organisation of the large, imperial estates in western *Africa Proconsularis* (modern Tunisia) which provide a likely model (though on a much larger scale).[459] In the case of the regions closer to the coast, there is a high likelihood that the owners of these estates lived in the cities, though the presence of the luxury features suggests that they would also have spent time at their country houses. A well-known literary example which provides support for this is Apuleius' mention in the *Apologia* of the *villae* in the region of *Oea*, owned by his rich wife Pudentilla.[460] A similar system probably operated in the territories around all of the coastal cities. A milestone marking 44 *milia* found in the *gebel* probably once marked the end of *Lepcis*' territory, attesting to the large area which included almost all of the sites from the central region discussed here, and which was probably under the control of the people in that city.[461] The *Antonine Itinerary* also gives us the names of six *villae* along the coastal route between *Tacape* and *Lepcis*, with Kolendo arguing that *Villa Magna*, *villa privata* (LT05-v) was potentially an imperial estate.[462]

We are far less informed about the socio-economic organisation and relationships between the farms in the eastern pre-desert and Syrtica. As previously argued by the authors of the *ULVS*, the larger courtyard farm buildings and in particular the use of ashlar masonry techniques in the pre-desert, combined with the presence of impressively large and well-built mausolea associated with these sites, were almost certainly indicative of an elite class, who perhaps controlled estates of various size.[463] However, how common this situation was, especially in earlier periods, or whether a greater number of farmers were more or less independent is not always clear, and probably there were examples of both systems. I would speculate that when buildings of a more or less similar form were clustered together as described in the previous section, however, these represented small hamlets of farms of equal status, perhaps related by family or other social ties; though this still does not exclude the possibility that they were attached or beholden in some way to larger estates, the centres of which were located further away.

In Syrtica, there is far less evidence for either the use of *opus africanum* or large-scale mausolea. In addition, as shown above, while there were still farms of a very large size, they were smaller in number and the largest of the Syrtica examples did not rival the scale of the largest farms found in the eastern pre-desert. This can partially be explained by the environmental factors already discussed determining the degree of agricultural productivity achievable in the region. It is probable that the degree of surplus and profit which would be necessary to construct the largest of the farms in the pre-desert, let alone acquire the luxury features of the *gebel* and coastal areas, was simply not achievable in Syrtica. On the other hand, the scarcity of both of these features might indicate that the elite class of this region chose not to display their status and wealth through domestic or funerary

[458] Finkelstein 1995: 46–49; Liverani 2005a: 397.

[459] Mattingly 1995: 147;1996a: 323–324. On the issue of private and imperial estates and tenancy in *Africa Proconsularis*: Kehoe 1988; 2007: 56–62, *et passim*, 2013; Hobson 2012: 41–83; de Vos 2013.

[460] For example, Apuleius, *Apologia*, 87–88.

[461] Mattingly 1995: 140.

[462] Kolendo 1986.

[463] Mattingly, Barker, & Jones 1996; Mattingly & Dore 1996: 118–119.

architecture. Mattingly has suggested that this difference could have, at least partly, been due to an actual lack of an elite class in this area, perhaps as a result of Roman campaigns which dealt harshly with the *Nasamones* in response to their revolt of the late first century AD.[464] The fact that in this region we find more instances of buildings clustered together into small settlements, normally without any single or central building that stands out, might support Mattingly's suggestion, and that the social organisation was much more egalitarian rather than based on elite estates.

We can also ask ourselves what the relationship of the people in the eastern pre-desert and Syrtica with their neighbours to the north, west and on the coast was, and how their involvement in wider imperial networks and economies compared. The presence of ceramics and other Roman goods clearly indicates that many peoples in the region, not only the elite, were involved in Roman trade networks to some extent. It also suggests that many of these unfortified farms were established in the late first or second century AD, potentially long before the southern expansion of the *limes* and the establishment of the major forts at Gheriat el-Garbia/*Myd[...]* and Bu Njem/*Gholaia*. If many of the owners of the farms of the central and western coastal and *gebel* regions actually lived in or had ties to the coastal cities, they were most likely tied into the larger imperial economic networks and systems, had to pay taxes, etc. But what was the legal or official status of these people who lived further from the coastal centres in the first two centuries AD and how might that have changed when the frontier was expanded? Did these people pay taxes? Evidence from other parts of North Africa suggests that indigenous leaders, through which the Roman state might have a degree of influence and control over tribal groups, were, as Brett and Fentress put it, co-opted, and in return their leadership was given legitimacy; they might even be given Roman citizenship, with the many advantages that could bring. It is probable that these sorts of schemes occurred in Tripolitania as well, though to what extent and how many people this directly affected is still unknown.[465]

[464] Mattingly 1998: 175–178. *Nasamonian* revolt: Mattingly 1995: 72–73; Dio 67.4.6.

[465] Brett & Fentress 1996: 50–80; Grahame 1998: 104–106.

chapter six

Fortified Architecture and Settlement

In this chapter, I will present analyses of some of the main physical characteristics of the fortified rural buildings and settlements of Tripolitania, as well as exploring the ways in which these buildings and settlements compared to their unfortified counterparts, and what this implies about the development of settlement in rural Tripolitania from the third century AD onwards. Fortified buildings are identified as those which are characterised by one or more features typically associated with defense, such as high external or enclosure walls, substantial, multi-storeyed construction, single, defensible entrances, few and small windows or surrounding ditches and banks, often combined with location in naturally defensible positions such as steep hilltops or isolated spurs. However, while defense was undoubtedly an important factor in the design and incorporation of many of the characteristics of these buildings, it was not necessarily the only one, and this chapter will also explore some of the other reasons why the adoption of fortified building types may have been desirable.

6.1 Fortified Farmhouses, Forts and *Gsur*: Terminology

For the same reasons discussed with respect to unfortified buildings, I will generally refer to civilian fortified structures simply as 'fortified (farm) buildings' in order to differentiate between farms as socio-economic settlements and the individual structures themselves. As discussed in Chapter 4, early reports and studies often used military terms, both modern and ancient, for any and all types of fortified buildings;[466] sometimes this was meant simply in the broad sense of 'stronghold', but in others, it was almost certainly due to confusion over the role of fortified buildings in the countryside and problems with differentiating between military and civilian buildings. Another term frequently used in North Africa and the Middle East for a wide variety of fortified buildings and settlements (and indeed, sometimes unfortified ones) is the Arabic word *gasr* (plural *gsur*).[467] This word can be variously translated as 'castle', 'palace', 'fort', or 'fortified village', and does not necessarily refer to any specific building type or any particular time period. In English sources concerned with Tripolitania, it is most commonly used interchangeably with 'fortified farmhouse', and usually refers specifically to the classic tower-like buildings for which the central pre-desert and *gebel* of modern Libya are particularly well-known, but also commonly for fortified sites from the Islamic period and beyond, in particular the iconic fortified granaries of southeast Tunisia. In order to avoid any confusion or ambiguity, I have tried to avoid using the term and will continue to do so, except where referring to older studies which used it or where it forms part of the proper name of a site or building.

Only two Latin terms attested epigraphically can be specifically connected with any confidence to non-military fortified buildings in Tripolitania. The first, *centenarium*, was already introduced in Section 4.1.1, known from two Latino-Punic inscriptions. As previously discussed, it is possible that the term originated in reference to granaries, but was perhaps extended to mean a fortified storehouse or structure more generally. The second term is *turris*, which was obviously also applicable in military contexts, but is attested at Henchir el-Gueciret/

[466] For example, Guérin 1862; Toussaint 1905; 1906; Cagnat & Merlin 1920, Goodchild 1950b; Trousset 1974. For discussion of the term *fortin* in particular, see also Lecat 2012; Mattingly, Sterry, & Leitch 2013: 170.

[467] The standard Arabic form قصر can also be found transliterated as *qasr* (pl. *qsur*) or *ksar* (pl. *ksour*), with the latter more commonly used in contexts where French was the colonial language, e.g. Tunisia. Interestingly, it may actually have come from the Latin word *castrum* (Shahîd 2002: 67–75; Kerr 2005: 1 fn.2; Munzi, Schirru, & Tantillo 2014: en.15).

Turris Maniliorum Arelliorum (RLT086-g), a building for which there is strong evidence of a civilian origin.[468]

As was the case with the unfortified farm buildings in the last chapter, we must also consider that Latin was probably not the common language of many rural peoples, an idea supported by the more or less equal use of non-Latin languages in the few known inscriptions associated with these buildings.[469] Krahmalkov has suggested that the Punic term *MGDL* might be translated as 'tall, tower-like building', though his reading of the example which he cites for its possible use in Tripolitania, probably from a tomb in the Wadi Scetaf (eastern pre-desert, south), is not universally accepted.[470] Otherwise, we are unfortunately in the dark as to what local terms may have existed for these buildings.

6.2 Physical Characteristics and Analyses

I have collected data on 810 structures which are certainly or probably classifiable as non-military fortified farm buildings across the nine regions of Tripolitania established in earlier chapters (Table 6.1; Figure 6.1). The number of fortified structures recorded is slightly more evenly spread across the nine regions than was the case with the unfortified buildings, but there are nevertheless areas with very small sample sizes and we must accept that until better samples can be incorporated, our analyses of these areas will carry less weight in our overall interpretations than others for which the data are more robust.

In the following sections, I will discuss and present quantitative and qualitative analyses for four main physical characteristics of these structures: plan, size, materials and construction, and decoration and inscriptions. In addition, as in the last chapter, I will include a discussion of how the presence of pressing facilities may relate to various features in fortified settlements and structures.

6.2.1 Form and Plan

As was the case with the unfortified structures discussed in the last chapter, there is a great deal of variability in the forms of fortified civilian settlement and architecture both between and within different regions of Tripolitania. In addition, it is useful to remind ourselves again, that the building forms analysed in this section are based on what is currently visible (or was at the time of their original recording), which is dependent on preservation conditions and usually representative of a building's latest phase. This is a particular issue with respect to the fortified buildings discussed here as our ignorance of possible alterations, additions or renovations that some of these buildings may have undergone potentially disguises the number of fortified buildings which actually began their lives as unfortified. Unfortunately, without more on-the-ground investigations at a larger sample of sites, the nature and timing of these types of activities remain poorly understood.

Previous Typologies

Because of their often excellent preservation, the fortified buildings of ancient Tripolitania have been the subject of drawings and descriptions of scholars and travellers for at least two centuries (longer, in many cases, than their unfortified counterparts). However, as in the last chapter, the differing methodologies and agendas of these previous investigations have resulted in inconsistency in the terminology and categorisation used for fortified buildings and settlement in different areas. As a result, even where existing typologies for fortified buildings are useful for particular regions or subsets of the data, most are inadequate for a discussion and comparative analysis of sites across Tripolitania as a whole.

Probably the earliest attempt at organising these fortified buildings of Tripolitania in a systematic manner was that undertaken by Goodchild, who investigated a number of examples from the eastern pre-desert and central *gebel* in the late 1940s and '50s. Goodchild identified the structures he found in both areas as fortified farmhouses, most of which were square or rectangular multi-storey structures, characterised by thick walls and a single, defensible entrance. These he divided into six types based on different internal arrangements of rooms around an open court or lightwell and in some cases the addition of external, projecting towers.[471]

Goodchild observed two main differences between the fortified farmhouses that he recorded in the *gebel* and those in the pre-desert. The first was that many of the *gebel* examples were surrounded by ditches, whereas this was a relatively rare occurrence in the pre-desert. Since Goodchild assumed that the function of the ditches would primarily have been defensive, his explanation for this was that ditches were largely unnecessary in the pre-desert because there were more naturally defensive sites available there on the steep wadi sides. Other than this, he concluded that in terms of their plan there was little difference between the fortified farmhouses of the *gebel* and those of the pre-desert. The second difference Goodchild noted was that the fortified structures of the *gebel* were generally in a more ruined state (which he attributed to the greater rainfall in that region), unfortunately making their internal plans far more difficult to

[468] *CIL* 8.22774.

[469] See Section 6.2.5.

[470] Krahmalkov 2000: 269. Cf. Brogan & Reynolds 1960: 54, no. 7; Kerr 2010: 208.

[471] Goodchild 1950b: 36, fig. 6.

	All	Published	%	Satellite	%
1. W. coastal	138	88	64	50	36
2. W. *gebel*	84	78	93	6	7
3. Southwest	13	5	38	8	62
4. Central coastal	6	6	100	–	–
5. Central *gebel*	153	122	80	31	20
6. E. pre-desert, north	289	239	83	50	17
7. E. pre-desert, south	92	82	89	10	11
8. W. Syrtica	19	9	47	10	53
9. E. Syrtica	16	–	–	16	100
Total	*810*	*629*	*78*	*181*	*22*

Table 6.1: *Number of fortified buildings identified in each sub-region of Tripolitania.*

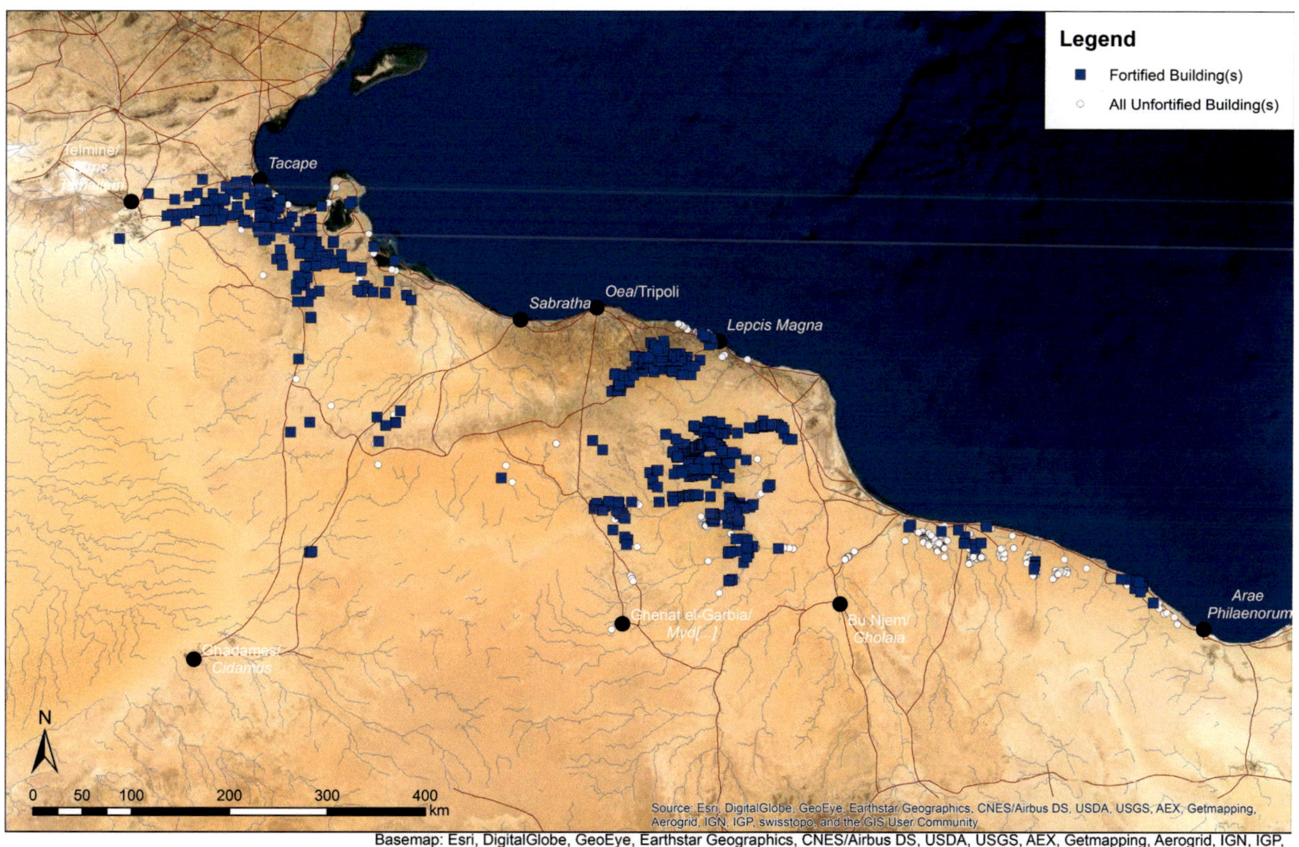

Basemap: Esri, DigitalGlobe, GeoEye, Earthstar Geographics, CNES/Airbus DS, USDA, USGS, AEX, Getmapping, Aerogrid, IGN, IGP, swisstopo, and the GIS User Community
Drainage: Lehner, B., Verdin, K., Jarvis, A. (2008): New global hydrography derived from spaceborne elevation data. Eos, Transactions, AGU, 89(10): 93-94. Retrieved from http://hydrosheds.cr.usgs.gov (15 sec Flow Accumulation)
Roads (Barrington Atlas): Ancient World Mapping Center (2012)

Figure 6.1: *Distribution of all catalogued fortified buildings (n=810).*

understand without excavation. As a result, his proposed typology was based more on the evidence of the pre-desert examples than the *gebel* ones.[472]

A few years after Goodchild published his initial work, Oates also published the results of the survey he had undertaken in the central *gebel*.[473] In addition to the free-standing tower-like *gsur* described by Goodchild, however, Oates also observed a number of structures which could still be considered defended by virtue of their location or surrounding ditches, but which more closely resembled the unfortified, open farm buildings discussed in the last chapter, consisting of a rectilinear enclosure with ranges of rooms or building complexes within; in some cases this included a multi-storeyed tower akin to the *gsur* described above, but not always. Like Goodchild, Oates emphasised the advanced state of ruin of many

[472] Goodchild 1950b: 34–37; 1951c: 59–62.

[473] Oates 1953; 1954.

of the farms of the *gebel*, and the difficulties associated with judging the original height or number of storeys a building may have had from the size of the rubble mound left.[474] He also noted that many *gsur* were located in close proximity to, or sometimes directly on top of, earlier, unfortified olive farms, often reusing the older masonry.

Slightly further east, Brogan recorded a number of fortified farm sites in the region southwest of Misurata where the coastal plain transitions into the pre-desert (overlapping slightly with the northeastern part of the *ULVS* area), dividing them into eight categories. Brogan deliberately did not use the term 'fortified farm' as it was her belief that "every building in this frontier territory was constructed with the problem of security very much in mind as a matter of course".[475] Her categories were descriptive and based on a combination of size, plan and construction, such as 'Very large farms, whose exterior walls have an outer facing of large dressed stones and an inner facing of small stones' or 'Medium-sized farms without ditches'.[476] Unfortunately, however, the use of subjective descriptions of size (e.g. large, medium, etc.) make it difficult to extend her system for comparisons with other areas. In addition, as I have already suggested elsewhere, these types of categories which incorporate different architectural characteristics are especially problematic, because they make it more difficult to assess how these different characteristics actually intersect, particularly when we do not always have all of this information for every building under investigation.

The investigators of the *ULVS* project proposed a similar system to Goodchild's original typology for the *gsur* recorded in that region, based largely on a number of well-preserved examples from the Wadis Umm el-Kharab and Buzra where they had undertaken relatively detailed investigations. The first three types identified in the *ULVS* publications were essentially the same as the six identified by Goodchild — tower-like buildings consisting of varying numbers of rooms arranged around a courtyard or lightwell. Then, in addition to the 'classic' tower-like *gsur*, they identified three further categories: very large examples with central courtyards, *gsur* of irregular plan (often due to siting on an irregular spur or hilltop) and other *gsur* which did not fit easily into the other categories, and which were usually interpreted as post-Roman. As the authors point out, however, it must be noted that since this system was largely developed after the bulk of the fieldwork had been completed, it was unfortunately not possible to apply it retroactively to all sites in their publications, and as a result, there is some inconsistency in its application. [477]

More recent surveys in both the central *gebel* and coastal plain in the hinterlands of *Lepcis Magna* have continued the work begun by Goodchild, Oates and Brogan, and made similar observations. During the *Tarhuna Archaeological Survey*, Ahmed re-recorded a number of fortified sites in the *gebel* which had been published by Goodchild and Oates, as well as identifying several previously unknown sites in the same region. Like Oates before him, Ahmed divided the fortified sites of the *gebel* into two types: those which had physically replaced and re-used material from earlier unfortified settlements and those which appeared to be new establishments, the latter often sited on hilltops.[478] It is notable, however, that the majority of the apparently new establishments recorded by Ahmed were still located within 300 m of earlier, unfortified sites, suggesting that there was still some relationship between the unfortified and fortified sites and, in some cases at least, probably an element of socio-economic replacement, if not a directly physical one.[479] In the coastal plain and hinterlands of *Lepcis Magna*, Cirelli *et al.* also described the fortified farm buildings in a similar way to Ahmed and Oates, differentiating between those which had clearly developed from earlier unfortified sites and those which appeared to be newly founded.[480] Beyond this distinction, however, from an architectural standpoint, neither Ahmed nor Cirelli *et al.* offer much detailed discussion about the form and construction of the fortified building themselves.

Comparatively few fortified buildings or settlements have been recorded in Syrtica and therefore little attempt has been made to organise them into a typological framework. Only four fortified structures, identified as *tours*, were reported by the *PVNL* project, described as "*proches des gsur de Tripolitaine*", by which the authors seem to have meant structures comparable to those recorded by the *ULVS* and earlier investigators in the pre-desert.[481] Further east, LeQuesne *et al.* likened the examples observed during the *Shell Sirte Basin* project, both east and west of *Arae Philaenorum*, more to those described by Goodchild in southwest Cyrenaica, surrounded by wide ditches, but the descriptions of these are unfortunately brief and vague.[482] In the western regions of Tripolitania, the study of fortified settlements and buildings has been largely directed by a particular

[474] Oates 1954: 93.

[475] Brogan 1977: 122.

[476] Brogan 1977: 122.

[477] Welsby 1992; Mattingly & Dore 1996: 127–129.

[478] Oates 1954: 116–117; Ahmed 2010: 70–78.

[479] Ahmed 2010: 78, fig. 2.25.

[480] Cirelli, Felici, & Munzi 2012: 764ff.

[481] Reddé 1988: 71.

[482] LeQuesne, Basell, & Sheibani 2010: 24; Goodchild 1951b.

interest in the *limes* and military on the part of French scholars working in Tunisia, as already discussed in Chapter 4. Trousset noted that a number of the smaller fortifications were similar in form to the 'fortified farms' identified by Goodchild, though made no attempt to further sub-divide them based on their plan.[483]

A more recent attempt to organise fortified architecture and settlement in North Africa into a usable typology was undertaken by Mattingly, Sterry and Leitch, in a study which encompassed all of late Roman and late antique North Africa, from Mauretania to Cyrenaica and Fazzan.[484] Their investigation divided the fortified buildings and settlements of the region into eight main types, each with further sub-types, based primarily on the plan of the buildings and features associated with them such as projecting towers and surrounding ditches. It is probably the most comprehensive and sensible typology for the region to date and my own analysis resembles this system most closely (though not exactly), in particular in the differentiation between tower-like buildings and compounds.

Revised Typology and Analyses

As suggested by the discussion above, it is clear that we are again faced with a complex and varied array of different building types, for which it was necessary to create a standardised typology in order to conduct region-wide comparisons and analyses. In addition, the analysis of fortified structures and settlements is slightly more complex than that of the unfortified farms because there were various components which were incorporated into these buildings in different combinations, including yards, batters, towers, wide surrounding ditches, enceintes and sometimes extensive associated settlements, all of which will be discussed in turn, below.

Of the 810 structures identified in my database as fortified, 435 (54%) had an identifiable building plan. The vast majority of fortified buildings identified here were divided into two general types, towers (or tower-like buildings) and compounds, each of which were then divided into further sub-types, the distribution of which are presented in Table 6.2 and Figure 6.2.

Towers or tower-like buildings are what are more often called to mind by the word *gasr* in eastern Tripolitanian contexts, particularly in the eastern pre-desert, though they were identified in all areas under study, accounting for around three-quarters of the buildings with identifiable plans (327/435) (Figure 6.3).[485] Most are essentially as Goodchild originally described them: multi-storeyed buildings of square or rectangular plan, with ranges of rooms facing onto a central lightwell or small courtyard. For most of the structures identified as towers it was not possible to make any further distinctions regarding their internal plan or layout, often due to the quantity of debris which has collapsed from upper storeys obscuring the interior plan of the building, both on satellite imagery and in cases where the sites were visited on the ground. However, in the case of the 133 for which we could say something more about their interior layout, these have been divided into three sub-types.

The first and most commonly identified form of towers was the 'central lightwell' type, which consisted of ranges of rooms on three or four sides of a small, centrally

	Towers				Compounds					
	central lightwell	range lightwell	block	unknown	courtyard	doubled	irregular	unknown	Range/ block	*Total*
1. W. coastal	2	–	–	7	1	–	–	5	–	*15*
2. W. *gebel*	9	–	–	27	6	–	2	23	–	*67*
3. Southwest	1	–	–	3	1	–	–	1	–	*6*
4. Central coastal	–	–	–	5	–	–	–	–	–	*5*
5. Central *gebel*	3	1	–	31	4	–	–	5	–	*44*
6. E. pre-desert, north	69	5	1	98	15	–	4	9	1	*202*
7. E. pre-desert, south	36	4	–	16	15	3	6	3	1	*84*
8. W. Syrtica	2	–	–	6	1	–	1	1	–	*11*
9. E. Syrtica	–	–	–	1	–	–	–	–	–	*1*
Total	*122*	*10*	*1*	*194*	*43*	*3*	*13*	*47*	*2*	*435*

Table 6.2: *Frequency of fortified building types by region.*

[483] Trousset 1974: 130–142.

[484] Mattingly, Sterry, & Leitch 2013.

[485] Nevertheless, it should be noted that any structures which were identified in the published sources only as '*gasr*' with no other description or accompanying photographs were catalogued as 'unknown' type, rather than making any assumptions about their form.

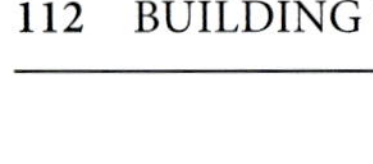

Figure 6.2: *Frequency of fortified plan types, in total and divided by region.*

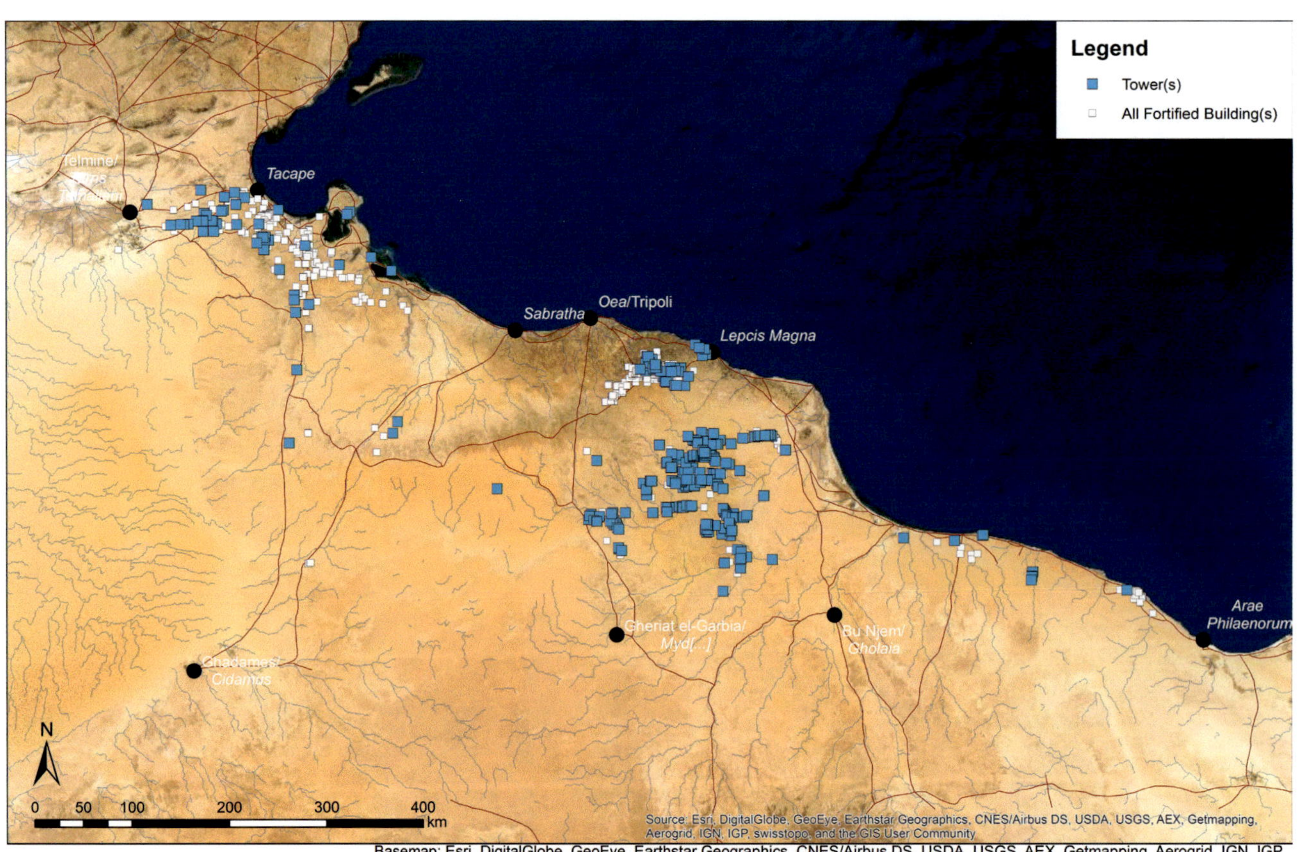

Basemap: Esri, DigitalGlobe, GeoEye, Earthstar Geographics, CNES/Airbus DS, USDA, USGS, AEX, Getmapping, Aerogrid, IGN, IGP, swisstopo, and the GIS User Community
Drainage: Lehner, B., Verdin, K., Jarvis, A. (2008): New global hydrography derived from spaceborne elevation data. Eos, Transactions, AGU, 89(10): 93-94. Retrieved from http://hydrosheds.cr.usgs.gov (15 sec Flow Accumulation)
Roads (Barrington Atlas): Ancient World Mapping Center (2012)

Figure 6.3: *Distribution of all tower-like fortified buildings.*

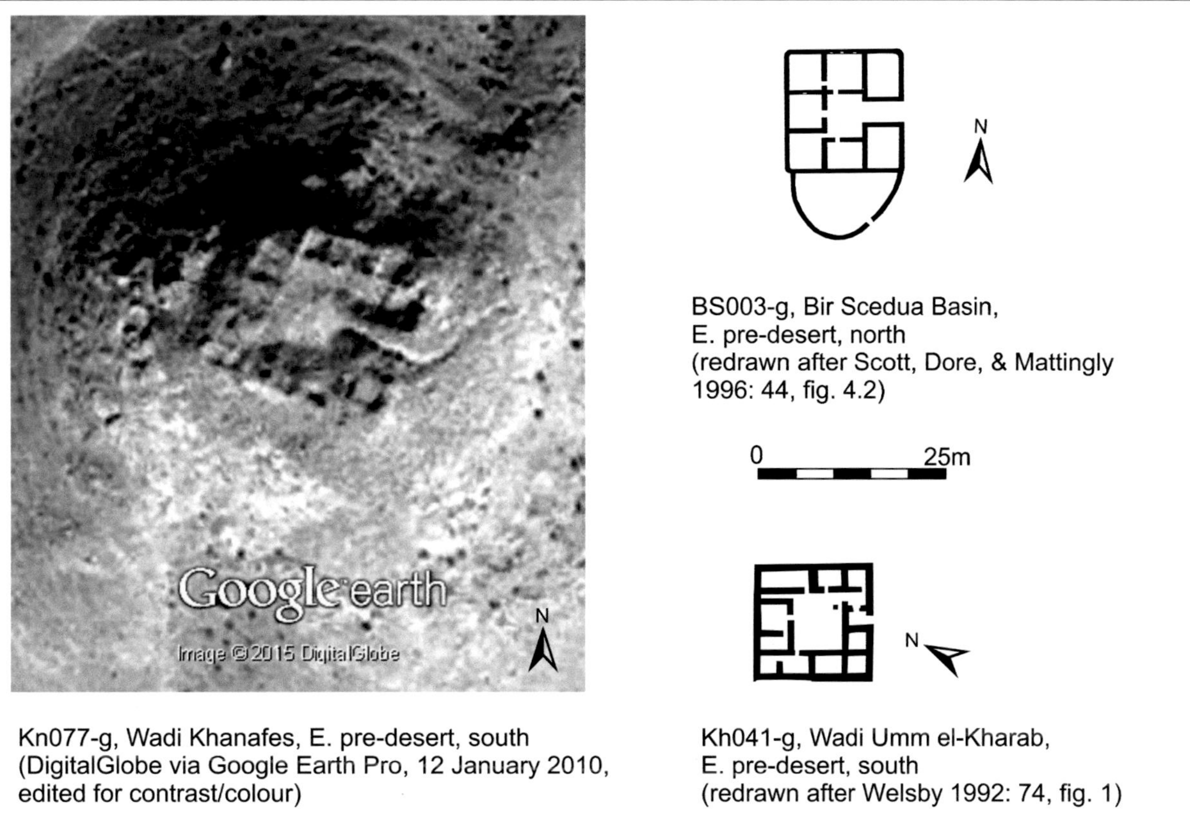

BS003-g, Bir Scedua Basin, E. pre-desert, north (redrawn after Scott, Dore, & Mattingly 1996: 44, fig. 4.2)

0 25m

Kn077-g, Wadi Khanafes, E. pre-desert, south (DigitalGlobe via Google Earth Pro, 12 January 2010, edited for contrast/colour)

Kh041-g, Wadi Umm el-Kharab, E. pre-desert, south (redrawn after Welsby 1992: 74, fig. 1)

Figure 6.4: *Examples of 'central lightwell' towers.*

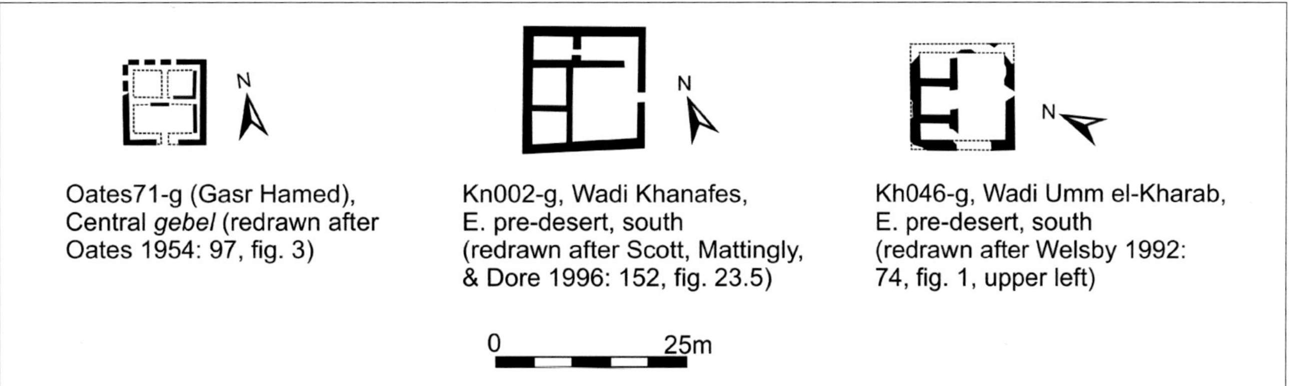

Oates71-g (Gasr Hamed), Central *gebel* (redrawn after Oates 1954: 97, fig. 3)

Kn002-g, Wadi Khanafes, E. pre-desert, south (redrawn after Scott, Mattingly, & Dore 1996: 152, fig. 23.5)

Kh046-g, Wadi Umm el-Kharab, E. pre-desert, south (redrawn after Welsby 1992: 74, fig. 1, upper left)

0 25m

Figure 6.5: *Examples of 'range lightwell' towers.*

positioned courtyard or lightwell (Figure 6.4). The second type, 'range lightwell' buildings, were very similar to the central lightwell towers, but with only a single range of rooms (or very rarely two) facing an open space (Figure 6.5). The known distribution of range lightwell types seems to be confined to the eastern pre-desert, where all but one of the ten of the examples identified were found; the last was located in the central *gebel*. Finally, there was a single explicitly recorded example of a structure which does not appear to have had a lightwell or courtyard which was open to the sky, and which can be termed a 'block' tower (Ms003-g[486]). Buildings of this type were interpreted in the *ULVS* study as "primarily of Islamic date", and any explicitly identified as such have not been included in my database.[487] However, it is entirely possible that this building type was more common in the Romano-Libyan period than the evidence suggests, due to the advanced state of ruin of many buildings and the fact that our knowledge concerning roofing is limited.[488] This is especially likely to be the case in many of the very

[486] See Scott, Dore, & Mattingly 1996: 248, fig. 30.1.

[487] Mattingly & Dore 1996: 129.

[488] See Section 6.2.4.

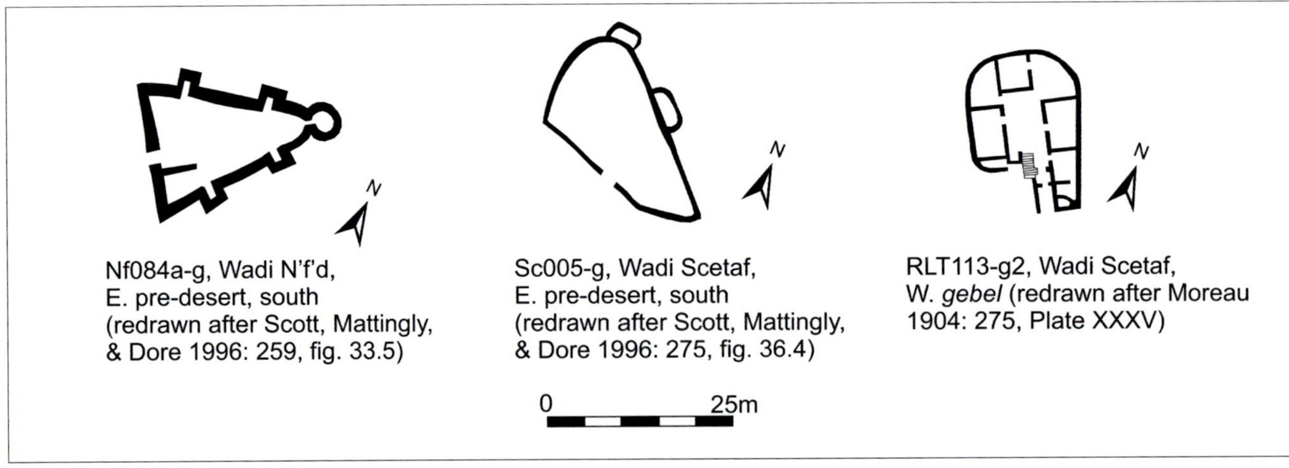

Figure 6.6: *Towers of non-rectangular shape.*

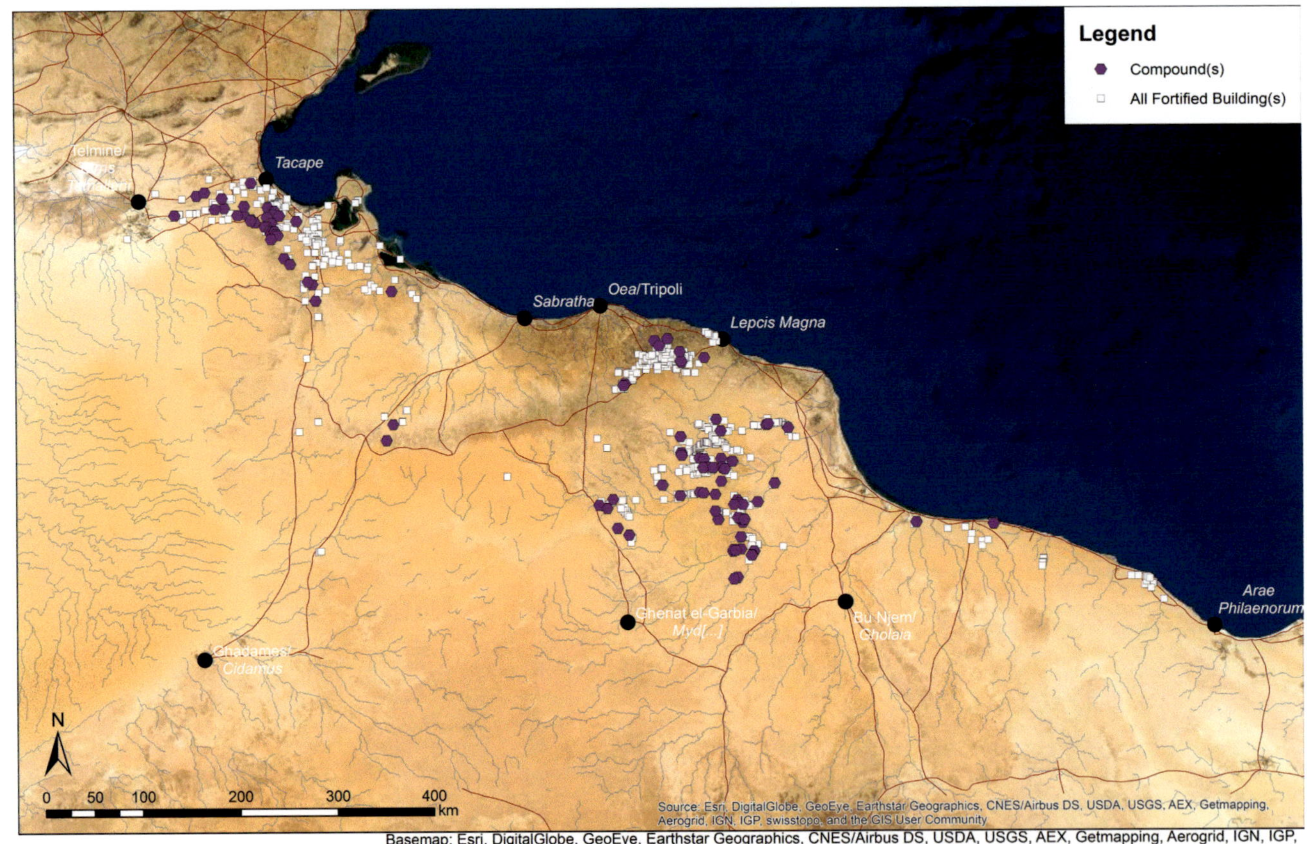

Basemap: Esri, DigitalGlobe, GeoEye, Earthstar Geographics, CNES/Airbus DS, USDA, USGS, AEX, Getmapping, Aerogrid, IGN, IGP, swisstopo, and the GIS User Community
Drainage: Lehner, B., Verdin, K., Jarvis, A. (2008): New global hydrography derived from spaceborne elevation data. Eos, Transactions, AGU, 89(10): 93-94. Retrieved from http://hydrosheds.cr.usgs.gov (15 sec Flow Accumulation)
Roads (Barrington Atlas): Ancient World Mapping Center (2012)

Figure 6.7: *Distribution of fortified compound buildings.*

small examples, which were possibly either watchtowers or storage towers, not intended for long-term human habitation. In addition, I suspect that in at least some cases, it is simply the case that this information has not been explicitly recorded.

Of the 327 fortified towers, 299 also had their external shape recorded, the vast majority of which were more or less rectangular, or slightly trapezoidal. Only nine examples were recorded as taking other shapes, including irregular, oval, round and triangular (Figure 6.6); this could usually be related to siting on an irregular landscape setting such as a hilltop or spur of land.

Structures identified as compounds account for around a quarter (106/435) of the fortified buildings with identifiable plans and were recorded in all areas except the central coastal region and eastern Syrtica (Figure 6.7). Unlike towers, compounds were not necessarily multi-storeyed, though individual rooms might have multiple storeys or they might have one or more tower-like elements incorporated into their construction. Compounds

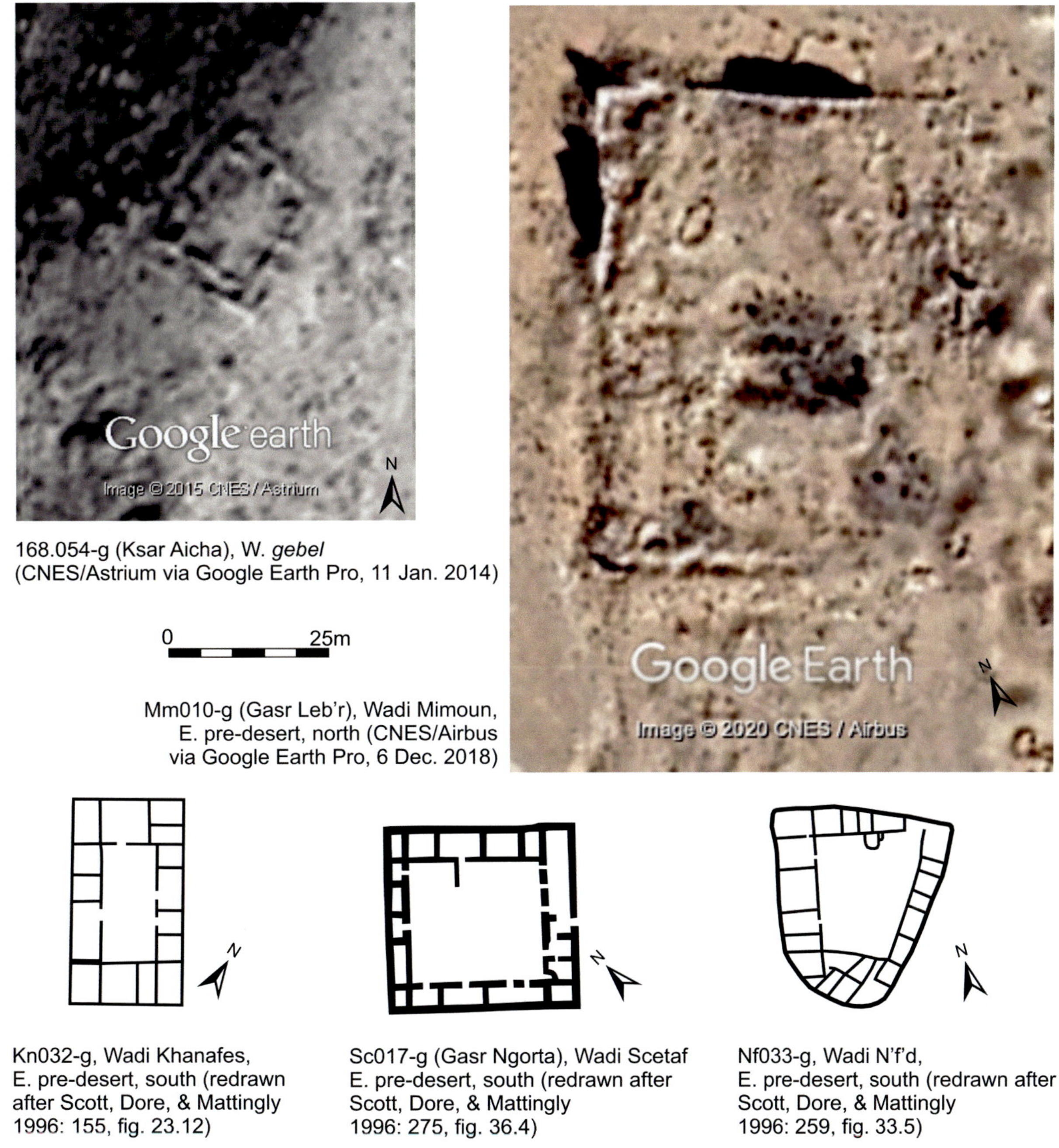

Figure 6.8: *Examples of fortified courtyard compounds.*

were also generally larger than towers,[489] and in particular, any internal open areas were more spacious, and could more properly be called courtyards rather than lightwells. Unfortunately, however, when the internal plan is unclear or it is not possible to tell if there were upper storeys or not, it can be difficult to differentiate between small compounds and large towers. In ambiguous cases, I have drawn an arbitrary limit in size between these two types at c.25 x 25 m (625 m^2), but in reality, the effective difference between a large lightwell tower and a small courtyard compound was probably minimal.

I have identified three different types of fortified compounds: courtyard, doubled and irregular, though again, there was unfortunately a large proportion of compounds for which it was not possible to identify a sub-type. The most common were courtyard compounds, which are defined the same way as unfortified courtyard buildings, that is, three or four continuous ranges of rooms facing onto an open courtyard (Figure 6.8). Differentiating between unfortified and fortified courtyard buildings is again difficult, particularly using satellite imagery. In general, fortified courtyard compounds tended to be more

[489] See Section 6.2.2.

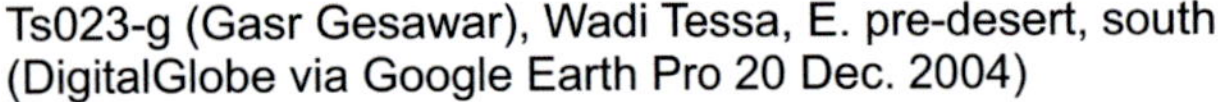
Ts023-g (Gasr Gesawar), Wadi Tessa, E. pre-desert, south (DigitalGlobe via Google Earth Pro 20 Dec. 2004)

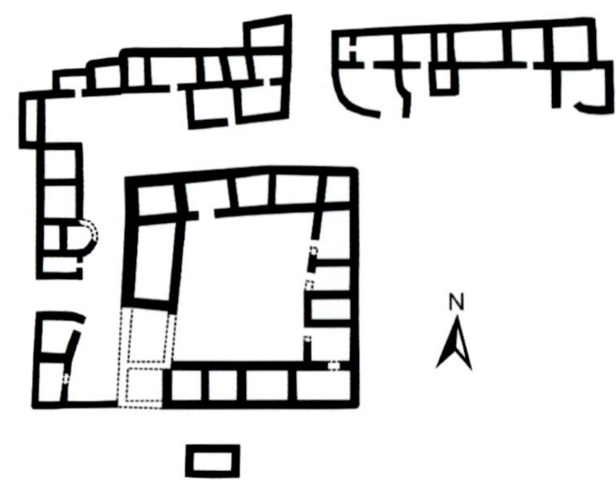

Gh127-01, Wadi Ghirza, E. pre-desert, south (redrawn after Brogan & Smith 1984: 48, fig. 4)

Figure 6.9: *Examples of doubled fortified compounds.*

substantially built, with taller exterior walls, and generally had only a single entrance, sometimes with defensive towers (whereas an unfortified courtyard building might have several, less defended entrances), and were located in conspicuously defensive locations such as the summits of steep hills. In addition, unlike their unfortified counterparts, fortified compounds were occasionally non-rectangular; at least five recorded in my catalogue were trapezoidal, six were irregular and one was triangular, again often due to siting in an irregular location.

The ambiguity is not aided by the fact that there were probably a number of buildings which, over the course of their lives, were fortified, for example, by the addition of a surrounding ditch or enceinte. We have at least one example which potentially shows the process by which a courtyard compound was fortified. At Mm008-g, the northeastern wall is of massive construction, but appears unfinished at either end, and seems to curve around the corner.[490] Brogan noted that the southeast wall abuts this huge wall, which might support the idea that it was a later addition or reconstruction (though admittedly it is unclear whether the other walls are keyed in or not), but for unknown reasons, this process does not appear to have been completed.[491]

Three fortified compounds can be identified as 'doubled compounds', all of which were found in the southern part of the eastern pre-desert, two at the settlement of Ghirza (Gh127) alone, and the third less than 20 km away in the Wadi Tessa. These have the appearance of a courtyard compound with another building (which may resemble a lightwell tower itself) occupying the centre of the courtyard, usually leaving a few metres of space between them, creating a kind of corridor (Figure 6.9). A possible example of a doubled compound in the process of being created has been identified at Ghirza: ranges of rooms can be seen along two sides of Gh127-01-g, separated from the fortified building by only a few metres, which could easily be later extended to surround the whole tower (Figure 6.9, right).

Thirteen examples were identified as irregular compounds; these are irregularly-shaped structures which have substantial enclosure walls and may have multiple and varied structures in their interior which are not arranged neatly around a central courtyard. Irregular compounds are slightly more common than irregular towers and in most cases seem to have derived their shape from the hilltop or spur on which they were situated (Figure 6.10). Finally, two examples of buildings

[490] Brogan 1977: 98–99, fig. 4; Scott, Dore, & Mattingly 1996: 213. The publication history reflects this uncertainty, where Brogan calls this site a *gasr*, while the *ULVS* publication identifies it only as a farm.

[491] Mattingly & Dore 1996: 129.

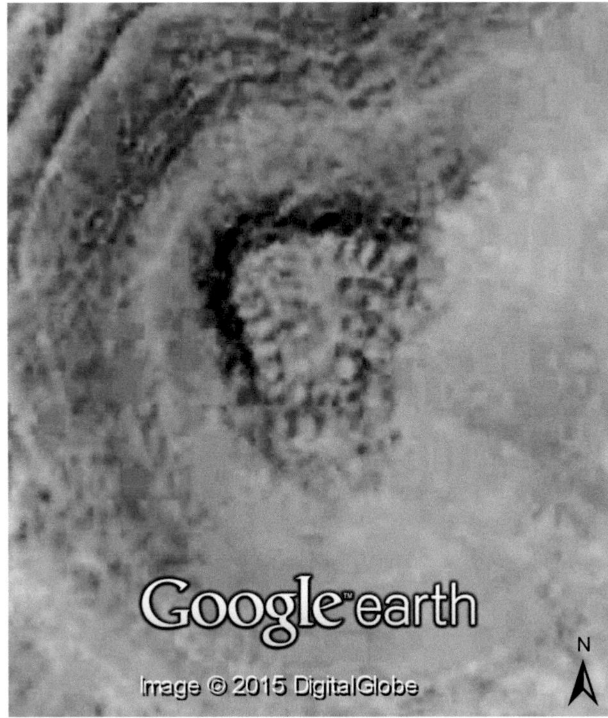

Kb002-g, Wadi Bey el-Kebir, W. Syrtica (DigitalGlobe via Google Earth, 1 May 2004 image adjusted for colour/contrast)

N

Kh7096-g, Wadi Umm el-Kharab, E. pre-desert, south (redrawn after Scott, Dore, & Mattingly 1996: 143, fig. 22.10)

0 25m

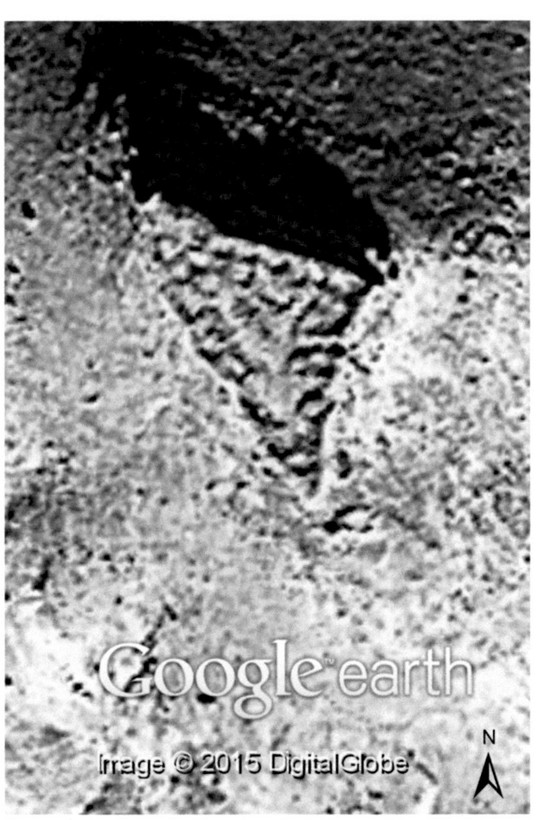

Dd-NS01-g, Wadi Dreder, E. pre-desert, north (DigitalGlobe via Google Earth, 31 Dec. 2012; image adjusted for colour/contrast)

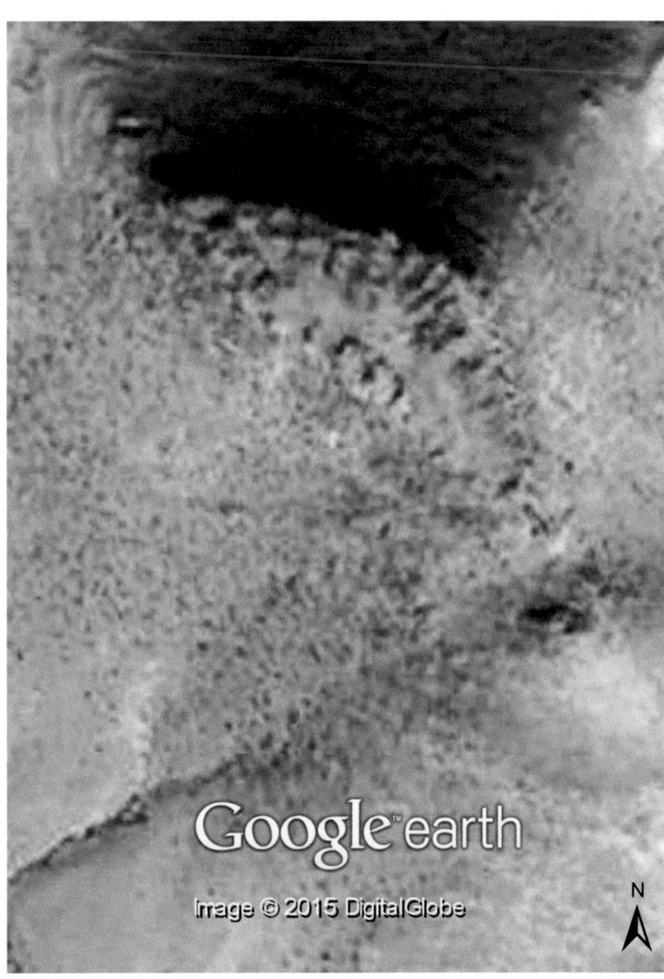

WT1-NS61-g, W. *gebel* (DigitalGlobe via Google Earth, 8 Jan. 2004; image adjusted for colour/contrast)

Figure 6.10: *Examples of irregular fortified compounds.*

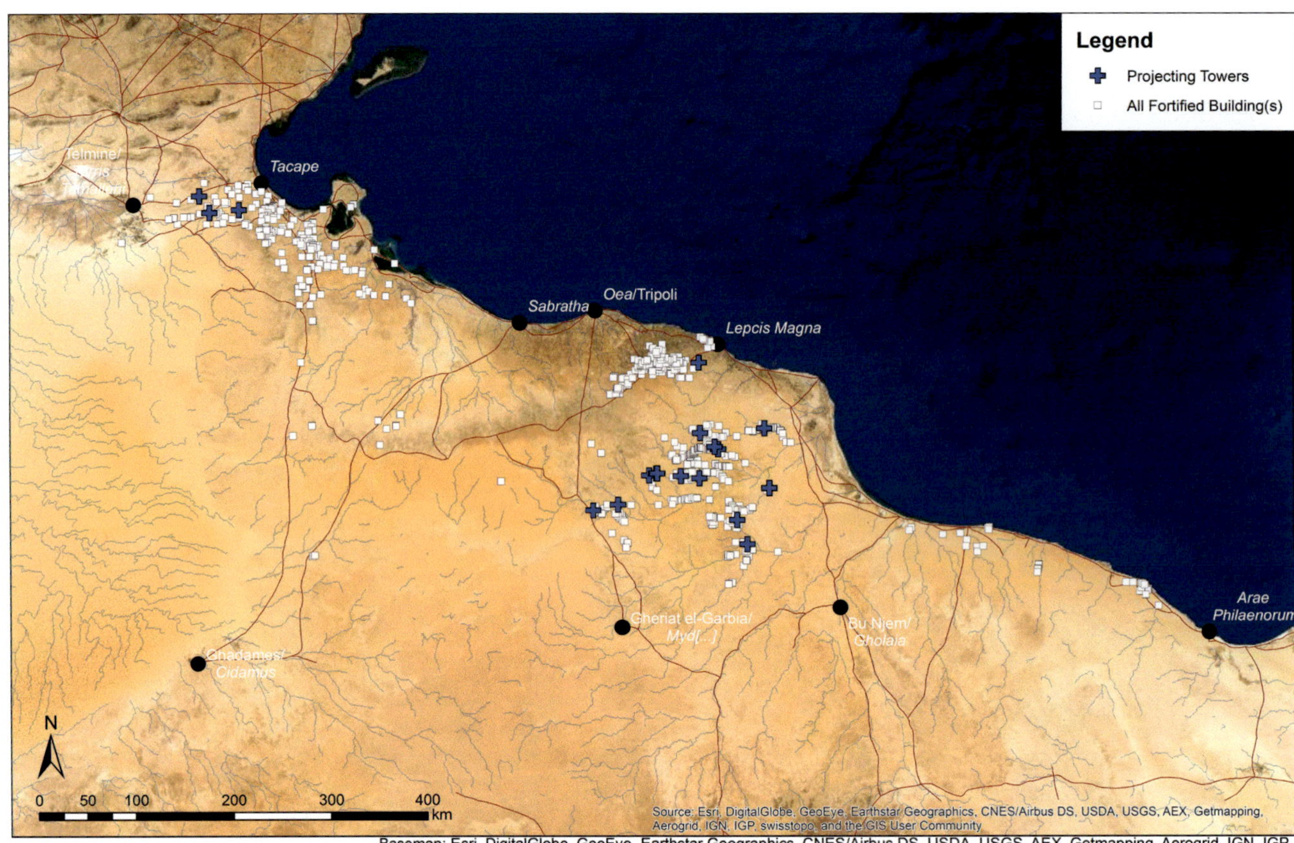

Basemap: Esri, DigitalGlobe, GeoEye, Earthstar Geographics, CNES/Airbus DS, USDA, USGS, AEX, Getmapping, Aerogrid, IGN, IGP, swisstopo, and the GIS User Community
Drainage: Lehner, B., Verdin, K., Jarvis, A. (2008): New global hydrography derived from spaceborne elevation data. Eos, Transactions, AGU, 89(10): 93-94. Retrieved from http://hydrosheds.cr.usgs.gov (15 sec Flow Accumulation)
Roads (Barrington Atlas): Ancient World Mapping Center (2012)

Figure 6.11: *Distribution of fortified buildings with externally projecting towers.*

can be identified as block or range types, similar to their unfortified counterparts, in that they were formed simply of a single-storeyed range of rooms. In this instance, however, these buildings are much more substantial than the unfortified examples and have thus been classified as fortified, though, here again, the distinction is a difficult one.

As with the unfortified buildings there is certainly a degree of overlap and ambiguity between the types. Nevertheless, it is a useful starting point for thinking about broad trends and patterns in distribution. In all areas, towers were the more commonly identified of the two main types. This imbalance is most pronounced in the northern part of the eastern pre-desert and the central *gebel*, where towers accounted for 86% (n=173) and 80% (n=35) of the total number of fortified buildings of identifiable type, respectively, and still more than two thirds in western Syrtica (73%, n=8) and the southern part of the eastern pre-desert (67%, n=56). In the western coastal zone and the western *gebel* we find something closer to an equal balance, with towers only making up 60% (n=9) and 54% (n=36) of the proportion, respectively.

The popularity of the fortified tower building over the courtyard type in many parts of Tripolitania, a very different form from any of the existing unfortified building types, points to changing architectural trends. However, there are two external factors which we can also bear in mind that potentially contributed to this apparent imbalance. First, there is the problem identified by Goodchild and Oates, that the fortified buildings of the more northern regions of the *gebel* and coastal areas were generally more ruined, and therefore there is a far larger proportion of buildings in that area for which we do not know what form the buildings actually took. Second, while the towers are more easily identifiable due to their height, the distinction between fortified compound structures and unfortified farm buildings can be more difficult to discern, particularly from satellite imagery alone.

Externally Projecting Towers and Batters

Two additional features which were sometimes incorporated into the construction of fortified buildings were externally projecting towers and batters. As discussed in Section 4.1.2, externally projecting towers were often seen in earlier reports and investigations as evidence supporting the military identification of the buildings on which they occurred, but it is now evident that at least some of these buildings were almost certainly civilian.[492]

[492] Mattingly, Sterry & Leitch 2013: 174.

Nineteen of the 435 (4%) civilian fortified structures for which plans or descriptions were available were recorded as having externally projecting towers attached to the main structure (Figure 6.11; Appendix Table 19).

Thirteen of the structures on which externally projecting towers were recorded were tower types themselves, all found in the eastern pre-desert, while the remaining six were compounds, spread across the eastern pre-desert, central *gebel* and western *gebel*. In the examples identified here, there were between one and seven towers projecting from the entrances, corners or sides of the buildings (Figure 6.12, see also examples in Figures 4.2, 4.3 and 4.9). Some past typologies of fortified buildings have distinguished structures with externally

Ms002-g, Wadi Meseuggi, E. pre-desert, north (*ULVS* Archive: F495/N16/14.10.1981)

Md121-g (Gasr Glul), Wadi Merdum, E. pre-desert, north (Scott, Dore, & Mattingly 1996: 189, fig. 26.22)

Figure 6.12: *Examples of fortified buildings with externally projecting towers.*

projecting towers as a separate building type.[493] However, while they were certainly a particularly distinctive feature, to the best of our (admittedly limited) knowledge, projecting towers do not seem to otherwise substantially change the character or function of the main structure, so it seems unnecessary to consider buildings with this feature as a different type altogether. In only three of the cases identified here (Bz028/Bz906-g, Sf116-g and Nf083-g; see Figure 4.9 for the latter) do towers seem to be definitely positioned at the entrance, suggesting a function associated with the defense or security of the gate. In the case of Md002-g (Gasr Burlarkan/Mselletin), none of the seven towers appears to have had any entrance, and this seems to be the case in other examples as well; Goodchild suggested that perhaps they were used for storage.[494]

The proportions of building types to which external towers were added approximately reflect the overall ratio of towers to compounds, suggesting that there was no preferential addition of externally projecting towers to one building type over the other. However, what may have had more bearing on their use on different sorts of fortified buildings is the region in which they are found. The few compounds with externally projecting towers were distributed across four regions, whereas the towers with additional externally projecting towers were found only in the eastern pre-desert.

This is potentially significant in how we should interpret the use of this feature on both military and civilian buildings. Although as discussed already, it is now generally accepted that we cannot automatically ascribe a military identification to buildings based solely on the presence of projecting towers, they were still a feature which was used at a much higher rate of frequency in military buildings, with eight (21%) of the 38 military buildings identified in Chapter 4 having them. For this reason, it is still tempting to assume that there was some relationship or influence at work in the adoption of this feature in civilian buildings. However, if we exclude the major forts, which were an exceptional building form and where all of the projecting towers were specifically gate-towers, the other four military buildings which had projecting towers (one minor fort, two fortlets and one outpost) were all located in one region: the western *gebel*. Only three of the 19 civilian fortified buildings with externally projecting towers, all compounds of a comparable size with the identified military fortlets or very large outposts, were also found in this region. The rest were found in the eastern pre-desert or the central *gebel*, where no military examples with externally projecting towers of comparable size and building type are currently known, making the idea of a direct military influence on this particular feature in the civilian buildings of that region more difficult to sustain.

All but one of the military examples with projecting towers were much larger than the typical civilian fortified tower building and were more closely comparable to fortified compounds, as described above. However, as pointed out elsewhere, examples of fortified towers with the same feature, of nearly identical size and plan to those found in the eastern pre-desert of Tripolitania have been recorded in Fazzan, (cf. Figure 4.2), and can be dated to approximately the same period, probably the third, or more likely, fourth century AD onwards.[495] While this is not to say that the feature's use on the *limes* was not a relevant factor in its adoption into civilian contexts, we can perhaps see its use in both eastern Tripolitania and Fazzan as part of a larger trend of the adoption of a Roman military building feature into what had become a common indigenous form of farm building.

Another feature that was sometimes incorporated into the construction of fortified buildings was a batter (or battered plinth), an angled construction built up against the lower parts of the exterior walls of a building, serving to reinforce and stabilise the structure (Figure 6.13). Some form of this feature occurs on 34 examples of the structures in my catalogue, or 8% of those for which the plan was known (Figure 6.14; Appendix Table 20).

The majority of the structures with batters were towers, while just three were identified as compounds, and a single example was of unknown building type, though its small size (81 m², MmA001-g) suggests that it was most likely a fortified tower as well. Thus, whereas the presence of externally projecting towers seems to have been less affected by building type, batters were a feature more clearly associated with fortified towers. They were also overwhelmingly found in the areas of the eastern pre-desert, a pattern which may be a consequence of their association with towers, since those are the areas in which towers were most commonly found.

Batters are commonly identified as a defensive feature and there can be no doubt that they would serve to strengthen walls and make them more difficult to damage if attacked.[496] Kenrick has also recently suggested, with reference to similar buildings in Cyrenaica, that they are also likely to have been constructed to repair and reinforce walls that had already been damaged, particularly by earthquakes.[497] He gives as an example Qasr az-Zaarura, where a 'massive sloping revetment' was added to a fortified tower and it is possible to see

[493] For example, Mattingly, Sterry & Leitch 2013: 174–175.

[494] Or prison cells, bearing in mind that he believed Gasr Burlarkan to be a military building. Goodchild 1950b: 34.

[495] Mattingly 2003b: 147–149; Mattingly *et al.* 2020a: 75–81.

[496] Mattingly 1995: 202; Goodchild 1953: 66; Emrage 2015: 96.

[497] Also suggested as a possible additional function by Isaac (2000: 66 fn. 11).

Ms003-g, Wadi Meseuggi, E. pre-desert, north
(*ULVS* Archive: F420/N16/15.10.1981; cropped for clarity)

Mn003-g, Wadi Mansur, E. pre-desert, north
(*ULVS* Archive: F112/N10/10.11.1980; cropped for clarity)

Figure 6.13: *Examples of fortified buildings with batters.*

that the original walls had large cracks in them.[498] This idea may be supported by the fact that in many cases in Tripolitania, the batter was not found on all sides of the building, as one might expect if its purpose was defensive. In addition, also potentially supporting Kenrick's view is the fact that despite the traditional association of batters with a defensive function, none of the military buildings identified in Chapter 4 seems to have had them. The more common occurrence of batters on towers rather than compounds mentioned above might also support the idea their main purpose was actually as structural reinforcement for towers since their greater height meant they were in more danger of collapse.

Eight examples had both projecting towers and batters,[499] all found in the eastern pre-desert regions, and all but one were fortified tower type buildings. Given the small numbers of buildings known to have had these features in the first place, this is not an insignificant proportion, where nearly half of the buildings with externally projecting towers also had batters, and a quarter of those with batters had one or more projecting towers, and suggests that the use of these features was associated in some way. On the other hand, the low numbers overall should indicate to us that these analyses should be approached with caution.

[498] Kenrick 2013: 124.

[499] For example, Lg001-g, see Mattingly & Dore 1996: 133, fig 5.22.

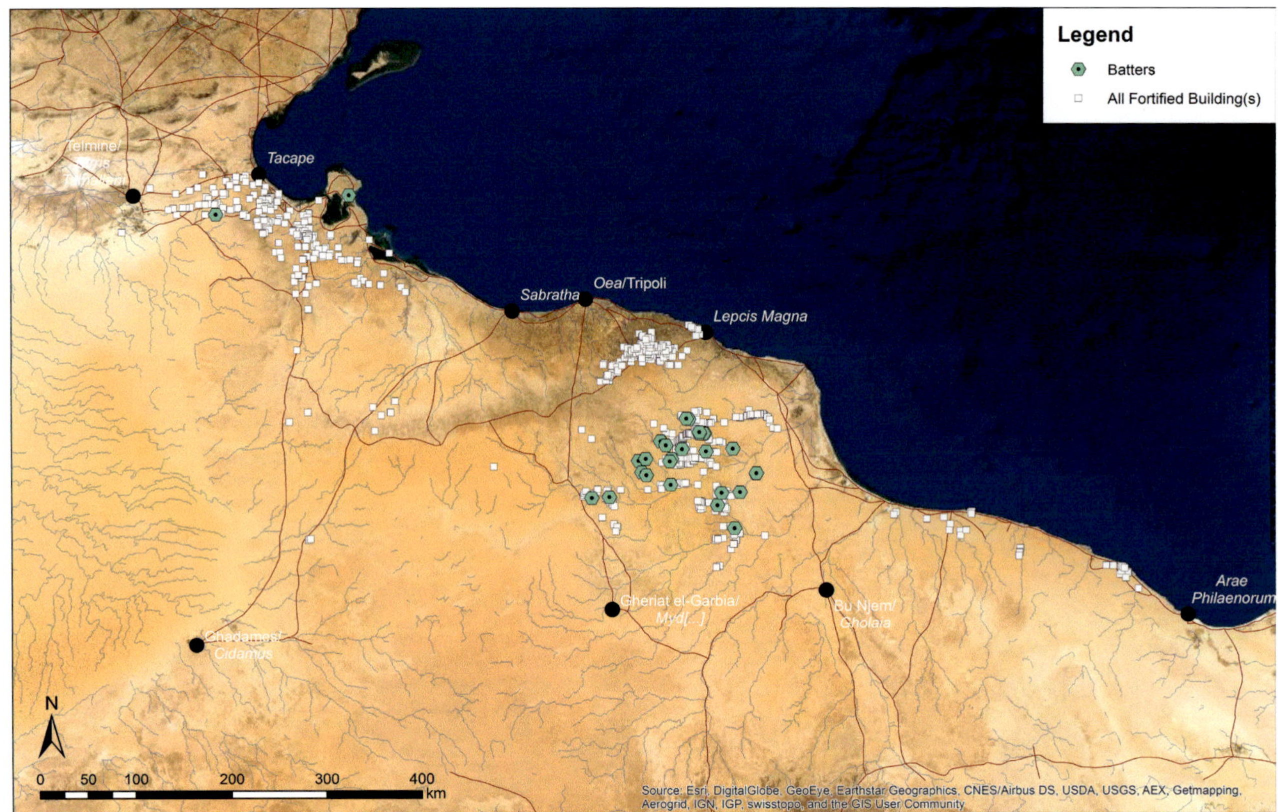

Basemap: Esri, DigitalGlobe, GeoEye, Earthstar Geographics, CNES/Airbus DS, USDA, USGS, AEX, Getmapping, Aerogrid, IGN, IGP, swisstopo, and the GIS User Community
Drainage: Lehner, B., Verdin, K., Jarvis, A. (2008): New global hydrography derived from spaceborne elevation data. Eos, Transactions, AGU, 89(10): 93-94. Retrieved from http://hydrosheds.cr.usgs.gov (15 sec Flow Accumulation)
Roads (Barrington Atlas): Ancient World Mapping Center (2012)

Figure 6.14: *Distribution of fortified buildings with batters.*

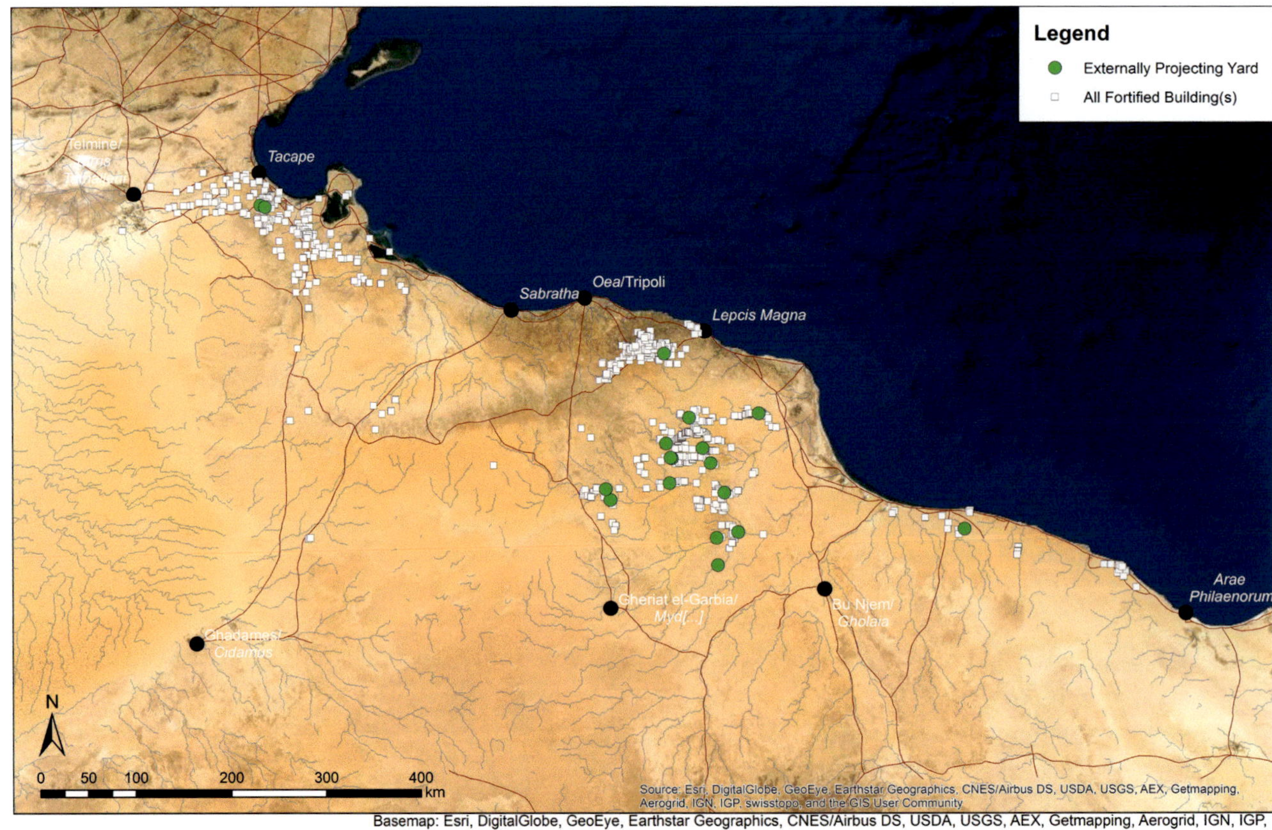

Basemap: Esri, DigitalGlobe, GeoEye, Earthstar Geographics, CNES/Airbus DS, USDA, USGS, AEX, Getmapping, Aerogrid, IGN, IGP, swisstopo, and the GIS User Community
Drainage: Lehner, B., Verdin, K., Jarvis, A. (2008): New global hydrography derived from spaceborne elevation data. Eos, Transactions, AGU, 89(10): 93-94. Retrieved from http://hydrosheds.cr.usgs.gov (15 sec Flow Accumulation)
Roads (Barrington Atlas): Ancient World Mapping Center (2012)

Figure 6.15: *Distribution of fortified buildings with externally projecting yards.*

External Yards, Ditches and Enceintes

Another group of features sometimes associated with fortified buildings were external farmyards, enceintes and ditches. Of the 810 fortified buildings identified in my catalogue, 364 (45%) were known to have had one or more of these features. Whereas farmyards (open-air spaces defined by a wall and extending from one or two sides of a building, but not itself lined with covered rooms or structures) were the defining feature of a large proportion of the unfortified buildings discussed in the last chapter, they were less commonly identified in association with fortified structures. Only 18 examples (2%) of the 810 fortified buildings in my catalogue were identified as having one or more possible externally projecting yards (Figure 6.15; Appendix Table 21). Only 15 of these were connected to a building of identifiable form, of which 11 were towers and four were compounds (Figure 6.16, see also Figure 6.4, BS003-g), approximately corresponding to the overall ratio of towers to compounds. Although this is an admittedly small sample from which to draw conclusions, this suggests there was no particular pattern to what types of buildings had

MDr-NS16-g, Wadi Mimun Darregh, E. pre-desert, north (DigitalGlobe via Google Earth, 2 March 2015)

Mn018-g, Wadi Mansur, E. pre-desert, north (DigitalGlobe via Google Earth Pro, 27 Dec. 2014)

157.118-g, W. *gebel* (DigitalGlobe via Google Earth Pro, 1 Oct. 2014)

Figure 6.16: *Examples of fortified buildings with externally projecting yards.*

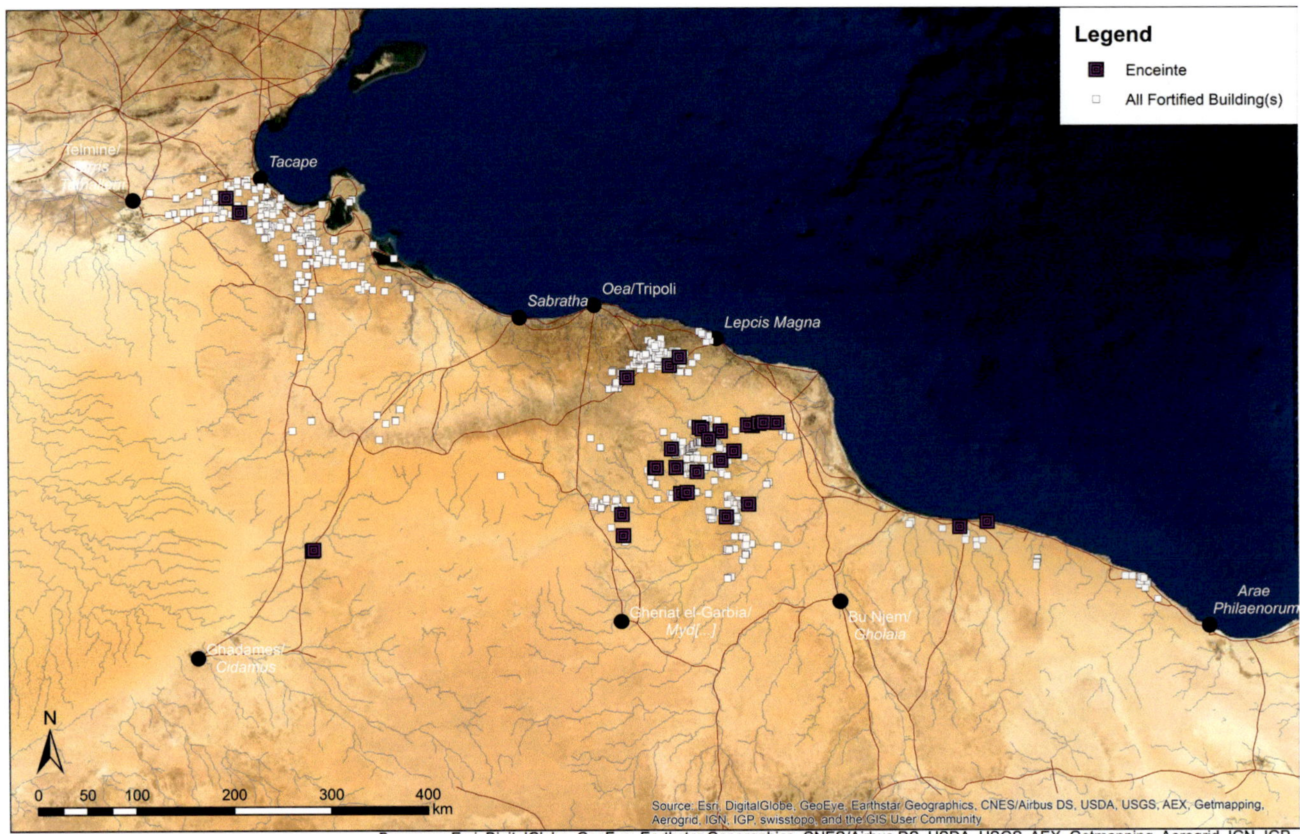

Basemap: Esri, DigitalGlobe, GeoEye, Earthstar Geographics, CNES/Airbus DS, USDA, USGS, AEX, Getmapping, Aerogrid, IGN, IGP, swisstopo, and the GIS User Community
Drainage: Lehner, B., Verdin, K., Jarvis, A. (2008): New global hydrography derived from spaceborne elevation data. Eos, Transactions, AGU, 89(10): 93-94. Retrieved from http://hydrosheds.cr.usgs.gov (15 sec Flow Accumulation)
Roads (Barrington Atlas): Ancient World Mapping Center (2012)

Figure 6.17: *Distribution of fortified buildings with external enceintes.*

yards. Considering the reduced space of tower buildings in particular, it is perhaps surprising that towers did not more often have this type of addition, potentially indicating a major shift in the distribution and use of covered and uncovered spaces (see Sections 6.2.2 and 6.2.3 below).

Another, similar feature sometimes associated with fortified buildings were enceintes, that is, a surrounding wall which was in addition to that which formed the outer wall of the main fortified structure. Enceintes can be differentiated from yards in that they surround at least three sides of a structure, rather than extending from one or two sides. Thirty-two buildings, or around 4% of the total fortified buildings, had surrounding enceintes (two of which were contained within a single enceinte) (Figure 6.17; Appendix Table 22). Of the buildings with enceintes, 26 were of an identifiable type, and all but one of these were towers while the last was a range/block type. In most of these cases, the tower was either still free-standing within the enceinte, or up against one of the walls (Figure 6.18). Most of the enceintes were rectilinear or sub-rectilinear in shape, but round and irregular examples were also recorded. The enclosed area created by the enceinte might also have a few small rooms or buildings scattered within, but had more the character of an open-air yard or enclosure which differentiated them from compounds or surrounding settlements, though it is entirely possible that buildings of perishable materials which are no longer present may have occupied the space. Where possible, they are also distinguished from field walls, which sometimes enclosed both buildings and large areas of agricultural land. On one hand, these features may simply have served the same function as farmyards, addressing the need for more open-air, but still bounded space, which was obviously limited in tower-type structures. However, since external enceintes enclosed three or more sides of the structures, they could also potentially be seen as defensive features. Contributing to this idea is the fact that three examples, one each from the eastern pre-desert, north, the western *gebel* and the southwest region, also seem to have had externally projecting towers of the type discussed in the last section incorporated into their construction.

By far the most common of the features discussed in this section were ditches, with 321 examples identified, 40% of the total number of fortified structures recorded (Table 6.3; Figure 6.19).[500]

[500] In two cases, two adjacent fortified buildings appear to share a single ditch which surrounded them both (sites 181.025 and 181.065, located less than 10 km apart in the western coastal area).

MDr05-g, Gasr al Jafiliyah, Wadi Mimun Darregh, E. pre-desert, north (DigitalGlobe via Google Earth Pro, 17 Aug. 2009)

0 25m

Ms002-g, Wadi Meseuggi, E. pre-desert, north (DigitalGlobe via Google Earth Pro, 14 Dec. 2014)

Md028-g (Gasr Azziz), Wadi Merdum, E. pre-desert, north (DigitalGlobe via Google Earth Pro, 21 Dec. 2004)

Figure 6.18: *Examples of fortified buildings with external enceintes.*

	Towers	Compounds	Unknown	*Total*	*% of total known sites*
1. W. coastal	4	5	122	131	95%
2. W. *gebel*	10	4	–	14	17%
3. Southwest	3	2	4	9	69%
4. Central coastal	1	–	1	2	33%
5. Central *gebel*	9	6	89	104	68%
6. E. pre-desert, north	14	3	24	41	14%
7. E. pre-desert, south	3	1	–	4	4%
8. W. Syrtica	–	1	3	4	21%
9. E. Syrtica	–	–	12	12	75%
Total	*44*	*22*	*257*	*321*	*40%*

Table 6.3: *Fortified buildings with ditches, divided by region and building type.*

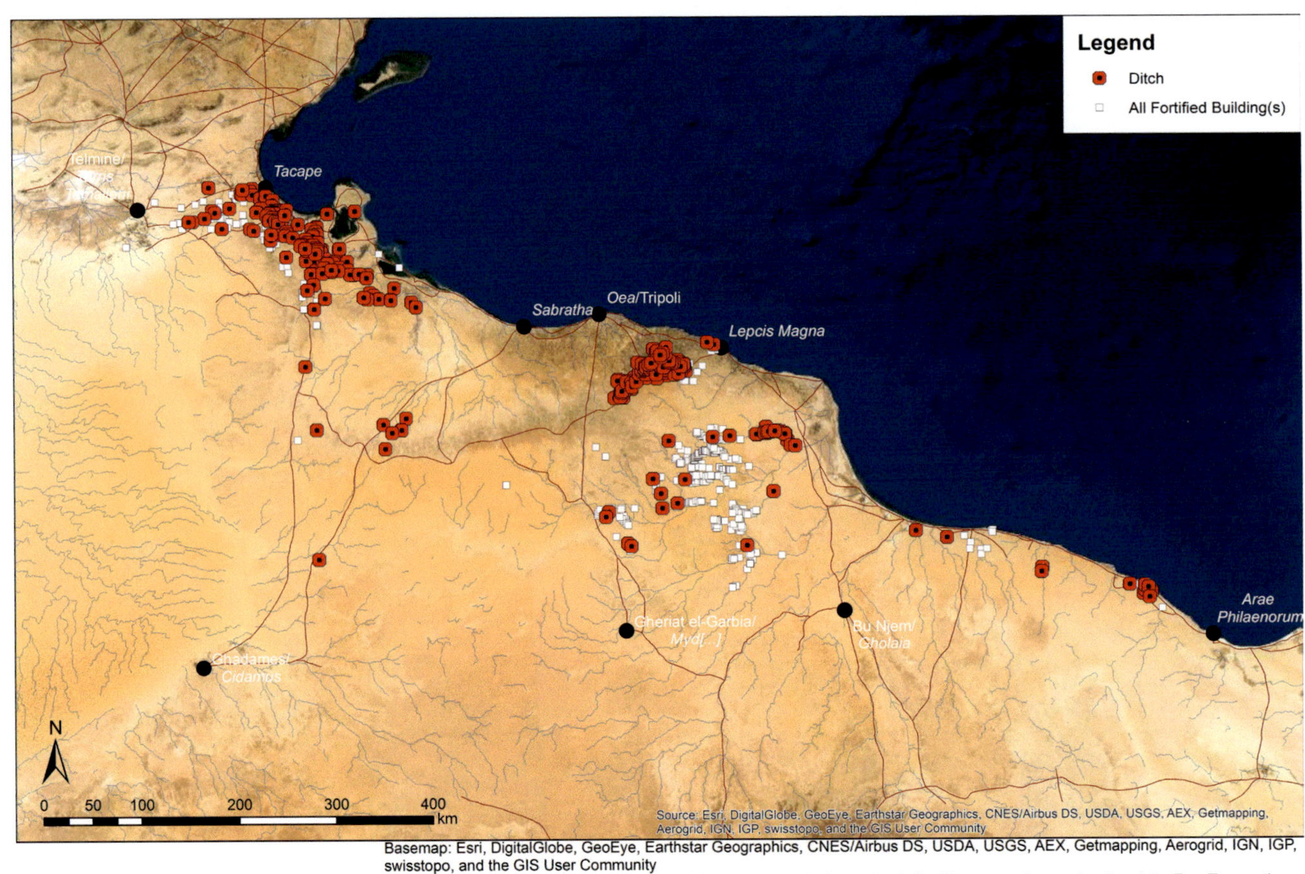

Figure 6.19: *Distribution of fortified buildings with ditches.*

Seven of these examples were rock-cut ditches which were clearly utilised to block off spurs of land; all but one of these were found in eastern pre-desert areas with one example in the southwest area. Far more common, however, were wide ditches which either surrounded or extended around two to three sides of the building (Figure 6.20). A single example was recorded as having a 'double-ditch', that is, it was ringed twice (180.029-g). Their use was clearly far more common in some areas than in others, with a near-total 95% of fortified sites identified in the western coastal region having ditches, and more than two-thirds in each of the southwest, central *gebel*, and eastern Syrtica regions. Though the absolute number of examples is small, the apparent popularity of ditches in eastern Syrtica but not western, is especially interesting, as surrounding ditches were also a frequent feature of fortified sites as one moved eastwards into Cyrenaica.[501] In the other regions, one-third

[501] Goodchild 1951b; LeQuesne, Basell & Sheibani 2010: 22.

Figure 6.20: *Examples of wide, surrounding ditches.*

or fewer of the known fortified sites had ditches, and indeed in the southern part of the eastern pre-desert, three of the four sites with ditches were of the rock-cut defensive barrier type, rather than the surrounding type.

It is important to note that while the ditches themselves are highly visible on satellite imagery, this is often the only evidence we have for the presence of a site at all and for the identification of that site as 'fortified'. I was only able to identify with any confidence the type of building associated with a ditch in 66 (21%) of the 321 examples listed above, and more often than not, a large central mound is all that attests that something once stood there. It is also sometimes the case, as mentioned above, that the structures found within these ditches would, on their own, potentially have been classified as unfortified; those noted by Mrabet in the western coastal area tended to be relatively small and simple structures.[502] Without further investigation,

[502] Mrabet 2011: 229–230.

we have no way of knowing how a ditch might relate chronologically to the structure within its bounds; it does not seem unlikely that in some cases, ditches may have been additions to pre-existing unfortified farm buildings.[503]

The type of ditches described here are often identified as defensive features and there is little doubt that they could serve this purpose; six examples had both a ditch and an enceinte. However, as with enceintes, they probably also served the same purpose as a farmyard, i.e. an open area in which one could keep animals and undertake other domestic, agricultural or productive activities.[504] Supporting the notion that the purpose of the ditches need not solely have been defensive is the fact that in some cases the ditches do not appear to completely surround the central mound or building, as TAR07-g or TAR09-g, where the ditch extends around only three sides. Emrage has also recently suggested, with reference to similar sites in Cyrenaica, that ditches were actually the by-product of extracting building material for the buildings that they surround.[505] Another theory we might consider is that they could be used for water collection (or drainage), essentially acting as large, wide reservoirs or even protected areas in which one could plant gardens, by taking advantage of the occasional periods of heavy rain.[506] Additionally, at the site of Gasr el-Heneia in southwestern Cyrenaica (c.150 km northeast of *Arae Philaenorum*), there were actually galleries cut into the outside wall of the ditch. Although this was almost certainly a military site, Goodchild's suggestion that "much of the daily life of the fort was carried on in the deep flat-bottomed ditch" and that in times of peace, it acted as the main stables for the horses, illustrates the possibilities of this feature.[507]

6.2.2 Size

Of the 810 fortified structures and settlements recorded in my catalogue, the total ground area defined by the exterior walls of each structure (not including any additional features discussed in the previous two sections) was recorded for 422 (52%). The minimum, maximum, mean and median figures of all fortified buildings divided by region are presented in Table 6.4.

Overall, it is immediately apparent that the mean and median sizes of the fortified structures are more uniform across the whole of Tripolitania and, in general, smaller than their unfortified counterparts (Figure 6.21); even those areas for which sample numbers are very small, i.e. eastern Syrtica, the central coastal area and the southwest, do not deviate significantly from this trend. The overall mean of the fortified buildings here of 423 m² is less than half that of the overall mean for the unfortified buildings (881 m²) discussed in the last chapter, and the fortified mean was smaller than the unfortified one in all the individual regions except the west *gebel*. Even there, it is only a small margin of difference and, while there were 71 fortified buildings measured, there were only seven unfortified buildings with recorded sizes. We should also note here, that as with the unfortified buildings, the medians were smaller than the means in all cases, and the same cautions therefore apply concerning the effect that a few exceptionally large examples have had on these calculations.

The areas with the largest overall means for fortified buildings are the southern part of the eastern pre-desert and the southwest region (579 and 578 m² respectively), followed by the western *gebel* region (498 m²). This is quite a different story from the unfortified

	Total buildings	Minimum size (m²)	Maximum size (m²)	Mean (m²)	Median (m²)
1. W. coastal	19	18	900	401	324
2. W. *gebel*	71	16	3,000	498	342
3. Southwest	6	320	1,225	578	400
4. Central coastal	4	134	306	205	189
5. Central *gebel*	45	64	1,892	365	224
6. E. pre-desert, north	183	12	4,125	346	210
7. E. pre-desert, south	80	12	2,500	579	373
8. W. Syrtica	12	25	1,258	381	225
9. E. Syrtica	2	400	400	400	400
Total	*422*	*12*	*4,125*	*423*	*282*

Table 6.4: *Minimum, maximum, mean and median total areas for all fortified buildings, divided by region.*

503 Mattingly 1987: 85 fn.76.

504 Mrabet 2011: 228–232; Mattingly, Sterry & Leitch 2013: 173.

505 Emrage 2015: 99.

506 McGrath & Boyd 2001. Cf. also Varro's description of the *militare* i.e. ditch and bank enclosure (*de re Rustica*, 1.14).

507 Goodchild 1951b: 173–181.

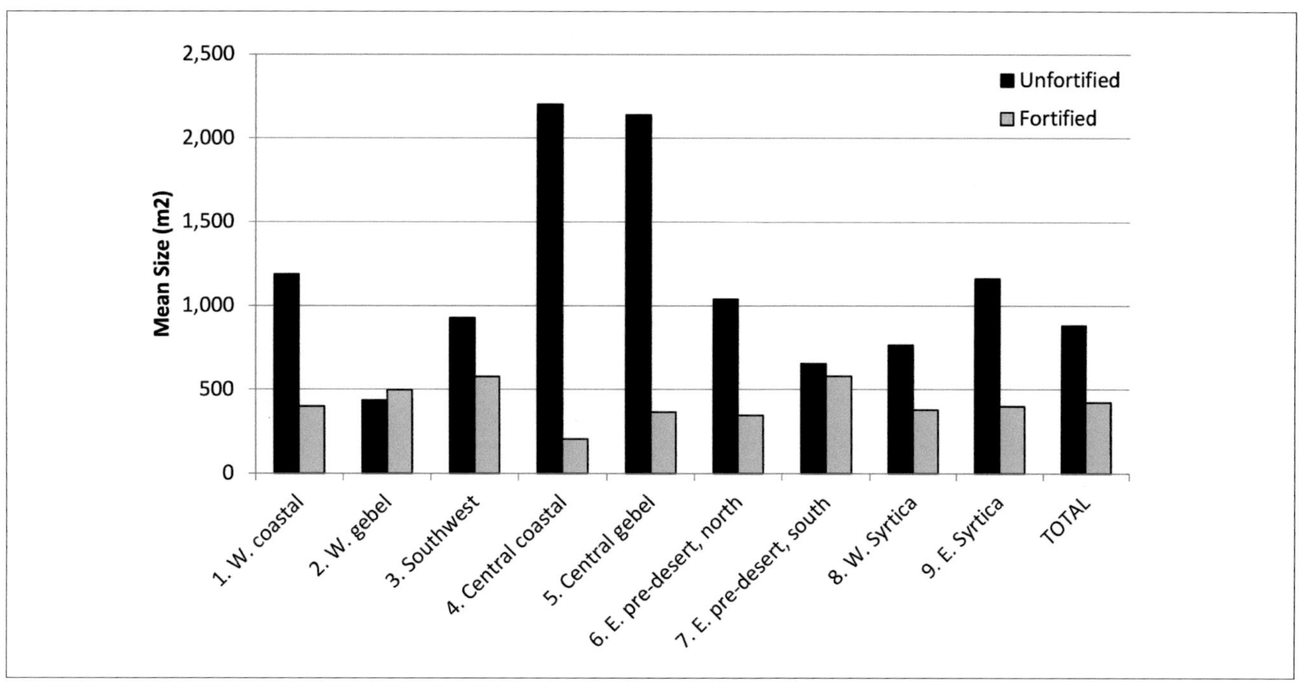

Figure 6.21: *Mean sizes of unfortified and fortified buildings.*

buildings, where the largest overall mean building sizes were found in the central *gebel* and coastal regions; in fact, the central coastal region has the smallest overall mean for fortified buildings. The western coastal region has undergone a similar drop in building size from the comparatively large unfortified buildings to smaller than average fortified ones.

It is especially striking that the southern part of the eastern pre-desert, which has the second smallest overall mean size of unfortified buildings is also the region with the largest overall mean for fortified buildings. Significantly, however, what we are seeing here is not an increase in the size of buildings in this region, but rather a decrease almost everywhere else. In terms of building size, if nothing else, this seems to suggest that there was a degree of stability in the southern parts of the eastern pre-desert that did not extend to other parts of Tripolitania. We can also perhaps relate this to the fact that the unfortified courtyard buildings of the southern part of the eastern pre-desert were the largest amongst those recorded in the four eastern pre-desert and Syrtica regions (see Section 5.2.2), perhaps hinting at the better establishment or success of the elite of that area.

In the last chapter, I argued that building size can be taken as a reasonable indicator of prosperity (albeit with exceptions), in that it reflects access and ability to marshal the resources necessary to construct buildings over a certain size. It is therefore tempting to view the overall trend of diminishing building sizes over time as a direct symptom of instability and decreasing prosperity in the region, particularly in the hinterlands of *Lepcis Magna*. However, while there may be some element of truth to this, there are more and complex factors to be taken into account when considering the significance of the size of fortified structures. In particular, it is important to understand that in many cases, this overall contraction in building sizes was not so much a straightforward loss of usable area as a change in the use and distribution of that space in different types of buildings and features. This is most evident in the introduction and popularity of multi-storey towers and the role of ditches (and to a lesser extent external yards and enceintes).

If we do separate analyses of the sizes of tower and compound buildings (Table 6.5 and Table 6.6; Figure 6.22), it is plain to see that there was a large margin of difference between the sizes of fortified towers and compounds as they were defined earlier, and that it is the small size of the tower buildings that have made the overall averages so low. It should be noted, however, that one of the defining characteristics actually used to differentiate towers from compounds in my classification, particularly in difficult cases was size. While I tried to limit the classification of buildings as towers only in cases where I was fairly confident that it had multiple storeys, buildings over c.25 x 25 m in size for which a plan could be discerned, were normally classified as compounds. Nevertheless, the separation of the buildings in this way does reveal some interesting trends.

In terms of their horizontal footprint, tower type buildings are clearly much smaller than most of the other building types discussed here, unfortified or fortified. The mean sizes of the towers remained within a relatively narrow range between regions, suggesting a degree of consistency across the entire region of Tripolitania, probably in part due to the practical difficulties

	Total buildings	Minimum size (m²)	Maximum size (m²)	Mean (m²)	Median (m²)
1. W. coastal	8	18	361	172	169
2. W. *gebel*	34	16	600	211	150
3. Southwest	4	320	400	374	387
4. Central coastal	4	134	306	205	189
5. Central *gebel*	31	64	672	195	156
6. E. pre-desert, north	151	12	575	211	180
7. E. pre-desert, south	52	12	575	266	252
8. W. Syrtica	7	25	304	167	144
9. E. Syrtica	1	400	400	400	400
Total	*292*	*12*	*672*	*220*	*196*

Table 6.5: *Minimum, maximum, mean and median total areas for fortified tower buildings, divided by region.*

	Total buildings	Minimum size (m²)	Maximum size (m²)	Mean (m²)	Median (m²)
1. W. coastal	5	225	900	650	899
2. W. *gebel*	31	165	3,000	862	750
3. Southwest	2	750	1,225	988	988
4. Central coastal	–	–	–	–	–
5. Central *gebel*	8	420	1,892	1,042	930
6. E. pre-desert, north	27	570	4,125	1,124	784
7. E. pre-desert, south	26	450	2,500	1,213	900
8. W. Syrtica	3	720	1,258	921	784
9. E. Syrtica	–	–	–	–	–
Total	*102*	*165*	*4,125*	*1,029*	*813*

Table 6.6: *Minimum, maximum, mean and median total areas for fortified compound buildings, divided by region.*

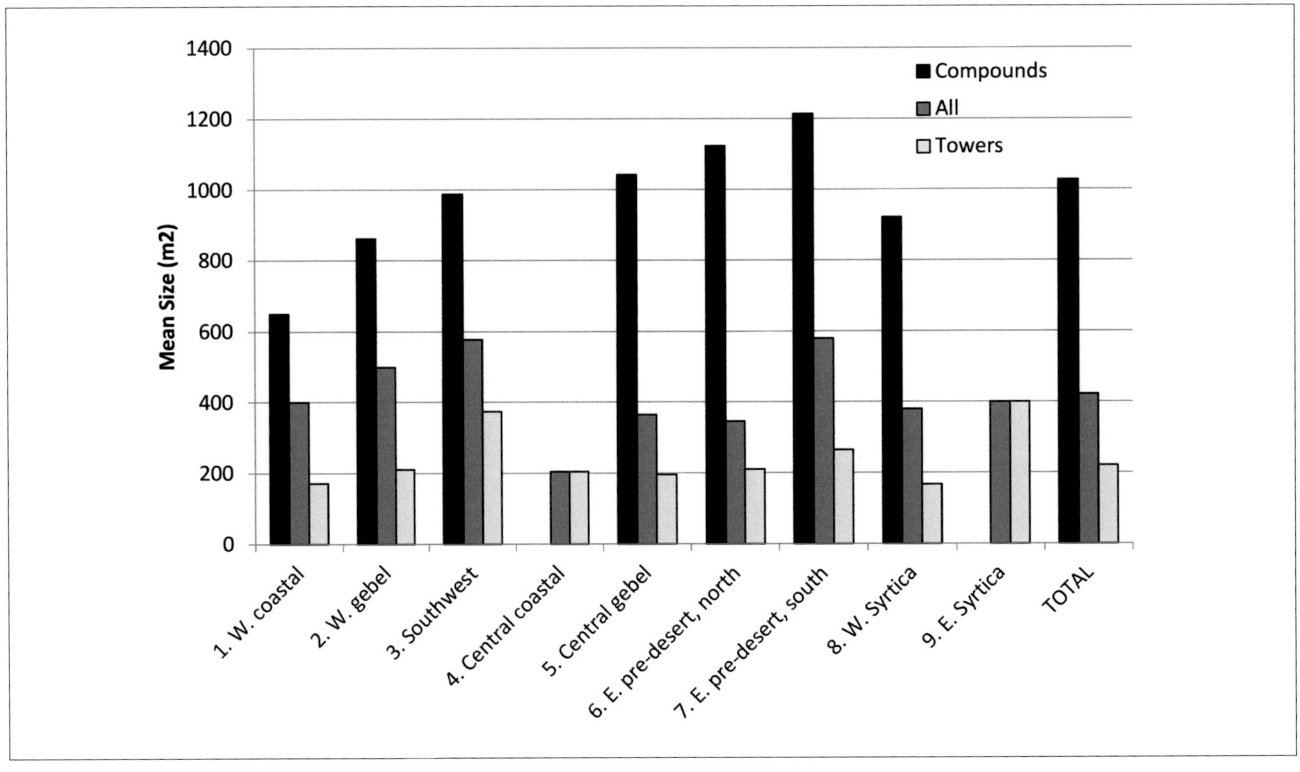

Figure 6.22: *Mean sizes (m²) of all fortified buildings, towers and compounds.*

and expense of constructing multi-storey structures over a certain size. The two areas with the highest means (eastern Syrtica and the southwest) both had very small sample sizes, lessening the reliability of these figures as representative. The areas with the next highest mean sizes were the southern and then the northern part of the eastern pre-desert, which as previously noted were the areas with some of the smallest unfortified buildings on average. Western Syrtica, the western coastal region and the central *gebel* had the smallest average sizes of buildings, all below 200 m^2.

If we consider the usable space that just one more storey would add to a building (and some towers had three or even more), this could have accounted for an additional 60–80% or more (depending on the size and arrangement of the lightwell). Nevertheless, even taking this into account, the usable space inside fortified tower buildings was, in most cases, more limited than in other types.

In particular, we cannot conclude that the small average horizontal footprint of fortified towers reflected a comparative lack of wealth when compared to other types of buildings, especially unfortified ones, with a larger recorded area; indeed, with regard to unfortified farmyard buildings at least, the opposite seems more likely to be true. Even if unfortified farmyard buildings had a larger horizontal footprint and usable area, much of that area was normally a simple open-air yard, bounded by a single, low stone wall. Fortified towers, on the other hand, even relatively small ones, because of their greater height and multiple storeys, represented a significant increase of investment in the resources, skills and effort necessary to construct and maintain them in the long term.

It is clear from the analysis of fortified compounds that some fortified buildings were still very large, a fact which the overall means disguise, skewed as they are by the very small sizes of the more common tower buildings. As already discussed, fortified compounds are in many ways similar to unfortified courtyard buildings in terms of their form and layout, and it is therefore more reasonable to make direct comparisons concerning their size (Table 6.7; Figure 6.23).

The overall difference in average size of the fortified compound buildings compared to the unfortified courtyard buildings is slight; however, a closer look indicates that this is because a significant change in size seems to have occurred only in some regions. The two areas in which the largest average sizes of unfortified courtyard buildings were found, the central *gebel* and the western coastal region, saw fortified compounds of a much smaller average size than unfortified buildings. By contrast, the fortified compounds of the regions of the eastern pre-desert and western Syrtica remained about the same size as their unfortified counterparts, placing them on a par with those in the central *gebel*, possibly indicating a degree of continuity that was not the case in other parts of the region. Unfortunately, the fact that there was only one example of a courtyard building in each of the west *gebel* and southwest regions means that it is not possible to make as meaningful a comparison about change in this regard, but we can note that the

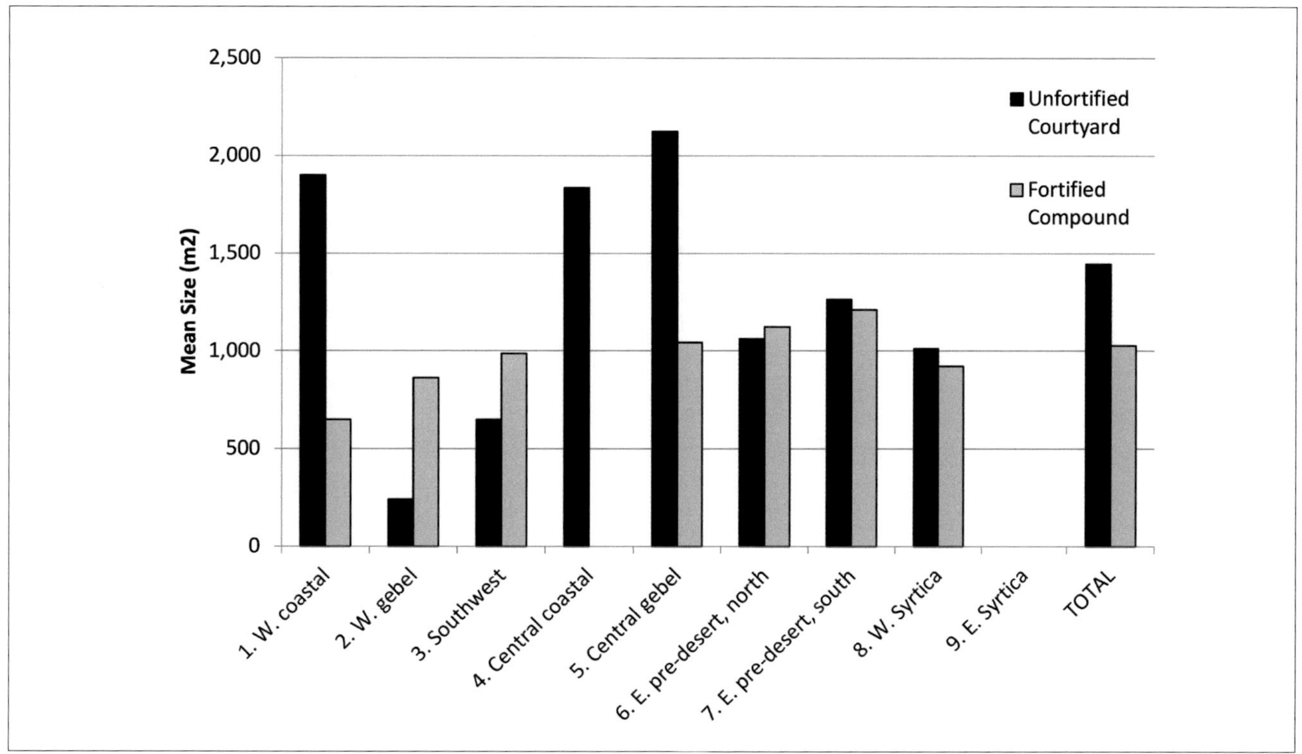

Figure 6.23: *Mean sizes of unfortified courtyard and fortified compound buildings, divided by region.*

	Unfortified courtyard buildings (#)	Unfortified courtyard mean (m²)	Fortified compound buildings (#)	Fortified compound mean (m²)
1. W. coastal	5	1,903	5	650
2. W. *gebel*	1	240	31	862
3. Southwest	1	650	2	988
4. Central coastal	5	1,838	–	–
5. Central *gebel*	29	2,125	8	1,042
6. E. pre-desert, north	30	1,063	27	1,124
7. E. pre-desert, south	32	1,267	26	1,213
8. W. Syrtica	11	1,011	3	921
9. E. Syrtica	–	–	–	–
Total	*114*	*1,445*	*102*	*1,029*

Table 6.7: *Mean sizes of unfortified courtyard and fortified compound buildings, divided by region.*

average sizes of the fortified compound buildings here were also of a comparable size, or slightly smaller than those found further east.

External Yards, Ditches and Enceintes

As discussed in the last section, external yards, surrounding ditches and enceintes all potentially increased the usable space associated with a given farm building. Given the apparent overall contraction in physical building sizes just outlined, this is potentially significant in that again, this would counteract any apparent loss of space.

Ten structures with external yards had their total size recorded (Appendix Table 23). Of these, all of them also had the size of the individual building without the yard also recorded, allowing me to calculate how much space was gained by the addition of an external yard. This increase ranged between 35 and 1,200% of the original building, on average, approximately a 400% increase.[508] The areas enclosed by enceintes surrounding fortified buildings was recorded for 26 examples (Appendix Table 24). Of these, 23 also had the size of the fortified building within recorded and the area gained by the addition of an external enceinte was between 54 and 2,165%, with an average increase of around 540%.[509] Finally, the area covered by structures plus surrounding ditches was recorded for 260 examples (Appendix Table 25). Of these, only 49 had a central building for which a size was recorded. Of these examples, the area gained by the addition of a surrounding ditch was between 49 and 2,300%, averaging around a 600% increase.

What these figures demonstrate is that there was a great deal of space which could be gained through the addition of one of these features, while still maintaining a degree of protection and privacy. As already mentioned, nearly half (46%) of the fortified buildings recorded in my database had one or more of these features, most of which were ditches. If we accept that one or all of these features were not only serving defensive purposes, but also added valuable room for agricultural and pastoral activities, then this potentially contradicts any idea that fortified farms had less usable space than their unfortified counterparts. It is perhaps true that the central buildings themselves were smaller, but these figures indicate that, in certain areas of Tripolitania, notably the western coastal region, the southwest, the central *gebel* and eastern Syrtica, the addition of a ditch, external yard or enceinte may have formed a significant part of a farm. As established earlier, however, external yards and enceintes were not that common anywhere, so despite the fact that in a few cases these types of features could clearly increase available space, either this was not considered a priority in the regions where ditches were not common, or other ways were found to achieve this.

This is not to suggest that the defensive aspect of these features with which they are normally associated was not still relevant. A building which is, itself, more fortified and in the centre of a ditched compound, rather than a range of rooms along the exterior compound wall, is indeed more defensible. However, it is important that the usable agricultural and pastoral space has not been lost, but rather it has simply been distributed in a different way that also, in fact, maximises defensibility (although, of course, anything left in the ditch area was at higher risk of being lost or damaged). Another factor

[508] This was measured by calculating the ratio of each building size alone and that with the additional space created by the feature. For example, if a 100 m² building, when measured with its yard is 500 m², this represents a 400% increase in size.

[509] Worth noting is that in one example recorded in my catalogue but not included in the calculations above, a single enceinte extended from the banks of the ditches to enclose two adjacent ditched sites (MDr-NS42-g1 and –g2) and part of the small wadi tributary they sit beside. The fact, however, that each fortified building also had its own ditch, may suggest that this very large enceinte (14,975 m²) was a later addition.

worth considering is that the creation of enclosures formed using ditches and banks, while potentially more labour-intensive in the construction itself, depending on the size of the ditch, required less technical ability than building a stone wall and required fewer physical resources, eliminating the need to acquire stone and any tools needed to work that stone. And indeed, these ditched and banked 'yards' could easily have been supplemented by the addition of fences, stakes or thorny plants which are common in the pre-desert.

6.2.3 Use of Space: Presses, Crops and Animals

Much of what was already discussed in Section 5.2.3 concerning how space was used in unfortified farm buildings is generally applicable here as well. Interior, covered spaces would most likely have been used for human and sometimes also animal habitation, domestic activities and certain production activities such as pressing. Outdoor spaces could be used for animals, further domestic or social activities, as well as other types of production or processing activities. However, in many fortified buildings, there were significant physical changes to the layout and relative sizes of covered and uncovered spaces in these buildings from what had come before, and this almost certainly would have had an impact on the ways in which those spaces were used. In addition, the very fortification of the buildings carries implications about the ways in which these spaces were used and perceived.

Tower buildings probably represented the most dramatic change in form and appearance of the architecture of the region. While it is clear that these buildings were certainly defensible, we know very little about how or in what ways the space in these buildings was used, particularly how the utilisation of the multiple storeys in the buildings may have differed. Upper storeys were reached by way of (often quite narrow) staircases, or presumably by ladders, wooden staircases or hand/foot grips in the cases where no stone stairs appear to have been found.[510] As a result, any activities requiring bulky or heavy equipment (at least any that had to be moved with any regularity) probably did not take place in these upper storeys.

The idea of these structures as fortified granaries was previously discussed with reference to the term *centenarium*. This potential function has been supported in some cases by the existence of rooms in some of these buildings which had no entrance. At Kh022-g, in the southern part of the eastern pre-desert, for example, several rooms on the ground floor had no apparent entrance and has thus been interpreted as a possible 'storage *gasr*' by the *ULVS* team. Similarly, at Henchir el-Gueciret/*Turris Maniliorum Arelliorum* (RLT086-g) in the western *gebel*, one room in the northeast corner appears to have had no opening.[511]

In some cases, like the military outpost of Ksar Tarcine/*Tibubuci* discussed in Chapter 4, an additional or alternative function for the ground floor could have been a stable for animals, while upper floors would be used for human habitation.[512] In addition to the ground floor functioning as a partial replacement for the space which was previously available in the external farmyards which were now a rare feature, a possible advantage of this set up is that during cold nights, the body heat from the animals would rise and help keep the rooms above warmer. More investigations into the interiors of a larger number of fortified tower buildings would be necessary to gain more insight into how common this arrangement might have been.

However, at the same time, while the ground floor of a fortified tower could house a certain number of animals for short periods of time, as demonstrated above, the ground area of these buildings would have been a fraction of the area previously put aside in farmyards. Given that I have suggested that the function and presence of farmyards in the last chapter would primarily have been associated with the corralling of animals, a particularly common and important feature in the eastern pre-desert and Syrtica, this raises some questions about both the reasons for and the consequences of them no longer being common features. It could suggest a general move to the use of perishable materials, such as branches or mudbrick to construct stock enclosures. In addition, it is possible that these enclosures were now more often detached from the main habitation buildings, which as discussed in the methodology, have not been included in my analyses.

Furthermore, as discussed in previous chapters, structures identified as stone huts are a ubiquitous feature of the eastern pre-desert and probably other regions where they are less visible, and although they are difficult to date, it is not improbable that those found in proximity to the larger buildings discussed here were associated with them in some way, as outbuildings for storage, stabling and even extra human accommodation. Even more than their unfortified counterparts, as will be discussed in more detail in Section 6.3 below, and particularly in the eastern pre-desert areas, fortified buildings were associated with small, clustered settlements composed of unfortified buildings and enclosures.

While the loss of farmyard space was a potential concern in the eastern pre-desert and Syrtica, tower buildings were not as common in other regions, where courtyard compounds made up a more significant proportion of the fortified buildings. However, as demonstrated in the

[510] Brogan & Smith 1984: 75.

[511] Welsby 1992: 97–98; Scott, Dore, & Mattingly 1996: 12; Trousset 1974: 85.

[512] Trousset 1974: 90–91.

previous sections, compound buildings were also often smaller than their unfortified courtyard counterparts in the same regions. In these areas, we see the rise in the popularity of the surrounding ditch, particularly in the western coastal area and the central *gebel*, which as discussed above could have made up for some of the lost space.

As in the last chapter, we can also investigate what the evidence for presses, as well as other archaeobotanical and faunal evidence can tell us about the kinds of activities that were happening on these farms and therefore how the buildings may have been used. The frequency of presses recorded in fortified buildings was much lower than in unfortified farm buildings, with only 39 sites (5% of the total) reported as having at least one press, compared to more than 200 unfortified sites (13% of the total) (Table 6.8, and cf. Table 5.10; Figure 6.24).

This overall decline is in large part due to the significant reduction in the central *gebel*, where 92% of unfortified buildings had one or more presses (143/156), but only 11% of fortified ones did (17/153). Despite this, the central *gebel* still remained the area with the most

	Total buildings	Total buildings with presses		1	2	3	4	5
1. W. coastal	138	5	4%	5	–	–	–	–
2. W. *gebel*	84	1	1%	1	–	–	–	–
3. Southwest	13	–	–	–	–	–	–	–
4. Central coastal	6	2	33%	2	–	–	–	–
5. Central *gebel*	153	17	11%	7	5	3	1	1
6. E. pre-desert, north	289	6	2%	6	–	–	–	–
7. E. pre-desert, south	92	8	9%	8	–	–	–	–
8. W. Syrtica	19	–	–	–	–	–	–	–
9. E. Syrtica	16	–	–	–	–	–	–	–
Total	*810*	*39*	*5%*	*29*	*5*	*3*	*1*	*1*

Table 6.8: *Distribution of fortified buildings with presses by region.*

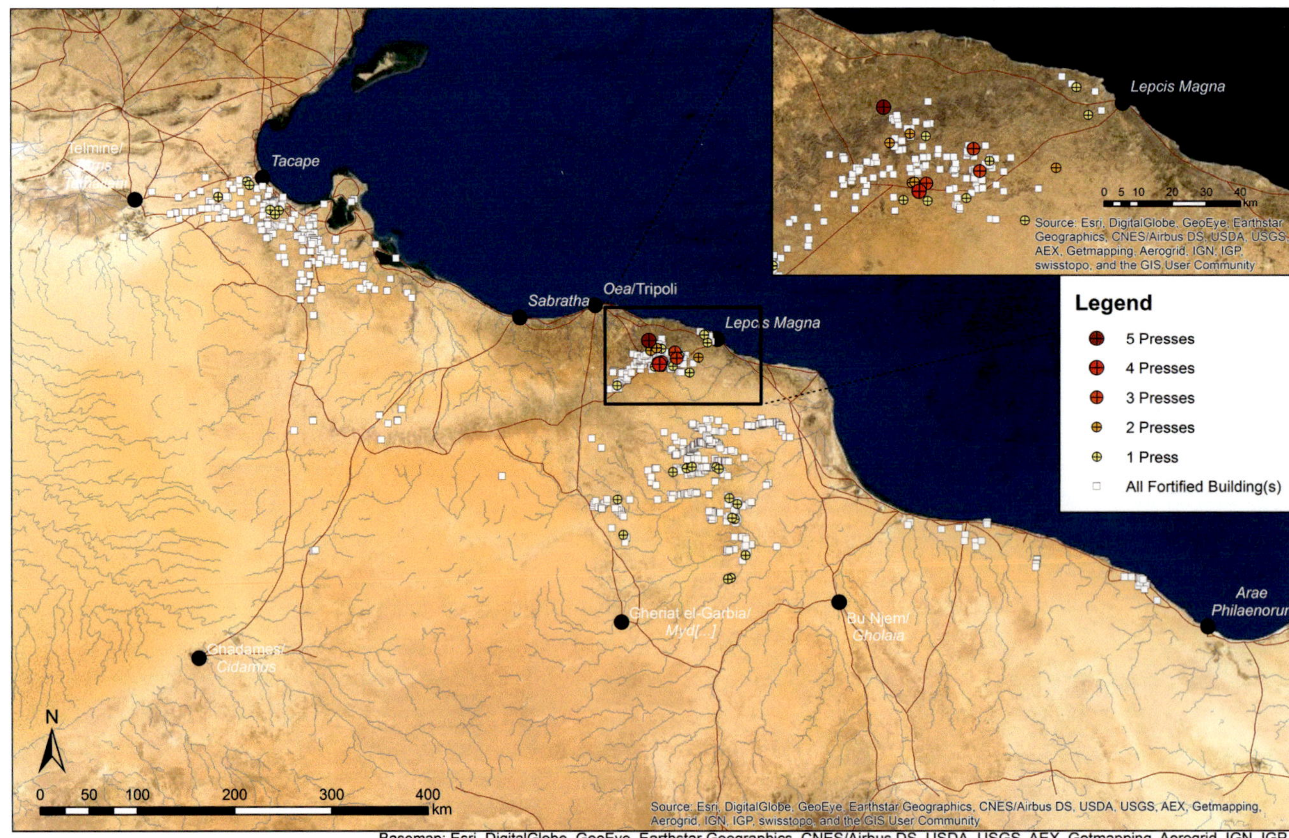

Figure 6.24: *Distribution of fortified buildings with presses.*

identified presses and the only area where more than one press was to be found at single site, to a maximum of five. In most of the other areas, there was a far less drastic decline in the numbers of sites between the unfortified and fortified buildings, probably, at least partly, because there were fewer to begin with. In the western regions, although the proportions of presses per numbers of sites recorded fell by 8–10%, the actual number of sites with presses across both areas only fell by one. The opposite occurred in the southern part of the eastern pre-desert, where the absolute number of sites with presses decreased (from 13 to 8), but the proportion of the sites that this represents actually tripled, from 3% to 9%. The lack of presses at fortified sites in the southwest and Syrtica regions is unsurprising, given the harsh conditions and the fact that they were already rare or unknown in unfortified buildings.

The comparative dearth of presses at fortified buildings compared to unfortified ones would appear to suggest that overall, there was a decline in olive oil and/ or wine production sites in the centuries following the rise in popularity of fortified buildings. One possible reason for this is that greater insecurity in the region during the third and fourth centuries AD[513] might have prompted people to reduce their reliance on olives as their main crop because they required long-term investment – the trees took years to mature, and so if anything happened to them, it could take quite a long time to recover. Instead, it is possible that annual crops became more important.[514]

However, it is important to bear in mind that there are several reasons why the low number of presses known to be associated with fortified buildings may be misleading. First of all, fortified farm buildings which appear to have 'replaced' unfortified farm buildings which had presses have not had those presses included in their numbers; it is difficult to know if and to what extent presses at these sites, or even sites which are otherwise abandoned, remained in use. There is also the problem of differentiating between presses which were actually found within fortified farm buildings and those that were found in buildings in surrounding settlements or outbuildings – the latter are not always reported with the fortified buildings themselves. In addition, the height of the fortified towers means that when they disintegrate, the ground floor of these structures, i.e. where one would expect to find a press, is often completely obscured.

Conversely, particularly if press elements are no longer standing *in situ*, it can be difficult to tell whether they are present on a site because they were being used for their original purpose, or whether they had been robbed from another site for use as building material, which is attested, for example at SLN19-g (Qasr Silin) and SLN49-g (Qasr al-Ahmar) in the central coastal zone.[515] High quality, monolithic press orthostats and other elements would have been expensive and difficult items to procure. It would be no surprise for them to be reused or even moved for their original purpose; but for them to be reused as building material suggests the failure of many olive farms (or vineyards) in the region, or at least a diminution in their production capacity. Alternatively, however, it could also be indicative of a change in pressing technology which rendered the large orthostats unnecessary.

Of the 39 fortified sites with presses, 26 had their building type also recorded (Appendix Table 26). Of these, 14 were found in compound buildings, while 12 were found in towers. As discussed above, the number of presses located at fortified sites is potentially unreliable, but it is perhaps significant that the number found at compound sites was actually slightly larger than the number associated with towers, a disproportionate amount considering there were three times as many towers identified as there were compounds in the first place. If this pattern is indeed representative, a probable explanation is that pressing required more room than was generally available in tower-like buildings, and so it therefore may have made more sense logistically for those who were still engaged in this activity to construct compound type buildings or to renovate/fortify existing unfortified buildings.

Twenty-five of the 39 fortified structures with one or more presses recorded, also had their size recorded (Appendix Table 27). As was the case with the unfortified buildings as demonstrated in Section 5.2.3, the overall average size of fortified buildings with presses (682 m^2) was considerably larger than the average size of fortified buildings overall (423 m^2). Again, the numbers with which we are dealing here are not that large and therefore unfortunately the degree to which they can be considered as representative of wider trends is in question. However, it was also the case when the data were broken down by region, that the buildings in which presses were found were on par, or more often, larger on average than the overall averages for fortified buildings.

When we further divide the analyses by building type, however, this was not always the case. The overall average size of tower-type buildings with presses (278 m^2) was larger than the overall average for all tower-type buildings (220 m^2), and the same was true in the central *gebel* and pre-desert regions (Appendix Table 28). The western and central coastal regions each only had one tower-type building with a press with its size recorded, but in both cases, the structure was smaller than the overall average for the region.

513 See Section 1.3.

514 A. Wilson, 2015. pers. comm.

515 Munzi *et al.* 2004: 48, 56.

Number of presses	Total buildings (w/ size recorded)	Minimum size (m²)	Maximum size (m²)	Mean (m²)	Median (m²)
1	21	120	2,473	670	500
2	2	672	729	701	701
3	1	132	132	132	132
5	1	1,444	1,444	1,444	1,444
Total	*25*	*120*	*2,473*	*682*	*570*

Table 6.9: *Minimum, maximum, mean and median sizes of fortified buildings with different numbers of presses.*

On average, fortified compound buildings with presses seem to have been of a comparable or slightly smaller size than the fortified compounds overall (Appendix Table 29). The only exception was in the eastern pre-desert, north, which maintained a higher average size for compound buildings with presses, though with only two examples of widely varying size (Mm012-g and Mm008-g, 952 and 2,090 m², respectively), we should not set too much store by this. This may be further evidence, therefore, that the production of olive oil and/or wine was no longer as lucrative a business as it had once been.

Four (of 25) fortified buildings with a recorded size had multiple presses (Table 6.9), but the correlation between size and number of presses is less clear than for the unfortified buildings. Nevertheless, if large building size can still be seen as reflective of wealth, the overall pattern could support the idea that despite the apparent overall decline in the industry of oil and/or wine production, those who stuck with it continued to do reasonably well for themselves. This is also supported by the analysis in Section 6.2.5 below which shows that as in the last chapter, the incidence of luxury features continued to be much higher at sites with presses than those without.

We can also look at archaeobotanical and faunal evidence to help us determine what kinds of plants and animals were present at these fortified buildings. Botanical and faunal samples were taken at five of the fortified sites included in my catalogue by the *ULVS* in the eastern pre-desert: Mm010-g (within building and middens), Gh075-g (midden, botanical evidence only), Gh127/Ghirza (middens, botanical samples collected during 1950s excavations, no faunal samples taken), Kh041-g (midden Kh1001), Bz028/906-g (midden, Bz908), Bz030/907-g (faunal evidence only).[516] Most of the samples from these were small, but those from Kh1001 and Bz908 were large enough for meaningful comparison.[517]

Overall, the archaeobotanical assemblages from the fortified structures were similar to those from the unfortified sites, with only a few differences. There were fewer remains of cereal grains overall recovered from the fortified sites of Kh1001 and Bz908 than at the unfortified farm site of Lm004. Barley was the most common grain identified at both the unfortified and fortified sites; however, while at Lm004 barley represented the vast majority, at Kh1001 and to a lesser extent Bz908, wheat species begin to make up a more substantial proportion of the identifiable assemblage. There were also more remains of grapes, figs and wild pistachio nutlets found at the fortified sites and the introduction at those sites of water melon and grass pea, 'replacing' the wild melon which was found at Lm004, as well as similar quantities of lentils, dates and safflower.[518] Again the relatively meagre evidence for olives is striking, which when coupled with the increase in the number of grape pips found over the unfortified sites seems to lend support to the idea that wine production was at least as common in this region as olive oil production.[519]

The faunal evidence for the fortified sites was also similar to that for the unfortified ones, with the bulk of the evidence coming from Mm010-g and Kh041-g (Kh1001). Again, and unsurprisingly, by far the most common species identified were sheep and goat, along with gazelle, antelope, camel and cattle in lesser quantities. The midden of Kh1001, associated with the tower Kh041, was the only site to produce bird bones (including chicken) and, interestingly for the pre-desert, a single fish veterbra (Couch's sea bream).[520] A single bone is scant evidence from which to make any significant conclusions, but its presence would seem to indicate that trade with the coast was still occurring during this later period (Kh1001 having been dated on the basis of the pottery evidence to the late third to sixth centuries AD).[521] A funerary inscription from Ghirza (fourth

516 Van der Veen, Grant, & Barker 1996: 229.

517 Van der Veen, Grant, & Barker 1996: 259.

518 Van der Veen, Grant, & Barker 1996: 234–238, Tables 8.1–8.3.

519 Van der Veen, Grant & Barker 1996: 259.

520 Van der Veen, Grant & Barker 1996: 241–242, 249–253.

521 Scott, Dore, & Mattingly 1996: 139.

century AD?) recording the sacrifice of 51 bulls and 38 goats also supports the idea of the continued importance of pastoralism, and sculptural evidence from Ghirza and elsewhere in the pre-desert attests to the presence of camels and other domestic animals in the region alongside agricultural activities.[522]

Other than these minor differences, and despite the significant architectural change that occurred with the swift rise in popularity of the tower-like building, based on the (admittedly very limited) botanical and faunal evidence, there does not appear to have been any major shift in the foods being produced and consumed and the animals being kept at the farms of the eastern pre-desert.[523] However, this is only one area, and one wonders how the assemblages from farms in other parts of the region might compare in this respect, and whether we might see more disruption in the agricultural patterns. Only more environmental analyses will tell. Nevertheless, for the eastern pre-desert at least, the agricultural and pastoral activities of the inhabitants of these buildings had not changed significantly, and we might ask what other aspects of the occupants' lives may have been changed by the new building forms they inhabited.

Finally, one additional advantage or consequence of the tower buildings especially, but also compound structures, was that these structures were more internally focussed and allowed for a greater degree of privacy.[524] A far larger proportion of the usable space in fortified buildings, particularly fortified towers, was covered, indoor space, and even the area of a central courtyard, while open to the air, would have been far more private and protected than an unfortified farmyard area. Domestic activities which previously would have taken place outside the home in the open yard, potentially moved to within the home, inside an enclosed courtyard. This could be related to a greater need for defense against the elements or other people, but we could also consider a shift in cultural norms in which privacy became more important, perhaps especially to an elite class who wanted to separate themselves physically from their dependents and/or those from lower classes.

6.2.4 Materials and Construction Techniques

Materials

Like their unfortified counterparts, fortified buildings were mainly constructed of local stone, and the discussion in the previous chapter on the sources of materials and quarrying for the construction of buildings is equally applicable here.[525] There is also evidence in a number of fortified buildings for the re-use of materials robbed from unfortified buildings, including press elements as mentioned in the last section. It is not particularly difficult to see why one would rob stone from nearby abandoned structures for the construction of new ones, rather than going to the effort and cost of obtaining new materials. However, because of the limited availability of these materials or perhaps because of their larger size, the robbed materials were often only used in the lower courses and/or the quoins of the fortified structures, while the rest of the structure was supplemented with smaller masonry (Figure 6.25).[526]

The re-use of material is important because it confirms that at least some of the unfortified structures were indeed abandoned by the time of the construction of the fortified buildings, and reflects a conscious decision to not continue to maintain or re-occupy these structures. Because our dating evidence is so poor, it is unknown for how long these buildings had been abandoned before they were robbed. In some cases, this may have entailed a deliberate dismantling of a structure and a rebuilding for the same person or family taking place over the course of a very short period of time, or in others the complete abandonment of a site by one group, only to be robbed much later by another when it was already falling apart.

The evidence for roofing in fortified buildings is somewhat better than for their unfortified counterparts, and although this evidence was not recorded consistently enough to allow for detailed analyses, it appears that similar techniques to that described in the previous chapter continued to be used. Slots which were probably for wooden roof and upper floor beams were noted in a number of towers in the *ULVS* area; in at least one instance (Lm003-g), a wooden beam was preserved *in situ* and was radiocarbon dated to the third or fourth century AD, and another at one of the fortified buildings at Ghirza (Gh127-34) was identified as acacia.[527] In the pre-desert especially, timber of sufficient size and quality for this purpose would probably not have been widely available, though clear evidence for its use in both roofing and in pressing installations means that it was coming from somewhere. Palm trees may have grown in some of the wadis, though probably not very many; perhaps timber was imported from the *gebel* and coastal areas or distributed from oases. Once wooden beams were in place, flat roofs could be formed using layers of palm fronds or other vegetation, consolidated with layers of mud which would bake and solidify in the

---

522 *IRT* 994; Brogan 1954; Brogan & Smith 1984: 220–221.

523 Van der Veen 1985: 25.

524 Fentress 2000: 15–16.

525 Section 5.2.4

526 See also Oates80-g (Gasr Haiuna), illustrated in Oates 1954: Plate XIV, c.

527 Brogan & Smith 1984: 72–73; Dore & Van der Veen 1986: 65–67.

Mm010-g (Gasr Leb'r), Wadi Mimoun, E. pre-desert, north (*ULVS* Archive: FB22/N26/1984; cropped for clarity)

Figure 6.25: *A fortified building with larger masonry in lower courses (possibly robbed/re-used from earlier buildings) and smaller masonry in upper courses.*

sun. Some of the aforementioned slots may also have been 'putlog' slots, which may be remnants of scaffolding used during construction, but could also be used as steps or handholds for climbing to upper storeys.

Another form of roofing used in the region was vaulting, and a number of fortified buildings recorded in my catalogue employed this technique. Vaulting does not seem to have been used in any unfortified farm buildings in the countryside of which I am aware, and only appears to become more common in domestic structures in the later Romano-Libyan period and more so in the Islamic period.[528] However, due to the low number of buildings in general for which we have definite evidence of the type of roofing used and once again, our poor understanding of the dating and phasing of individual buildings, we should not discount the possibility that vaulted roofs may have been more commonly employed in the Romano-Libyan period than the evidence currently suggests.

Construction Techniques: Previous Investigations

Goodchild first noted very early on in his investigations of fortified farm buildings that there were recognisable variations in the quality of masonry. He described three classes, starting with careful courses of large, regular blocks (though not of ashlar quality) which he dated to the early third century AD, followed by the gradual decline in quality of both the regularity and size of the stones use and the regularity of the coursing.[529] A few years later at Ghirza, Brogan and Smith encountered only the second of Goodchild's masonry classifications (smaller blocks but still in relatively regular courses) and further subdivided it into five grades, again based on the regularity of the blocks and the coursing, applying them to all of the buildings at Ghirza, not only the fortified buildings.[530]

As already briefly outlined in the previous chapter, at the beginning of their investigations, the *ULVS* team initially followed Goodchild's basic masonry classification system for both fortified and unfortified buildings, though putting much less emphasis on the chronological aspect. They soon realised, however, that his system did not reflect the variability that they were seeing, particularly in what was originally Goodchild's middle class, into which the majority of the fortified farm buildings seemed to fall.[531] In addition, the *ULVS* began noting a significant number of buildings of near- or semi-ashlar

[528] Mattingly 1995: 202; Mattingly & Dore 1996: 133.

[529] Goodchild 1950b: 35–36.

[530] Brogan & Smith 1984: 47.

[531] Mattingly & Dore 1996: 129.

construction which did not fit comfortably into any of Goodchild's original categories. As a result, they eventually developed a new classification system but again, it was too late to apply it retroactively or systematically.[532] While other surveys in Tripolitania have obviously discussed and described the masonry used in fortified buildings, noting a variety of techniques, no other projects have explicitly conducted any detailed comparative analyses or attempted to construct any type of typology.[533]

Construction Techniques: Analyses

Although it will become obvious that some of the techniques used in the construction of fortified farm buildings were never used in unfortified buildings and vice versa, I have used essentially the same masonry typology for fortified buildings as was established for unfortified buildings in the last chapter. Despite some of the differences, by applying the same classification system to all types of buildings, with the understanding that some masonry classes might never appear in certain types of buildings, it becomes far easier to detect patterns in the types and quality of masonry used and how they changed along with other architectural features.[534]

Also important to note is that my analyses are largely based on the construction technique recorded for the exterior walls of the buildings in question. It can be demonstrated that in some cases, the construction techniques used for the interior walls of a structure were different than that used for the exterior, as in the example of Oates15-g, which was described as having on its exterior 'a fine ashlar face', while the interior face used regular, but non-ashlar masonry, and interior partitions walls utilised *opus africanum*.[535] Unfortunately, again due to the overall poor and inconsistent recording of masonry techniques across the region, the exterior or most dominant masonry technique used in a building was more often the only one recorded.

Of the masonry techniques which were identified in the last chapter in unfortified buildings,[536] the following were also noted in fortified buildings: ashlar masonry (Figure 6.26, though as mentioned above, this often seems to have been re-used from earlier buildings), *opus africanum*, regular and irregular masonry (*petit appareil*) (Figure 6.27 and Figure 6.28), mortared

Cowper35-g (Kasr Zuguseh), Central *gebel* (Cowper 1897: 162, fig. 47)

An013-g, Wadi Antar, E. pre-desert, north (*ULVS* Archive: F447/N35/14.10.1981; cropped for clarity)

Figure 6.26: *Ashlar masonry.*

[532] Mattingly & Dore 1996: 129; Scott, Dore & Mattingly 1996: 8–11.

[533] Cf. also Emrage's division of masonry used in fortified buildings in the Wadi al-Kuf (Cyrenaica), into 'ashlar work', 'small and medium roughly dressed and irregular blockwork with ashlar quoins', and 'mixture of ashlar work and medium and small blocks' (Emrage 2015: 86–92).

[534] It also addresses one of the problematic building-types identified by the *ULVS*, namely the '*gasr*-type farms', as "what distinguishes these sites from other [unfortified] farms is simply the quality of their masonry, which is equivalent to the carefully-coursed blockwork of the typical *gasr*" (Mattingly & Dore 1996: 121–122), a potentially misleading association.

[535] Oates 1953: 103.

[536] Section 5.2.4.

BS068-g, Bir Scedua Basin, E. pre-desert, north (*ULVS* Archive: F463/N9/17.10.1981; cropped for clarity)

Gb004-g, Wadi Gobbeen, E. pre-desert, north (*ULVS* Archive: F129/N24/12.11.1980; cropped for clarity)

Figure 6.27: *Regular masonry.*

Hm001-g, Wadi H'mee, E. pre-desert, north (*ULVS* Archive: F422/N20/4.10.1981; cropped for clarity)

Hq001-g, Wadi Harqus, E. pre-desert, north (*ULVS* Archive: F492/N2/30.9.1981; cropped for clarity)

Figure 6.28: *Irregular masonry.*

Gj006/BUW022-g, Wadi Garjuma, E. pre-desert, north (*ULVS* Archive: F130/N16/13.11.1980)

Figure 6.29: *Coursed rubble/drystone.*

BS028-g, Bir Scedua Basin, E. pre-desert, north
(*ULVS* Archive: F453/N30/14.10.1981; cropped for clarity)

Kh041-g, Wadi Umm el-Kharab, E. pre-desert, south
(*ULVS* Archive: F131/N17/16.11.1980; cropped for clarity)

Figure 6.30: *Very regular masonry.*

rubble, and coursed rubble/drystone (Figure 6.29). A new category which does seem to have been limited to fortified buildings, and which I have termed 'very regular masonry' (often recorded as 'Class 2/near ashlar' by the *ULVS*),[537] consisting of exceptionally well-coursed blocks of a relatively small but consistent size, of a similar quality to ashlar construction but on a smaller scale (Figure 6.30, see also Mg003-g2 and Ms004-g in Figure 6.33, below). In addition, another new category was added to reflect instances where very high quality, larger masonry has been used in the lower courses, with smaller and/or rougher masonry being used in the upper courses, sometimes the result of the reuse of masonry from earlier sites, as already discussed (see Figure 6.25). No examples of the large orthostats, small orthostats or the 'Syrtica group' techniques as discussed in the last chapter were identified in fortified buildings.

[537] Scott, Dore & Mattingly 1996: 13.

	ashlar	ashlar lower & other upper	opus africanum	very regular masonry	regular masonry	irregular masonry	coursed rubble/ drystone	mortared rubble	Total
1. W. coastal	4	–	20	–	–	–	5	2	31
2. W. *gebel*	8	–	9	–	7	2	2	–	28
3. Southwest	–	–	1	–	–	–	–	–	1
4. Central coastal	1	–	–	–	3	–	–	1	5
5. Central *gebel*	3	3	1	–	6	4	5	1	23
6. E. pre-desert, north	1	2	–	44	44	11	4	–	106
7. E. pre-desert, south	2	–	–	20	24	2	6	–	54
8. W. Syrtica	–	–	–	–	3	1	1	–	5
Total	*19*	*5*	*31*	*64*	*87*	*20*	*23*	*4*	*253*

Table 6.10: *Distribution of construction techniques employed in fortified buildings, divided by region.*

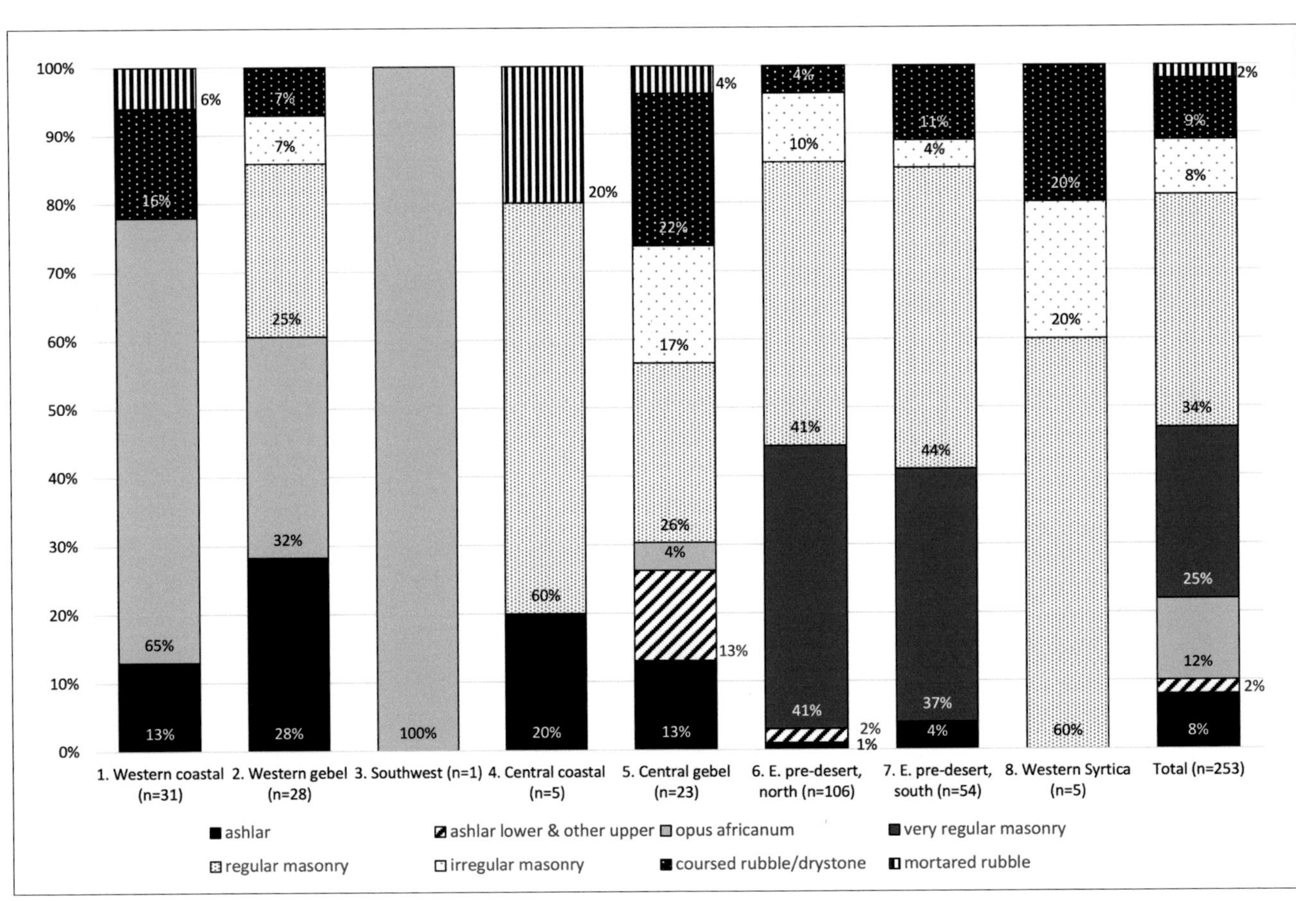

Figure 6.31: *Ratios of construction techniques employed in fortified buildings in different regions of Tripolitania.*

Of the 810 individually catalogued fortified structures, I was able to record the construction technique used for 253 (31%) (Table 6.10; Figure 6.31 and Figure 6.32). As in the last chapter, unfortunately, no data on construction techniques were available for eastern Syrtica, so it has not been included in the analyses or tables in this section. The most commonly recorded building type overall was regular masonry, followed by very regular masonry, though the latter was recorded only in the eastern pre-desert. The former is the most commonly recorded type in all of the central and eastern regions, whereas *opus africanum* and coursed rubble/drystone respectively were the most frequently recorded masonry types of unfortified buildings. In fact, in the central regions in particular, *opus africanum* has gone from the most commonly used technique in unfortified

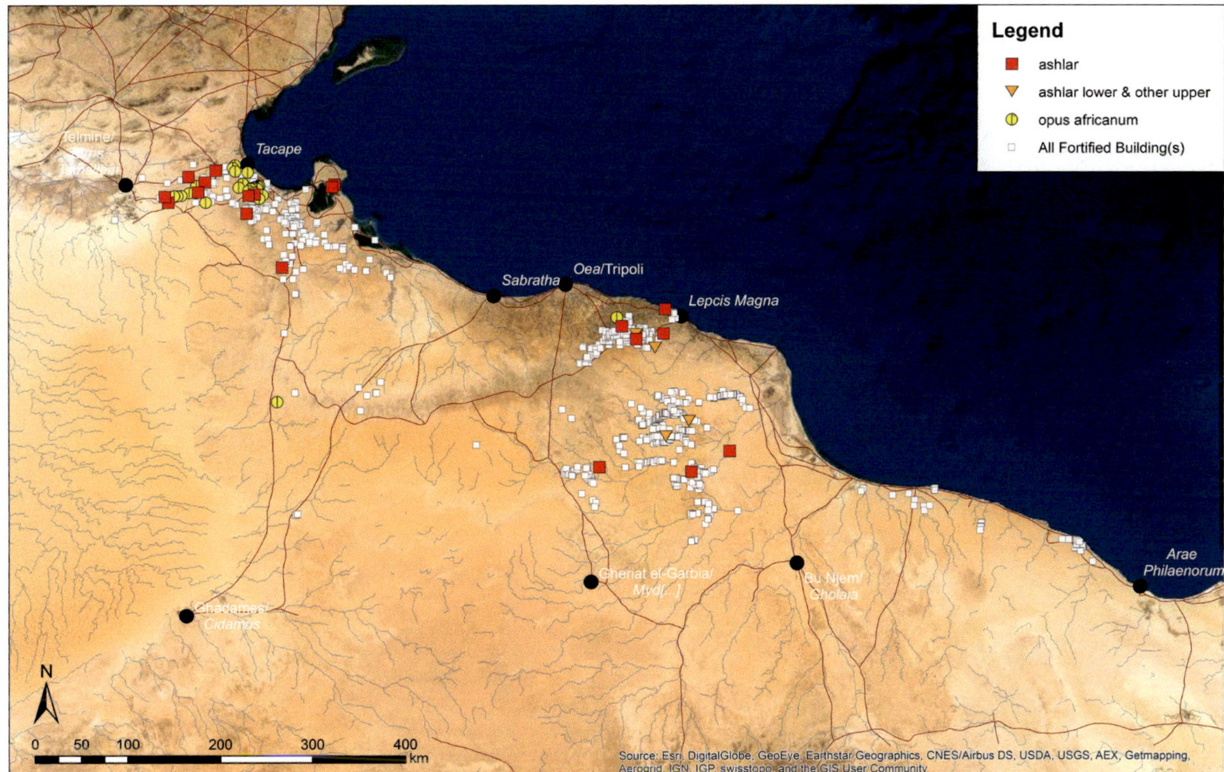

Basemap: Esri, DigitalGlobe, GeoEye, Earthstar Geographics, CNES/Airbus DS, USDA, USGS, AEX, Getmapping, Aerogrid, IGN, IGP, swisstopo, and the GIS User Community
Drainage: Lehner, B., Verdin, K., Jarvis, A. (2008): New global hydrography derived from spaceborne elevation data. Eos, Transactions, AGU, 89(10): 93-94. Retrieved from http://hydrosheds.cr.usgs.gov (15 sec Flow Accumulation)
Roads (Barrington Atlas): Ancient World Mapping Center (2012)

Figure 6.32a: *Geographical distribution of construction techniques used in fortified buildings: ashlar and* opus africanum.

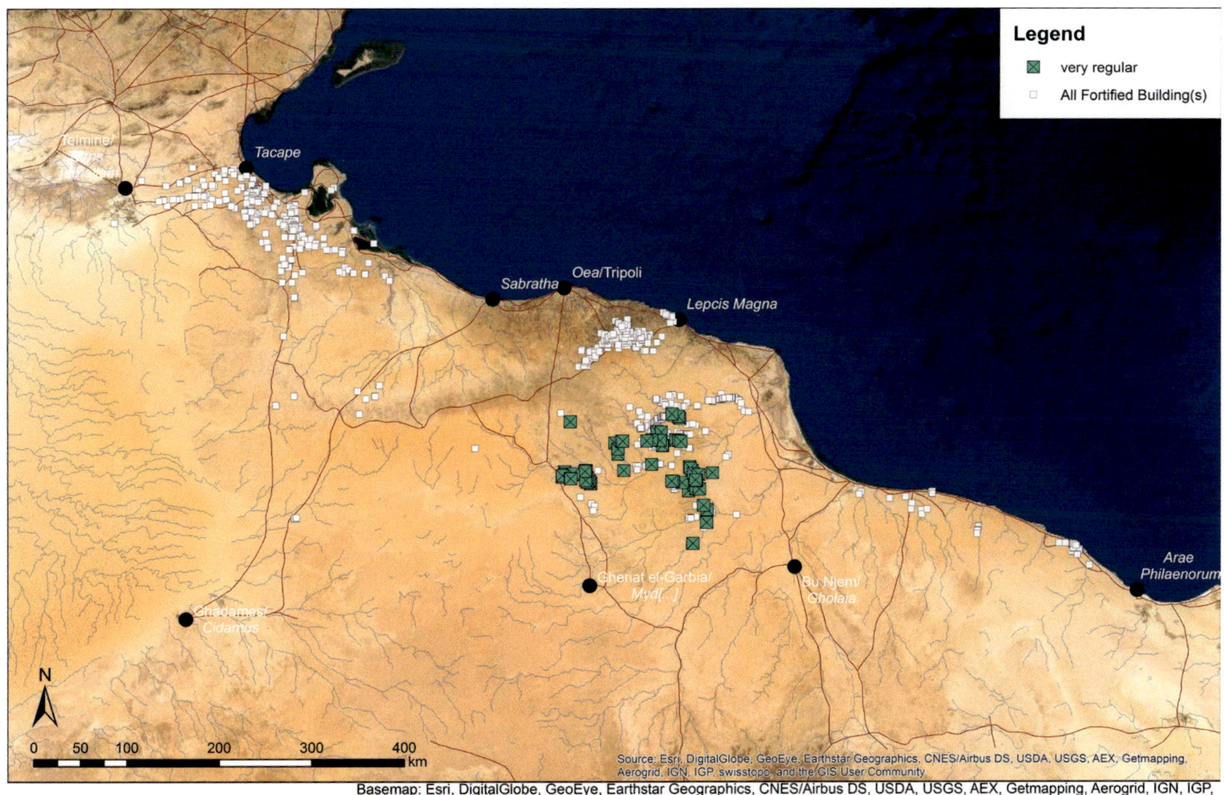

Basemap: Esri, DigitalGlobe, GeoEye, Earthstar Geographics, CNES/Airbus DS, USDA, USGS, AEX, Getmapping, Aerogrid, IGN, IGP, swisstopo, and the GIS User Community
Drainage: Lehner, B., Verdin, K., Jarvis, A. (2008): New global hydrography derived from spaceborne elevation data. Eos, Transactions, AGU, 89(10): 93-94. Retrieved from http://hydrosheds.cr.usgs.gov (15 sec Flow Accumulation)
Roads (Barrington Atlas): Ancient World Mapping Center (2012)

Figure 6.32b: *Geographical distribution of construction techniques used in fortified buildings: very regular masonry.*

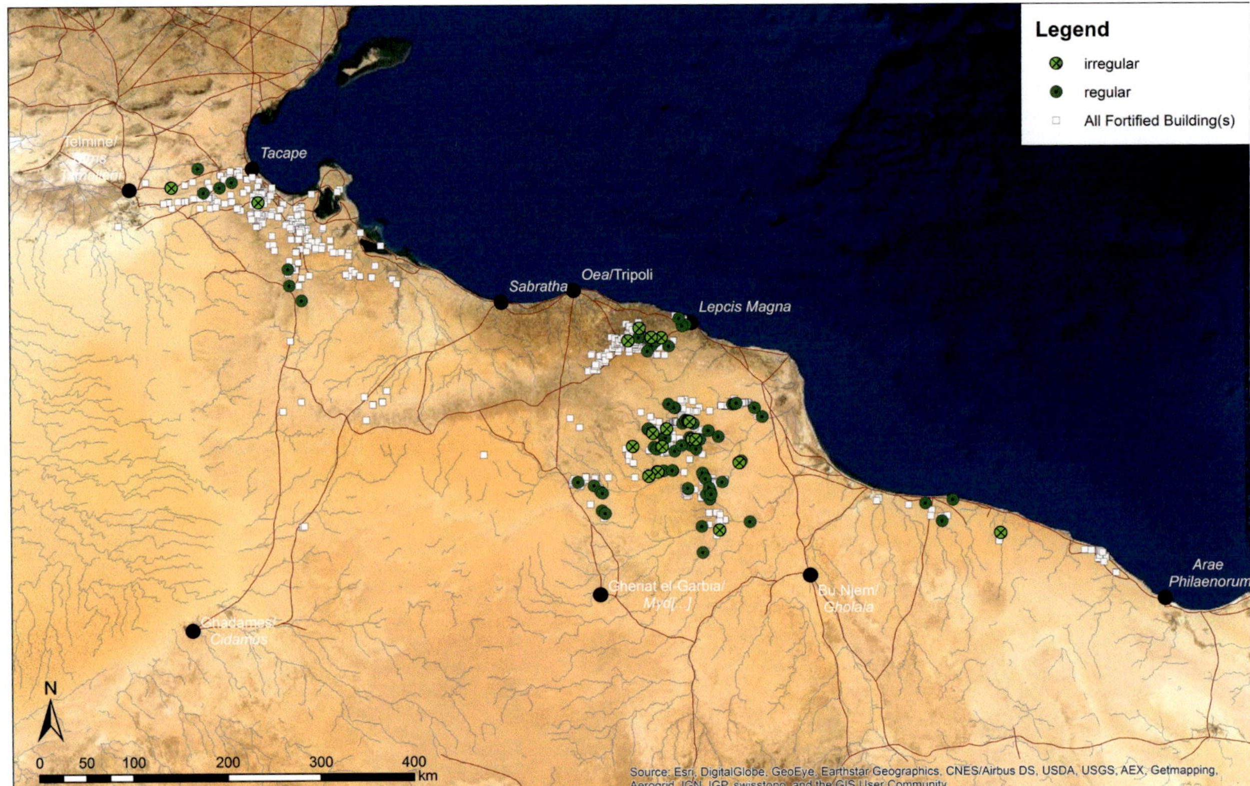

Basemap: Esri, DigitalGlobe, GeoEye, Earthstar Geographics, CNES/Airbus DS, USDA, USGS, AEX, Getmapping, Aerogrid, IGN, IGP, swisstopo, and the GIS User Community
Drainage: Lehner, B., Verdin, K., Jarvis, A. (2008): New global hydrography derived from spaceborne elevation data. Eos, Transactions, AGU, 89(10): 93-94. Retrieved from http://hydrosheds.cr.usgs.gov (15 sec Flow Accumulation)
Roads (Barrington Atlas): Ancient World Mapping Center (2012)

Figure 6.32c: *Geographical distribution of construction techniques used in fortified buildings: regular and irregular masonry.*

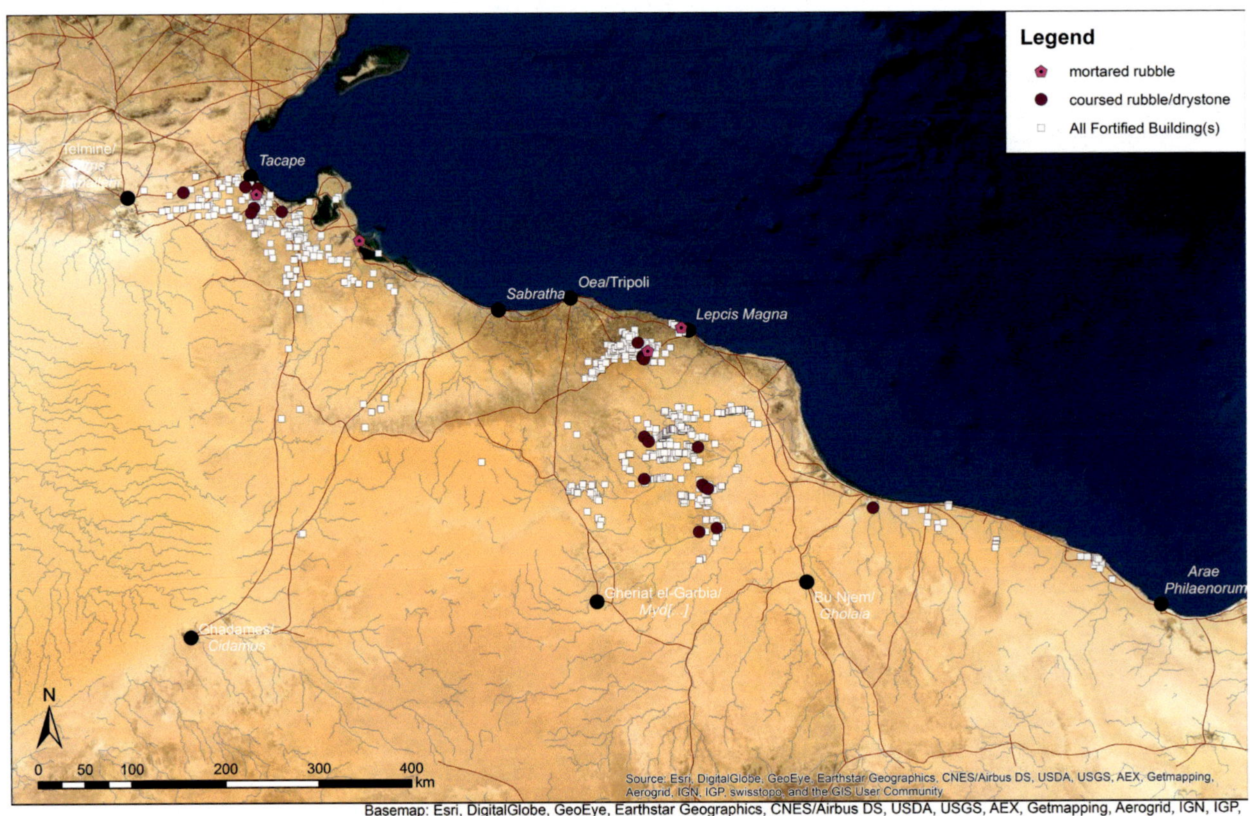

Basemap: Esri, DigitalGlobe, GeoEye, Earthstar Geographics, CNES/Airbus DS, USDA, USGS, AEX, Getmapping, Aerogrid, IGN, IGP, swisstopo, and the GIS User Community
Drainage: Lehner, B., Verdin, K., Jarvis, A. (2008): New global hydrography derived from spaceborne elevation data. Eos, Transactions, AGU, 89(10): 93-94. Retrieved from http://hydrosheds.cr.usgs.gov (15 sec Flow Accumulation)
Roads (Barrington Atlas): Ancient World Mapping Center (2012)

Figure 6.32d: *Geographical distribution of construction techniques used in fortified buildings: mortared rubble and coursed rubble/drystone.*

buildings to virtually non-existent in fortified buildings, with only one single example of the latter recorded, in the central *gebel*. There is now a far more evenly spread distribution of masonry types in the central *gebel*. In the western regions, *opus africanum* continues to be popular in fortified buildings as it was in unfortified ones, though in the western *gebel*, it is closely followed by ashlar and then regular masonry.

If the very low proportion of fortified buildings constructed of *opus africanum* in the central *gebel* and coastal regions is not simply a result of preservation and recording, this is an interesting trend, as the technique was used for more than 75% of the unfortified buildings for which this information was recorded. I suspect, however, that we might find that a number of the ditched sites for which no building information is yet available were constructed in *opus africanum*. In addition, as mentioned above, the issue of exterior vs. interior construction techniques may also be an issue here, as it is possible that *opus africanum* continued to be used for the interior partitions.

The more frequent use of the higher quality regular and very regular masonry in the pre-desert regions over the previously dominant coursed rubble/drystone, is also interesting as it indicates a greater level of investment in quality of construction. A similar trend was perhaps also

Mg003-g2, Wadi Migdal, E. pre-desert, north
(*ULVS* Archive: F422/N9/3.10.81; cropped for clarity)

Ms004-g, Wadi Meseuggi, E. pre-desert, north
(*ULVS* Archive: F420/N17/15.10.81; cropped for clarity)

Figure 6.33: *Fortified structures with ashlar and rounded corners.*

	ashlar	ashlar lower & other upper	opus africanum	very regular masonry	regular masonry	irregular masonry	coursed rubble/ drystone	mortared rubble	Total
Tower	10	3	10	51	69	15	7	2	169
Central lightwell	3	1	5	39	25	5	1	–	80
Range lightwell	–	1	–	1	4	1	–	–	7
Block	–	–	–	–	1	–	–	–	1
Unknown	7	1	5	11	39	9	6	2	82
Compound	5	1	4	12	14	2	8	1	48
Courtyard	3	1	1	6	10	–	2	1	25
Doubled	–	–	–	1	–	1	–	–	2
Irregular	–	–	–	1	3	–	2	–	6
Unknown	2	–	3	4	1	1	4	–	15
Range/block	–	–	–	–	–	–	1	–	1
Total	*15*	*4*	*14*	*63*	*83*	*17*	*16*	*3*	*218*

Table 6.11: *Frequency of construction techniques used in different fortified building types and sub-types across Tripolitania.*

seen in western Syrtica, but a sample of only five here makes the evidence more tenuous. The fact that in these regions people were more frequently constructing buildings which not only utilised well-coursed, neat masonry but were also two to three storeys in height, nearing 8–10 m or more in some cases, is indicative of a certain level of access to and command of resources, which was very likely only available to a wealthy and elite segment of the population.

Also worth noting, though not explicitly recorded as a separate type (due again to inconsistency in the recording of the original data and the inability to distinguish in satellite imagery), were buildings where special care seems to have been taken by the builders in the construction of the corners. A number of instances were recorded in which larger, or even ashlar blocks (sometimes robbed from unfortified buildings) were used for the corners of buildings and additionally or alternatively, the blocks used for corners were rounded off, rather than being left squared (Figure 6.33). Both of these features are again indicative of the ability and resources to obtain and shape large blocks of stone and served to strengthen the building. They also potentially indicate a concern for defense; corners are the weak point in building construction and both using more substantial blocks and rounding them off made them less vulnerable to damage from projectiles.[538]

Masonry Type and Plan

Of the buildings with their masonry type recorded, 218 also had a known building plan (Table 6.11). In both towers and compounds, regular and very regular masonry were, respectively, the most commonly utilised construction techniques. In Figure 6.34, we can see that the distribution of different types of masonry used in fortified tower and compounds buildings is similar, though slightly more evenly spread in fortified compounds, with larger proportions of coursed rubble/drystone and ashlar recorded for compounds than for towers. If masonry type can be seen as a reflection of wealth and status, this would seem to indicate that towers and compounds both had the potential to have been constructed by people of similar wealth and status, as there was little difference in the materials and techniques preferred.[539]

Masonry Type and Building Size

Of the 253 fortified structures for which the construction technique was recorded, 214 also had their building size recorded; 160 of these could be identified as towers, 46 as compounds. Given the significant difference in size between fortified towers and compounds demonstrated in Section 6.2.2, separate analyses were undertaken for each building type to assess the relationship between masonry type and size.

[538] See Section 4.1.2, fn. 244.

[539] A large proportion of the buildings of unknown plan type (17/35) and not included in Table 6.11 were constructed using *opus africanum*, and it would be interesting to know where these fit in.

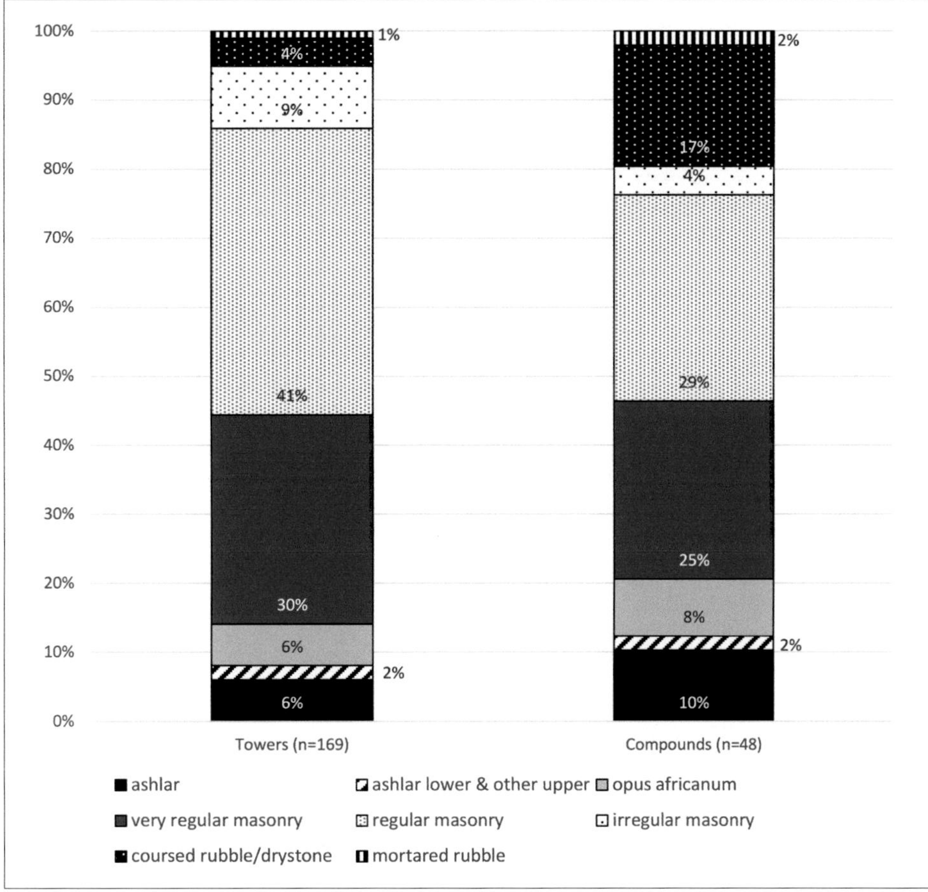

Figure 6.34: *Proportions of different types of masonry used in fortified tower and compound buildings.*

In Table 6.12 we see that, overall, the largest towers were not those constructed using ashlar blocks, but rather, those of very regular masonry, though this technique is recorded only in the eastern pre-desert. Those using ashlar masonry throughout or in the lower courses are the next two largest groups, followed by regular masonry, indicating that there was still a relationship between the use of ashlar masonry and larger buildings. Exceptionally, the largest towers in the central *gebel* appear to have been constructed of irregular masonry, with ashlar constructions having the second largest average, whereas in other regions, buildings constructed of irregular masonry were generally much smaller.

	ashlar (n=12)	ashlar lower & other upper (n=3)	opus africanum (n=10)	very regular masonry (n=49)	regular masonry (n=64)	irregular masonry (n=14)	coursed rubble/ drystone (n=6)	mortared rubble (n=2)
1. W. coastal	253	–	120	–	–	–	–	26
2. W. *gebel*	205	–	159	–	154	–	–	–
3. Southwest	–	–	320	–	–	–	–	–
4. Central coastal	183	–	–	–	165	–	–	306
5. Central *gebel*	218	178	–	–	101	279	81	–
6. E. pre-desert, north	361	–	–	259	180	159	325	–
7. E. pre-desert, south	216	–	–	335	260	–	17	–
8. W. Syrtica	–	–	–	–	225	144	24	–
All regions	*231*	*178*	*171*	*281*	*194*	*184*	*142*	*166*

Table 6.12: *Average size (m^2) of fortified towers in different regions, divided by construction technique.*

	ashlar	ashlar lower & other upper	opus africanum	very regular masonry	regular masonry	irregular masonry	coursed rubble/ drystone	mortared rubble
# of examples	*5*	*1*	*4*	*12*	*13*	*2*	*8*	*1*
1. W. coastal	–	–	483	–	–	–	–	–
2. W. *gebel*	1,209	–	–	–	–	1,452	663	–
3. Southwest	–	–	–	–	–	–	–	–
4. Central coastal	–	–	–	–	–	–	–	–
5. Central *gebel*	729	–	1,444	–	1,320	–	–	672
6. E. pre-desert, north	–	4,125	–	830	1,551	–	985	–
7. E. pre-desert, south	900	–	–	1,125	1,152	1,978	1,670	–
8. W. Syrtica	–	–	–	–	1,258	–	–	–
All regions	*1,051*	*4,125*	*723*	*977*	*1,326*	*1,715*	*1,247*	*672*

Table 6.13: *Average size (m^2) of fortified compounds in different regions, divided by construction technique.*

The pattern observed for the fortified compounds differed from that seen in the towers (Table 6.13). By far the largest single fortified building was Mm010-g (Gasr Leb'r) which measured 4,125 m^2, employing ashlar masonry in the lower courses and smaller masonry in the upper ones. Otherwise, the largest overall average was that for buildings constructed in irregular masonry (though here only two examples were noted), followed by regular masonry, coursed rubble/drystone, and only then, ashlar. Unfortunately, particularly when divided by region, the numbers begin to get too small for the patterns observed to be reliable indicators of wider trends; however, the average sizes of the buildings employing both regular and irregular masonry remain consistently large. It may be that as seen with the unfortified courtyard buildings in Chapter 5, there was no strong link between masonry technique and size of fortified compound buildings.

6.2.5 Inscriptions, Decoration and Luxury

I have recorded 94 fortified sites which have one or more features which could be broadly interpreted as decorative or luxury elements (Table 6.14; Figure 6.35). Overall, the table shows that around 12% of fortified buildings recorded in my catalogue had one or more of these luxury elements, though we must again take into account the particular issues of recovery and preservation

	Total buildings	Total buildings with luxury elements		Inscription	Bath	Marble	Plaster	Sculpture
1. W. coastal	138	14	10%	–	3	1	12	–
2. W. *gebel*	84	8	10%	2	–	–	–	8
3. Southwest	13	1	8%	–	–	–	–	1
4. Central coastal	6	1	17%	–	–	1	1	–
5. Central *gebel*	153	14	9%	6	–	–	2	12
6. E. pre-desert, north	289	33	11%	3	–	–	10	25
7. E. pre-desert, south	92	22	24%	3	–	–	3	21
8. W. Syrtica	19	1	5%	–	–	–	1	–
9. E. Syrtica	16	–	–	–	–	–	–	–
Total	*810*	*94*	*12%*	*14*	*3*	*2*	*29*	*67*

Table 6.14: *Frequency of fortified buildings at which luxury elements were observed.*[540]

[540] As in the last chapter, when more than one type of luxury feature occurred at the same site, this was counted only as one in the 'Total Buildings with luxury elements' column.

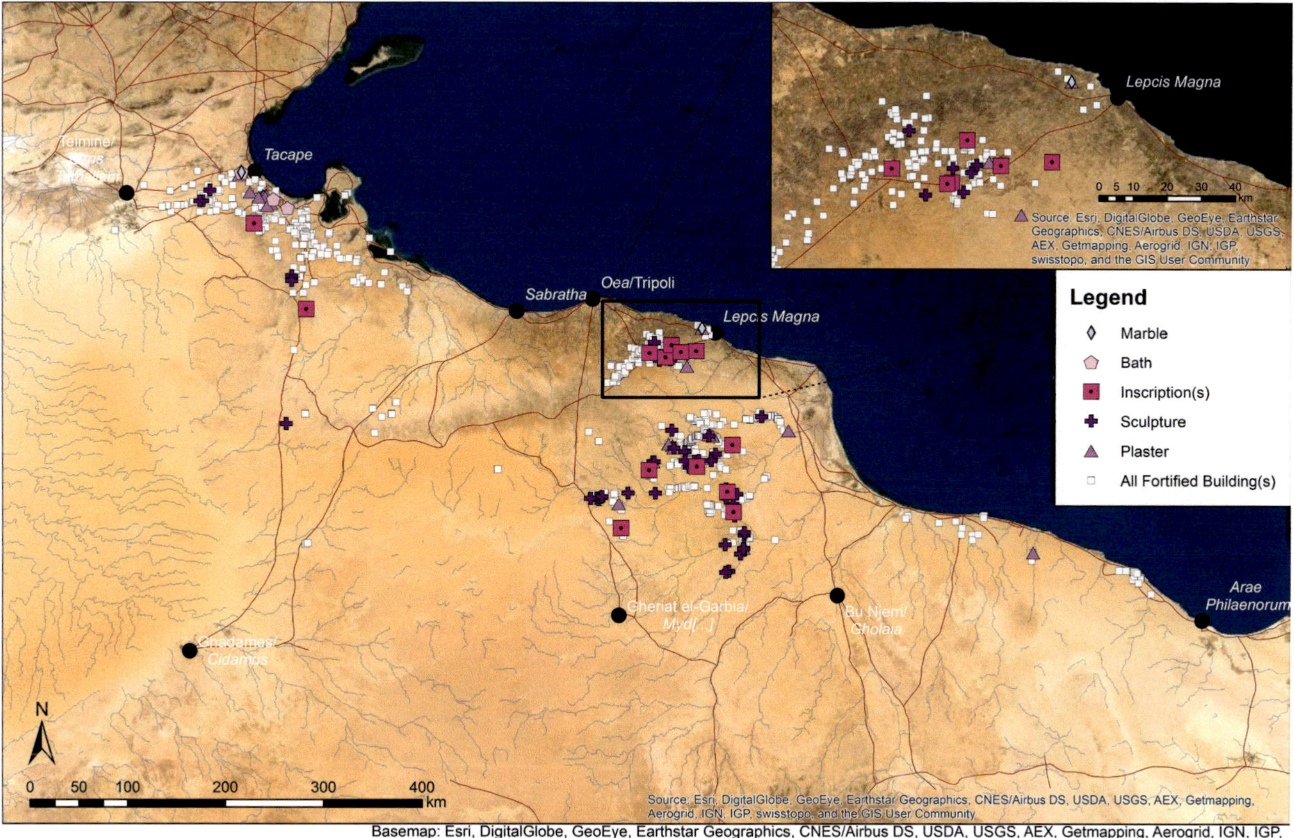

Figure 6.35: *Distribution of fortified buildings with luxury features.*

associated with this type of evidence discussed for unfortified buildings in Section 5.2.5. This is triple the proportion of unfortified buildings which had similar features, though the overall increase is really due only to the major increase in two regions. While the incidence of these features in unfortified and fortified buildings has remained approximately the same in the western regions and in Syrtica, and actually decreased by about half in the central coastal and *gebel* areas, there has been a substantial increase in the eastern pre-desert regions, particularly in the presence of architectural sculpture. While only seven unfortified sites out of 779 in the eastern pre-desert regions together, or less than 1%, had any of these features, 55 out of 381 (14%) fortified sites did; indeed, in the southern part of the pre-desert in particular, nearly one in four sites had one or more of these features. Yet again, this supports the idea that while the areas in the regions around *Lepcis* were potentially experiencing decline, clearly this did not extend to the pre-desert, especially the more southern parts, where building sizes remained large, and some people still had the means and the motivation to include these features.

In contrast to the unfortified buildings for which no inscriptions are currently known, I recorded 14 civilian fortified buildings in my catalogue which had one or more inscriptions that were (probably) originally associated with the building itself (as opposed to funerary inscriptions, milestones, etc. which sometimes found their way into other buildings) (Appendix D).[541] These inscriptions were in Latin, or nearly as often Latino-Punic (or possibly Latino-Libyan in some cases), or bilingual, and were commonly placed over the main entrance of fortified buildings (Figure 6.36). A few of the translatable inscriptions appear to have recorded the construction or restoration of a building, e.g. the bilingual inscription at Mg006-g, which probably recorded the construction of the building in Latin by a group of men, followed by the information in Latino-Punic that the engraving was done by 'their son'.[542] At Lm003-g, as mentioned previously, an inscription seems to record an instance where a fortified building replaced an unfortified

[541] N.B. these are not the only known inscriptions from the region, but I have not included those which could not be confidently associated with a particular building in my catalogue.

[542] Brogan & Reynolds 1960; Wilson 2012a: 311–312.

Md028-g, *IRT*893, Wadi Merdum, E. pre-desert, north (*ULVS* Archive: F128/N35/10.11.1980)

Figure 6.36: *An example of an inscription above a sculpted doorway on a fortified building.*

one.[543] Other inscriptions have already been discussed above, with reference to the use of terminology such as *turris* (RLT086-g) or *centenarium* (Oates101-g).[544] A number of examples unfortunately remain untranslated or are too fragmentary, but we might surmise that at least some of these were similar in content.

These inscriptions are important in that they begin to give us a better idea of the identities of the inhabitants of these buildings, or at least the ones who could afford inscriptions; even when the inscriptions were in Latin, it is notable that the names recorded almost always had Libyan or Punic components, e.g. Marcius Metasan Fidelis or M. Caecilius Bumupal.[545] There does not seem to be any particular geographic pattern as to the languages used in different areas, as Latin and Latino-Punic/Libyan inscriptions are found in both the central *gebel* and the eastern pre-desert; of the two identified in the western *gebel*, one was in Latin, while the content and language of the other is unknown. At least three sites, all from the central *gebel* area (Goodchild26-g, Oates83-g and Oates84-g) also had explicitly Christian inscriptions, featuring Chi-Rho monograms (see further discussions about Christian churches in Section 6.3.2).[546]

A number of apparently Libyan inscriptions were also recorded at Ghirza, Bu Njem/*Gholaia* and in other areas of the pre-desert, frequently scratched onto the voussoirs or lintels of doors and entranceways. These are often described as graffiti, but Brogan notes that their repeated occurrence on and around doorways, i.e. where more traditional inscriptions are often found, may suggest that they were more deliberate than that. Unfortunately, however, because we can neither translate nor date them, there is little else that can be said about them at this time.[547]

Also in contrast to the unfortified farm buildings, are the relatively large number of fortified buildings at which some form of sculpture is recorded, whether in the form of decorative architectural elements such as columns, or relief sculpture. A number of the inscriptions noted and illustrated above had relief decoration accompanying them. A common form of relief sculpture seems to have been that which decorated the lintels and frames of doorways, both external and internal (Figure 6.37). The doorways themselves could be arched or have flat lintels and it would perhaps be interesting to know if there was any pattern to this in itself, but unfortunately this information was not recorded systematically

[543] Brogan 1964: 52; Reynolds 1985: 23–25; Mattingly 1996a: 329.

[544] See Section 6.1

[545] Lm003-g, Brogan 1964: 52; Oates 101-g, *IRT* 877, Jongeling & Kerr 2005: 63–64.

[546] Nave 1914; Ward-Perkins & Goodchild 1953: 48–49; Oates 1954: 106, 113–114. The first of these (Goodchild26-g, Henscir Uheda) may not be in its original context.

[547] Brogan 1975; Rebuffat 1975b; Brogan & Smith 1984: 250–257. See also on the Libyan language: Galand 1989; 2003; Ait Kaci 2007.

enough to make a judgment. However, even without any other form of decoration, many doorways were often constructed using very large ashlar blocks, either as doorjambs and lintels, or to form an arch, which would also have been impressive on their own.

There were no recorded examples of fortified structures with evidence for mosaics. However, just as with the presses above, this could potentially be because the size and overall substantiality of fortified buildings is such that their floors are more often obscured, so it is difficult to know whether there may indeed be mosaic or tile pavements hidden beneath. Only two examples were noted to have any architectural marble remains: one from the western coastal zone and one from the central

Tn003-g, Wadi Tininai, E. pre-desert, north
(Scott, Dore, & Mattingly 1996: 305, fig. 40.4)

Sf112-g, Wadi Sofeggin, E. pre-desert, north
(*ULVS* Archive: F433/N2/21.10.1981)

Kh014-g, Wadi Umm el-Kharab, E. pre-desert, south
(Welsby 1992: 83, fig. 12)

Sf116-g, Wadi Sofeggin, E. pre-desert, north
(*ULVS* Archive: F434/N28/21.10.1981)

Kh041-g, Wadi Umm el-Kharab, E. pre-desert, south
(Scott, Dore, & Mattingly 1996: 137, fig. 22.7, b)

Figure 6.37: *Sculpted doorframes.*

BS003-g, Bir Scedua Basin, E. pre-desert, north (*ULVS* Archive: F442/N24/16.10.1981)

Figure 6.38: *Interior niches.*

coastal zone. Although two examples are hardly enough to make any real judgments, it is unsurprising that both of these were found in coastal regions, suggesting that trade in this costly and cumbersome material was no longer making it very far inland.

Very few examples seem to have had bath facilities incorporated into or associated with them. Two, both located in the western coastal zone (157.064-g, 158.037-g), have been potentially identified through the presence of vaulting tubes, which were commonly used for roofing bathhouses in Roman times, since their hollow form retained heat. At another site in the same region (147.030-g) the presence of *'hypocaustes réemployés'* were noted, and it was at this site where one of the fragments of marble was also recorded. Unfortunately, we cannot be sure about the identification of any of these examples, but in all cases, their proximity to the coastal urban centres, from where the necessary supplies could be obtained, is unsurprising. Of course, some of the bathhouses identified in the previous chapter may have remained in use, especially when new fortified buildings were built in proximity to or directly on top of earlier farm buildings, but without better investigations, we cannot know to what extent.

A number of examples of the use of plaster or stucco, sometimes decorated in some way, have been noted at fortified buildings. Instances of vaults with moulded stucco decoration in particular are sometimes assumed to be Islamic in date, but as always, without more investigation, it can be difficult to know for certain whether some might not date from the later Romano-Libyan periods.[548] Also noted in a number of instances, but not recorded systematically in my catalogue, were interior niches, often arched, which could be functional storage compartments, but could also be seen as decorative, as a place for display (Figure 6.38).[549]

Luxury Elements and Building Plan, Size and Construction

Of the 94 fortified buildings which had recorded luxury elements associated with them, 74 also had their building plan recorded (none of which were range/block buildings) (Appendix Table 30). Towers and compounds were approximately equally likely to have one or more type of decorative or luxury element (17 and 19% of the overall number respectively). Like the relationship between masonry type and plan, there seems to have been no preferential use of higher status elements or materials in one or the other type of building.

Of the buildings with recorded plan, 73 also had their size recorded, 53 towers and 20 compounds (Appendix Tables 31 & 32). In most areas, buildings with

[548] For example, Md150, described by the *ULVS* investigators as having 'Islamic rope-moulded decoration' (Scott, Dore, & Mattingly 1996: 190).

[549] Jones & Barker 1983: 44.

luxury elements were slightly larger than the averages overall; however, in most cases these were not substantial increases. Unlike the unfortified buildings, where luxury features were clearly associated with buildings which were of a larger size, in fortified buildings, size does not seem to be as much of a factor.

Also, as already briefly mentioned in Section 6.2.3, we can illustrate the relationship between presses and luxury elements (Appendix Table 33). Interestingly, neither of the buildings with four or five presses had any luxury elements recorded but nevertheless, a significant proportion (36% or 14/39) of sites with presses also had luxury elements. However, where more than half of the unfortified buildings with luxury elements also had presses, here only 15% (14/94) of the fortified buildings with recorded luxury elements did.

Finally, of the 94 fortified sites with luxury elements, 69 also had their construction technique recorded (Appendix Table 34). Whereas 83% of the unfortified buildings with luxury elements were recorded in buildings which utilised ashlar blocks in some way, here, ashlar block techniques only accounted for 32% of the buildings with luxury elements. A larger proportion of buildings with decorative or luxury elements (57%), were found in buildings constructed of very regular and regular masonry, suggesting that in the eastern pre-desert at least, this type of masonry was more commonly associated with the kinds of luxury and decoration that probably only the elite could afford.

6.3 Fortified Settlements and Other Rural Structures

Having analysed and discussed the characteristics and features of individual fortified buildings above, we can now investigate how fortified structures related to each other spatially, along with other types of buildings with which they were often associated.

6.3.1 Settlements

In order to determine the number and nature of settlement groups into which fortified buildings could be grouped and the number of buildings which make up those settlements, I conducted the same analyses used for unfortified buildings, described in Section 5.3.1, and similarly, all types of fortified farm buildings discussed in the previous sections were given equal weight. It should be remembered that, as in the last chapter, there were many other types of buildings and structures that may have formed part of these settlements but were not included in these analyses, some of which will be discussed further in Section 6.3.2 below. Nevertheless, this type of analysis gives us a starting point for comparing broad patterns in the make-up and formation of settlements across the region.

Of the 810 fortified farm buildings in my catalogue, accurate co-ordinates were recorded for 722. These fortified buildings were grouped into 'settlements' based on how many buildings were found within arbitrary distances of each other (Table 6.15). The proportion of settlements with two or more fortified buildings never rises above 25% (compared to unfortified buildings, in which upwards of half the settlement groups had two or more buildings in them when a distance of 500 m was allowed) (Figure 6.39). In addition, the largest grouping of fortified buildings was six, compared to groups of more than 20 unfortified buildings.

The density of fortified buildings recorded within each of the settlement groups was also much lower than that recorded for the unfortified buildings (Table 6.16). What is immediately clear from these data is that in comparison to the unfortified buildings, fortified buildings more rarely occurred in close groups. There is still some variation in different areas, with the eastern pre-desert retaining a comparatively high average number of fortified buildings per settlement, along with the western coastal area. The overall number of fortified buildings recorded in Syrtica is far fewer compared

	Individual buildings	Number of 'settlement' groups			
		50 m	100 m	200 m	500 m
1. W. coastal	136	134	124	115	111
2. W. *gebel*	73	73	72	72	70
3. Southwest	10	10	10	10	9
4. Central coastal	5	5	5	5	5
5. Central *gebel*	138	138	138	135	123
6. E. pre-desert, north	247	236	228	220	187
7. E. pre-desert, south	83	80	78	71	64
8. W. Syrtica	14	14	14	13	13
9. E. Syrtica	16	15	15	15	12
Total	*722*	*705*	*684*	*656*	*594*

Table 6.15: *Number of 'settlements' into which fortified buildings can be grouped based on different distances.*

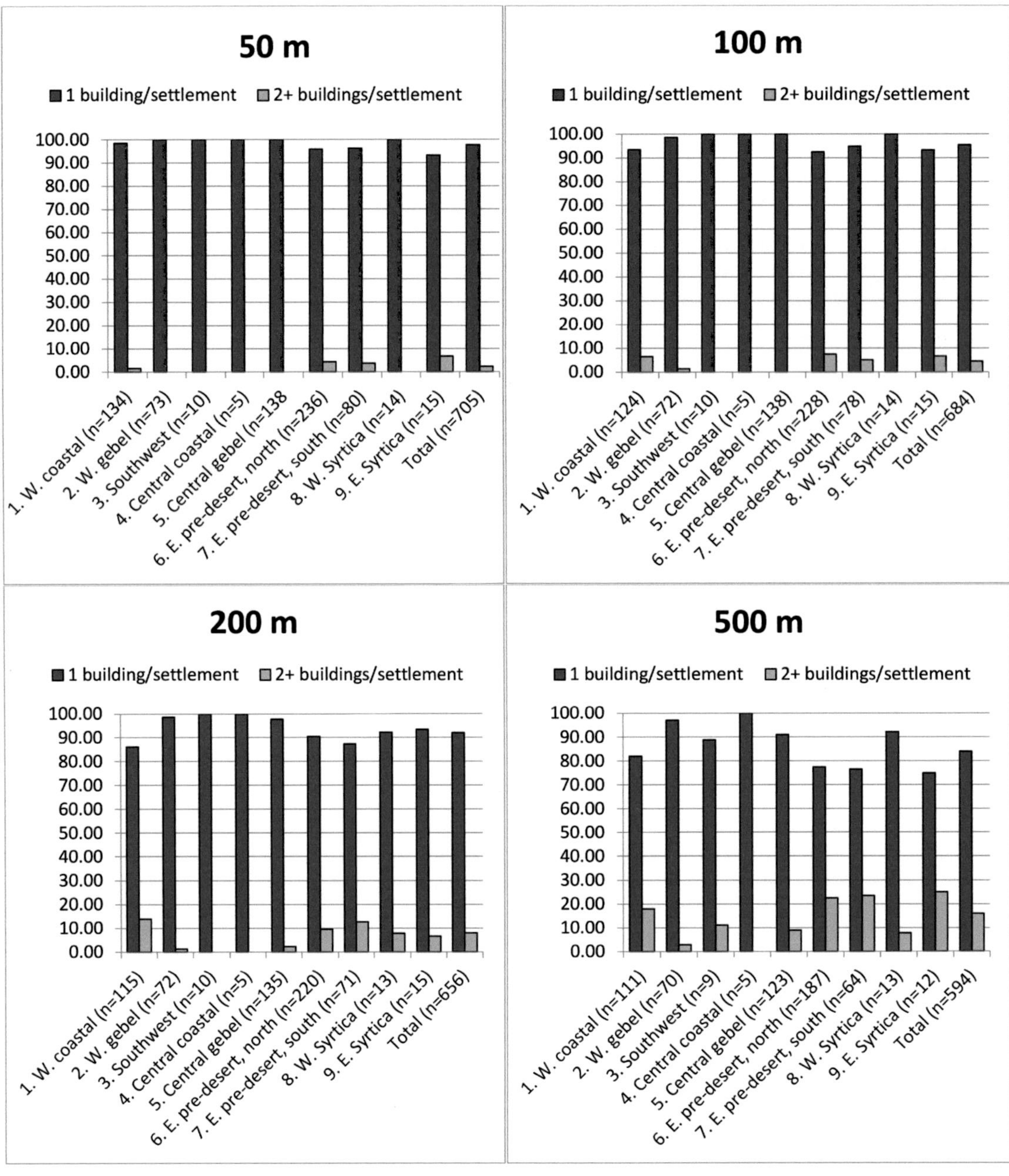

Figure 6.39: *Proportions of settlements with one vs. two or more individual fortified buildings recorded.*

	Individual Buildings	Average number of buildings per settlement at various distances			
		50 m	100 m	200 m	500 m
1. W. coastal	136	1.01	1.10	1.18	1.23
2. W. *gebel*	73	1.00	1.01	1.01	1.04
3. Southwest	10	1.00	1.00	1.00	1.11
4. Central coastal	5	1.00	1.00	1.00	1.00
5. Central *gebel*	138	1.00	1.00	1.02	1.12
6. E. pre-desert, north	247	1.05	1.08	1.12	1.32
7. E. pre-desert, south	83	1.04	1.06	1.17	1.30
8. W. Syrtica	14	1.00	1.00	1.08	1.08
9. E. Syrtica	16	1.07	1.07	1.07	1.33
Total	*722*	*1.02*	*1.06*	*1.10*	*1.22*

Table 6.16: *Average number of fortified buildings in recorded settlements.*

to the numbers of unfortified buildings so the averages are less reliable, as are those in the southwest and in the central coastal region. Overall, however, the average number of fortified buildings per settlement never rises above 1.33 in eastern Syrtica at the 500 m range, a significantly smaller number compared with the maximum of 3.21 unfortified buildings per settlement in western Syrtica.

However, while the fortified buildings themselves occurred less often in clusters than their unfortified counterparts, this does not mean that these buildings were more isolated. Rather, in many areas, fortified buildings occur alongside or within settlements consisting of groups of small buildings and enclosures which could be densely clustered (Figure 6.40) or slightly dispersed (Figure 6.41). These settlements ranged widely in

Mm002-g, E. pre-desert, north
(DigitalGlobe via Google Earth Pro, 28 Dec. 2014)

Md306-g, E. pre-desert, north
(DigitalGlobe via Google Earth Pro, 28 Dec. 2014)

BS004-g, E. pre-desert, north
(DigitalGlobe via Google Earth Pro, 9 Dec. 2014)

Oates80-g, Central *gebel*
(DigitalGlobe via Google Earth Pro, 22 Jan. 2015)

Figure 6.40: *Fortified buildings with closely clustered settlements.*

their size, from 400 m^2 to over 5 ha, though most were less than 1 ha in area and were normally not as substantially built as the fortified buildings with which they were associated (Figure 6.42). There were 191 fortified buildings which had associated settlements or structures of this type; in ten examples, a single settlement incorporated two towers, resulting in 181 of these types of settlement (Table 6.17; Figure 6.43).

This phenomenon was most commonly associated with towers, and the largest number of known examples was in the northern part of the eastern pre-desert. Although relatively uncommon in other areas, in the eastern pre-desert, more than a third of all fortified buildings had a clustered settlement associated with them. The fortified buildings of Syrtica also had a notable percentage, but the absolute numbers of these

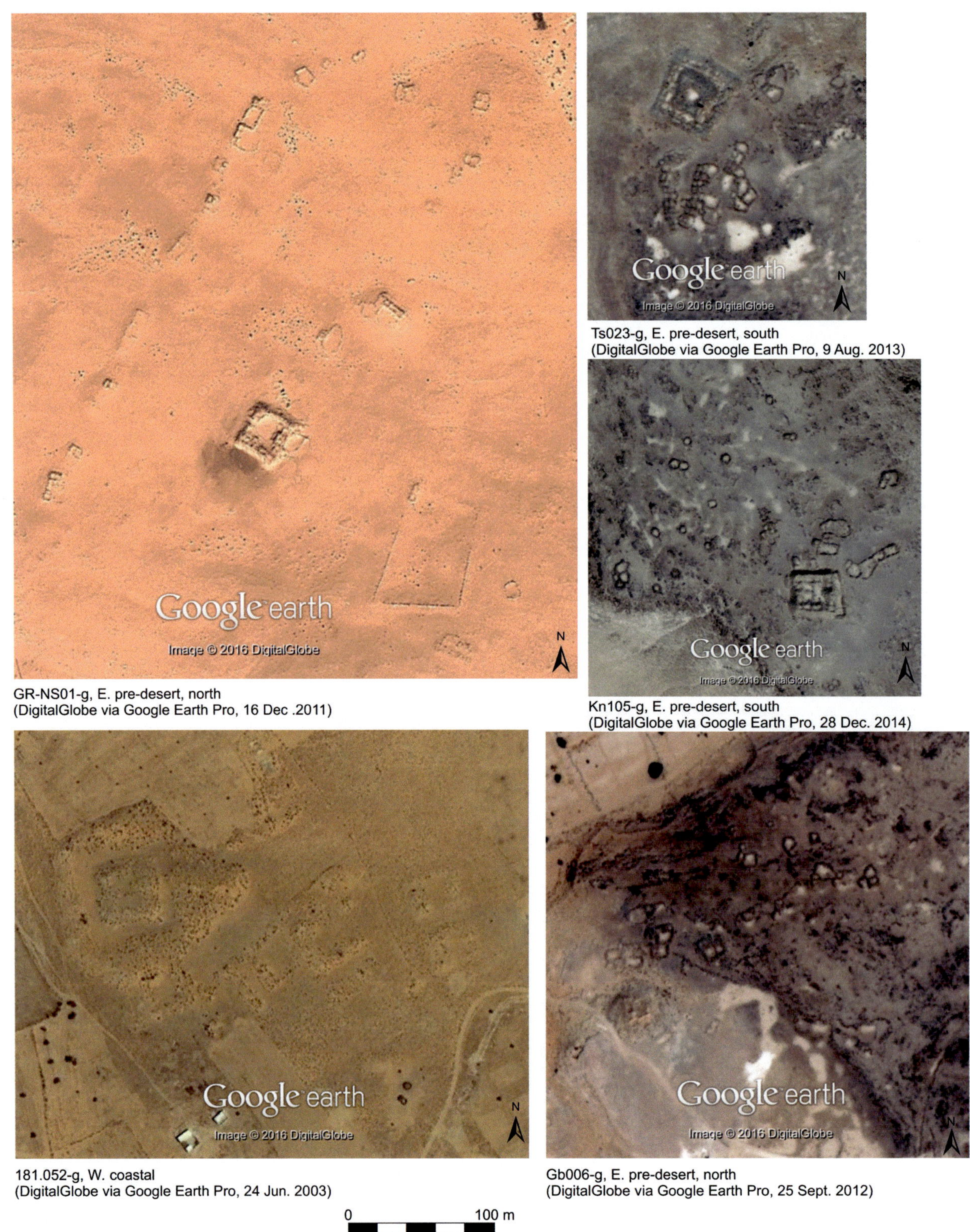

Figure 6.41: *Fortified buildings with dispersed settlements.*

Figure 6.42: *Fortified building with clustered settlement.*

	Buildings with settlements	% of total	Towers	Compounds	Unknown
1. W. coastal	10	7%	1	1	8
2. W. *gebel*	4	5%	–	1	3
3. Southwest	1	8%	–	1	–
4. Central coastal	–	–	–	–	–
5. Central *gebel*	13	8%	12	1	–
6. E. pre-desert, north	114	39%	90	10	14
7. E. pre-desert, south	32	35%	21	11	–
8. W. Syrtica	3	16%	2	–	1
9. E. Syrtica	4	25%	–	–	4
Total	*181*	*22%*	*126*	*25*	*30*

Table 6.17: *Distribution of settlements associated with fortified structures, divided by building type, region and in total.*

are smaller, making the statistical significance of these examples less certain.

In addition, we must also take into account when fortified settlement groups occurred in close proximity to unfortified settlement groups of the type recorded in the last chapter (Table 6.18; Figure 6.44). In all areas except the two western regions, between 20 and 40% of all fortified structures were within half a kilometre of at least one unfortified building. The significance of this is difficult to know at this level of analysis and certainly varied in individual examples. In some cases, the unfortified building(s) probably pre-dated the fortified ones, with the latter sometimes even being built directly on top of or re-used construction materials from the former. In other cases, the unfortified buildings may have been occupied at the same time as the fortified buildings, perhaps by tenants, or as additional accommodation or outbuildings for the community.

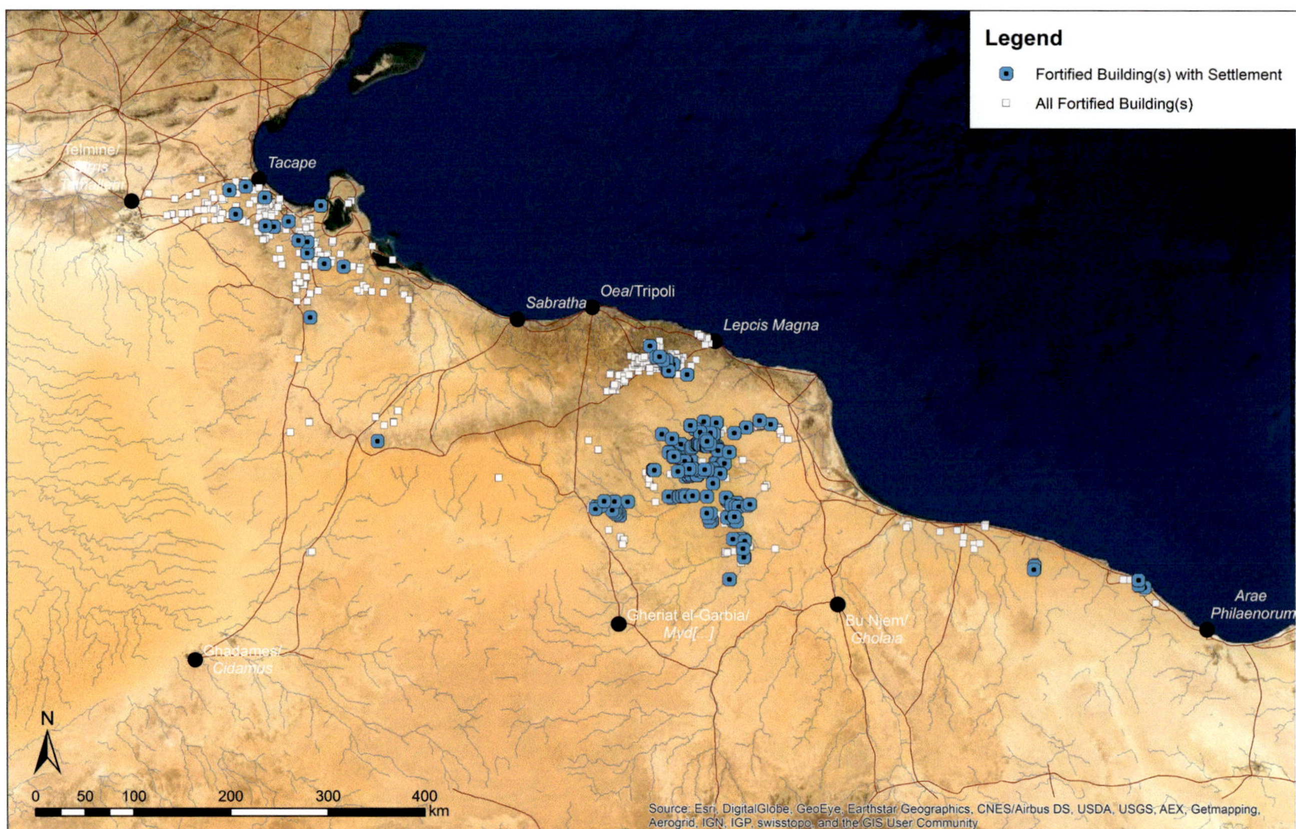

Basemap: Esri, DigitalGlobe, GeoEye, Earthstar Geographics, CNES/Airbus DS, USDA, USGS, AEX, Getmapping, Aerogrid, IGN, IGP, swisstopo, and the GIS User Community
Drainage: Lehner, B., Verdin, K., Jarvis, A. (2008): New global hydrography derived from spaceborne elevation data. Eos, Transactions, AGU, 89(10): 93-94. Retrieved from http://hydrosheds.cr.usgs.gov (15 sec Flow Accumulation)
Roads (Barrington Atlas): Ancient World Mapping Center (2012)

Figure 6.43: *Distribution of fortified buildings with associated settlements.*

	50 m		100 m		200 m		500 m	
	#	%	#	%	#	%	#	%
1. W. coastal	–	–	1	0.8%	2	2%	4	4%
2. W. *gebel*	2	3%	1	1%	1	1%	2	3%
3. Southwest	–	–	–	–	–	–	2	22%
4. Central coastal	2	40%	2	40%	2	40%	2	40%
5. Central *gebel*	13	9%	14	10%	17	13%	27	22%
6. E. pre-desert, north	7	3%	20	9%	31	14%	51	27%
7. E. pre-desert, south	9	11%	16	21%	16	23%	24	38%
8. W. Syrtica	2	14%	2	14%	3	23%	5	39%
9. E. Syrtica	–	–	–	–	1	7%	3	25%
Total	*35*	*5%*	*56*	*8%*	*73*	*11%*	*120*	*20%*

Table 6.18: *Number and percentage of fortified settlement groups which intersect at least one unfortified group at different distances.*

There is clearly some ambiguity between these two 'types' of settlement, and the decision to record unfortified buildings in close proximity to fortified ones as dependent outbuildings or settlements as opposed to individual unfortified farm buildings has, in many cases, been subjective and dependent on how they were recorded by previously published surveys. Nevertheless, what the previous analyses make clear is that a large proportion of fortified buildings in most areas of Tripolitania had nearby settlements of one type or another. Furthermore, many of these settlements may have been far more extensive than we now know, since parts of them may not have survived or are no longer distinguishable above ground due to robbing, taphonomic processes or the use of perishable materials such as wood or mudbrick.

DOG65-g, DOG66-f, Central *gebel*
(DigitalGlobe via Google Earth Pro, 21 Dec. 2012)

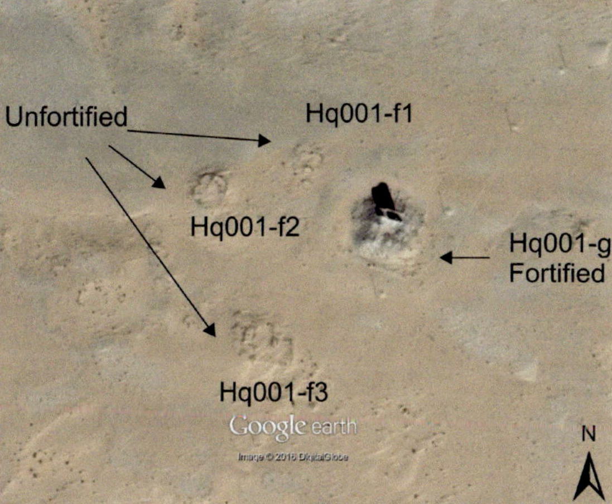

Hq001-g, Hq001-f1, -f2, & f3, E. pre-desert, north
(DigitalGlobe via Google Earth Pro, 20 Nov. 2014)

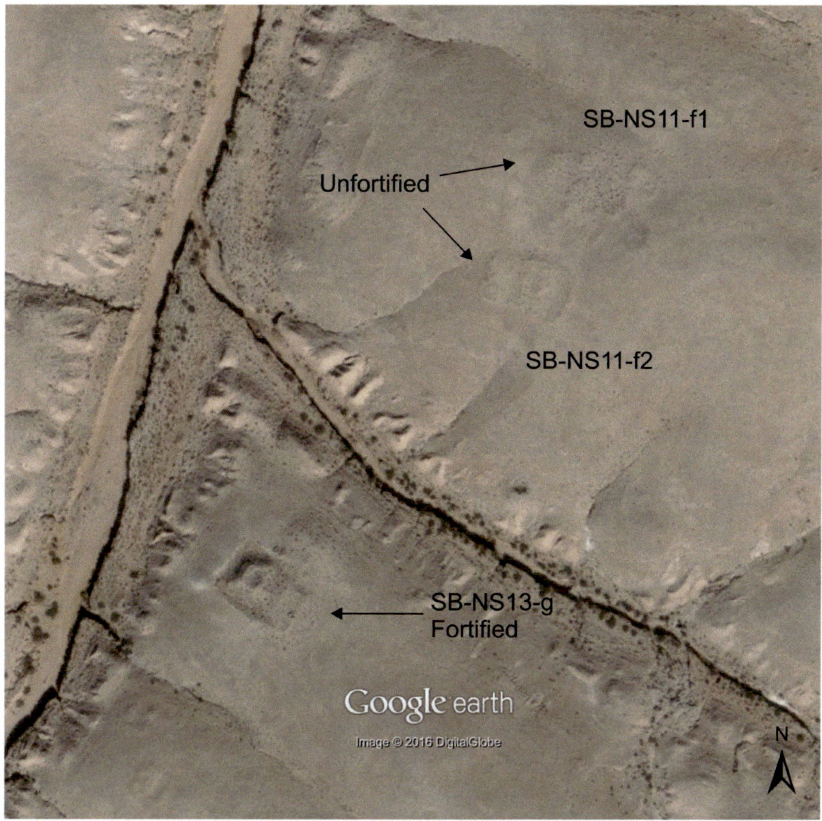

SB-NS13-g, SB-NS11-f1 & -f2, W. Syrtica (DigitalGlobe via Google Earth Pro, 7 Dec. 2014)

Figure 6.44: *Examples of fortified building settlement groups in close proximity to unfortified settlement groups.*

It is difficult to be more precise than this or to draw firm conclusions about the significance of these data because of our ignorance concerning the chronological relationships between most of these buildings. While we can be more confident of at least some degree of contemporary occupation when the buildings are physically attached, this is clearly not always the case. And indeed, the fact that these clustered groups of buildings and enclosures were often (though not always) rather haphazardly arranged, suggests that in many cases these settlements developed gradually over years or even decades or more as families and settlements grew. This might support the idea of a nucleation process whereby people gradually abandoned their unfortified farms and moved closer to fortified farm buildings, rather than this happening very quickly.

This clustering of several small buildings around a clearly larger and more significant one to form small settlements is not something that seems to have occurred in the same way with the unfortified buildings. Oates noted that the clustered settlement around Gasr Hamed (Oates71-g) seemed to be composed of smaller groups of buildings, which in fact resemble unfortified farmyard buildings, arranged around a courtyard, and which did not have access to the others around them. He theorised that each of these belonged to individual family groups "living together for mutual protection under the shadow of the *gsur* in which they could take refuge in times of trouble", suggesting as argued above for farmyard buildings, that the attached yards were for livestock.[550] We could also conceive of a situation in which the central building was a communal one, for the storage of produce and indeed, for protection should the need arise. However, the evidence strongly suggests that in many cases, the adoption of fortified building types was a reflection of a new architectural hierarchy. Rather than larger clusters of buildings which were of more or less similar sizes and forms, we begin to see individual fortified buildings surrounded by groups of much smaller, unfortified, and less well-constructed buildings. This points to the formation of discrete estates, possibly with well-defined boundaries, centred on fortified buildings. The actual relationship between the elite owners of these buildings and the people living around them is not always clear. Were they community leaders or the equivalent of local 'lords' with the people they ruled living around them? To what extent might the people living around the fortified buildings actually have been dependent on or indentured to their elite occupants? Or was this a more mutually beneficial arrangement? Probably the situation varied in different examples, and further investigations are clearly needed to illuminate this issue.

6.3.2 Other Structures

Other types of buildings also accompanied fortified buildings and settlements, as they did unfortified ones. Many of these were, of course, the same types of structures and most of what was already discussed in the last chapter regarding wadi walls, cisterns, enclosures and other structures associated with agricultural activities is applicable here also. An interesting avenue of further work would be more detailed investigations into how structures of these kinds differed (or not) when associated with unfortified versus fortified settlements.

As mentioned in the previous chapter, most of the identified mausolea can be dated to the first to fourth centuries AD,[551] but a number of these were almost certainly associated with the fortified buildings discussed in this chapter, as was the case at Ghirza. Furthermore, many originally built by the inhabitants of the unfortified buildings probably continued to be significant monuments when their descendants moved into new buildings. The few temples identified in the last chapter are difficult to date or associate with particular farm buildings and again, while many of them were potentially originally built in the first centuries AD, they could potentially have continued to be utilised long afterwards.

One building type which we know to have been more associated with the later, fortified buildings, however, are Christian churches. Although never as common as in other areas of North Africa or in the urban centres, churches and other evidence of Christianity are also found scattered across Tripolitania's countryside. Ward-Perkins and Goodchild discussed the remains of churches and Christian inscriptions in the central coastal and *gebel* regions, and the northern part of the eastern pre-desert, and a few more churches were identified and investigated by the *ULVS* team in the eastern pre-desert area, but little work has subsequently been done on these physical remains. These rural churches were frequently to be found in defensible locations and fortified themselves, sometimes closely associated with one or more fortified farm buildings. Altogether, fewer than ten churches are known from rural contexts in Tripolitania, and not many more explicitly Christian inscriptions (mentioned briefly in Section 6.2.5), and these few are mostly located in the *gebel*, suggesting that the religion was probably not adopted as widely beyond the coastal urban centres as it was in other parts of North Africa.[552]

[550] Oates 1954: 96.

[551] Nikolaus 2016; 2017.

[552] Ward-Perkins & Goodchild 1953: 35–56; Mattingly 1995: 209–213; 1996a: 337–338. Cf. Dossey 2010; Leone 2013.

	Unfortified	Fortified	*Total*
1. W. coastal	50	138	*188*
2. W. *gebel*	9	84	*93*
3. Southwest	11	13	*24*
4. Central coastal	94	6	*100*
5. Central *gebel*	156	153	*309*
6. E. pre-desert, north	365	289	*654*
7. E. pre-desert, south	414	92	*506*
8. W. Syrtica	487	19	*506*
9. E. Syrtica	67	16	*83*
Total	*1,653*	*810*	*2,463*

Table 6.19: *Total number of unfortified and fortified buildings catalogued, divided by region.*

6.4 Discussion

The analyses and discussions above have revealed a number of patterns in the form and construction of fortified architecture and settlement of Tripolitania, as well as some of the ways that they differ from the unfortified buildings which were the focus of the last chapter. In this section I will summarise what the quantitative analyses in the previous sections have revealed about fortified architecture and settlement in Tripolitania and investigate further what the reasons for some of these patterns might have been.

Overall, it is evident that there were far fewer examples of fortified buildings (n=810) catalogued than unfortified ones in the same areas (n=1,653) (Table 6.19). The fall in the number of recorded buildings overall seems quite drastic, but as much of the evidence presented in previous sections suggests, in some areas of Tripolitania at least, this was not necessarily due to decrease in population or settlement, but rather a change in the ways those buildings and settlements were formed and distributed.

As established in Chapter 3, most fortified buildings in the region can be dated to between the third and seventh centuries AD, though unfortunately we cannot often be more specific than this. While the unfortified farm buildings seem to have been at their peak between the first and third centuries AD, a not insignificant proportion also had dating evidence from the fourth and fifth centuries, and some beyond even that. It seems likely, then, that there was a significant period of overlap, in which many unfortified farms were still occupied and operational at the time that the fortified buildings began to be constructed. Although the ceramic evidence as well as the examples of the reuse of building materials from unfortified buildings in the construction of fortified ones does still attest to an eventual overall move to the new building type, the period of co-existence may have lasted two centuries or more. In addition, as discussed in the last section, many of the unfortified buildings may have been replaced not only by the fortified buildings themselves, but also by the sometimes extensive settlements which accompanied them, which have not been counted separately.

Furthermore, while the overall number of fortified buildings recorded is smaller than unfortified ones, this decrease in building numbers did not occur equally in all parts of Tripolitania. The southern part of the eastern pre-desert, Syrtica and the central coastal region have all seen a significant fall in the number of recorded buildings. In the latter case, however, this may be somewhat misleading, in that the low number of fortified buildings recorded is probably at least partly due to the substantial amount of modern development and agriculture in the area. Surveys around *Lepcis Magna*, by the *Università Roma Tre* project identified at least 23 fortified structures not included in my catalogue, largely dated between the second and sixth centuries AD, as well as 21 in the Wadi Caam-Taraglat system, further east and south.[553] The decrease in the northern part of the eastern pre-desert is much less dramatic, and the number of buildings recorded in the central *gebel* and the southwest remained approximately the same. In the two western regions, the number of sites recorded as fortified actually represent a drastic increase. This is almost certainly the result of disproportionate preservation and recording techniques, but it is clear nevertheless that we cannot assume that the overall pattern is representative of the situation in all areas.

Finally, it is also notable that while the numbers of overall buildings appears to have fallen significantly, the number of settlement groups as defined in the previous section has not (Table 6.20). In several individual regions, the number of fortified settlement groups has actually increased over the number of unfortified ones because they were less often clustered together; this is obviously unsurprising in regions where the recorded fortified buildings outnumber the unfortified ones in the first

[553] Munzi *et al.* 2014: 215–223.

place. However, when we allow for relatively dispersed settlements at a 500 m range, the overall number of fortified building settlement groups for the entire region is actually greater than the unfortified ones. Notably, in the northern part of the eastern pre-desert, while there were fewer individual fortified buildings than unfortified ones recorded, in all instances starting from the smallest distance allowance, the number of settlements based on fortified buildings has actually gone up.

The reasons for the patterns observed above obviously differ by region. In Syrtica, the almost complete lack of fortified buildings and settlement groups compared to the large number of unfortified ones does seem to suggest a major societal change and/or decline in the population of the region. While the numerous unfortified buildings attest to the adoption of a sedentary, agricultural lifestyle along the wadis during the first few centuries AD, permanent settlement does not seem to have lasted beyond this period in any significant way. What fortified buildings have been recorded were also far more isolated than the unfortified ones, which were often clustered into groups. While we cannot assume that the overall population of the region necessarily decreased, if people were still living in the region, they were probably no longer using stone buildings, or at least no longer living in them permanently.

Of the few fortified buildings which were recorded in Syrtica, only about a third had a building form which could be assigned with any confidence (12/35), none of which are known to have had projecting towers or batters, although a few did have yards or enceintes, and at least 16 of the 35 appear to have had ditches. These buildings were not notably large or small and the masonry used ranged from coursed rubble/drystone to regular masonry, with no evidence for any very regular masonry or any of the techniques which utilised ashlar blocks. Only a single site in western Syrtica had any evidence for luxury materials, which amounted to some remains of plaster and there are no known presses, though a substantial proportion of the already small number of identified sites were identified by remote sensing, including every site from eastern Syrtica, so we cannot be certain about the presence or not of such features.

This apparent shift away from permanent settlement which is attested by the building evidence can potentially be explained by a couple of factors. The first is that Syrtica is probably one of the most difficult regions in Tripolitania to farm; it has extremely low levels of rainfall and but for a narrow coastal strip, the region is basically desert. It would have required a great deal of effort to maintain any level of agricultural activity in the region, and if the economy of the region overall had taken a downturn, after a certain point, it made more sense for the people occupying these farms probably to move away and/or move to semi-nomadic pastoral lifestyles.

In the eastern pre-desert regions, for the most part and unlike in Syrtica, permanent settlement apparently remained the norm; however, the form of these settlements and the architecture of individual buildings underwent some drastic changes. Fortified tower buildings appear to have been especially popular in these regions, particularly the north where 86% (173/202) of the fortified buildings of known form were identified as towers, though we must not forget that the remarkable preservation of buildings in this area compared to others may have contributed to this situation. The vast majority of buildings with externally projecting towers and batters were recorded in these two regions, as were most of the examples known to have externally projecting yards and surrounding enceintes. Furthermore, nearly 40% of fortified buildings in these regions had clustered settlements associated with them, a much larger proportion than anywhere else, and a fair number also intersected groups of separately recorded unfortified farm buildings.

The number of presses known to have been associated with fortified buildings in the eastern pre-desert fell from the already small number associated with unfortified buildings (though in the southern part of the

	Buildings		50 m		100 m		200 m		500 m	
	U	F	U	F	U	F	U	F	U	F
1. W. coastal	43	136	37	134	34	124	33	115	32	111
2. W. *gebel*	7	73	5	73	5	72	4	72	4	70
3. Southwest	10	10	10	10	8	10	7	10	7	9
4. Central coastal	15	5	15	5	15	5	15	5	15	5
5. Central *gebel*	82	138	82	138	82	138	79	135	71	123
6. E. pre-desert, north	262	247	219	236	178	228	152	220	107	187
7. E. pre-desert, south	336	83	252	80	205	78	178	71	134	64
8. W. Syrtica	388	14	315	14	226	14	176	13	121	13
9. E. Syrtica	67	16	63	15	54	15	44	15	32	12
Total	*1,210*	*722*	*998*	*705*	*807*	*684*	*688*	*656*	*523*	*594*

Table 6.20: *Number of unfortified (U) and fortified (F) buildings of known location and settlement groups.*

pre-desert this now represented a larger proportion of the recorded buildings). Nevertheless, the construction of substantial fortified buildings in the eastern pre-desert indicate a certain level of access to wealth and resources, so perhaps it is possible that oil and/or wine production was never the most important part of the pre-desert economy to begin with. The largest recorded fortified building in my entire database (Mm010-g, 4,125 m^2) was found in the northern part of the pre-desert, and the fortified buildings of the southern part of the eastern pre-desert had the largest overall average size recorded in Tripolitania. The majority of those for which the construction technique was known were constructed in very regular or regular masonry (132/160, 83%).

Furthermore, the southern part of the eastern pre-desert has the highest proportion of buildings with recorded luxury elements (24%), while the northern part also had a fair number (11%), compared to unfortified buildings of the same region (1%). This is largely due to a trend of sculptural decoration that became more common, as well as recorded uses of plaster and inscriptions. All of these things point to continued, if not increased, accumulation of wealth, at least by the elite in the region. It is difficult to know, however, whether the success of the elite in these areas benefited the people of the lower classes or was at their expense. These trends are exemplified in the settlement of Ghirza (Gh127), located in the southern part of the eastern pre-desert, which was one of the largest and wealthiest known rural settlements in Tripolitania. While I have occasionally mentioned this site above, I have deliberately avoided focussing too much attention on it because of its exceptional nature, but with its five large fortified buildings, several unfortified ones, a temple and a number of monumental mausolea, the elite occupants of this settlement were clearly wealthy, and this was probably an important rural centre.[554]

Although not exactly the same, the trends of the unfortified buildings in the central *gebel* and coastal areas were comparable enough to be grouped together. However, at the point where fortified buildings begin to rise in prominence, the architectural trends in these two areas appear to diverge. In the central *gebel*, the number of unfortified and fortified buildings recorded was approximately the same. We know far less for certain about the physical characteristics of the fortified buildings in this region due to poor preservation and modern agricultural activity. A major feature which came to characterise the fortified buildings of the central *gebel* was the surrounding ditch, with more than two-thirds of the fortified structures recorded with one. Amongst the few buildings which had their construction technique recorded there were comparable numbers of all construction techniques, with the exception of very regular masonry. A reasonable number still had luxury features, mostly inscriptions or sculptural decoration (9%), though this is fewer than what was found at the unfortified buildings. The number of fortified buildings with recorded presses (n=17) has fallen drastically compared to the number of unfortified buildings (n=143), but the central *gebel* remains the only region which has any sites with more than one press.

The central coastal area, on the other hand, may have suffered a more severe downturn in rural settlement, perhaps gradual at first, but more dramatic by the later fifth and sixth centuries AD.[555] Only six fortified buildings, compared to the 94 unfortified ones have been recorded in the region (although that may be in part due to the higher levels of modern development and agriculture in this area), and as such little can be concluded with certainty about the region as a whole based on these few sites. All those for which a plan could be identified were recorded as tower buildings, of around average size, none of which had any associated features except two with ditches. A few buildings were constructed in regular masonry, and one was even constructed of ashlar (SLN19-g), with another site (SLN57-g) producing evidence of marble and plaster; two of these six sites were recorded as having presses which is potentially significant, all of which suggests that the region was not completely impoverished. As suggested in the last chapter, however, many of the farms in the hinterland of *Lepcis Magna* actually probably belonged to people who lived in the city itself, with their farms being run by tenants and/or slaves. As the urban economy began to take a downturn (and its population decreased) many of the unfortified farms were probably closed down, rather than being replaced. Similarly, for those who were living on the farms, if security was becoming an issue, they would potentially have moved to the safety of the city.

In the western coastal and *gebel* regions, there were far more fortified buildings recorded than unfortified, but this is almost certainly down to issues of preservation and problems with identifying unfortified structures in these regions. Of the buildings for which a form could be identified, towers and compounds were identified in approximately equal numbers. Only a few examples had externally projecting towers (n=3) or batters (n=2). One of the buildings with a recorded batter was found on the island of Jerba (148.020-g), while the others (RLT025-g, RLT059-g, RLT043-g, RLT079-g) were all clustered in the northwest part of *gebel* region in the vicinity of the *limes* and military sites in this area.

Very few sites were recorded in either the western *gebel* or coastal areas with either projecting yards or enceintes. The defining characteristic of the fortified buildings identified in the western coastal zone were

[554] Brogan & Smith 1984.

[555] Munzi *et al.* 2016: 110. See also Section 3.2.2.

ditches, with 95% of the known buildings recorded having them, while 17% of those in the *gebel* did. While the tower buildings of these regions were of comparable size to those in other areas, the compounds of the western coastal and *gebel* regions were on average smaller than those found to the east, measuring 650 and 862 m^2, respectively, whereas the average compound sizes in the central *gebel*, and the eastern pre-desert regions were all over 1,000 m^2. The number of fortified buildings with known presses in the western regions has remained around the same as for unfortified buildings, though this now represents a much smaller proportion of the known sites. It seems likely, however, that as in the central coastal and *gebel* areas, pressing did continue at fortified sites, but on a slightly smaller scale. The most common construction technique recorded in both of these regions remained *opus africanum* and ashlar. If these buildings were being constructed *de novo* this would again suggest that there was a degree of continued prosperity in the region, but without better investigations it is not clear how much of this represents reuse of earlier sites and materials. Nevertheless, around 10% of sites in both the western coastal and *gebel* regions had evidence of some luxury decoration (most commonly plaster or architectural decoration), which is around the same proportion as the unfortified buildings. Compared to other regions of Tripolitania very few sites had recorded clustered settlement or were within close proximity to unfortified buildings (although in the latter case, the comparatively small number of unfortified buildings recorded in the first place has obviously contributed to this).

Finally, in the southwest, not much fortified settlement was recorded, though unlike in other areas, this is not very different from the situation with the unfortified buildings. Both towers and compounds were identified, none of which had externally projecting towers, batters, or yards. Two, however, had enceintes and nine (69%) had ditches. Based on the few examples for which area was recorded, the fortified buildings recorded in the southwest were on the larger side, particularly compared with the other western regions. No fortified buildings in this area had presses that we know of, though this is unsurprising given the environment and the fact that no unfortified buildings had them either. Only one example (RLT135-g) had its construction technique recorded, and this was built in *opus africanum*; this same example is also the only one for which any evidence for luxury was found, in the form of sculpted architectural decoration. A single example had evidence for surrounding settlement (WT3-NS10-g).

The analyses in each of the regions summarised above point to some substantial changes in the architecture and settlement of rural Tripolitania, which probably began happening around the third century AD. The most significant trend to note, obviously, is the one on which this entire chapter is based, that buildings which can be identified as fortified begin to rise in popularity, particularly visible in the adoption of tower-like building and the addition of wide, surrounding ditches to various types of buildings. In many cases, these new fortified buildings can be shown to have replaced unfortified ones, though we do not know whether this was done by the same occupants or new ones. Epigraphic evidence seems to attest to a need for greater security in the rural parts of the region which provides a likely explanation for this trend;[556] the inscription from the military outpost of Gasr Duib (Db001) mentions barbarian incursions,[557] and an inscription from what was most likely a civilian fortified site in the central *gebel* also discusses *incursi[o]ni barbarorum seu gentili[um]*.[558] The latter is particularly interesting in that it mentions a threat from not only barbarians but *gentiles*; it is not clear how this should be interpreted, though Reynolds has suggested that this may refer to the people already settled in the *limes* zone who perhaps found "common cause with the [barbarian] invaders".[559]

There is no reason to understate the importance of the defensive aspects of these buildings or to dismiss the idea that security was a primary motivation in the construction of these new building types and the analyses undertaken in this chapter have shown that this was manifested in different ways in different parts of Tripolitania. However, they have also indicated that there were other reasons why these new buildings forms and features may have been practical or desirable, in addition to their defensive advantages. One factor which probably contributed to the design and construction of these new types of buildings was an increased stratification of society. The evidence points to the idea that an elite class constructed and occupied these imposing buildings, which were often, as we have seen above, surrounded by settlements of far less impressive buildings, as people congregated closer together and to leaders who could provide them with more security. In addition to providing security both for themselves and their dependent settlements, these elite buildings were a means by which to make cultural or political statements, both in the fortification and impressiveness of the buildings themselves and their location in more defensible and therefore visible and commanding locations in the landscape. The

[556] Mattingly 1995: 202–205.

[557] *IRT* 880.

[558] *IRT* 871. I was not able to determine the exact location of this building, but based on the description of its location and appearance it almost certainly must be one of TAR03–04, 07–09, 12–14, or Cowper53.

[559] Reynolds, in Goodchild 1976a: 111–112.

decoration on many fortified buildings which was not present in unfortified ones supports the idea that these buildings were meant to impress and to make a statement.[560] Welsby has concluded that the masonry and the decoration of examples in the Wadi Umm el-Kharab (eastern pre-desert, south), was probably professional, specialist work, which strongly suggests that the owners of these buildings went to great effort and cost to make them appear impressive.[561]

Based on their defensive function and similarity of certain forms, a relationship to Roman military architecture has often been suggested for these buildings; on one hand this does not necessarily have to have been the case, but some inspiration or a desire to emulate these buildings on the part of the indigenous elite is not out of the question. As discussed with regards to the hillforts in Section 3.1.2, there was a pre-existing indigenous tradition of fortified settlement in North Africa that long predated Roman contact and hegemony. Also, as outlined in Section 5.4, the basic idea of the courtyard form, i.e. a building comprised of ranges of rooms surrounding an open space, was one which was used throughout the Punic and Roman worlds, in both civilian and military contexts, and there is no reason to think that in terms of architectural design the fortified versions were all that different from unfortified ones. This type of structure had known defensive advantages and was well-suited to the environmental conditions on the frontier, as pointed out in Section 4.2.3 with respect to minor forts which took essentially the same form, but these features were not solely applicable to military buildings. The degree to which this similarity of form may have represented similar patterns of usage in terms of the function of various spaces, however, e.g. habitation rooms, stables, storage, etc., is more difficult to determine.

It is more difficult to dismiss the similarities between civilian fortified towers and Roman military outposts, especially as the military buildings which were of more or less the same design do seem to be the earlier in the region. The impressiveness of the latter, particularly the high, imposing towers in the stark landscape, would not have escaped local peoples, and it is not so difficult to imagine that they might have inspired emulation. This association would have added significant layers of meaning to the impression the civilian versions of these buildings might have made in referencing such obvious symbols of Roman military power, for both the owners of these buildings, and those who lived in their shadow (figuratively or literally). Also relevant, however, is the tradition of the impressive mausolea discussed in Sections 5.3.2 and 6.3.2, and in particular the so-called tower tombs, the height of which was clearly an important feature; it is not difficult to see how notions of power, of literally being situated above others around you and the landscape, which others have argued were integral to the funerary monuments, could be equally applicable to domestic structures.[562] Another factor already mentioned above, was potentially changing social norms which demanded more privacy.[563] In addition, a number of studies of similar buildings in the Middle East have shown that the features of both fortified compounds and towers, in that they had fewer entrances and windows and had thicker walls, were in fact ideal for the environmental conditions, as it helped regulate the temperature and kept out dust and sand.[564]

Once again, we can also wonder what, then, the status of the people occupying these fortified buildings was, and how their relationship with the peoples on the coast and in the cities had potentially changed. While we are still very much in the dark about these issues, the use of Latin in the inscriptions cited above and on mausolea, for example, is highly suggestive of people who still had some connection to Roman networks and the presence of finewares implies continued participation in the trade of and desire for those goods, at least when the first of these structures were being built in the third and perhaps also fourth century AD, and probably only amongst the elite.

By the fifth and sixth centuries AD, however, it seems likely that whatever stability had been provided by the integration of the region into the Roman Empire which had made the widespread sedentarisation of the first century AD possible, was again on the wane. Outside the coastal regions, many people probably returned to the socio-economic systems of semi-nomadic pastoralism that their ancestors had previously practised and indigenous leaders and groups once again gained control over the interior.[565] While agriculture and permanent settlement certainly continued into the Islamic period and beyond, it was probably on a reduced scale. While the evidence proves that settled agriculture was certainly possible in the pre-desert regions, it required substantially more work to maintain it, and it is possible that without the incentive and support of being part of wider Mediterranean economic systems it was no longer worth investing in this form of production and subsistence.[566]

[560] Mattingly 1996a: 326–331.

[561] Welsby 1992: 97.

[562] Nikolaus 2016.

[563] Fentress 2000.

[564] Jones & Barker 1983: 52–53.

[565] Mattingly 1995: 202–217; Brett & Fentress 1996: 76–77.

[566] Gilbertson, Hunt & Gillmore 2000. Cf. parallels in the Negev (southern Jordan): Rosen 2000.

chapter seven

Conclusions

Even though the majority of the rural population lived and worked in small vernacular buildings, these have often been overlooked in favour of larger ones, except in more limited research areas. However, in addition to providing evidence of the domestic and farming activities that took place in and around them, these rural buildings, large and small, represent the outcomes of deliberate choices, informed by and reflecting the economic and socio-cultural landscapes in which people lived and acted, and the ways in which these landscapes developed and changed over the centuries.

In this book, I have brought together data collected during archaeological survey projects from across Tripolitania and incorporated new evidence collected using satellite imagery, in order to investigate and highlight this significant but understudied aspect of Tripolitania's rich archaeological record. I have deliberately focussed my attention on regional patterns in order to give equal weight and attention to a wide variety of building types and features, and avoided placing disproportionate focus on the exceptional but not representative buildings and settlements which have commanded the most attention in the past.

The result is the first standardised, region-wide synthesis and analysis of the form and construction of rural farm buildings and settlements in Tripolitania from the first century BC until the seventh century AD. This has included not only wide-scale, regional comparisons between buildings in different parts of Tripolitania, but also, for the first time, an examination of the ways in which the use of different physical characteristics and features intersected and related, all of which has been made possible by the new collation and standardisation of the available material undertaken here. In addition, it has also incorporated and assessed the significance of data from several areas, particularly Syrtica, which have not previously been factored into discussions of settlement and architecture in the region.

As discussed in previous sections, before the first century BC, rural settlement in Tripolitania does not appear to have extended far beyond the immediate hinterlands of the coastal urban centres. Small rural centres at oases and fortified hilltops were scattered across the region and semi-nomadic pastoralists were moving through and utilising the landscape, but otherwise, the majority of the rural areas remained unsettled. However, the relatively sudden appearance of unfortified, stone buildings across Tripolitania testifies to widespread sedentarisation over large parts of the region, probably made possible by the pacification of the inland peoples of the region in the first century AD. As demonstrated in Chapter 5, the unfortified farm buildings constructed as part of this new sedentarisation varied in their form and construction, reflecting similarities and differences in the character and development of those settlements in different areas. This process of sedentarisation created new opportunities for rural peoples to take part in the wide-ranging economic systems of the Roman Empire and enabled certain individuals or families to consolidate and secure positions of power, ultimately allowing a new elite class to emerge and increasing the stratification of the local societies.

Overall, the architectural evidence for the unfortified farm buildings studied here supports previous findings pointing to the significant wealth and prosperity of the central coastal and *gebel* regions, particularly during the first few centuries AD. This success was based on agricultural production and processing, particularly of olive oil and wine, evidenced by the high number of presses known to be associated with buildings in these regions. Similar observations can be made for the western coastal and *gebel* areas, though not quite on the same scale. In all of these regions, large, well-built unfortified courtyard buildings were the norm during this period; their size, construction and in some cases luxury features, were physical testaments to the resources available to those who built them. These buildings seem to have occurred in groups less often than in the eastern regions, suggesting that they were potentially the centres of larger estates which were the property of wealthy landowners who lived in the urban centres. In addition, both the courtyard form itself and the construction technique commonly used in them, *opus africanum*, can be identified with wider Hellenistic-Punic architectural traditions and could be seen as an indication of participation in wider Mediterranean systems.

By contrast, the farmyard buildings that were the most common building type constructed in the eastern pre-desert and Syrtica during the same period were distinct both in form and origin from courtyard buildings. While the construction of the buildings themselves, in addition to the establishment of irrigation systems (wadi walls) and pressing facilities, are clear evidence of the adoption of sedentary agriculture, the large open-air enclosed spaces suitable for stock-keeping which were the defining feature of these buildings testified to the continued economic and cultural importance of pastoralism alongside agriculture in the lives of the people living in these regions.

The existence of probable elite versions of these buildings in the eastern pre-desert region potentially indicate the presence of estate systems in some areas. However, it is notable that the unfortified buildings in both this area and especially in Syrtica were more often clustered together than in the more northern regions, suggesting that even if an estate system was in place, different factors contributed to how settlement was organised, perhaps with families or other social groups opting to live near each other.

By the time sedentarisation and the construction of unfortified buildings was reaching its peak, between the first and fourth centuries AD, the Roman military had established and was maintaining a presence in the region, which was physically manifested in the imposing fortified buildings that the soldiers occupied. Strategically located at oases that were probably originally tribal centres and important points in both east-west and north-south trade routes, we can imagine that these buildings would have made a significant impression on the peoples living in the region.

As early as the third century AD, fortified civilian buildings began gaining popularity in many parts of rural Tripolitania. Undoubtedly there was a period of overlap, but what little dating evidence we have suggests that during this time many independent unfortified buildings were abandoned in favour of fortified buildings and the more closely clustered settlements that frequently surrounded them. This major transition in the architecture and settlement of the region has often been seen as having been connected to two major, related factors: a decrease in the stability and security of the regions and, perhaps driven by the former, an increase in the stratification of society. While many of the characteristics and features associated with these buildings had defensive roles, the present study has emphasised that they could also serve other purposes which enabled them to continue to be useful and appropriate for the same sorts of agricultural and pastoral activities that had been practised in association with unfortified buildings. The move towards the fortification of farm buildings seems to have been a region-wide phenomenon, but was physically manifested in different ways in different parts of Tripolitania, from the fortified tower buildings in the pre-desert areas to the ditched sites of the coastal and *gebel* regions

It appears that agricultural and pastoral activities continued in the pre-desert and *gebel* regions in much the same way as they had when unfortified buildings were more common, but the forms and arrangements of the fortified buildings and their settlements indicate that these activities were now probably far more frequently based around estates, conspicuously centred on these elite structures. The construction of impressive, well-built fortified towers and compounds, often with decorative embellishments and large, presumably dependent settlements, is indicative of a society in which a select group of people had both the means and the desire to advertise their wealth, as well as the status and power that came with it. The substantiality and height of fortified tower buildings especially made them an ideal means by which to convey this message in a far more emphatic way than had been the case with the unfortified buildings, and the contrast between these new buildings and those that already existed in the landscape would have been striking. It would have been clear to all that viewed these buildings that their construction and maintenance were only achievable by a select group of wealthy and powerful people; their prominence in the landscape would have drawn attention to them, unmissable, constant reminders of the power and resources available to the elite. Their similarity to Roman military architecture may also have led people to view them as symbols of military power, authority and legitimacy.

If building size, the presence of surplus production facilities (i.e. presses) and luxury-type features such as bath buildings, mosaics and sculpture, can be taken as evidence for prosperity, the central and western coastal regions appear to have suffered some decline from the peak associated with the unfortified settlement. This pattern is consistent with the decline of the coastal cities to which the farms in these areas were probably connected, though there is still evidence for settlement in this period. By contrast, in Syrtica, after the third to fourth centuries AD, there was widespread, if not total, abandonment of sedentary rural settlement, suggesting that whatever agricultural or pastoral economy had been established there in the first three centuries AD was no longer worth pursuing. This move can perhaps even be seen as a conscious rejection of sedentary settlement in favour of a semi-nomadic pastoralism.

As outlined briefly in Chapter 1, during the same periods, the settlement of neighbouring regions and provinces was developing in different ways from Tripolitania, though there were some important similarities as well. In the more agriculturally fertile parts of *Africa Proconsularis* in modern Tunisia to the northwest, regional surveys and other investigations have revealed abundant evidence for large-scale agricultural production and large and imperial estates.[567] The *Kasserine Archaeological Survey*, for example, recorded around 200 sites in the region of the ancient cities of *Cillium* and *Thelepte* in western Tunisia. The most commonly recorded sites were rectilinear courtyard farm buildings with a single press, many of a similar size and layout to the unfortified courtyard buildings recorded in Tripolitania, particularly those in the *gebel* and coastal regions. In the Kasserine region, however, these farm buildings seem to have been more clearly part of a settlement hierarchy which was centred on larger villas and agrovilles, some over 50 ha in size, a system for which we do not have as much evidence in Tripolitania.[568]

Further north, the *Rus Africum* survey recorded over 600 sites in the region of ancient *Thugga*, nearly 300 of which were interpreted as farms, dating from the Punic and Late Republican periods through to late antiquity.[569] The buildings they recorded were again, largely rectilinear in their form and frequently constructed in *opus africanum*. Many of these buildings had long, narrow rooms specifically built to accommodate the beams of olive and wine presses and had abundant evidence of mills for both olives and grains.[570] Unlike Tripolitania, however, in addition to the larger centre of *Thugga*, the landscape in which these farms were located was also home to a number of other small- and medium-sized towns and inscriptions provide clearer evidence for the existence of estates on which many of the smaller farms were almost certainly dependent.[571]

The *Project Africa Proconsularis* employed a dedicated architecture team, who recorded 193 sites in the region of *Segermes*, with just over a hundred of these identified as 'agriculturally-based habitation' dating from the first century BC until the seventh century AD, and around half of those of sufficient preservation to comment on their architectural form.[572] As elsewhere, *opus africanum* was commonly used in the construction of the farm buildings they recorded. The recorded site plans show that many of these can be identified as rectilinear courtyard buildings, with sizes ranging from below 500 m^2 to complexes of up to 3000 m^2; these were also sometimes found in groups forming larger settlements. Similarities were already noted by the authors to the buildings and settlements recorded in the *Kasserine Archaeological Survey*, though an important difference was that while evidence for the production of olive oil was found at some of the sites, nothing comparable to the large production facilities found in other surveys were identified during their investigations.[573]

The evidence of the three projects mentioned here briefly offer only a few examples of relevant comparisons; other projects, and especially the on-going work of the *Institut Nationale du Patrimoine* of Tunisia on the *Carte Nationale des Sites Archéologiques et des Monuments Historiques*, continue to add new data and information on rural settlement and architecture in the region.[574] However, it is clear that there were notable similarities in the architecture of the known farms of *Africa Proconsularis* with the unfortified courtyard farms found in the *gebel* and coastal regions of Tripolitania, often with one or more presses, reflecting a similar emphasis on agricultural production in both regions.[575] A more detailed comparison of the architecture and construction of the farm buildings in these two regions would potentially offer interesting insight into how the use and distribution of space in these buildings compared in different rural contexts.

Unsurprisingly, however, the situation differs substantially from the patterns we see in the eastern pre-desert regions and in Syrtica, where the more common farmyard building form reflected the importance of pastoralism. In addition, and especially in later periods, with the move to fortified farm buildings, the architectural trends in Tripolitania seem to have had more in common with Fazzan to the south, which also saw an increase in fortified architectures and settlements from the third century AD,[576] and Cyrenaica to the east, where fortified tower farm buildings and surrounding ditches were also common.[577]

Apt comparisons for the settlement and agricultural systems of Tripolitania's eastern pre-desert and Syrtica especially, can also be found in the Near East. While

[567] Hobson 2012: 41–83, *et passim*.

[568] Hitchner 1988; 1989; 1993; Hitchner *et al.* 1990.

[569] De Vos 2013: 153. See also de Vos 2000; de Vos Raaijmakers & Attoui 2013.

[570] De Vos 2013: 187. See also site plans in de Vos Raaijmakers & Attoui 2013, e.g. Site 207 (Plate 80) and Site 049 (Plate 20).

[571] De Vos 2013: 152–162.

[572] Hansen 1995: 349. See also Carlsen & Tvarnø 1990; Dietz, Ladjimi Sebaï, & Ben Hassen 1995; Ørsted *et al.* 2000.

[573] Hansen 1995: 371–377; Carlsen 2000: 118–119.

[574] http://www.inp.rnrt.tn/Carte_archeo/html/index_fr.htm.

[575] Though this is not to say that pastoralism was not also practised in these regions, see, for example, Hitchner 1994.

[576] Mattingly 2003b: 361, et passim; 2007; 2010; Liverani 2005b.

[577] Goodchild 1951b; Emrage 2015.

there were wide differences in historical development and experiences with Roman imperialism, these regions both have extremely low levels of rainfall, and extensive wadi systems cutting deeply into plateaus. Similar farm buildings, including fortified tower buildings have been recorded by surveys in parts of modern Syria, Jordan and the Negev,[578] and a more directed study comparing the rural landscapes of these regions could help illuminate how these forms developed and whether these similarities may have a common root or they are simply the result of similar solutions being found to deal with similar environments.

The rural landscape of Tripolitania and its buildings have already provided scholars over the last hundred years with an astonishing wealth of information about the ancient peoples who once lived in this region, but as this study has highlighted, we have only scratched the surface. For example, I have mentioned already the need for more systematic and detailed recording and analysis of construction techniques. While my analyses on that subject have revealed some broad trends, I was completely reliant on photographs and descriptions in order to make my own categorisations. In order to do a proper analysis of construction techniques, this is clearly insufficient and on-the-ground investigations are absolutely essential. A more detailed study of the materials and construction techniques used for these buildings would give us greater insight into the development and spread of building technology and trends.[579] More archaeobotanical and faunal analyses from sites throughout the region are also needed to round out our understanding of what rural life and farming was really like beyond what is attested by the remains of olive and wine presses.

Finally, and more pressing, however, is the fact that the archaeological heritage of rural Tripolitania is under threat from a variety of factors, including the expansion of modern settlements, agriculture, development, looting, conflict and climate change.[580] Local heritage authorities and archaeologists are working tirelessly to record sites and mitigate these threats, and collaborating with international projects to provide training and incorporate new methodologies of heritage recording and damage and threat assessment into their work.[581] However, many of the sites which were recorded by surveys such as the *ULVS*, for example, have been damaged or lost,[582] not to mention those recorded in the late nineteenth and early twentieth centuries. In particular, smaller structures and settlements are at greater risk because they are less often recorded systematically; however, even small, unassuming structures have something to tell us about the past. The potential that this landscape offers in archaeological and historical terms is practically immeasurable and we can only hope that we will be able to continue to learn and benefit from what it has to offer for many years to come.

[578] For example, Tchalenko 1953–1958; Rubin 1991; Nevo 1991; Tate 1992; 1997; Finkelstein 1995; Foss 1995; Hirschfeld 1997; Decker 2006; Barker, Gilbertson, & Mattingly 2007.

[579] See, for example, work done in *Mauretania Tingitana* (Morocco): Camporeale 2011; Gliozzo *et al.* 2011.

[580] Nebbia *et al.* 2016; Munzi & Zocchi 2017; Rayne, Sheldrick, & Nikolaus 2017.

[581] For example, *Endangered Archaeology in the Middle East and North Africa (EAMENA)*, www.eamena.org; Nikolaus *et al.* 2018; Hobson 2019; *Training in Action*, www.traininginaction.org; Leone *et al.* 2020.

[582] See, for example, sites MmA001, with a modern road cutting directly through the site, or Gb069 which is being encroached upon by modern development.

BIBLIOGRAPHY

Abbreviations

AE	*L'Année Épigraphique*
AfrIt	*Africa Italiana*
AfrRom	*L'Africa Romana*
AJA	*American Journal of Archaeology*
AntAfr	*Antiquités Africaines*
BCTH	*Bullétin archéologique du comité des travaux historiques et scientifiques*
CIL	*Corpus Inscriptionum Latinarum*
CNSA	*Carte Nationale des Sites Archéologiques et des Monuments Historiques* (Available at: http://www.inp.rnrt.tn/Carte_archeo/html/index_fr.htm)
CRAI	*Comptes Rendus à l'Académie des Inscriptions et Belles Lettres*
ILAf	*Inscriptions Latines d'Afrique* (= Cagnat, Merlin, & Chatelain 1923)
ILT	*Inscriptions Latines de la Tunisie* (= Merlin 1944)
IRT	*Inscriptions of Roman Tripolitania* (= Reynolds & Ward-Perkins 1952)
JRA	*Journal of Roman Archaeology*
JRS	*Journal of Roman Studies*
LibAnt	*Libya Antiqua*
LibStud	*Libyan Studies*
OJA	*Oxford Journal of Archaeology*
PBSR	*Papers of the British School at Rome*
QAL	*Quaderni di Archeologia della Libia*

Abdussaid, A. (1996). The restoration of the North Mausoleum of Wadi Nfed. *LibAnt* n.s.2. 73–78.

Abdussaid, A. (1998). Bir el-Uaar Mausoleum (Al-Urban, Djebel Garian). *LibAnt* n.s.4. 147–156.

Abitino, G. (1979). I confini della Libia Antica e le Are dei Fileni. *Rivista Geografica Italiana* 86. 54–72.

Adams, J.N. (2007). *The Regional Diversification of Latin.* Cambridge: Cambridge University Press.

Ahmed, M.A.M. (2010). *Rural Settlement and Economic Activity: Olive Oil and Amphorae Production on the Tarhuna Plateau during the Roman Period.* PhD Thesis, University of Leicester.

Ahmed, M.A.M. (2019). *Rural Settlement and Economic Activity: Olive Oil, Wine and Amphorae Production on the Tarhuna Plateau during the Roman Period.* London: Society for Libyan Studies.

Ait Kaci, A. (2007). Recherche sur l'ancêtre des alphabets libyco-berbères. *LibStud* 38. 13–38.

al-Mahjub, O. (1978–1979). I mosaici della villa Romana di Silin. *LibAnt* 15–16. 69–74.

al-Mahjub, O. (1983). I mosaici della villa romana di Silin. In R. Farioli Campanati (ed.), *III Colloquio internazionale sul mosaico antico*, I. Ravenna. 299–306.

Alcock, L. (1950). A Seaside Villa in Tripolitania. *PBSR* 18. 92–100.

Alcock, S.E., Dey, H.W., & Parker, G. (2001). Sitting down with the *Barrington Atlas. JRA* 14. 454–461.

Allan, J.A. & Richards, T.S. (1983). Use of satellite imagery in archaeological surveys. *LibStud* 14. 4–8.

Allison, P.M. (2013). *People and Spaces in Roman Military Bases.* Cambridge: Cambridge University Press.

Altekamp, S. (2004). Italian Colonial Archaeology in Libya 1912–1942. In M.L. Galaty & C. Watkinson (eds), *Archaeology Under Dictatorship.* New York: Springer.

Arata, F.P. (1996). L'Arco di Marco Aurelio a Tripoli (Oea): una nuova ipotesi esegetica. In L. Bachhielli & M. Bonanno Aravantinos (eds), *Scritti di Antichità in memoria di Sandro Stucchi.* Vol. II. Rome: "L'Erma" di Bretschneider. 9–30.

Arthur, P. (1982). Amphora Production in the Tripolitanian Gebel. *LibStud* 13. 61–72.
Asmia, M.A., & al-Haddad, M.A. (1997). Tarhuna, Wadi Guman area: recent finds. *LibAnt* n.s.3. 218–220.
Attema, P.A.J., & Schörner, G. (eds). (2012). *Comparative Issues in the Archaeology of the Roman Rural Landscape. Site classification between survey, excavation, and historical categories*. Portsmouth, RI: JRA.
Aurigemma, S. (1914). Colonna miliare dell'imperatore Tacito in località Sciáabet el-Ain (Homs). *Studi Romani* 11. 471–474.
Aurigemma, S. (1915). *Notizie Archeologiche sulla Tripolitania*. Rome: G. Bertero.
Aurigemma, S. (1916). Le fortificazioni della città di Tripoli. *Notiziario Archeologico* 2. 217–300.
Aurigemma, S. (1926). *I Mosaici di Zliten*. Rome/Milan.
Aurigemma, S. (1929). Mosaici di Leptis Magna tra l'uadi Lebda e il circo. AfrIt 2. 246–261.
Aurigemma, S. (1930). Federico Halbherr e la missione archeologica Italiana in Cirenaica e in Tripolitania. *AfrIt* 3(3–4). 237–250.
Aurigemma, S. (1940). Sculpture del Foro vecchio di Leptis Magna raffiguranti la dea Roma e Principi della casa di Guilio Claudio. *AfrIt* 8. 1–94.
Aurigemma, S. (1954). Il Mausoleo di Gasr Dóga in Territorio di Tarhúna. *QAL* 3. 13–31.
Aurigemma, S. (1960). *L'Italia in Africa. Le Scoperte Archeologiche.* (Vol. 1 – I Monumenti d'Arte Decorativa. Pt.1 - I mosaici). Rome: Istituto Poligrafico dello Stato.
Aurigemma, S. (1962). *L'Italia in Africa. Le Scoperte Archeologiche.* (Vol. 1 – I Monumenti d'Arte Decorativa. Pt.2 - Le Pitture d'Età Romana). Rome: Istituto Poligrafico dello Stato.
Aurigemma, S. (1967). L'ubicazione e la funzione urbanistica dell'arco quadrifonte di Marco Aurelio in Tripoli, e le sopravvivenze Italiane, medievali e moderne, degli archi quadrifronti ("sedili", "loggie", "gallerie"). *QAL* 5. 65–78.
Aurigemma, S. (1970). *L'arco di M. Aurelio e di Lucio Vero in Tripoli*. Rome.
Ayoub, M.S. (1967). *Excavations in Germa between 1962 and 1966*. Tripoli: Ministry of Education.
Babelon, E., Cagnat, R., & Reinach, S. (1893). *Atlas archéologique de la Tunisie. Edition spéciale des cartes topographiques publiées par la Ministère de la Guerre*. Paris.
Bacchielli, L. (1991). L'Arco Severiano di Leptis Magna: storia e programma del restauro. *AfrRom* 9. 763–770.
Băjenaru, C. (2010). *Minor fortifications in the Balkan-Danubian area from Diocletian to Justinian*. Cluj-Napoca: Editura Mega.
Bakir, T. (1967). Archaeological News 1965–1967: Tripolitania. *LibAnt* 3–4. 241–251.
Bakir, T. (1968a). Archaeological News 1968: Tripolitania. *LibAnt* 5. 195–204.
Bakir, T. (1968b). *Historical and Archaeological Guide to Leptis Magna*. Libya: Press of the Ministry of Information and Culture.
Balice, M. (2010). *Libia: Gli Scavi Italiani 1922–1937: Restauro, Riconstruzione o Propaganda?* Rome: "L'Erma" di Bretschneider.
Baradez, J. (1949). *Fossatum Africae: recherches aériennes sur l'organisation des confins sahariens à l'époque romaine*. Paris: Arts et métiers graphiques
Barker, G. (1981). Early agriculture and economic change in north Africa. In J.A. Allan (ed.), *Sahara: Ecological Change and Early Economic History*. London: Menas Press. 131–145.
Barker, G. (1986). ULVS XVI: prehistoric rock carvings in the Tripolitanian pre-desert. *LibStud* 17. 69–86.
Barker, G. (1989). From Classification to Interpretation: Libyan Prehistory, 1969-1989. LibStud 20. 31–43.
Barker, G. (1996a). Castles in the Desert. In G. Barker (ed.), *Farming the Desert: The UNESCO Libyan Valleys Archaeological Survey*. Vol. One: Synthesis. 1–20.
Barker, G. (1996b). Prehistoric Settlement. In G. Barker (ed.), *Farming the Desert: The UNESCO Libyan Valleys Archaeological Survey.* Vol. One: Synthesis. 83–110.
Barker, G. (ed.). (1996c). *Farming the Desert: The UNESCO Libyan Valleys Archaeological Survey* (Vol. One: Synthesis). Paris/Tripoli/London: UNESCO/The Department of Antiquities, SPLAJ/Society for Libyan Studies.
Barker, G., & Gilbertson, D.D. (1996a). *Farming the Desert: Retrospect and Prospect. In G. Barker (ed.), Farming the Desert: The UNESCO Libyan Valleys Archaeological Survey*. Vol. One: Synthesis. 343–363.
Barker, G., & Gilbertson, D.D. (1996b). The UNESCO Libyan Valleys Archaeological Survey: Methodologies. In G. Barker (ed.), *Farming the Desert: The UNESCO Libyan Valleys Archaeological Survey*. Vol. One: Synthesis. 21–48.
Barker, G., Gilbertson, D.D., Hunt, C.O., & Mattingly, D.J. (1996). Romano-Libyan Agriculture: Integrated Models. In G. Barker (ed.), *Farming the Desert: The UNESCO Libyan Valleys Archaeological Survey.* Vol. One: Synthesis. 265–290.
Barker, G., Gilbertson, D.D., Jones, B., & Welsby, D.A. (1991). ULVS XXIII: The 1989 season. *LibStud* 22. 31–60.

Barker, G., Gilbertson, D.D., & Mattingly, D.J. (eds). (2007). *Archaeology and Desertification: the Wadi Faynan Landscape Survey, southern Jordan*. Oxford: Oxbow.

Barker, G., & Jones, B. (1981). The UNESCO Libyan Valleys Survey 1980. *LibStud* 12. 9–48.

Barker, G., & Jones, B. (1982). The UNESCO Libyan Valleys Survey 1979-1981: Palaeoeconomy and Environmental Archaeology in the Pre-Desert. *LibStud* 13. 1–34.

Barker, G., & Jones, B. (1984). The UNESCO Libyan Valleys Survey VI: Investigations of a Romano-Libyan Farm Part I. *LibStud* 15. 1–44.

Barnett, T. (2002). Rock-art, landscape and cultural transition in the Wadi al-Ajal, Fazzan. *LibStud* 33. 71–84.

Barnett, T. (2005). Patterns on the rocks: report on recent work to survey rock art sites in the Wadi al-Haya, Fezzan. *LibStud* 36. 121–134.

Barnett, T. (2006). Dancing girls and insect-headed gods: results of the rock art recording project in the Wadi al-Haya, Fazzan, 2006. *LibStud* 37. 95–116.

Barnett, T. (2009). DMP VII: Style, Symbolism and cultural identity in the Wadi al-Hayat: results of fieldwork in 2008 and 2009. *LibStud* 40. 155–170.

Barth, H. (1857). *Travels and Discoveries in North and Central Africa. Being a Journal of an Expedition Undertaken under the Auspices of H.BM's government in the years 1849–1855.* (2nd ed. Vol. 1). London: Longman, Brown, Green, Longmans, & Roberts.

Bartoccini, R. (1926). Le antichità della Tripolitania. *Aegyptus* 7(1/2). 49–96.

Bartoccini, R. (1927a). *Guida di Leptis (Leptis Magna).* Rome-Milan.

Bartoccini, R. (1927b). *Guida di Sabratha.* Rome-Milan.

Bartoccini, R. (1929a). *Le terme di Leptis.* Bergamo: Istituto italiano d'arto grafiche.

Bartoccini, R. (1929b). Scavi e rinvenimenti in Tripolitania negli anni 1926–27 - Asàbaa, Tripoli, Gurgi, En-Ngila, Henscir Suffit. *AfrIt* 2. 77–110.

Bartoccini, R. (1931). L'Arco quadrifonte dei Severi a Lepcis (Leptis Magna). *AfrIt* 4. 35–152.

Bartoccini, R. (1958). Il porto romano di Leptis Magna. Rome: Il centro studi per la storia dell'architettura.

Bartoccini, R. (1961). Il foro Severiano di Leptis Magna – Campagna di scavo 1958. *QAL* 4. 105–126.

Bates, O. (1914). *The Eastern Libyans. An Essay.* London: MacMillan and Co.

Bauer, G. (1935). Le due necropoli di Ghirza. *AfrIt* 6. 61–78.

Beechey, H.W., & Beechey, F.W. (1828). *Proceedings of the Expedition to explore the Northern Coast of Africa from Tripoli Eastward 1821–1822.* London.

Ben Hassen, H., & Maurin, L. (1998). *Oudhna (Uthina): La découverte d'une ville antique de Tunisie.* Paris: Ausonius.

Ben Rabha, K.A., & Masturzo, N. (1997). Wadi al-Fani (Khoms): villa, mausoleum and gasr. *LibAnt* n.s.3. 214–216.

Bianchi, B. (2002). Pittura residenziale nella Tripolitania romana: lo stato degli studi e i nuovi dati. *AfrRom* 15. 1729–1750.

Bianchi Bandinelli, R., Vergara Caffarelli, E., & Caputo, G. (1966). *The Buried City. Excavations at Leptis Magna* (D. Ridgway, Trans.). New York: Frederick A. Praeger, Inc.

Bigi, F., Di Vita-Evrard, G., Fontana, S., & Schingo, G. (2009). The Mausoleum of Gasr Doga. *LibStud* 40. 25–46.

Blanchet, P. (1898). Sur quelques points fortifiés de la frontière saharienne de l'empire romain. *Recueil des notices et mémoires de la Société archéologique de la province de Constantine.* 32. 71–96.

Blanchet, P. (1899). Mission archéologique dans le centre et le sud de la Tunisie. *Nouvelles archives des missions scientifiques et littéraires* 9. 103–156.

Blázquez Martinez, J.M., López Monteagudo, G., Neira Jimenez, M.L., & San Nicolas Pedraz, M.P. (1990). Pavimentos africanos con espectaculos de toros. Estudio comparativo a proposito del mosaico de Silin (Tripolitania). *AntAfr* 26. 155–204.

Boizot. (1913). Fouilles exécutées en 1912 dans le camp Romain de Ras-el-Aïn-Tlalet (Tunisie). *BCTH* 1913. 260–266.

Bonacasa, N., & Bonacasa Carra, R.M. (2003). Gli edifici termali di Sabratha. Nota preliminare. *QAL* 18. 403–420.

Boni, G., & Mariani, L. (1915). Relazione intorno al consolidamento e al ripristino dell'arco di Marco Aurelio in Tripoli. *Notiziario Archeologico* 1. 13–34.

Bonifay, M. (2004). *Études sur la céramique romaine tardive d'Afrique.* Oxford: Archaeopress.

Bonifay, M. (2013). Africa: Patterns of consumption in coastal regions versus inland regions. The ceramic evidence (300–700 A.D.). *Late Antique Archaeology* 10. 529–566.

Bonifay, M. (2017). Can we speak of pottery and amphora 'import substitution' in inland regions of Roman Africa? In D.J. Mattingly, V. Leitch, C.N. Duckworth, A. Cuenod, M. Sterry & F. Cole (eds), *Trade in the Ancient Sahara and Beyond.* Cambridge: Cambridge University Press. 341–368.

Borgerhoff Mulder, M., Fazzio, I., Irons, W., McElreath, R.L., Bowles, S., Bell, A., Hertz, T., & Hazzah, L. (2010). Pastoralism and Wealth Inequality: Revisiting an Old Question. *Current Anthropology* 51(1). 35–48.

Borsari, F. (1888). *Geografia, Etnologica e Storica della Tripolitania, Cirenaica e Fezzan.* Naples: L. Pierro.

Bosio, L. (1983). *La Tabula Peutingeriana: una descrizione pittorica del mondo antico.* Rimini: Maggioli Editore.

Bradley, R. (1998). *The Significance of Monuments: On the shaping of human experience in Neolithic Bronze Age and Europe.* London: Routledge.

Brett, M. (1978). The Arab conquest and the rise of Islam in North Africa. In J.D. Fage (ed.), *The Cambridge History of Africa, Volume 2, from c. 500 BC to AD 1050.* Cambridge: Cambridge University Press. 490–555.

Brett, M., & Fentress, E. (1996). *The Berbers.* Oxford: Blackwell.

Brogan, O. (1954). The camel in Roman Tripolitania. *PBSR* 22. 126–131.

Brogan, O. (1964). The Roman remains in the Wadi el-Amud. *LibAnt* 1. 47–56.

Brogan, O. (1965a). Henscir el-Ausaf by Tigi (Tripolitania) and some related tombs in the Tunisian Gefara. *LibAnt* 2. 47–56.

Brogan, O. (1965b). Notes on the Wadis Neina and Bei el-Kebir and some pre-desert tracks. *LibAnt* 2. 57–64.

Brogan, O. (1968). First and Second Century Settlement in the Tripolitanian Pre-Desert. In F. Gadallah (ed.), *Libya in History.* Libya: Faculty of Arts, University of Libya. 121–130.

Brogan, O. (1975a). Inscriptions in the Libyan alphabet from Tripolitania, and some notes on the tribes of the region. In J. Bynon & T. Bynon (eds), *Hamito-Semitica: proceedings of a colloquium held by the Historical Section of the Linguistics Association, Great Britain at the School of Oriental and African Studies, University of London, on the 18th, 19th and 20th of March 1970.* The Hague: Mouton. 267–289.

Brogan, O. (1975b). Round and about Misurata. *LibStud* 6. 49–58.

Brogan, O. (1977). Some ancient sites in Eastern Tripolitania. *LibAnt* 13–14. 93–129.

Brogan, O. (1978). Es-Senama Bir el-Uaar: a Roman tomb in Libya. In P.R.S. Moorey & P. Parr (eds), *Archaeology in the Levant: essays for Kathleen Kenyon.* Warminster: Aris & Phillips. 233–237.

Brogan, O. (1980). Hadd Hajar, a clausura in the Tripolitanian Gebel Garian south of Asabaa. *LibStud* 11. 45–52.

Brogan, O., & Reynolds, J.M. (1960). Seven new inscriptions from Tripolitania. *PBSR* 28. 51–54.

Brogan, O., & Reynolds, J.M. (1964). Inscriptions from the Tripolitanian Hinterland. *LibAnt* 1. 43–46.

Brogan, O., & Smith, D.J. (1967). Notes from the Tripolitanian pre-desert 1967. *LibAnt* 3–4. 139–144.

Brogan, O., & Smith, D.J. (1984). *Ghirza. A Libyan Settlement in the Roman Period.* Tripoli: Department of Antiquities.

Brouquier-Reddé, V. (1992). *Temples et Cultes de Tripolitaine.* Paris: Éditions CNRS.

Brun, J.-P. (2004). *Archéologie du Vin et de l'Huile dans l'Empire Romain.* Paris: Éditions Errance.

Büchsenschütz, O. (2001). De la hutte à la maison, de Vitruve aux trois petits cochons. In J.R. Brandt & L. Karlsson (eds), *From huts to houses: transformations of ancient societies. Proceedings of an International Seminar organized by the Norwegian and Swedish Institutes in Rome, 21–24 September 1997.* Stockholm: Paul Åströms Förlag. 223–231.

Bullo, S. (2002). *Provincia Africa. Le città e il territoria dalla caduta di Cartagine a Nerone.* Roma: "L'Erma" di Bretschneider.

Cadotte, A. (2007). *La Romanisation des Dieux. L'interpretatio romana en Afrique du Nord sous le Haut-Empire.* Leiden/Boston: Brill.

Cagnat, R. (1901). Les Ruines de Leptis Magna a la fin du XVIIe siècle. *Mémoires de la Societé Nationale des Antiquaires de France* 60. 63–78.

Cagnat, R. (1913). *L'armée Romaine d'Afrique et l'occupation militaire de l'Afrique sous les empereurs.* Paris: Imprimerie Nationale.

Cagnat, R., & Merlin, A. (1920). *Atlas Archéologique de la Tunisie. Édition Spéciale des cartes topographiques publiées par le Ministère de la Guerre, accompagnée d'un texte explicatif.* Paris: Éditions Ernest Leroux.

Cagnat, R., Merlin, A., & Chatelain, L. (eds). (1923). *Inscriptions Latines d'Afrique* (Tripolitaine, Tunisie, Maroc). Paris.

Callegarin, L. (2009). Le Gétule: Cet autre insaisissable (première partie). In M.-F. Marein, P. Voisin & J. Gallego (eds), *Figures de l'étranger autour de la Méditerranée antique. Actes de Colloque International. Antiquité méditerranéenne: à la rencontre de "l'autre". Perceptions et représentations de l'étranger dans les littératures antiques.* Paris: L'Harmattan. 203–214.

Camporeale, S. (2011). Military Building Techniques in *Mauretania Tingitana*: the Use of Mortar and Rubble at *Thamusida* (Sidi Ali ben Ahmed, Morocco). In Å. Ringbom & R.L. Hohlfelder (eds), *Building Roma Aeterna. Current Research on Roman Mortar and Concrete. Proceedings of the conference March 27–29 2008.* Helsinki: Societas Scientarium Fennica. 169-186.

Camporeale, S. (2013). *Opus africanum*: Problems of origin, diffusion, and uses in the western Mediterranean. Paper presented at the Ancient Architecture Discussion Group, Oxford.

Caputo, G. (1939). *Il Teatro Romano di Sabratha* (2nd ed.). Tivoli: Arti Grafiche A. Chicca.

Caputo, G. (1940). Il tempio oeense al Genio della colonia. *AfrIt* 7(1–2). 35–45.

Caputo, G. (1942). Notizario di scavi, scoperte, studi relativi all'Impero Romano: Provincie Africane. *Bullettino del Museo dell'Impero Romano* 13. 151–154.

Caputo, G. (1987). *Il Teatro Augusteo di Leptis Magna: Scavo e Restauro (1937–1951).* Roma: "L'Erma" di Bretschneider.

Caputo, G., & Ghedini, F. (1984). *Il Tempio d'Ercole di Sabratha.* Rome: "L'Erma" di Bretschneider.

Carlsen, J. (2000). Property and Production in the Segermes Valley during the Roman Era. In P. Ørsted, J. Carlsen, L. Ladjimi Sebaï, & H. Ben Hassen (eds), *Africa Proconsularis: Regional studies in the Segermes Valley of Northern Tunisia* (Vol. 3, Historical Conclusions). Århus: Aarhus University Press. 105–134.

Carlsen, J., & Tvarnø, H. (1990). The Segermes Valley Archaeological Survey (Region of Zaghouan). An Interim Report. *AfrRom* 7. 803–813.

Carton, D. (1888). Essai sur les travaux hydrauliques des Romains dans le sud de la Régence de Tunis. *BCTH* 1888. 438–465.

Casana, J. (2020). Global-Scale Archaeological Prospection using CORONA Satellite Imagery: Automated, Crows-Sourced, and Expert-led Approaches. *Journal of Field Archaeology* 45(S1). S89–S100.

Casana, J., & Cothren, J. (2008). Stereo analysis, DEM extraction and orthorectification of CORONA satellite imagery: Archaeological application from the Near East. *Antiquity* 82. 732–749.

Cerrata, L. (1933). *Sirtis (Studio Geografico-Storico).* Avellino: Tipografia Pergola.

Chastagnol, A. (1967). Les Gouverneurs de Byzacène et de Tripolitaine. *AntAfr* 1. 119–134.

Chiesa, C. (1949). Sui materiali da costruzione di provenienza locale usati dagli antichi in Tripolitania. *Reports and Monographs of the Department of Antiquities in Tripolitania* 2. 25–28.

Christides, V. (2000). *Byzantine Libya and the March of the Arabs toward the West of North Africa.* Oxford: BAR.

Cifani, G., Munzi, M., Felici, F., & Cirelli, E. (2003). Ricerche topografiche nel territorio di Leptis Magna: rapporto preliminare. In M. Khanoussi (ed.), *Actes du VIIIe Colloque International sur l'Histoire et l'Archéologie de l'Afrique du Nord - 1er colloque international sur l'Histoire et l'Archéologie du Maghreb (Tabarka, 8–13 mai 2000).* Tunis. 395–414.

Cirelli, E., Felici, F., & Munzi, M. (2012). Insediamenti fortificati nel territorio di Leptis Magna tra III e XI secolo. In P. Galetti (ed.), *Paesaggi, Comunità, Villaggi Medievali. Atti del Convegno internazionale di studio. Bologna, 14–16 gennaio 2010.* Spoleto: Fondazione Centro Italiano di Studi sull'Alto Medioevo. 763–774.

Cività, A. (1994). *A Morphological Study of Undefended Sites in the Tripolitanian Pre-desert.* MA dissertation, University of Leicester.

Clark, G. (1986). ULVS XIV: Archaeozoological Evidence for Stock-Raising and Stock-management in the Pre-desert. *LibStud* 17. 49–64.

Clark, J.D. (1982). *The Cambridge History of Africa, Volume 1: From the Earliest Times to c. 500 BC.* Cambridge: Cambridge University Press.

Clarke, J.R. (2007). *Looking at Laughter: Humor, Power, and Transgression in Roman Visual Culture, 100 B.C. - A.D. 250.* Berkeley: University of California Pres.

Colantoni, E. (2012). Straw to Stone, Huts to Houses. Transitions in building practices and society in protohistoric Latium. In M.L. Thomas & G.E. Meyers (eds), *Monumentality in Etruscan and early Roman architecture: ideology and innovation.* Austin: University of Texas Press. 21–40.

Comer, D.C., & Harrower, M.J. (eds). (2013). *Mapping Archaeological Landscapes from Space.* New York: Springer.

Conant, J. (2012). *Staying Roman: Conquest and Identity in Africa and the Mediterranean, 439–700.* Cambridge: Cambridge University Press.

Constans, L.A. (1916). *Gigthis. Étude d'histoire et d'archéologie sur un emporium de la Petite Syrte.* Paris: Imprimerie Nationale.

Corò, F. (1928). *Vestigia di colonie agricole Romane.* Gebel Nefusa. Rome.

Courtois, C. (1955). *Les Vandales et l'Afrique.* Paris: Arts et Métiers Graphiques.

Cowper, H.S. (1897). *The Hill of the Graces. A Record of Investigation Among the Trilithons and Megalithic Sites of Tripoli.* London: Methuen & Co.

Cunliffe, E.L. (2013). *Satellites and Site Destruction: An Analysis of Modern Impacts on the Archaeological Resource of the Ancient Near East.* PhD Thesis, Durham University.

Daniels, C.M. (1968). The Garamantes of Fazzan. In F. Gadallah (ed.), *Libya in History.* Libya: Faculty of Arts, University of Libya. 261–287.

Daniels, C.M. (1970). *The Garamantes of Southern Libya*. North Harrow, Middlesex: Oleander Press.

Daniels, C.M. (1975). An Ancient People of the Libyan Sahara. In J. Bynon & T. Bynon (eds), *Hamito-Semitica: proceedings of a colloquium held by the Historical Section of the Linguistics Association, Great Britain at the School of Oriental and African Studies, University of London, on the 18th, 19th and 20th of March 1970*. The Hague: Mouton. 249–265.

Daniels, C.M. (1989). Excavation and fieldwork amongst the Garamantes. *LibStud* 20. 45–61.

De Meyer, M. (2004). Archaeological research using Satellite Remote Sensing Techniques (Corona) in the Valleys of Shirwan and Chardawal (Pusht-i Kuh, Luristant), Iran. *Iranica Antiqua* 39. 43–103.

De Miro, E., & Polito, A. (2005). *Leptis Magna. Dieci anni di scavo archeologici nell'area del Foro Vecchio. I livelli fenici, punici e romani (Missione dell'Università di Messina)*. Rome: "L'Erma" di Bretschneider.

de Vos, M. (2000). *Rus Africum : terra, acqua, olio nell'Africa settentrionale : scavo e ricognizione nei dintorni di Dougga (Alto Tell Tunisino)*. Trento; Tunis: Università degli studi di Trento; INP.

de Vos, M. (2013). The Rural Landscape of Thugga: Farms, Presses, Mills, and Transport. In A.K. Bowman & A. Wilson (eds), *The Roman Agricultural Economy: Organisation, Investment, and Production*. Oxford: Oxford University Press. 143–218.

de Vos Raaijmakers, M., & Attoui, R. (2013). *Rus Africum. Tome I. Le paysage rural antique autour de Dougga et Téboursouk: cartographie, relevés et chronologie des établissements*. Bari-S. Spirito: Edipuglia.

Decker, M. (2006). Towers, Refuges, and Fortified Farms in the Late Roman East. *Liber Annuus* 56. 499–520.

Degrassi, N. (1951). Il Mercato Romano di Leptis Magna. *QAL* 2. 27–70.

Desanges, J. (1962). *Catalogue des tribus africaines de l'Antiquité classique à l'ouest du Nil*. Dakar: Université de Dakar.

Desanges, J. (1969). Un drame africain sous Auguste: le meutre du Proconsul L. Cornelius Lentulus par les Nasamons. In J. Bibauw (ed.), *Hommages à Marcel Renard*. Vol. 2. Bruxelles: Latomus. 197–213.

di Lernia, S. (2013). The Emergence and Spread of Herding in Northern Africa: A Critical Reappraisal. In P. Mitchell & P. Lane (eds), *The Oxford Handbook of African Archaeology*. Oxford: Oxford University Press.

Di Vita, A. (1964). Il 'limes' romano di Tripolitania nella sua concretezza archeologica e nella sua realtà storica. *LibAnt* 1. 65–98.

Di Vita, A. (1966). *La Villa della "Gara delle Nereidi" presso Tagiura: un contributo alla storia del mosaico Romano. Ed Altri Recenti Scavi e Scoperte in Tripolitania (Supplements to Libya Antiqua II)*. Tripoli, Libya: The Directorate-General of Antiquities, Museums and Archives.

Di Vita, A. (1968). Influences grecques et tradition orientale dans l'art punique de Tripolitaine. *Mélanges d'archéologie et d'histoire* 80(1). 7–84.

Di Vita, A. (1982). Gli *Emporia* di Tripolitania dall'età di Massinissa a Diocleziano: un profilo storico-istituzionale. *Aufstieg und Niedergang der Romischen Welt. Principat II* 10(2). 515–595.

Di Vita, A. (1983). Architettura e società nelle città di Tripolitania fra Massinissa e Augusto: qualche nota. In *Architecture et Société de l'archaisme grec à la fin de la république romaine*. Paris: CNRS. 355–376.

Di Vita, A. (1990). Sismi, urbanistica e cronologia assoluta. Terremoti e urbanistica nelle città di Tripolitania fra il I secolo a.C. ed il IV d.C. In *L'Afrique dan l'occident Romain (Ier siècle av. J.-C. – IVe siècle ap. J.-C.)*. Rome: École française de Rome.

Di Vita, A. (1992). L'urbanistica nelle città punico-romane della Tripolitania. *AfrRom* 10. 685–688.

Di Vita, A., & Liviadotti, M. (eds). (2005). *I Tre Templi del Lato Nord-Ovest del Foro Vecchio a Leptis Magna*. Rome: "L'Erma" di Bretschneider.

Di Vita-Evrard, G. (1984). *L. Volusius Bassus Cerealis*, légat du proconsul d'Afrique *T. Claudius Aurelius Aristobulus*, et la création de la province de Tripolitaine. *AfrRom* 2. 149–177.

Di Vita-Evrard, G. (1985). Regio Tripolitana. A Reappraisal. In D.J. Buck & D.J. Mattingly (eds), *Town and Country in Roman Tripolitania. Papers in honour of Olwen Hackett*. Oxford: BAR. 143–159.

Díaz-Andreu, M. (2007). *A World History of Nineteenth-Century Archaeology: Nationalism, Colonialism and the Past*. New York: Oxford University Press.

Díaz-Andreu, M., Lucy, S., Babic, S., & Edwards, D.N. (2005). *The Archaeology of Identity: Approaches to gender, age, status, ethnicity and religion*. London: Routledge.

Dietler, M. (2010). *Archaeologies of Colonialism: Consumption, Entanglement, and Violence in Ancient Mediterranean France*. Berkeley and Los Angeles: University of California Press.

Dietz, S., Ladjimi Sebaï, L., & Ben Hassen, H. (eds). (1995). *Africa Proconsularis: Regional studies in the Segermes Valley of Northern Tunisia* (Vol. 1). Århus: Aarhus University Press.

Dobres, M.-A., & Robb, J.E. (eds). (2000). *Agency in Archaeology*. London: Routledge.

Donau, R. (1904). Le Castellum de Benia-Guedah-Ceder. Fouilles exécutées en 1904. *BCTH* 1904. 467–477.

Donau, R. (1906). Note sur des ruines du sud Tunisien. *BCTH* 1906. 113–122.

Donau, R. (1915). Une note sur des sépultures berbères de Tunisie. *BCTH* 1915. cxx–cxxiv.

Donau, R., & Pervinquière, L. (1912). Notes archéologiques sur la frontière tuniso-tripolitaine. *Bullétin de Géographie historique et descriptive* 1912(3). 465–507.

Dore, J. (1985). Settlement chronology in the pre-desert zone: the evidence of the fineware. In D.J. Buck & D.J. Mattingly (eds), *Town and Country in Roman Tripolitania. Papers in honour of Olwen Hackett*. Oxford: BAR. 107–125.

Dore, J. (1988). Pottery and the History of Roman Tripolitania: Evidence from Sabratha and the UNESCO Libyan Valleys Survey. *LibStud* 19. 61–86.

Dore, J. (1996). Part 2. The UNESCO Libyan Valleys Archaeological Survey Pottery. In D.J. Mattingly (ed.), *Farming the Desert: The UNESCO Libyan Valleys Archaeological Survey*. Vol. Two: Gazetteer and Pottery. 319–389.

Dore, J., & Keay, N. (1989). *Excavations at Sabratha 1948-1951. Volume II The Finds Part 1 The Amphorae, Coarse Pottery and Building Materials*. London: The Society for Libyan Studies in behalf of The Department of Antiquities, Tripoli.

Dore, J., & van der Veen, M. (1986). ULVS XV: Radio-carbon Dates from the Libyan Valleys Survey. *LibStud* 17. 65–68.

Dorsett, J.E., Gilbertson, D.D., Hunt, C.O., & Barker, G.W.W. (1984). The UNESCO Libyan Valleys Survey VIII: image analysis of Landsat satellite data for archaeological and environmental surveys. *LibStud* 15: 71–80.

Dossey, L. (2010). *Peasant and Empire in Christian North Africa*. Berkeley: University of California Press.

Drine, A. (2002). Autour du lac El Bibèn: les sites d'El Mdeina et de Bou Garnin. *AfrRom* 14(3). 2001–2014.

Dunbabin, K. (1978). *The Mosaics of Roman North Africa: Studies in iconography and patronage*. Oxford: Clarendon Press.

Duveyrier, H. (1864). *Exploration du Sahara: Les Touareg du Nord*. Paris: Challamel Ainé.

Dyson, S.L. (2006). *In Pursuit of Ancient Pasts. A History of Classical Archaeology in the Nineteenth and Twentieth Centuries*. New Haven: Yale University Press.

Emrage, A. (2015). *Roman Fortified Farms (Qsur) and Military Sites in the Region of the Wadi al-Kuf, Cyrenaica (Eastern Libya)*. PhD Thesis, University of Leicester.

Euzennat, M. (1972). Quatre années de recherches sur la frontière romaine en Tunisie mèridionale. *Comptes Rendus des Séances de l'Académie des Inscriptions et Belles-lettres* 116(1). 7–27.

Euzennat, M. (1973). Tillibari, forteresse du "limes Tripolitanus". *BCTH* 1973. 143–144.

Euzennat, M. (1977). Les recherches sur la frontière romaine d'Afrique. In Fitz (ed.), *Acten des Internationalen Limeskongress, 1976*. Budapest.

Euzennat, M. (1985). L'olivier et le "limes", considerations sur la frontière romaine de Tripolitaine. *BCTH* n.s.19B. 161–171.

Euzennat, M. (1986). Les camps Marocains d'Aïn Schkour et de Sidi Moussa Bou Fri et l'introduction du "quadriburgium" en Afrique du Nord. In *Histoire et Archéologie de L'Afrique du Nord. Actes du IIIe Colloque International*. Paris: CTHS. 373–376.

Euzennat, M., & Trousset, P. (1978). Le Camp de Remada: Fouilles Inédites du Commandant Donau (Mars-Avril 1914). *Africa. Fouilles, monuments et collections archéologiques en Tunisie* 5–6. 111–189.

Fage, J.D. (1978). *The Cambridge History of Africa, Volume 2: from c. 500 BC to AD 1050*. Cambridge: Cambridge University Press.

Faraj, M.O. (1996). Jebel Msellata. Roman mausolea and farms at Rumia (el-Khamri). *LibAnt* n.s.2. 169–170.

Felici, F., Munzi, M., & Tantillo, I. (2006). *Austuriani* e *Laguatan* in Tripolitania. *AfrRom* 16. 591–687.

Felici, F., & Pentiricci, M. (2002). Per una definizione delle dinamiche economiche e commerciali del territorio di *Leptis Magna*. *AfrRom* 14. 1875–1900.

Fellman, R. (1992). *La Suisse Gallo-Romaine: Cinq Siècles d'Histoire*. Lausanne: Editions Payot.

Fentress, E. (1979). *Numidia and the Roman Army: Social, Military and Economic Aspects of the Frontier Zone*. Oxford: BAR.

Fentress, E. (2000). Social Relations and Domestic Space in the Maghreb. In A. Bazzana & É. Hubert (eds), *Castrum 6. Maisons et espaces domestiques dans le monde méditerranéen au Moyen Âge*. Rome-Madrid: École française de Rome-Casa de Velázquez. 15–26.

Fentress, E. (2001). Villas, Wines and Kilns: the landscape of Jerba in the late Hellenistic period. *JRA* 14. 249–268.

Fentress, E., & Docter, R.F. (2008). North Africa: Rural Settlement and Agricultural Production. In P. van Dommelen & C. Gómez Bellard (eds), *Rural Landscapes of the Punic World*. London: Equinox.

Fentress, E., Drine, A., & Holod, R. (2009). *An Island Through Time: Jerba Studies* (Vol. 1: The Punic and Roman Periods). Portsmouth, Rhode Island: JRA.

Fentress, E., Fontana, S., Hitchner, R.B., & Perkins, P. (2004). Accounting for ARS: Fineware and Sites in Sicily and Africa. In S.E. Alcock & J.F. Cherry (eds), *Side-by-Side Survey: Comparative Regional Studies in the Mediterranean World.* Oxford: Oxbow. 147–162.

Fentress, E., & Perkins, P. (1988). Counting African Red Slip Ware. *AfrRom* 5. 205–214.

Fentress, E., & Wilson, A.I. (2016). The Saharan Berber Diaspora and the Southern Frontiers of Byzantine North Africa. In S.T. Stevens & J.P. Conant (eds), *North Africa under Byzantium and Early Islam.* Washington, D.C.: Dumbarton Oaks.

Fenwick, C. (2013). From Africa to Ifrīqiya: Settlement and Society in Early Medieval North Africa (650–800). *Al-Masaq: Islam and the Medieval Mediterranean* 25(1). 9–33.

Ferchiou, N. (1984). *Gigthis* à une époque mal connue: la phase julio-claudienne. *BCTH* n.s.17B. 65–74.

Ferchiou, N. (1988). Le temple de Mercure à Gigthis. Recherches sur le décor architectonique. *Africa. Revue des études et recherches préhistoriques, antiques, islamiques et ethnographiques* 10. 174–189.

Ferchiou, N. (1990a). Habitats fortifiés pré-impériaux en Tunisie antique. *AntAfr* 26. 43–86.

Ferchiou, N. (1990b). L'habitat fortifié pré-impérial en Tunisie antique: aperçus sur la typologie des sites perchés et des sites de versant, illustrés par quelques exemples. In *Histoire et Archéologie de l'Afrique du Nord. Actes du IVe Colloque International réuni dans la cadre du 113e Congès national des Sociétés savantes (Strasbourg, 5–9 avril 1988). Tome I: Carthage et son territoire dans l'antiquité.* Paris: Editions du CTHS. 229–252.

Fergusson, J. (1872). *Rude Stone Monuments in All Countries: Their Age and Uses.* London: John Murray.

Finkelstein, I. (1995). *Living on the Fringe: The Archaeology and History of the Negev, Sinai and Neighbouring Regions in the Bronze and Iron Ages.* Sheffield: Sheffield Academic Press.

Fishwick, D. (1993). On the Origins of Africa Proconsularis, I: The amalgamation of Africa Vetus and Africa Nova. *AntAfr* 29. 53–62.

Fishwick, D. (1994). On the Origins of Africa Proconsularis, II: The administration of Lepidus and the commission of M. Caelius Phileros. *AntAfr* 30. 57–80.

Fishwick, D., & Shaw, B.D. (1977). The Formation of Africa Proconsularis. *Hermes* 105. 369–380.

Floriani Squarciapino, M. (1966). *Leptis Magna.* Basel: Raggi Verlag.

Floriani Squarciapino, M. (1974). *Sculture del Foro Severiano di Leptis Magna.* Rome: "L'Erma" di Bretschneider.

Flower, C.P.J., & Mattingly, D.J. (1995). ULVS XXVII: Mapping and Spatial Analysis of the Libyan Valleys Data using GIS. *LibStud* 26. 49–78.

Fontana, S. (1995). I manufatti romani nei corredi funerari del Fazzan: Testimonianza dei commerci e della cultura dei Garamanti (I–III sec. d.C.). In *L'Afrique du Nord Antique et Médiévale, VIe colloque international: Productions et exportations africaines, Actualités archéologiques.* Paris: Éditions du CTHS. 405–420.

Fontana, S. (1997). Il predeserto tripolitano: mausolei e rappresentazione del potere. *LibAnt* n.s.3. 149–162.

Fontana, S., Munzi, M., & Ricci, G. (1996). Insediamenti agricoli di età ellenistica e romana nell'area dell'uadi Bendar (Leptis Magna). *LibAnt* n.s.2. 67–72.

Foss, C. (1995). The Near Eastern countryside in late antiquity: a review article. In J.H. Humphrey (ed.), *The Roman and Byzantine Near East: Some recent archaeological research.* Ann Arbor: JRA. 213–234.

Foucher, L. (1964). Sur les mosaïques de Zliten. *LibAnt* 1. 9–20.

Frankovich, R., Patterson, H., & Barker, G. (eds). (2000). *Extracting meaning from ploughsoil assemblages.* Oxford: Oxbow.

Frere, S.S., & St Joseph, J.K.S. (1983). *Roman Britain from the Air.* Cambridge: Cambridge University Press.

Fulford, M., & Tomber, R. (1994). *Excavations at Sabratha 1948–1951. Volume II: The Finds. Part 2: The Finewares and Lamps.* London: The Society for Libyan Studies on behalf of the Department of Antiquities, Tripoli.

Galand, L. (1989). Les alphabets libyques. *AntAfr* 25. 69–82.

Galand, L. (2003). Interrogations sur le Libyque. *AntAfr* 38–39. 259–266.

Ganci, R. (1995). La Spedizione di Dorieo in Libia. *Hesperìa* 5. 223–231.

Garnsey, P. (1978). Rome's African Empire under the Principate. In P. Garnsey & C.R. Whittaker (eds), *Imperialism in the Ancient World.* Cambridge: Cambridge University Press.

Gascou, J. (1984). La carrière de Marcus Caelius Phileros. *AntAfr* 20. 105–120.

Gascou, J. (1987). Les Sacerdotes Cererum de Carthage. *AntAfr* 23. 95–128.

Gauckler, P. (1896). *L'Archéologie de la Tunisie.* Paris: Berger-Levrault.

Gauckler, P. (1897). *Enquête sur les Installations Hydrauliques Romaines en Tunisie* (Vol. I). Tunis: Imprimerie Rapide.

Gauckler, P. (1899). *Enquête sur les Installations Hydrauliques Romaines en Tunisie* (Vol. III). Tunis: Imprimerie Rapide.

Gauckler, P. (1900). Note sur les fouilles exécutées dans le Sahara tunisien. *CRAI* 44(5). 541–547.

Gauckler, P. (1902). Le centenarius de Tibubuci (Ksar Tarcine - sud Tunisien). *CRAI* 46(3). 321–340.
Gentilucci, I. (1933). Resti di antichi edifici lungo l'uàdi Sofeggìn. *AfrIt* 5. 172–187.
GHF/J.M. Kaplan Award Funds Documentation of Over 3,000 Endangered Heritage Sites in MENA. (2019, 7 November). *EAMENA Blog*. Retrieved 10 June 2020 from http://eamena.arch.ox.ac.uk/ghf-j-m-kaplan-award-funds-documentation-of-over-3000-endangered-heritage-site-in-mena/.
Gichon, M. (1990). The courtyard pattern castellum in the limes Palaestinae — strategic and tactical features. In H. Vetters & M. Kandler (eds), *Akten des 14. Internationalen Limeskongresses 1986 in Carnuntum*. Wien: Verlag der Österreichischen Akademie der Wissenschaften. 193–214.
Gilbert. (1885). Fouilles d'El-Kantara en 1882. *BCTH* 1885. 119–124.
Gilbertson, D.D. (1996). Explanations: Environment as Agency. In G. Barker (ed.), *Farming the Desert: The UNESCO Libyan Valleys Archaeological Survey.* Vol. One: Synthesis. 291–318.
Gilbertson, D.D., & Chisholm, N.W.T. (1996). ULVS XXVIII: Manipulating the Desert Environment: Ancient Walls, Floodwater Farming and Territoriality in the Tripolitanian Pre-Desert of Libya. *LibStud* 27. 17–52.
Gilbertson, D.D., Hayes, P.P., Barker, G., & Hunt, C.O. (1984). The UNESCO Libyan Valleys Survey VII: An Interim Classification and Functional Analysis of Ancient Wall Technology and Land Use. *LibStud* 15. 45–70.
Gilbertson, D.D., Hunt, C., & Gillmore, G. (2000). Success, longevity, and failure of arid-land agriculture: Romano-Libyan floodwater farming in the Tripolitanian pre-desert. In G. Barker & D.D. Gilbertson (eds), *The Archaeology of Drylands: Living at the margin*. London: Routledge. 133–155.
Gilbertson, D.D., & Hunt, C.O. (1990). ULVS XXI: Geomorphological Studies of the Romano-Libyan Farm, its Floodwater Control Structues and Weathered Building Stone at the Site LM4, at the Confluence of Wadi el Amud and Wadi el Bagul in the Libyan Predesert. *LibStud* 21. 25–42.
Gilbertson, D.D., & Hunt, C.O. (1996). Romano-Libyan Agriculture: Walls and Floodwater Farming. In G. Barker (ed.), *Farming the Desert: The UNESCO Libyan Valleys Archaeological Survey.* Vol. One: Synthesis. 191–226.
Gilman, A. (1974). Neolithic of Northwest Africa. *Antiquity* 48. 273–282.
Gliozzo, E., Damiani, D., Camporeale, S., Memmi, I., & Papi, E. (2011). Building materials from *Thamusida* (Rabat, Morocco): a diachronic local production from the Roman to the Islamic period. *Journal of Archaeological Science* 38. 1026–1036.
Goldsworthy, A., & Haynes, I.P. (eds). (1999). *The Roman Army as a Community: Including papers of a conference held at Birkbeck College, University of London on 11–12 January 1997.* Portsmouth, RI: JRA.
Gombeaud. (1901). Fouilles du Castellum d'el-Hagueuff (Tunisie). *BCTH* 1901. 81–94.
Gómez Bellard, C. (2008). Ibiza: the Making of New Landscapes. In P. van Dommelen & C. Gómez Bellard (eds), *Rural Landscapes of the Punic World.* London: Equinox. 44–75.
Goodchild, R.G. (1948). *The Roman Roads and Milestones of Tripolitania.* Tripoli: Department of Antiquities, British Military Administration, Tripolitania.
Goodchild, R.G. (1949). The Organisation and Work of the Antiquities Department, 1943–1948. *Reports and Monographs of the Department of Antiquities in Tripolitania* 2. 9–14.
Goodchild, R.G. (1950a). The Latino-Libyan inscriptions of Tripolitania. *Antiquaries Journal* 30. 135–144.
Goodchild, R.G. (1950b). The *Limes Tripolitanus* II. *JRS* 40. 30–38.
Goodchild, R.G. (1950c). Roman Tripolitania: Reconnaissance in the Desert Frontier Zone. *The Geographical Journal* 115(4/6). 161–178.
Goodchild, R.G. (1951a). Boreum of Cyrenaica. *JRS* 41. 11–16.
Goodchild, R.G. (1951b). "Libyan" Forts in South-west Cyrenaica. *Antiquity* 25(99). 131–144.
Goodchild, R.G. (1951c). Roman sites on the Tarhuna plateau of Tripolitania. *PBSR* 19. 43–65.
Goodchild, R.G. (1952). Arae Philaenorum and Automalax. *PBSR* 20. 94–110.
Goodchild, R.G. (1953). The Roman and Byzantine Limes in Cyrenaica. *JRS* 43. 65–76.
Goodchild, R.G. (1954). Oasis Forts of *Legio III Augusta* on the routes to the Fezzan. *PBSR* 22. 56–68.
Goodchild, R.G. (1964). Medina Sultan (Charax - Iscina - Sort). *LibAnt* 1. 99–106.
Goodchild, R.G. (1968). The Roman Roads of Libya and their Milestones. In F. Gadallah (ed.), *Libya in History.* Libya: Faculty of Arts, University of Libya. 155–171.
Goodchild, R.G. (1976a). Inscriptions from Western Tarhuna. In J.M. Reynolds (ed.), *Libyan Studies: Select Papers of the late R.G. Goodchild.* London: Elek Books. 107–113.
Goodchild, R.G. (1976b). *Libyan Studies: Selected papers of the late R.G. Goodchild (ed. J.M. Reynolds).* London: Elek Books.
Goodchild, R.G., & Ward-Perkins, J.B. (1949). The *Limes Tripolitanus* in the light of Recent Discoveries. *JRS* 39. 81–95.
Goodchild, R.G., & Ward-Perkins, J.B. (1953). The Roman and Byzantine Defences of Lepcis Magna. *PBSR* 21. 42–73.
Goodman, P.J. (2007). *The Roman City and its Periphery: From Rome to Gaul.* London: Routledge.

Gosden, C. (2005). What do objects want? *Journal of Archaeological Method and Theory* 12(3). 193–211.

Govoni, L., Custodi, A., & Sciortino, L. (2002). Un metodo per la definizione dei parametri elastici dell'opera a telaio. *Università di Bologna, DISTART, nota tecnica* 91. 19 pages.

Grahame, M. (1998). Rome without Romanization: Cultural Change in the Pre-Desert of Tripolitania (First-Third Centuries AD). *OJA* 17(1). 93–111.

Graves-Brown, P. (1996). All things bright and beautiful? Species, ethnicity and cultural dynamics. In P. Graves-Brown, S. Jones & C. Gamble (eds), *Cultural Identity and Archaeology: The Construction of European Communities*. London: Routledge. 81–95.

Graves-Brown, P., Jones, S., & Gamble, C. (eds). (1996). *Cultural Identity and Archaeology: The Construction of European Communities*. London: Routledge.

Graziosi, P. (1942). *L'Arte Rupestre della Libia*. Naples: Mostra d'Oltremare.

Gregory, S. (1989). Not "Why not playing cards?" but "Why playing cards in the first place?". In D.H. French & C.S. Lightfoot (eds), *The Eastern Frontier of the Roman Empire. Proceedings of a colloquium held at Ankara in September 1988*. Oxford: BAR. 169–175.

Gregory, S. (1997). *Roman Military Architecture on the Eastern Frontier* (Vol. 1). Amsterdam: Adolf M. Hakkert.

Gsell, S. (1921). *Histoire Ancienne de l'Afrique du Nord* (Vol. 1). Paris: Hachette.

Guédon, S. (2018). *La frontière romaine de l'*Africa *sous le Haut-Empire*. Madrid: Casa de Velázquez.

Guérin, V. (1862). *Voyage archéologique dans la Régence de Tunis* (Vol. 1). Paris: Henri Plon.

Guéry, R. (1986). Chronologie de quelques établissements de la frontière romaine du sud tunisien à partir de la céramique collectée sur les sites. In *Studien zu den Militärgrenzen Roms III. 13. Internationaler Limeskongress, Aalen 1983: Vorträge*. Stuttgart: Konrad Theiss Verlag. 600–604.

Guidi, G. (1931). I recenti scavi di Leptis Magna e di Sabratha e l'ordinamento dei musei archeologici in Tripolitania. In *Atti del Primo Congresso di Studi Coloniali, Firenze, 8–12 aprile 1931*. 1–9.

Guidi, G. (1933). La villa del Nilo. *AfrIt* 5(1–2). 1–56.

Guidi, G. (1935). I Monumenti della Tripolitania Romana. In U. Hoepli (ed.), *Africa Romana*. Milan: Istituto di Studi Romani.

Haensch, R., & Mackensen, M. (2011). Das tripolitanische Kastell Gheriat el-Garbia im Licht einer neuen spätantiken Inschrift: Am Tag als der Regen. *Chiron* 41. 263–286.

Hales, S., & Hodos, T. (eds). (2010). *Material Culture and Social Identity in the Ancient World*. Cambridge: Cambridge University Press.

Hammond, N. (1964). Cambridge *Limes Tripolitanus* Expedition Report.

Hammond, N. (1967). The *Limes Tripolitanus*: A Roman Road in North Africa. *The Journal of the British Archaeological Association* 30. 1–18.

A Handbook of Libya. Compiled by the Geographical Section of the Naval Intelligence Division, Naval Staff, Admiralty. (1920). London: H.M. Stationary Office.

Hanel, N. (2007). Military Camps, *Canabae*, and *Vici*. The Archaeological Evidence. In P. Erdkamp (ed.), *A Companion to the Roman Army*. Oxford: Blackwell Publishing. 395–416.

Hanoune, R. (2009). La construction romaine en "opus Africanum" et ses renaissances: innovation technique? continuité accidentale? In J.-R. Gaborit (ed.), *Tradition et innovation en histoire de l'art (Grenoble, 2006)*. Paris: CTHS. 29–39.

Hansen, C.G. (1995). Architectural Studies. In S. Dietz, L. Ladjimi Sebaï, & H. Ben Hassen (eds), *Africa Proconsularis: Regional studies in the Segermes Valley of Northern Tunisia* (Vol. 1). Århus: Aarhus University Press. 177–379.

Hanson, J.W. (2011). The Urban System of Roman Asia Minor and Wider Urban Connectivity. In A. Wilson & A.K. Bowman (eds), *Settlement, Urbanization, and Population*. Oxford: Oxford University Press. 229–275.

Hanson, W.S., & Oltean, I.A. (eds). (2013). *Archaeology from Historical Aerial and Satellite Archives*. New York: Springer-Verlag.

Harmand, J. (1951). Sur la valeur archéologique du mot 'villa'. *Revue Archéologique* 38. 155–158.

Hayes, J.W. (1972). *Late Roman Pottery*. London: British School at Rome.

Hayes, J.W. (1980). *A Supplement to Late Roman Pottery*. London: British School at Rome.

Haynes, D.E.L. (1946). *A short historical and archaeological introduction to Ancient Tripolitania*. Tripoli: The Department of Antiquities of Tripolitania, Libya.

Haynes, D.E.L. (1955). *The Antiquities of Tripolitania*. Tripoli: The Department of Antiquities of Tripolitania, Libya.

Hijmans, R.J., Cameron, S.E., Parra, J.L., Jones, P.G., & Jarvis, A. (2005). Very high resolution interpolated climate surfaces for global land areas. *International Journal of Climatology* 25. 1965–1978. Retrieved 31 March 2016 from http://www.worldclim.org/current.

Hilaire. (1900). Compte Rendu de feuilles exécutées en 1898 sur l'emplacement de Tacape. *BCTH* 1900. 115–125.
Hilaire. (1901). Note sur la voie stratégique Romaine qui longeait la frontière militaire de la Tripolitaine. Essai d'identification des gìtes d'étapes de la portion de cette voie comprise entre *Ad Templum* et *Tabuinati. BCTH* 1901. 95–105.
Hillier, B., & Hanson, J. (1984). *The social logic of space*. Cambridge: Cambridge University Press.
Hingley, R. (2005). *Globalizing Roman Culture: Unity, diversity and empire*. New York: Routledge.
Hirschfeld, Y. (1997). Farms and Villages in Byzantine Palestine. *Dumbarton Oaks Papers* 51. 33–71.
Hitchner, R.B. (1988). The University of Virginia-INAA Kasserine Archaeological Survey 1982–1986. *AntAfr* 24. 7–41.
Hitchner, R.B. (1989). The organization of rural settlement in the Cillium-Thelepte region (Kasserine, Central Tunisia). *AfrRom* 6. 387–402.
Hitchner, R.B. (1993). The Kasserine Archaeological Survey 1982–1985. *Africa. Fouilles, monuments et collections archéologiques en Tunisie* 11–12. 158–198.
Hitchner, R.B. (1994). Image and Reality. The changing face of pastoralism in the Tunisian High Steppe. In J. Carlsen, P. Ørsted, & J.E. Skydsgaard (eds), *Landuse in the Roman Empire*. Rome: "L'Erma" di Bretschneider. 27–44.
Hitchner, R.B., Ellis, S., Graham, A., Mattingly, D.J., & Neuru, L. (1990). The Kasserine Archaeological Survey 1987. *AntAfr* 26. 231–260.
Hobson, M.S. (2012). *The African Boom? Evaluating Economic Growth in the Roman Province of Africa Proconsularis*. PhD Thesis, University of Leicester.
Hobson, M.S. (2019). EAMENA Training in the use of satellite remote sensing and digital technologies in heritage management: Libya and Tunisia workshops 2017–2019. *LibStud* 50. 63–71.
Holtorf, C.J. (1997). Megaliths, Monumentality, and Memory. *Archaeological Review from Cambridge* 14(2). 45–66.
Horden, P., & Purcell, N. (2001). *The Corrupting Sea. A Study of Mediterranean History*. Oxford: Blackwell.
Hornby, A.J.W. (1945). Northern Tripolitania: A Dry Mediterranean Coastal Region. *Economic Geography* 21(4). 231–251.
Howard Carter, T. (1965). Western Phoenicians at Lepcis Magna. *AJA* 69(2). 123–132.
Humphrey, J., Sear, F., & Vickers, M. (1973). Aspects of the Circus at Lepcis Magna. *LibAnt* 9–10. 25–98.
Humphrey, J., Sear, F., & Vickers, M. (1974). Aspects of the Circus at Lepcis Magna. *LibStud* 5. 4–12.
Hunt, C.O., Mattingly, D.J., Gilbertson, D.D., Dore, J., Barker, G., Burns, J.R., Fleming, A.M., & van der Veen, M. (1986). ULVS XIII: Interdisciplinary Approaches to Ancient Farming in the Wadi Mansur, Tripolitania. *LibStud* 17. 7–48.
Isaac, B. (2000). *The Limits of Empire: The Roman Army in the East (Revised Edition)*. Oxford: Clarendon Press.
Izzet, V.E. (2001). Putting the house in order: the development of Etruscan domestic architecture. In J.R. Brandt & L. Karlsson (eds), *From huts to houses: transformations of ancient societies. Proceedings of an International Seminar organized by the Norwegian and Swedish Institutes in Rome, 21–24 September 1997*. Stockholm: Paul Åströms Förlag. 41–49.
James, S. (2001). Soldiers and civilians: identity and interaction in Roman Britain. In S. James & M. Millett (eds), *Britons and Romans: advancing an archaeological agenda*. York: Council for British Archaeology.
Johns, C. (1982). *Sex or Symbol: Erotic Images of Greece and Rome*. London: British Museum Publications.
Johnston, D.E. (1982). Some mosaics and murals in Roman Tripolitania. In J. Liversidge (ed.), *Roman Provincial Wall Painting of the Western Empire*. Oxford: BAR.
Joly, E., & Tomasello, F. (1984). *Il tempio a divinità ignota di Sabratha*. Rome: "L'Erma" di Bretschneider.
Jones, A.H.M. (1968). Frontier defence in Byzantine Libya. In F. Gadallah (ed.), *Libya in History*. Libya: Faculty of Arts, University of Libya. 289–298.
Jones, B., & Barker, G. (1980). Libyan Valleys Survey. *LibStud* 11. 11–36.
Jones, B., & Barker, G. (1983). The UNESCO Libyan Valleys Survey IV: The 1981 Season. *LibStud* 14. 39–68.
Jones, G.D.B. (1983). The Development of Gheriat el-Garbia. *LibStud* 14. 64–68.
Jones, G.D.B. (1985). The UNESCO Libyan Valleys Survey: the Development of Settlement Survey. In D.J. Buck & D.J. Mattingly (eds), *Town and Country in Roman Tripolitania. Papers in honour of Olwen Hackett*. Oxford: BAR. 263–289.
Jones, R.H. (2012). *Roman Camps in Britain*. Stroud: Amberley.
Jongeling, K., & Kerr, R.M. (2005). *Late Punic Epigraphy. An Introduction to the Study of Neo-Punic and Latino-Punic Inscriptions*. Tübingen, Germany: Mohr Siebeck.
Kaegi, W.E. (2010). *Muslim expansion and the Byzantine collapse in North Africa*. Cambridge: Cambridge University Press.

Kehoe, D.P. (1988). *The Economics of Agriculture on Roman Imperial Estates in North Africa.* Gottingen: Vandenhoeck & Ruprecht.

Kehoe, D.P. (2007). *Law and the Rural Economy in the Roman Empire.* Ann Arbor: University of Michigan Press.

Kehoe, D.P. (2013). The State and Production in the Roman Agricultural Economy. In A.K. Bowman & A. Wilson (eds), *The Roman Agricultural Economy: Organisation, Investment, and Production.* Oxford: Oxford University Press. 33–54.

Kennedy, D., & Bewley, R. (2004). *Ancient Jordan from the Air.* London: Council for British Research in the Levant.

Kennedy, D., & Bishop, M.C. (2011). Google Earth and the archaeology of Saudi Arabia: a case study from the Jeddah area. *Journal of Archaeological Science* 38(6). 1284–1293.

Kennedy, D., & Riley, D. (1990). *Rome's Desert Frontier from the Air.* London: Batsford.

Kenrick, P. (1986). *Excavations at Sabratha 1948-1951. A report on the excavations conducted by Dame Kathleen Kenyon and John Ward-Perkins.* London: The Society for the Promotion of Roman Studies.

Kenrick, P. (2009). *Tripolitania.* London: Silphium Press, The Society for Libyan Studies.

Kenrick, P. (2013). *Cyrenaica.* London: Silphium Books, The Society for Libyan Studies.

Kent, S. (1994). Activity areas and architecture: an interdisciplinary view of the relationship between use of space and domestic built environments. In S. Kent (ed.), *Domestic architecture and the use of space: An interdisciplinary cross-cultural study.* Cambridge: Cambridge University Press. 1–8.

Kerr, R.M. (2005). North African Centenaria and Hebrew נציבים, Some remarks relating to the Latino-Punic Inscription from Gasr el-Azaiz (IRT 893). In L.E. Kogan (ed.), *Memoriae Igor M. Diakonoff.* Winona Lake, Ind.: Published for the Russian State University for the Humanities by Eisenbrauns. 475–512.

Kerr, R.M. (2010). *Latino-Punic Epigraphy.* Tübingen, Germany: Mohr Siebeck.

Khalaf, N. & Insoll, T. (2019). Monitoring Islamic archaeological landscapes in Ethiopia using open source satellite imagery. *Journal of Field Archaeology* 44(6). 401–419.

King, G.R.D. (1989). Islamic Archaeology in Libya, 1969–1989. *LibStud* 20. 193–207.

Kolendo, J. (1986). Les grand domaines en Tripolitaine d'après l'Itinéraire Antonin. In *Histoire et archéologie de l'Afrique du Nord, Actes du IIIe Colloque international (Montpellier 1985).* Paris: CTHS. 149–162.

Kotula, T. (1974). L'Affaire des Emporia: Probleme d'histoire et de chronologie (Tite-Live, XXXIV 62; Polybe, XXXI 21). *Africana Bulletin* 20. 47–61.

Krahmalkov, C.R. (2000). *Phoenician-Punic Dictionary.* Leuven: Peeters.

Krimi, H. (2007). L'architecture militaire romaine dans le système défensif du *Limes Tripolitanus* occidental (sud de la Tunisie). *Revue des Études Militaires Anciennes* 4. 131–148.

Lancel, S. (1995). *Carthage. A History.* (A. Nevill, Trans.). Oxford: Blackwell.

Laronde, A. (1987). *Cyrène et la Libye Hellénistique. Libykai Historiai de l'époque républicaine au principat d'Auguste.* Paris: Éditions CNRS.

Laronde, A. (1988). Le port de Lepcis Magna. *CRAI* 132(2). 337–353.

Laronde, A. (1994). Nouvelles recherches archéologiques dans le port de Lepcis Magna. *CRAI* 138(4). 991–1006.

Law, R.C.C. (1978). North Africa in the Hellenistic and Roman period, 323 BC to AD 305. In J.D. Fage (ed.), *The Cambridge History of Africa.* Vol. 2 from c. 500 BC to AD 1050. London: Cambridge University Press. 148–209.

Le Bohec, Y. (1989). *La Troisième Légion Auguste.* Paris: Éditions CNRS.

Le Bohec, Y. (2005). *Histoire de L'Afrique Romaine (146 avant J.-C. – 439 après J.-C.).* Paris: Éditions A. et J. Picard.

Le Coeur, C. (1937). Les "mapalia" numides et leur survivance au Sahara. *Hespéris: Archives berbères et bulletin de l'Institut des Hautes Etudes Marocaines* 24. 29–45.

Le Quellec, J.-L. (1987). *L'Art Rupestre du Fezzan Septentrional (Libye): Widyan Zreda et Tarut (Wadi Esh-Shati).* Oxford: BAR.

Lecat, Z. (2012). Les "fortins", témoins matériels de l'insécurité ou marqueurs de l'organisation du contrôle du territoire à l'époque byzantine? *AfrRom* 19. 1123–1140.

Lecoy de la Marche, H. (1894). Recherche d'une voie Romaine du Golfe de Gabès vers Ghadamès. *BCTH* 1894. 389–413.

Lehner, B., Verdin, K., & Jarvis, A. (2008). New global hydrography derived from spaceborne elevation data. *Eos, Transactions, AGU* 89(10). 93–94. Retrieved 30 September 2015 from http://hydrosheds.cr.usgs.gov.

Leitch, V. (2010). *Production and trade of Roman and late Roman Africa cookwares.* DPhil Thesis, University of Oxford.

Leitch, V., Duckworth, C., Cuénod, A., Mattingly, D.J., Sterry, M., & Cole, F. (2017). Early Saharan Trade: The Inorganic Evidence. In D.J. Mattingly, V. Leitch, C.N. Duckworth, A. Cuenod, M. Sterry & F. Cole (eds), *Trade in the Ancient Sahara and Beyond.* Cambridge: Cambridge University Press. 287–340.

Lemaire, C. (1706). Mémoire des observations que le Sieur Claude Lemaire, consul de France au Royaume de Tripoly, a fait en voiagent le long de la coste de derne et du golfe de la Sidre, en 1705 et 1706, et sur diverces relations qu'il a eu du Soudan, qui signiffie païs de nègre. In H.A. Omont (ed.), *(1902) Missions archéologiques françaises en Orient aux XVIIe et XVIIIe siècles.* Paris: Imprimerie Nationale. 1037–1050.

Lemak, J. (2006). *Pastoralism in the Roman Empire: A Comparative Approach.* PhD Thesis, State University of New York at Buffalo.

Lenoir, M. (2011). *Le Camp Romain: Proche-Orient et Afrique du Nord.* Rome: École Française de Rome.

Leone, A. (2007). *Changing Townscapes in North Africa from Late Antiquity to the Arab Conquest.* Bari: Edipuglia.

Leone, A. (2013). *The End of the Pagan City: Religion, Economy, and Urbanism in Late Antique North Africa.* Oxford: Oxford University Press.

Leone, A., & Mattingly, D.J. (2004). Vandal, Byzantine and Arab Rural Landscapes in North Africa. In N. Christie (ed.), *Landscapes of Change: Rural Evolutions in Late Antiquity and the Early Middle Ages.* Aldershot: Ashgate.

Leone, A., Wootton, W., Fenwick, C., Nebbia, M., Alkhalaf, H., Jorayev, G., Othman, A., Belzic, M., Emrage, A., Hddad, M., Siala, Z., & Voke, P. (2020). An integrated methodology for the documentation and protection of cultural heritage in the MENA region: a case study from Libya and Tunisia. *LibStud* 51. 141–168.

LeQuesne, C. (2011). Libyan Uprisings: Conflict in the Sirte Basin. *Current World Archaeology* 47(June/July). 22–29.

LeQuesne, C., Basell, L.S., & Sheibani, R. (2010). Archaeology in the Sirte Basin: Preliminary Results of Mitigation Surveys carried out for Shell 2007–2009. *LibStud* 41. 7–32.

Leschi, L. (1941). Centenarium quod "Aqua Viva" appellatur... *CRAI* 85(2). 163–176.

Leveau, P. (2002). Les incertitudes du terme *villa* et la question du *vicus* en Gaule Narbonnaise. *Revue archéologique de Narbonnaise* 35. 5–26.

Lewis, C.T., & Short, C. (1879). *A Latin Dictionary. Founded on Andrews' edition of Freund's Latin Dictionary. Revised, enlarged, and in great part rewritten.* Oxford: Clarendon Press.

Liverani, M. (2005a). The household level analysis. In M. Liverani (ed.), *Aghram Nadharif: The Barkat Oasis (Sha'abiya of Ghat, Libyan Sahara) in Garamantian Times.* Florence: Edizioni all'Insegna del Giglio. 395–409.

Liverani, M. (ed.). (2005b). *Aghram Nadharif: The Barkat Oasis (Sha'abiya of Ghat, Libyan Sahara) in Garamantian Times.* Florence: Edizioni all'Insegna del Giglio.

Locock, M. (1994). Meaningful Architecture. In M. Locock (ed.), *Meaningful Architecture: Social Interpretations of Buildings.* Aldershot: Avebury. 1–13.

Lodewijckx, M., & Pelegrin, R. (eds). (2011). *A View from the Air. Aerial Archaeology and Remote Sensing Techniques: Results and opportunities.* Oxford: Archaeopress.

Longerstay, M. (1999). Prospection archéologique dans cinq vallées de la région syrtique (Libye) et fouille d'un bâtiment antique de la vallée du Wadi Harawah: rapport préliminaire. *BCTH* n.s.25. 53–68.

Longerstay, M. (2000). La mise en valeur des vallées syrtiques durant l'Antiquité. In *Actes du colloque du 25–26 octobre 1999 Aux rivages des Syrtes : la Libye, espace et développement de l'Antiquité à nos jours.* Paris: Centre des hautes études sur l'Afrique et l'Asie modernes. 19–27.

Longerstay, M. (2003). Les vestiges de la vie aux confins du désert: les vallées syrtiques dans l'Anqituité. *Bulletin de la Société Nationale des Antiquaires de France.* 205–207.

López Castro, J.L. (2008). The Iberian Peninsula: Landscapes of Tradition. In P. van Dommelen & C. Gómez Bellard (eds), *Rural Landscapes of the Punic World.* London: Equinox. 76–100.

Luisi, A. (1992). Getuli, dei popoli libici il più grande (Strab. 17, 826). In M. Sordi (ed.), *Autocoscienza e rappresentazione dei popoli nell'antichità.* Milan: Vita e Pensiero. 145–151.

Lund, J. (2009). Methodological constraints affecting the precise dating of African Red Slip Ware. In J. Humphrey (ed.), *Studies on Roman pottery of the provinces of Africa Proconsularis and Byzacena (Tunisia). Hommage à Michel Bonifay.* Portsmouth, RI: JRA.

Lyon, G.F. (1821). *A narrative of travels in North Africa in the years 1818, 1819 and 1820.* London.

MacKendrick, P. (1980). *The North African Stones Speak.* London: Croom Helm.

Mackensen, M. (2005). *Militärlager oder Marmorwerkstätten. Neue Untersuchungen im Ostbereich des Arbeits- und Steinbruchlagers von Simitthus/Chemtou, Simitthus III.* Mainz am Rhein: Verlag Philipp von Zabern.

Mackensen, M. (2008). Mannschaftsunterkünfte und Organisation einer severischen Legionsvexillation im tripolitanischen Kastell *Gholaia*/Bu Njem (Libyen). *Germania* 86. 271–306.

Mackensen, M. (2009). Gasr Wames, eine burgusartige Kleinfestung des mittleren 3. Jahrhunderts am tripolitanischen *limes Tentheitanus* (Libyen). *Germania* 87. 75–104.

Mackensen, M. (2010a). Das Commoduszeitliche Kleinkastell *Tisavar*/Ksar Rhilane am südtunesischen *limes Tripolitanus. Kölner Jahrbuch* 43. 451–468.

Mackensen, M. (2010b). Das severische Vexillationskastell Myd(---)/Gheriat el-Gharbia am limes Tripolitanus (Libyen). Bericht über die Kampgne 2009. *Mitteilungen des Deutschen Archäologischen Instituts Römische Abteilung* 116. 363–458.

Mackensen, M. (2011a). Am Rand der Wüste. Das römische Kastell Gheriat el-Garbia am l*imes Tripolitanus. Antike Welt* 2011(1). 77–84.

Mackensen, M. (2011b). Das severische Vexillationskastell Myd(---) und die spätantike Besiedlung in Gheriat el-Garbia (Libyen). Bericht über die Kampagne im Frühjahr 2010. *Mitteilungen des Deutschen Archäologischen Instituts Römische Abteilung* 117. 247–375.

Mackensen, M. (2012). New fieldwork at the Severan fort of *Myd(---)*/ Gheriat el-Garbia on the l*imes Tripolitanus. LibStud* 43. 41–60.

Madau, M. (1997). Popolazioni rurali tra Cartagine e Roma: Sa Tanca ʻe sa Mura a Mon teleone Roccadoria. In P. Bernardini, R. D'Oriano & P.G. Spanu (eds), *Phoinikes B Shrdn: I Fenici in Sardegna*. Cagliari: La Memoria Storica. 142–145.

Malkin, I. (1990). Territorialisation Mythologique: Les "Autels des Philènes" en Cyrénaïque. *Dialogues d'histoire ancienne* 16(1). 219–229.

Manetti, O. (1914). Gli asnam del gebel Tripolitano. Note di archeologia agraria Tripolitana. *Agricoltura Coloniale* 8. 421–451.

Marcy, G. (1942). Remarques sur l'habitation berbère dans l'Antiquité. À propos des Mapalia. *Hesperis* 29. 23–40.

Marelli, M. (1933). Relazione al progetto di sistemazione dell'arco di Marco Aurelio in Tripoli. *AfrIt* 5(3–4). 162–171.

Marichal, R. (1992). *Les Ostraca du Bu Njem*. Tripoli.

Marzano, A. (2007). *Roman Villas in Central Italy. A Social and Economic History*. Leiden: Brill.

Masturzo, N. (1997). Haleg al-Karuba (Silin): remains of a coastal villa. *LibAnt* n.s.3. 216–217.

Masturzo, N. (2003). Le città della Tripolitania fra continuità ed innovazione: i fori di Leptis Magna e Sabratha. *Mélanges de l'école française de Rome* 115(2). 705–753.

Matoug, J.M. (1998). Wadi al-Fani (Khoms): Mausoleum with subterranean tomb. *LibAnt* n.s.4. 274–275.

Mattingly, D.J. (1982). The Roman Road-Station at Thenadassa (Ain Wif). *LibStud* 13. 73–80.

Mattingly, D.J. (1983). The Laguatan: A Libyan Tribal Confederation in the Late Roman Empire. *LibStud* 14. 96–108.

Mattingly, D.J. (1985a). *IRT* 895 and 896: Two Inscriptions from Gheriat el-Garbia. *LibStud* 16. 67–76.

Mattingly, D.J. (1985b). Olive Oil Production in Roman Tripolitania. In D.J. Buck & D. Mattingly (eds), *Town and Country in Roman Tripolitania: Papers in Honour of Olwen Hackett*. Oxford: BAR. 27–46.

Mattingly, D.J. (1987). Libyans and the 'Limes': Culture and Society in Roman Tripolitania. *AntAfr* 23. 71–94.

Mattingly, D.J. (1988a). Megalithic madness and measurement. Or how many olives could an olive press press? *OJA* 7(2). 177–195.

Mattingly, D.J. (1988b). Oil for Export? A comparison of Libyan, Spanish, and Tunisian olive oil production. *JRS* 1. 33–56.

Mattingly, D.J. (1988c). The Olive Boom. Oil Surpluses, Wealth and Power in Roman Tripolitania. *LibStud* 19. 21–42.

Mattingly, D.J. (1989). Farmers and Frontiers. Exploiting and Defending the Countryside of Roman Tripolitania. *LibStud* 20. 135–154.

Mattingly, D.J. (1992). War and Peace in Roman North Africa. Observations and Models of State-Tribe Interaction. In R.B. Ferguson & N.L. Whitehead (eds), *War in the Tribal Zone: expanding states and indigenous warfare*. Sante Fe, N.M.: School of American Research Press. 31–60.

Mattingly, D.J. (1993). Maximum figures and maximizing strategies of oil production? Further thoughts on the processing capacity of Roman olive presses. In M.-C. Amouretti & J.-P. Brun (eds), *La production du vin et de l'huile en Méditerranée*. Paris: Diffusion de Boccard. 483–497.

Mattingly, D.J. (1994). Olive Presses in Roman Africa: Technical Evolution or Stagnation. *AfrRom* 11. 577–595.

Mattingly, D.J. (1995). *Tripolitania*. London: Batsford.

Mattingly, D.J. (1996a). Explanations: People as Agency. In G. Barker (ed.), *Farming the Desert: The UNESCO Libyan Valleys Archaeological Survey*. Vol. One: Synthesis. 319–342.

Mattingly, D.J. (ed.). (1996b). *Farming the Desert: The UNESCO Libyan Valleys Archaeological Survey* (Vol. Two: Gazetteer and Pottery). Paris/Tripoli/London: UNESCO/Department of Antiquities SPLAJ/Society for Libyan Studies.

Mattingly, D.J. (1997). Modèles d'occupation agricole et archéologie des paysages dans les oueds de la Tripolitaine romaine. In J. Burnouf, J.-P. Bravard & G. Chouquer (eds), *La dynamique des paysages protohistoriques, antiques, médiévaux et modernes. XVII*[e] *Rencontres internationales d'archéologie et d'histoire d'Antibes: actes des reconcontres 19 - 20 - 21 octobre 1996*. Paris: Éditions CNRS. 195–209.

Mattingly, D.J. (1998). Landscapes of Imperialism in Roman Tripolitania. *AfrRom* 12. 163–179.

Mattingly, D.J. (1999). The Art of the Unexpected: Ghirza in the Libyan pre-desert. In *Histoire et archéoloie de l'Afrique du Nord, 7e Colloque International Nice.* Paris: Editions comité historiques et scientifiques.
Mattingly, D.J. (2003a). Family Values: Art and Power at Ghirza in the Libyan Pre-Desert. In S. Scott & J. Webster (eds), *Roman Imperialism and Provincial Art.* Cambridge: Cambridge University Press. 153–170.
Mattingly, D.J. (ed.). (2003b). *The Archaeology of Fazzan* (Vol. 1, Synthesis). London: Society for Libyan Studies.
Mattingly, D.J. (2004). Being Roman: expressing identity in a provincial setting. *JRA* 17. 5–25.
Mattingly, D.J. (ed.). (2007). *The Archaeology of Fazzan* (Vol. 2, Site Gazetteer, Pottery and other survey finds). London: Society for Libyan Studies.
Mattingly, D.J. (ed.). (2010). *The Archaeology of Fazzan* (Vol. 3, Excavations of C.M. Daniels). Tripoli and London: Department of Antiquities (Socialist People's Libyan Arab Jamahariya) and The Society for Libyan Studies.
Mattingly, D.J. (2011). *Imperialism, Power, and Identity: Experiencing the Roman Empire.* Princeton, NJ: Princeton University Press.
Mattingly, D.J. (2013). The south and north: Saharan trade in antiquity. In H. Eckardt & S. Rippon (eds), *Living and Working in the Roman World. Essays in honour of Michael Fulford on his 65th birthday.* Portsmouth, RI: JRA. 169–190.
Mattingly, D.J., Barker, G., & Jones, B. (1996). Architecture, technology and society: Romano-Libyan settlement in the Wadi Umm-el Agerem, Tripolitania. In L. Bacchielli & M. Bonanno Aravantinos (eds), *Scritti di Antichità in memoria di Sandro Stucchi.* Vol. II. Rome: "L'Erma" di Bretschneider. 101–114.
Mattingly, D.J., & Dore, J. (1996). Romano-Libyan Settlement: Typology and Chronology. In G. Barker (ed.), *Farming the Desert: The UNESCO Libyan Valleys Archaeological Survey.* Vol. One: Synthesis. 111–158.
Mattingly, D.J., & Flower, C. (1996). Romano-Libyan Settlement: Site Distributions and Trends. In G. Barker (ed.), *Farming the Desert: The UNESCO Libyan Valleys Archaeological Survey.* Vol. One: Synthesis. 159–191.
Mattingly, D.J., & Jones, B. (1986). A New *Clausura* in Western Tripolitania: Wadi Skiffa South. *LibStud* 17. 87–96.
Mattingly, D.J., Lahr, M., Armitage, S., Barton, H., Dore, J., Drake, N., Foley, R., Merlo, S., Salem, M., Stock, J., & White, K. (2007). Desert Migrations: people, environment and culture in the Libyan Sahara. *LibStud* 38. 115–156.
Mattingly, D.J., Leitch, V., Duckworth, C.N., Cuenod, A., Sterry, M., & Cole, F. (eds). (2017). *Trade in the Ancient Sahara and Beyond.* Cambridge: Cambridge University Press.
Mattingly, D.J., Rushworth, A., Sterry, M., & Leitch, V. (2013c). The African Frontiers / Die Grenzen in Afrika / Les frontières africaines. In *Frontiers of the Roman Empire / The African Frontiers.* Edinburgh. 40–96.
Mattingly, D.J., & Sterry, M. (2013). The first towns in the central Sahara. *Antiquity* 87(336). 503–518.
Mattingly, D.J., Sterry, M., & Leitch, V. (2013). Fortified Farms and Defended Villages of Late Roman and Late Antique Africa. *Antiquité Tardive* 21. 167–188.
Mattingly, D.J, Sterry, M., & Ray, N. (2019). Dying to be Garamantian: burial, migration and identity in Fazzan. In M.C. Gatto, D.J. Mattingly, N. Ray, & M. Sterry (eds), *Burials, Migration and Identity in the Ancient Sahara and Beyond.* Cambridge: Cambridge University Press. 53–107.
Mattingly, D.J., Thomas, D., Sterry, M., & Preston, J. (2013a). Public and Domestic Architecture of Garama. In D.J. Mattingly (ed.), *The Archaeology of Fazzan. Volume 4, Survey and Excavations at Old Jarma (Ancient Garama) carried out by C.M. Daniels (1962–69) and the Fazzan Project (1997–2001).* Tripoli, London: Department of Antiquities, Society for Libyan Studies. 287–297.
Mattingly, D.J., Thomas, D., Sterry, M., & Preston, J. (2013b). Public and Domestic Architecture of Islamic Jarma. In D.J. Mattingly (ed.), *The Archaeology of Fazzan. Volume 4, Survey and Excavations at Old Jarma (Ancient Garama) carried out by C.M. Daniels (1962–69) and the Fazzan Project (1997–2001).* Tripoli, London: Department of Antiquities, Society for Libyan Studies. 299–321.
Mattingly, D.J., Merlo, S., Mori, L., & Sterry, M. (2020a). Garamantian Oasis Settlements in Fazzan. In M. Sterry & D.J. Mattingly (eds), *Urbanisation and State Formation in the Ancient Sahara and Beyond.* Cambridge: Cambridge University Press. 53–111.
Mattingly, D.J., Sterry, M., Rayne, L., & Al-Haddad, M. (2020b). Pre-Islamic Oasis Settlements in the Eastern Sahara. In M. Sterry & D.J. Mattingly (eds), *Urbanisation and State Formation in the Ancient Sahara and Beyond.* Cambridge: Cambridge University Press. 112–146.
Mattingly, D.J., Sterry, M., Al-Haddad, M., & Trousset, P. (2020c). Pre-Islamic Oasis Settlements in the Northern Sahara. In M. Sterry & D.J. Mattingly (eds), *Urbanisation and State Formation in the Ancient Sahara and Beyond.* Cambridge: Cambridge University Press. 187–238.
McBurney, C.B.M. (1960). *The Stone Age of Northern Africa.* London: Penguin.
McBurney, C.B.M. (1967). *The Haua Fteah (Cyrenaica) and the Stone Age of the South-East Mediterranean.* Cambridge: Cambridge University Press.

McGrath, R.J., & Boyd, W.E. (2001). The chronology of the Iron Age 'moats' of northeast Thailand. *Antiquity* 75. 349–360.

Méhier de Mathuisieulx, H. (1903). *A Travers: la Tripolitaine*. Paris: Hachette.

Mekki, H. (2021). Documentation et gestion du patrimoine archéologique de la chaîne montagneuse Tuniso-libyenne via l'utilisation de la nouvelle technologie: résultats préliminaires. *LibStud* 52.

Merlin, A. (1915). Séance de la commission de l'Afrique du Nord. *BCTH* 1915. clxxxviii–cxciv.

Merlin, A. (1919). Séance de la commission de l'Afrique du Nord. *BCTH* 1919. clv–clxii.

Merlin, A. (1921). Le fortin de Bezereos sur les "limes" Tripolitain. *CRAI* 65(3). 236–249.

Merlin, A. (ed.). (1944). *Inscriptions Latines de la Tunisie*. Paris.

Merrills, A.H. (ed.). (2004). *Vandals, Romans, and Berbers: New Perspectives on late antique North Africa*. Aldershot: Ashgate.

Merrills, A.H., & Miles, R. (2010). *The Vandals*. Oxford: Wiley-Blackwell.

Meyers, G.E. (2012). Introduction: the experience of monumentality in Etruscan and early Roman architecture. In M.L. Thomas & G.E. Meyers (eds), *Monumentality in Etruscan and early Roman architecture: ideology and innovation*. Austin: University of Texas Press. 1–20.

Micacchi, R. (1934). L'arco di Marco Aurelio in Tripoli e la sistemazione della zone adiacente. *Rivista delle Colonie Italiane* 8(10). 824–839.

Millett, M. (1990). *The Romanization of Britain: an essay in archaeological interpretation*. Cambridge: Cambridge University Press.

Millett, M. (1991). Pottery: Population or Supply Patterns? The Ager Tarraconensis Approach. In G. Barker & J.A. Lloyd (eds), *Roman Landscapes: Archaeological Survey in the Mediterranean Region*. London: British School at Rome. 18–26.

Mitchell, P., & Lane, P. (eds). (2013). *The Oxford Handbook of African Archaeology*. Oxford: OUP.

Modéran, Y. (2003). *Les Maures et l'Afrique Romain*. Rome: École française de Rome.

Monlezun. (1885). Les ruines de Tacape (Gabès). *BCTH* 1885. 126–131.

Moore, J.D. (2012). *The Prehistory of Home*. London: University of California Press.

Moreau. (1904). Le castellum de Ras-Oued-El-Gordab près de Ghoumrassen. *BCTH* 1904. 369–376.

Moreau, J. (2009). Le Gétule: Cet autre insaisissable (deuxième partie). In M.-F. Marein, P. Voisin & J. Gallego (eds), *Figures de l'étranger autour de la Méditerranée antique. Actes de Colloque International. Antiquité méditerranéenne: à la rencontre de "l'autre". Perceptions et représentations de l'étranger dans les littératures antiques*. Paris: L'Harmattan. 215–222.

Mori, F. (1965). *Tadrart Acacus: Arte rupestre e culture del Sahara preistorico*. Turin: Einaudi.

Morley, N. (2011). Cities and Economic Development in the Roman Empire. In A. Wilson & A.K. Bowman (eds), *Settlement, Urbanization, and Population*. Oxford: Oxford University Press. 143–160.

Morton, T.J. (2003). *The Impact of Luxury: The Forum of Meninx, an architectural investigation*. PhD Thesis, University of Pennsylvania.

Morton, T.J. (2006). *Meninx*: The Luxury of the Purple Dye Industry and the Richness of Architecture. *AfrRom* 17. 951–962.

Mrabet, A. (1998). *Carte Nationale des Sites Archeologiques et des Monuments Historiques. Carte au 1/50.000. Gabes 147*. Tunis: Institut National du Patrimoine. Retrieved 3 February 2014 from http://www.inp.rnrt.tn/Carte_archeo/html/147_fr.htm.

Mrabet, A. (2000a). *Carte Nationale des Sites Archeologiques et des Monuments Historiques. Carte au 1/50.000. Kettana 157*. Tunis: Institut National du Patrimoine. Retrieved 11 March 2014 from http://www.inp.rnrt.tn/Carte_archeo/html/157_fr.htm.

Mrabet, A. (2000b). *Carte Nationale des Sites Archeologiques et des Monuments Historiques. Carte au 1/50.000. Mareth 158*. Tunis: Institut National du Patrimoine. Retrieved 11 March 2014 from http://www.inp.rnrt.tn/Carte_archeo/html/158_fr.htm.

Mrabet, A. (2011). Identité de la Tripolitaine occidentale: de quelques signalements archéologiques. In C. Briand-Ponsart & Y. Modéran (eds), *Provinces et identités provinciales dans l'Afrique romaine*. Caen: CRAHM. 221–240.

Munzi, M. (1998). Missione Archeologica dell'Università Roma Tre a Leptis Magna, 1997: Uadi er-Rsaf, area sud. Lo scavo della villa suburbana. *LibAnt* n.s.4. 189–193.

Munzi, M. (2001). *L'Epica del Ritorno. Archeologia e Politica nella Tripolitania Italiana*. Rome: "L'Erma" di Bretschneider.

Munzi, M. (2004). Italian Archaeology in Libya: From Colonial Romanità to Decolonization of the Past. In M.L. Galaty & C. Watkinson (eds), *Archaeology Under Dictatorship*. New York: Springer. 73–107.

Munzi, M. (2010). Il territorio di Leptis Magna. Insediamenti rurali, strutture produttive e rapporti con la città. In I. Tantillo & F. Bigi (eds), *Leptis Magna: una città e le sue iscrizioni in epoca tardoromana*. Cassino: Università degli Studi di Cassino. 45–80.

Munzi, M., & Abd el-Aziz el-Nemsi, M. (1998). Leptis Magna-Khoms, villa romana al porto: un contesto monetale di età giulianea. *LibAnt* n.s.4. 99–128.

Munzi, M., & Felici, F. (2006). La villa del wadi er-Rsaf (*Leptis Magna*): stratigrafia e contesti. *AfrRom* 17. 2317–2338.

Munzi, M., Felici, F., Cifani, G., Cirelli, E., Gaudiosi, E., Lucarini, G., & Matug, J. (2004). A topographic research sample in the territory of Lepcis Magna: Silin. *LibStud* 35. 11–66.

Munzi, M., Felici, F., Cifani, G., & Lucarini, G. (2004–2005). Leptis Magna: città e campagna dall'origine alla scomparsa del sistema sedentario antico. *Scienze dell'Antichità* 12. 433–471.

Munzi, M., Felici, F., Cirelli, E., Schingo, G., & Zocchi, A. (2010). Il territorio di *Leptis Magna*: recognizioni tra Ras el-Mergheb e Ras el-Hammam (2007). *AfrRom* 18. 723–746.

Munzi, M., Felici, F., Matoug, J., Sjöström, I., & Zocchi, A. (2016). The Lepcitanian landscape across the ages: the survey between Ras el-Mergheb and Ras el-Hammam (2007, 2009, 2013). *LibStud* 47. 67–116.

Munzi, M., Felici, F., Sjöström, I., & Zocchi, A. (2014). La Tripolitania rurale tardoantica, medievale et ottomana alla luce delle recenti indagini archeologiche territoriali nella regione di Leptis Magna. *Archeologia Medievale* 41. 215–245.

Munzi, M., & Pentiricci, M. (1997). Missione Archeologica dell'Università Roma Tre a Leptis Magna, 1996: Lo scavo della villa suburbana di uadi er-Rsaf. *LibAnt* n.s.3. 272–275.

Munzi, M., Schirru, G., & Tantillo, I. (2014). *Centenarium*. *LibStud* 45. 49–64.

Munzi, M. & Zocchi, A. (2017). The Lepcitanian territory: cultural heritage in danger in war and peace. *LibStud* 48. 51–67.

Musso, L. (1995). Leptis Magna. *Enciclopedia dell'arte antica, II Supplemento*. 333–347.

Musso, L. (2008). La romanizzazione di Leptis Magna nel primo periodo imperiale: Augusto e Roma nel 'Foro Vecchio'. In D. Kreikenbom (ed.), *Augustus, der Blick von aussen : die Wahrnehmung des Kaisers in den Provinzen des Reiches und in den Nachbarstaaten; Akten der internationalen Tagung an der Johannes Gutenberg-Universität Mainz vom 12. bis 14. Oktober 2006*. Wiesbaden: Harrassowitz. 161–196.

Musso, L., Baldoni, D., Bianchi, B., Calì, M.G., Davidde, B., Di Vita-Evrard, G., Munzi, M., Petriaggi, R., Pinna Caboni, B., Ponti, G., & Shebani, R. (2010). Missione Archeologica dell'Università Roma Tre, 1998-2007. *LibAnt* n.s.5. 49–78.

Muzzolini, A. (1986). *L'Art Rupestre Préhistorique des Massifs Centraux Sahariens*. Oxford: BAR.

Myres, J.L. (1899). On the age and purpose of the megalithic structures of Tripoli and Barbary. *Proceedings of the Society of Antiquaries, 2nd Series* 17. 280–293.

Napoli, J. (1997). *Recherches sur les fortifications linéaires Romaines*. Rome: École Française de Rome.

Nave, G. (1914). Frammenti indigeni d'arte Cristiana a Tarhuna ed Henscir Uhéda Tripolitania. Bollettino d'Arte 8(3). 96–104.

Nebbia, M., Leone, A., Bockmann, R. Hddad, M., Abdouli, H., Masoud, A.M., Elkendi, N., Hamoud, H., Adam, S., & Khatab, M. (2016). Developing a collaborative strategy to manage and preserve cultural heritage during the Libyan conflict: the case of the Gebel Nāfusa. *Journal of Archaeological Method and Theory* 23(4). 971–988.

Nevo, Y.D. (1991). *Pagans and Herders: A re-examination of the Negev runoff cultivation systems in the Byzantine and early Arab periods*. Midreshet Ben-Gurion, Negev, Israel: IPS Ltd.

Nikolaus, J. (2016). Beyond Ghirza: Roman-period mausolea in Tripolitania. In N. Mugnai, J. Nikolaus & N. Ray (eds), *De Africa Romaque, Merging Cultures Across North Africa*. London: Society for Libyan Studies. 199–214.

Nikolaus, J. (2017). *Roman Funerary Reliefs and North African Identity: A Contextual Investigation of Tripolitanian Mausolea and their Iconography*. PhD Thesis, University of Leicester.

Nikolaus, J., Mugnai, N., Rayne, L., Zerbini, A., Mattingly, D.J., Walker, S., Abdrbba, M., al-Haddad, M.A., Buzian, A., & Emrage, A. (2018). Training, partnerships, and new methodologies for ptoecting Libya's cultural heritage. *QAL* 21, n.s.1. 351–358.

Oates, D. (1953). The Tripolitanian Gebel: settlement of the Roman period around Gasr ed-Daun. *PBSR* 21. 81–117.

Oates, D. (1954). Ancient Settlement in the Tripolitanian Gebel, II: The Berber Period. *PBSR* 22. 91–117.

OED. (2015). hut, n. *Oxford English Dictionary Online*. Oxford University Press. Retrieved 3 July 2015.

Oliverio, G. (ed.). (1936). *Il Decreto di Anastasio I su l'ordinamento politico-militare della Cirenaica. Inscrizioni di Tocra, El Chamís, Tolemaide, Cirene*. Bergamo: Istituto Italiano d'Arti Grafiche.

Omont, H.A. (ed.). (1902). *Missions archéologiques françaises en Orient aux XVIIe et XVIIIe siècles*. Paris: Imprimerie Nationale.

Ørsted, P., Carlsen, J., Ladjimi Sebaï, L., & Ben Hassen, H. (eds). (2000). *Africa Proconsularis: Regional studies in the Segermes Valley of Northern Tunisia* (Vol. 3, Historical Conclusions). Århus: Aarhus University Press.

Parker, S.T. (1995). The Typology of Roman and Byzantine Forts and Fortresses in Jordan. *Studies in the History and Archaeology of Jordan* 5. 251–260.

Parrish, D. (1985). The date of the mosaics from Zliten. *AntAfr* 21. 137–158.

Peña, J.T. (2007). *Roman Pottery in the Archaeological Record*. Cambridge: Cambridge University Press.

Pensabene, P. (1988). Architettura e decorazione architettonica nelAfrRom: osservazioni. AfrRom 6. 431–458.

Pensabene, P. (1990). Riflessi sull'architettura dei cambiamenti socio-economici dal tardo II e III secolo in Tripolitania e nella Proconsolare. *AfrRom* 8. 447–448.

Pensabene, P. (2001). Pentelico e proconnesio in Tripolitania: coordinamento o concorrenza nella distribuzione? *Archeologia Classica* 52 n.s.2. 63–127.

Pensabene, P. (2003). La porta Oea e l'arco di Marco Aurelio a Leptis Magna: Contributo alla definizione dei marmi e del loro costo, delle officine e delle committenze. *QAL* 18. 341–368.

Percival, J. (1976). *The Roman Villa. An Historical Introduction*. London: Batsford.

Pericaud, & Gauckler, P. (1905). La T*urris Maniliorum Arelliorum* dans la massif des Matmata (Tunisie). *BCTH* 1905. 259–269.

Pesce, G. (1953). *Il Tempio d'Iside in Sabratha*. Rome: "L'Erma" di Bretschneider.

Petragnani, E. (1928). *Il Sahara Tripolitano*. Rome: Sindacato Italiano Arti Grafiche.

Picard, G. (1985). La villa du Taureau à Silin (Tripolitaine) *CRAI* 129(1). 227–241.

Picard, G. (1990). Mosaïques et société dans l'Afrique romaine. Les mosaïques d'El Alia (Tunisie). In *L'Afrique dans l'Occident romain (Ier siècle av. J.-C. – IVe siècle ap. J.-C.) Actes du colloque de Rome (3-5 décembre 1987)*. Rome: École Française de Rome. 3–14.

Ponsich, M. (1970). *Recherches Archéologiques A Tanger et dans sa Région*. Paris: Éditions CNRS.

Preziosi, D. (1979). *The Semiotics of the Built Environment. An Introduction to Architectonic Analysis*. Bloomington: Indiana University Press.

Pringle, D. (1981). *The Defence of Byzantine Africa from Justinian to the Arab Conquest*. Oxford: BAR.

Purcaro, V. (1996). Osservazioni su alcuni rilievi delle necropoli di Ghirza con scene di sacrificio e di cerimonia. In L. Bacchielli & M. Bonanno Aravantinos (eds), *Scritti di Antichità in memoria di Sandro Stucchi*. Vol. II. Rome: "L'Erma" di Bretschneider. 141–148.

Purcell, N. (1995). The Roman villa and the landscape of production. In T.J. Cornell & K. Lomas (eds), *Urban Society in Roman Italy*. London: University College London Press.

Quinn, J.C. (2004). The Role of the 146 Settlement in the Provincialization of Africa. *AfrRom* 15. 1593–1602.

Quinn, J.C. (2014). A Carthaginian perspective on the Altars of the Philaeni. In J.C. Quinn & N.C. Vella (eds), *The Punic Mediterranean: Identities and Identification from Phoenician Settlement to Roman Rule*. Cambridge: Cambridge University Press. 169–179.

Rae, E. (1877). *The Country of the Moors, a journey from Tripoli in Barbary to the city of Karwan*. London.

Ramón, J. (1995). *Ses païsses de cala d'Hort. Un establiment rural d'època antiga al sud-oest d'Eivissa*. Ibiza: Consell insular d'Eivissa i Formentera.

Raven, S. (1984). *Rome in Africa* (2nd ed.). New York: Longman Inc.

Ray, N. & Nikolaus, J. (2019). Buried in the archives: cemeteries and mausolea in Tripolitania. *LibStud* 50: 93–98.

Rayne, L., Bradbury, J., Mattingly, D., Philip, G., Bewley, R., & Wilson, A. I. (2017). From Above and on the Ground: Geospatial Methods for Recording Endangered Archaeology in the Middle East and North Africa. *Geosciences* 7. Article 100.

Rayne, L., Gatto, M.C., Abdulaati, L., Al-Haddad, M., Sterry, M., Sheldrick, N., & Mattingly, D.J. (2020). Detecting change at archaeological sites in North Africa using open-source satellite imagery. *Remote Sensing* 12(22): 3694.

Rayne, L., Sheldrick, N., & Nikolaus, J. (2017). Endangered archaeology in Libya: recording damage and destruction. *LibStud* 48. 23–49.

Rebuffat, R. (1970a). Bu Njem 1968. *LibAnt* 6–7. 9–105.

Rebuffat, R. (1970b). Bu Njem 1970. *LibAnt* 6–7. 107–168.

Rebuffat, R. (1970c). Zella et les routes d'Égypte. *LibAnt* 6–7. 181–187.

Rebuffat, R. (1972). Nouvelles Recherches dans le sud de la Tripolitaine. *CRAI* 116(2). 319–339.

Rebuffat, R. (1973a). L'arrivée des Romains à Bu Njem. *LibAnt* 9–10. 121–134.

Rebuffat, R. (1973b). Les inscriptions des portes du camp de Bu Njem. *LibAnt* 9–10. 99–120.

Rebuffat, R. (1975a). Bu Njem, 1971. *LibAnt* 11–12. 189–242.

Rebuffat, R. (1975b). Graffiti en "Libyque de Bu Njem". *LibAnt* 11–12. 165–188.
Rebuffat, R. (1977a). Bu Njem 1972. *LibAnt* 13–14. 37–77.
Rebuffat, R. (1977b). Une zone militaire et sa vie économique: le limes de Tripolitaine. In *Armées et Fiscalité dans l e Monde Antique*. Paris: Éditions CNRS. 395–419.
Rebuffat, R. (1980). A propos du "limes Tripolitanus". *Revue Archeologique* n.s.1980. 105–124.
Rebuffat, R. (1982). Recherches dans la desert de Libye. *CRAI* 126(2). 188–199.
Rebuffat, R. (1985). L'arrivée des Romains en Tripolitaine interieure. *BCTH* n.s.19B. 249–256.
Rebuffat, R. (1988). Les fermiers du désert. *AfrRom* 5. 33–68.
Rebuffat, R. (1989). Notes sur le Camp Romain de *Gholaia* (Bu Njem). *LibStud* 20. 155–168.
Rebuffat, R. (1990a). Divinités de l'oued Kebir (Tripolitaine). *AfrRom* 7. 119–159.
Rebuffat, R. (1990b). Où étaient les Emporia? *Semitica* 39. 111–126.
Rebuffat, R. (1995). Le centurion M. Porcius Iasucthan à Bu Njem (Notes et documents XI). *LibAnt* n.s.1. 79–124.
Rebuffat, R. (2006). Notes d'onomastique ethnique. Les *Maces*. *AfrRom* 16. 403–444.
Rebuffat, R., Deneauve, J., & Hallier, G. (1967). Bu Njem 1967. *LibAnt* 3–4. 49–138.
Rebuffat, R., Gassend, J.M., Guéry, R., & Hallier, G. (1969). Bu Njem 1968. *LibAnt* 6–7. 9–106.
Reddé, M. (1985). Occupation humaine et mise en valeur économique dans les vallées du nord de la Libye: L'exemple du Wadi Tlal. *BCTH* n.s.19B. 173–182.
Reddé, M. (1988). *Prospection des vallées du nord de la Libye (1979–1980). La région de Syrte à l'époque romaine.* Paris: Presses de l'école normale supérieure.
Reddé, M. (1995). Dioclétian et les fortifications militaires de l'Antiquité tardive. *Antiquité Tardive* 3. 92–124.
Reinach, S. (1885). Fouilles de Gigthis (Henchir sidi Salem Bou-Ghrara). *BCTH* 1885. 124–126.
Reinach, S. (1888). *Atlas de la province Romaine d'Afrique.* Paris: Imprimerie Nationale.
Reinach, S., & Babelon, E. (1886). Recherches Archéologiques en Tunisie. *BCTH* 1886. 4–78.
Renault, H. (1901). Note sur l'inscription de Ras-el-Aïn et le "limes" Tripolitain à la fin du IIIe siècle. *BCTH* 1901. 429–437.
Reynolds, J.M. (1977). The Austuriani and Tripolitania in the early 5th century. *LibStud* 8. 13–15.
Reynolds, J.M. (1985). Inscriptions in the pre-desert of Tripolitania. In D.J. Buck & D.J. Mattingly (eds), T*owns and Country in Roman Tripolitania. Papers in Honour of Olwen Hackett.* Oxford: BAR. 23–25.
Reynolds, J.M., & Simpson, W.G. (1967). Some inscriptions from el-Auenia near Yefren in Tripolitania. *LibAnt* 3–4. 45–47.
Reynolds, J.M., & Ward-Perkins, J.B. (eds). (1952). *The Inscriptions of Roman Tripolitania.* Rome, London: British School at Rome.
Ribichini, S. (1991). I fratelli Fileni e i confini del territorio Cartaginese. In *Atti del Il Congresso Internazionale di Studi Fenici e Punici. Roma, 9–14 Novembre 1987.* Rome: Consiglio Nazionale delle Ricerche. 393–400.
Richardson, A. (2000). The Numerical Basis of Roman Camps. *OJA* 19(4). 425–437.
Richardson, A. (2002). Camps and Forts of Units and Formations of the Roman Army. *OJA* 21(1). 92–107.
Richardson, A. (2003). Space and Manpower in Roman Camps. *OJA* 22(3). 303–313.
Ritter, S., & Ben Tahar, S. (2020). New insights into the urban history of *Meninx* (Jerba). *AntAfr* 56. 101–128.
Romanelli, P. (1916). Scavi e scoperte nella città di Tripoli. *Notiziario Archeologico* 2. 301–364.
Romanelli, P. (1925). *Leptis Magna.* Rome.
Romanelli, P. (1970). Topografia e archeologica delAfrRom *Enciclopedia Classica* (Vol. 10 sez. III).
Rosen, S.A. (2000). The decline of desert agriculture: a view from the classical period Negev. In G. Barker & D.D. Gilbertson (eds), *The Archaeology of Drylands: Living at the margin.* London: Routledge. 44–61.
Rossiter, J. (1978). *Roman Farm Buildings in Italy.* Oxford: BAR.
Rossiter, J. (1994). *Suburbana Oeensia*: Roman Villas in the Region of Tripoli, Libya. Paper presented at the 96th Annual Meeting of the Archaeological Institute of America, Atlanta, Georgia.
Roth, R. (2007). Ceramic integration? Typologies and the perception of identities in Republican Italy. In R. Roth & J. Keller (eds), *Roman by Integration: Dimensions of Group Identity in Material Culture and Text.* Portsmouth, RI: JRA. 59–70.
Roth, R., & Keller, J. (eds). (2007). *Roman by Integration: Dimensions of Group Identity in Material Culture and Text.* Portsmouth, RI: JRA.
Rowan, E. (2015). The utility of olive oil pressing waste as a fuel source in antiquity. *AJA* 119(4). 465–482.
Rubin, R. (1991). Settlement and Agriculture on an Ancient Desert Frontier. *Geographical Review* 81(2). 197–205.
Rushworth, A. (2004). From Arzuges to Rustamids: State Formation and Regional Identity in the Pre-Saharan Zone. In A.H. Merrills (ed.), *Vandals, Romans and Berbers. New Perspectives on Late Antique North Africa.* Aldershot: Ashgate. 77–98.

Russell, B.J. (2013). *Gazetteer of Stone Quarries in the Roman World.* Version 1.0. Retrieved 23 May 2013. oxrep.classics.ox.ac.uk/databases/stone_quarries_database/

Saladin, H. (1902). Fouilles à Henchir-bou-Guerba (Tunisie) exécutées par M. du Breil de Pontbriand. *BCTH* 1902. 405–411.

Salza Prina Ricotti, E. (1971). Le ville marittime di Silin (Leptis Magna). *Atti della Pontificia Accademia Romana di Archeologia: Rendiconti* 43. 135–164.

Scheidel, W. (2014). The Shape of the Roman World. *JRA* 27. 7–32.

Schimmer, F. (2012). New evidence for a Roman fort and *vicus* at Mizda (Tripolitania). *LibStud* 43. 33–39.

Schörle, K., & Leitch, V. (2012). Report of the preliminary season of the Lepcis Magna Coastal Survey. *LibStud* 43. 149–154.

Schörner, G. (2012). Comparing surface, topsoil and subsurface ceramic assemblages: the case of Il Monte, San Gimignano. In P.A.J. Attema & G. Schörner (eds), *Comparative Issues in the Archaeology of the Roman Rural Landscape. Site classification between survey, excavation, and historical categories.* Portsmouth, RI: JRA. 31–42.

Scott, E. (1993). *A Gazetteer of Roman Villas in Britain.* Leicester: School of Archaeological Studies, University of Leicester.

Scott, E., Dore, J., & Mattingly, D.J. (1996). Part 1. The UNESCO Libyan Valleys Archaeological Survey Gazetteer 1979-1989. In D.J. Mattingly (ed.), *Farming the Desert: The UNESCO Libyan Valleys Archaeological Survey.* Vol. Two: Gazetteer and Pottery. 1–316.

Sears, G. (2007). *Late Roman African Urbanism. Continuity and transformation in the city.* Oxford: Archaeopress.

Sears, G. (2011). *The Cities of North Africa.* Stroud: History Press.

Sever, T.L., & Parry, J.T. (2006). Archaeological Remote Sensing of Early Human Settlements. In M.K. Ridd & J.D. Hipple (eds), *Remote Sensing of Human Settlements.* Bethesda, Maryland: American Society for Photogrammetry and Remote Sensing. 431–520.

Shahîd, I. (2002). *Byzantium and the Arabs in the Sixth Century. Volume II, Part 1: Toponymy, Monuments, Historical Geography, and Frontier Studies.* Washington, D.C.: Dumbarton Oaks Research Library and Collection.

Shaw, B.D. (1984). Water and Society in the Ancient Maghrib: Technology, Property and Development. *AntAfr* 20. 121–173.

Sjöström, I.W. (1993). *Tripolitania in Transition: Late Roman to Islamic Settlement, with a catalogue of sites.* Aldershot: Avebury.

Slim, H., Trousset, P., Paskoff, R., & Oueslati, A. (2004). *Le Littoral de la Tunisie. Étude géoarchéologique et historique.* Paris: Éditions CNRS.

Smith, D.J. (1968). The *Centenaria* of Tripolitania and their antecedents. In F. Gadallah (ed.), *Libya in History.* Libya: Faculty of Arts, University of Libya. 299–320.

Smith, J.T. (1997). *Roman Villas. A Study in Social Structure.* London: Routledge.

Speidel, M.P. (1988). Outpost duty in the desert. Building the Fort at Gholaia (Bu Njem, Libya). *AntAfr* 24. 99–102.

Sterry M. & Mattingly D.J. (eds). (2020). *Urbanisation and State Formation in the Ancient Sahara and Beyond.* Cambridge: Cambridge University Press.

Sutter, J.W. (1987). Cattle and Inequality: Herd Size Differences and Pastoral Production among the Fulani of Northeastern Senegal. *Africa: Journal of the International African Institute* 57(2). 196–218.

Symonds, M. (2007). *The Design and Purpose of Roman Fortlets in the North-Western Frontier Provinces of the Empire.* DPhil Thesis, University of Oxford.

Talbert, R.J.A. (ed.). (2000). *Barrington Atlas of the Greek and Roman World.* Princeton: Princeton University Press.

Tapete, D. (ed.). (2017). *Remote Sensing and Geosciences for Archaeology.* Printed Edition of Special Issue Published in *Geosciences*. Basel: MDPI.

Tapete, D. (ed.). (2019). *Earth Observation, Remote Sensing and Geoscientific Ground Investigations for Archaeological and Heritage Research.* Printed Edition of Special Issue Published in *Geosciences*. Basel: MDPI.

Tate, G. (1992). *Les campages de la Syrie du Nord.* Paris: P. Geuthner.

Tate, G. (1997). The Syrian Countryside during the Roman Era. In S.E. Alcock (ed.), *The Early Roman Empire in the East.* Oxford: Oxbow. 55–71.

Tchalenko, G. (1953–1958). *Villages antiques de la Syrie du Nord; le massif du Bélus à l'époque romaine.* Paris: P. Geuthner.

Terrenato, N. (2001). The Auditorium site in Rome and the origins of the villa. *JRA* 14. 5–32.

Thompson, L.A. (1968). Roman and Native in the Tripolitanian Cities in the Early Empire. In F. Gadallah (ed.), *Libya in History.* Libya: Faculty of Arts, University of Libya. 235–250.

Tissot, C. (1884). *Géographie Comparée de la Province Romaine d'Afrique* (Vol. 1). Paris: Imprimerie Nationale.

Tissot, C. (1888). *Géographie Comparée de la Province Romaine d'Afrique* (Vol. 2). Paris: Imprimerie Nationale.

Tomasello, F. (1992). L'architettura del II secolo in Tripolitania, a proposito della sima del Tempio a divinità ignota di Sabratha. *QAL* 15. 253–282.

Tomasello, F. (2005). *Fontane e Ninfei Minori di Leptis Magna*. Rome: "L'Erma" di Bretschneider.

Tomasello, F. (2011). *Il Tempio sul Decumano Maggiore di Leptis Magna*. Rome: "L'Erma" di Bretschneider.

Toussaint, P.-M. (1905). Résumé des Reconnaissances Archéologiques Exécutées par les Officiers des Brigades Topographiques d'Algérie et de Tunisie pendant la campagne de 1903-1904. *BCTH* 1905. 56–74.

Toussaint, P.-M. (1906). Résumé des Reconnaissances Archéologiques Exécutées par les Officiers des Brigades Topographiques d'Algérie et de Tunisie pendant la campagne de 1903-1904. *BCTH* 1906. 223–241.

Toutain, J. (1895). Note sur quelques voies Romaines de l'Afrique Proconsulaire (Tunisie Méridionale et Tripolitaine). *Mélanges d'archéologie et d'histoire* 15. 201–229.

Toutain, J. (1896). Les Romains dans la Sahara. *Mélanges de l'école française de Rome* 16. 63–77.

Toutain, J. (1903). Notes et Documents sur les voies stratégiques et sur l'occupation militaire du sud Tunisien à l'époque Romaine par Mm. les Capitaines Donau et Le Boeuf, les Lieutenants De Pontbriand, Goulon et Tardy. *BCTH* 1903. 272–409.

Townsend, P.W. (1938). The significance of the arch of the Severi at Lepcis. *AJA* 42(4). 512–524.

Tribalet. (1901). Notes sur des recherches archéologiques aux environs de Tatahouine. BCTH 1901. 284–289.

Trigger, B. (1990). Monumental Architecture: A Thermodynamic Explanation of Symbolic Behaviour. *World Archaeology* 22(2). 119–132.

Trousset, P. (1974). *Recherches sur le Limes Tripolitanus*. Paris: Éditions CNRS.

Trousset, P. (1982). Le franchissement des chotts du Sud tunisien dans l'Antiquité. *AntAfr* 18. 45–60.

Trousset, P. (1984). Note sur un type d'ouvrage linéaire du 'limes' d'Afrique. *BCTH* n.s.17B. 383–398.

Trousset, P. (1985). Les 'fines Antiquae' et la reconquête Byzantine en Afrique. *BCTH* n.s.19B. 361–376.

Trousset, P. (1990). Tours de guet (watch-towers) et système de liaison optique sur le limes Tripolitanus. In H. Vetters & M. Kandler (eds), *Akten des 14. Internationalen Limeskongresses 1986 in Carnuntum*. Wien: Verlag der Österreichischen Akademie der Wissenschaften. 249–278.

Trousset, P. (2002). Pénétration romaine et organisation de la frontière dans le prédésert tunisien. *AfrRom* 15. 59–88.

Trousset, P. (2011). Une entière frontalière tardive et sa genèse: des Nybgenii aux Arzuges. In C. Briand-Ponsart & Y. Modéran (eds), *Provinces et identités provinciales dans l'Afrique romaine*. Caen: Publications de CRAHM. 201–220.

van der Veen, M. (1985). The UNESCO Libyan Valleys Survey X: Botanic Evidence for Ancient Farming in the Pre-Desert. *LibStud* 16. 15–28.

van der Veen, M., Grant, A., & Barker, G. (1996). Romano-Libyan Agriculture: Crops and Animals. In G. Barker (ed.), *Farming the Desert: The UNESCO Libyan Valleys Archaeological Survey*. Vol. One: Synthesis. 227–264.

van Dommelen, P., & Finocchi, S. (2008). Sardinia: Divergent Landscapes. In P. van Dommelen & C. Gómez Bellard (eds), *Rural Landscapes of the Punic World*. London: Equinox. 159–201.

van Dommelen, P., & Gómez Bellard, C. (eds). (2008). *Rural Landscapes of the Punic World*. London: Equinox.

von Bary, E. (1883). Senams et tumuli de la chaine des montagnes de la côte Tripolitaine. *Revue d'Ethnographie* 2. 426–437.

Von Petrikovits, H. (1971). Fortifications in the North-Western Roman Empire from the Third to the Fifth Centuries A.D. *JRS* 61. 178–218.

Wallace-Hadrill, A. (1994). *Houses and Society in Pompeii and Herculaneum*. Princeton: Princeton University Press.

Wallace-Hadrill, A. (2008). *Rome's Cultural Revolution*. Cambridge: Cambridge University Press.

Ward-Perkins, J.B. (1951). The Arch of Septimius Severus at Lepcis Magna. *Archaeology* 4(4). 226–231.

Ward-Perkins, J.B. (1968). Pre-Roman Elements in the Architecture of Roman Tripolitania. In F. Gadallah (ed.), *Libya in History*. Libya: Faculty of Arts, University of Libya. 101–116.

Ward-Perkins, J.B., & Goodchild, R.G. (1953). The Christian antiquities of Tripolitania. *Archaeologia* 95. 1–83.

Ward-Perkins, J.B., Jones, B., Ling, R., & Kenrick, P. (1993). *The Severan Buildings of Lepcis Magna, an Architectural Survey*. London: The Society for Libyan Studies on behalf of the Department of Antiquities, SPLAJ.

Welfare, H., & Swan, V. (1995). *Roman Camps in England: The Field Archaeology*. London: HMSO.

Welsby, D.A. (1983). The Roman Fort at Gheriat el-Garbia. *LibStud* 14. 57–64.

Welsby, D.A. (1991). ULVS XXIV: A Late Roman and Byzantine church at Souk el Awty in the Tripolitanian Pre-Desert. *LibStud* 22. 61–80.

Welsby, D.A. (1992). ULVS XXV: The *Gsur* and Associated Settlements in the Wadi Umm el Kharab: An Architectural Survey. *LibStud* 23. 73–100.

Whyte, W. (2006). How do buildings mean? Some Issues of Interpretation in the History of Architecture. *History and Theory* 45(2). 153–177.

Wilson, A. (1997). Book Review: *Tripolitania*, by D.J. Mattingly. *LibStud* 28. 71–73.

Wilson, A. (2011). City Sizes and Urbanization in the Roman Empire. In A.K. Bowman & A. Wilson (eds), *Settlement, Urbanization and Population*. Oxford: Oxford University Press. 161–195.

Wilson, A. (2012a). Neo-Punic and Latin inscriptions in Roman North Africa: function and display. In A. Mullen & P. James (eds), *Multilingualism in the Greco-Roman Worlds*. Cambridge: Cambridge University Press. 265–316.

Wilson, A.I. (2012b). Saharan Trade in the Roman Period: Short-, Medium-, and Long-Distance Trade Networks. *Azania* 47(4). 409–449.

Wilson, A.I. (2017). Trade across Rome's southern frontier: the Sahara and the Garamantes. In A.I. Wilson & A.K. Bowman (eds), *Trade, Commerce, and the State in the Roman World*. Oxford: Oxford University Press. 599–624.

Wilson, D.R. (1974). Roman camps in Britain. In D.M. Pippidi (ed.), *Actes du IXe Congrès International d'Etudes sur les Frontières Romaines. Mamaïa, 6–13 septembre 1972*. Bucharest: Editura Academiei. 341–350.

Witcher, R. (2012). 'That from a long way off look like farms': the classification of Roman rural sites. In P.A.J. Attema & G. Schörner (eds), *Comparative Issues in the Archaeology of the Roman Rural Landscape. Site classification between survey, excavation, and historical categories*. Portsmouth, RI: JRA. 11–30.

Appendix Tables

Rank	Tripolitania		Africa Proconsularis		Cyrenaica	
	#	**Names**	**#**	**Names**	**#**	**Names**
1	1	Lepcis Magna	1	Carthage	0	–
2	3	Tacape, Sabratha, Oea	2	Hadrumetum, Hippo Regius	2	Cyrene, Ptolemais
3	15	Turris Tamalleni, Cidamus, Gigthis, Meninx, Tipasa, Girba?[1], Zitha, Pisida, Thubactis, Macomades, Iscina, Digdida Selorum, Tillibari, Thenteos, Gholaia	63	Thagaste, Madauros, Thuburnica, Thabraca, Bulla Regia, Simitthu, Sicca Veneria, Lares, Belalis Maior, Vaga, Numluli, Thignica, Thubursicu Bure, Thugga, Agbia, Aunobari, Musti, Uchi Maius, Zama Regia, Hippo Diarrhytus, Matar, Thizika, Ureu, Uzali Sar, Membressa, Abitina, Chidibbia, Bisica Lucana, Avitta Bibba, Thuburbo Maius, Apisa Maius, Semta, Seressi, Limisa, Utica, Uthina, Abbir Maius, Segermes, Biia, Abthugni, Pheradi Maius, Carpi, Neapolis, Pupput, Althiburos, Thala, Cillium, Theveste, Ammaedara, Thelepte, Capsa, Assuras, Uzappa, Mactaris, Thugga Terebenthina, Sufes, Sufetula, Uluzibbira, Lepti Minus, Thysdrus, Bararus, Thaenae, Thapsus	6	Berenice/ Euesperides, Hadrianopolis, Taucheira, Barke, Apollonia, Darnis

Appendix Table 1: *Urban settlements of Tripolitania (Maps 35 and 37),* Africa Proconsularis *(Maps 32, 33, and 34) and* Cyrenaica *(Maps 37 and 38) in the* Barrington Atlas *(Talbert 2000).*

[1] Neither *Girba* nor *Tipasa* is known archaeologically, and it has been argued that the former may actually have been a later name for *Meninx* (Fentress, Drine, & Holod 2009: 81–85).

Years	1 – Jerba	2 – *Lepcis Magna*	3 – Silin and coast	4 – Wadi Caam-Taraglat	5 – Tarhuna	6 – *ULVS*
500–450	6	–	–	–	–	–
450–400	6	–	–	–	–	–
400–350	6	–	1	–	–	–
350–300	6	–	1	–	–	–
300–250	19	12	1	–	–	–
250–200	79	12	1	–	–	–
200–150	79	72	13	1	1	–
150–100	79	72	13	1	1	–
100–50	79	98	18	3	7	–
50–0	93	98	18	3	7	–
0–50	93	130	52	74	62	–
50–100	93	130	52	74	62	172
100–150	93	129	55	83	84	172
150–200	53	129	55	83	84	172
200–250	53	94	44	69	85	274
250–300	53	94	28	58	85	274
300–350	46	66	28	78	83	274
350–400	46	66	28	78	83	274
400–450	46	65	27	77	53	209
450–500	46	65	9	9	53	209
500–550	50	13	8	7	46	35
550–600	50	13	5	2	46	35
600–650	50	–	–	1	28	35
650–700	50	2	–	1	28	38

Appendix Table 2: *Number of sites with finewares dated to 50-year periods between 500 BC and AD 700 in six survey areas. (N.B. Not all of the data were originally divided by 50-year periods; numbers were repeated for those which used broader divisions).*[2]

	Minimum (m²)	Maximum (m²)	Mean (m²)
Total area	29	6,295	779
Open area	0	4,053	616
Covered area	13	2,648	292

Appendix Table 3: *Summary of results of an analysis of the total open and covered areas for 166 unfortified farms in the* ULVS *area (after Cività 1994: 39–42).*

[2] Data sources: 1. Jerba – Fentress, Drine, & Holod 2009: Appendix 1. 2. *Lepcis Magna* – Munzi *et al.* 2010: 725–729; Munzi *et al.* 2016: 69–72. 3, 4. Silin and coast, and Wadi Caam-Taraglat – Munzi *et al.* 2004–2005: 436, Tables 1–2 (see also, Musso *et al.* 2010). 5. Gebel Tarhuna – Ahmed 2010: 166–167. 6. *ULVS* – Mattingly & Flower 1996: 159–169.

	With 1+ press(es)		Farmyard	Courtyard	Open (undiff.)	Open complex	Range
	Total #	# with plan recorded					
1. W. coastal	6	5	1	3	1	–	–
2. W. *gebel*	1	–	–	–	–	–	–
3. Southwest	–	–	–	–	–	–	–
4. Central coastal	28	3	–	3	–	–	–
5. Central *gebel*	143	46	–	32	14	–	–
6. E. pre-desert, north	22	16	2	6	5	1	2
7. E. pre-desert, south	13	13	4	7	1	–	1
8. W. Syrtica	2	–	–	–	–	–	–
9. E. Syrtica	–	–	–	–	–	–	–
Total	*215*	*83*	*7*	*51*	*21*	*1*	*3*

Appendix Table 4: *Unfortified buildings with presses, divided by building type and region.*

	With 1+ press(es)			All (from Table 5.3)		
	Total #	# with size recorded	Average size	Total #	# with size recorded	Average size
1. W. coastal	6	5	1,914	50	38	1,188
2. W. *gebel*	1	–	–	9	7	435
3. Southwest	–	–	–	11	10	929
4. Central coastal	28	7	1,486	94	15	2,201
5. Central *gebel*	143	34	2,182	156	35	2,138
6. E. pre-desert, north	22	19	1,277	365	217	1,038
7. E. pre-desert, south	13	12	790	414	349	655
8. W. Syrtica	2	–	–	487	402	766
9. E. Syrtica	–	–	–	67	66	1,161
Total	*215*	*77*	*1,661*	*1653*	*1,139*	*881*

Appendix Table 5: *Frequency and average size of unfortified buildings with presses vs. overall.*

	With 1+ press(es)			All (from Table 5.5)		
	Total #	# with size recorded	Average size	Total #	# with size recorded	Average size
1. W. coastal	3	3	2589	50	5	1,903
2. W. *gebel*	–	–	–	9	1	240
3. Southwest	–	–	–	11	1	650
4. Central coastal	3	3	1553	94	5	1,838
5. Central *gebel*	32	28	2178	156	29	2,125
6. E. pre-desert, north	6	6	1860	365	30	1,063
7. E. pre-desert, south	7	6	1094	414	32	1,267
8. W. Syrtica	–	–	–	487	11	1,011
9. E. Syrtica	–	–	–	67	–	–
Total	*51*	*46*	*1981*	*1653*	*114*	*1,445*

Appendix Table 6: *Frequency and average size of unfortified courtyard buildings with presses vs. overall.*

	With 1+ press(es)			All (from Table 5.6)		
	Total #	# with size recorded	Average size	Total #	# with size recorded	Average size
1. W. coastal	1	1	850	50	11	580
2. W. *gebel*	–	–	–	9	–	–
3. Southwest	–	–	–	11	–	–
4. Central coastal	–	–	–	94	–	–
5. Central *gebel*	–	–	–	156	–	–
6. E. pre-desert, north	2	1	750	365	95	598
7. E. pre-desert, south	4	4	437	414	223	585
8. W. Syrtica	–	–	–	487	338	667
9. E. Syrtica	–	–	–	67	43	820
Total	*7*	*6*	*558*	*1653*	*710*	*640*

Appendix Table 7: *Frequency and average size of unfortified farmyard buildings with presses vs. overall.*

	ashlar	ashlar & opus africanum	opus africanum	large orthostats	small orthostats	regular masonry	irregular masonry	coursed rubble/ drystone	mortared rubble	Syrtica group
1. W. coastal	–	–	2	–	–	–	–	–	1	–
2. W. *gebel*	–	–	–	–	–	–	–	–	–	–
4. Central coastal	–	–	3	–	–	–	–	–	–	–
5. Central *gebel*	3	2	23	–	–	–	–	–	–	–
6. E. pre-desert, north	–	–	4	2	–	8	2	7	–	–
7. E. pre-desert, south	–	1	1	1	–	7	5	4	–	–
8. W. Syrtica	–	–	–	–	–	–	–	–	2	3
Total	*3*	*3*	*33*	*3*	–	*15*	*7*	*11*	*3*	*3*

Appendix Table 8: *Frequency of courtyard buildings in different regions using different construction techniques.*

	ashlar	ashlar & opus africanum	opus africanum	large orthostats	small orthostats	regular masonry	irregular masonry	coursed rubble/ drystone	mortared rubble	Syrtica group
1. W. coastal	–	–	–	1	–	–	–	–	–	–
2. W. *gebel*	–	–	–	–	–	–	–	–	–	–
4. Central coastal	–	–	–	–	–	–	–	–	–	–
5. Central *gebel*	–	–	–	–	–	–	–	–	–	–
6. E. pre-desert, north	–	–	1	4	6	4	6	50	2	–
7. E. pre-desert, south	–	–	–	–	21	19	16	49	–	–
8. W. Syrtica	–	–	–	–	–	–	–	7	–	27
Total	–	–	*1*	*5*	*27*	*23*	*22*	*106*	*2*	*27*

Appendix Table 9: *Frequency of farmyard buildings in different regions using different construction techniques.*

	ashlar	ashlar & opus africanum	opus africanum	large orthostats	small orthostats	regular masonry	irregular masonry	coursed rubble/ drystone	mortared rubble	Syrtica group
1. W. coastal	–	–	3	–	–	–	–	–	–	–
2. W. *gebel*	–	–	–	–	–	1	–	–	–	–
4. Central coastal	–	–	3	–	–	–	–	–	–	–
5. Central *gebel*	–	1	7	–	–	–	–	–	–	–
6. E. pre-desert, north	–	–	2	1	–	9	2	21	–	–
7. E. pre-desert, south	–	–	1	–	1	3	–	19	–	–
8. W. Syrtica	–	–	–	1	–	–	–	4	3	3
Total	–	*1*	*16*	*2*	*1*	*13*	*2*	*44*	–	–

Appendix Table 10: *Frequency of open (undifferentiated) buildings in different regions using different construction techniques.*

	ashlar	ashlar & opus africanum	opus africanum	large orthostats	small orthostats	regular masonry	irregular masonry	coursed rubble/ drystone	mortared rubble	Syrtica group
1. W. coastal	–	–	–	–	–	–	–	–	–	–
2. W. *gebel*	–	–	–	–	–	–	–	–	–	–
4. Central coastal	–	–	–	–	–	–	–	–	–	–
5. Central *gebel*	–	–	–	–	–	–	–	–	–	–
6. E. pre-desert, north	–	–	–	1	1	2	2	18	–	–
7. E. pre-desert, south	–	–	–	–	–	3	–	1	–	–
8. W. Syrtica	–	–	–	–	–	–	–	–	–	–
Total	–	–	–	*1*	*1*	*5*	*2*	*19*	–	–

Appendix Table 11: *Frequency of open complexes in different regions using different construction techniques.*

	ashlar	ashlar & opus africanum	opus africanum	large orthostats	small orthostats	regular masonry	irregular masonry	coursed rubble/ drystone	mortared rubble	Syrtica group
1. W. coastal	–	–	–	–	–	–	–	–	–	–
2. W. *gebel*	1	–	–	–	–	–	–	–	–	–
4. Central coastal	–	–	–	–	–	–	–	–	–	–
5. Central *gebel*	–	–	–	–	–	–	–	–	–	–
6. E. pre-desert, north	–	–	1	–	–	4	–	3	–	–
7. E. pre-desert, south	–	1	1	–	1	3	7	1	–	–
8. W. Syrtica	–	–	–	1	–	–	–	–	1	–
Total	*1*	*1*	*2*	*1*	*1*	*7*	*7*	*4*	*1*	–

Appendix Table 12: *Frequency of range/block buildings in different regions using different construction techniques.*

	ashlar	ashlar & opus africanum	opus africanum	large orthostats	small orthostats	regular masonry	irregular masonry	coursed rubble/ drystone	mortared rubble	Syrtica group
# of examples	*3*	*3*	*30*	*3*	–	*15*	*7*	*9*	*2*	*3*
1. W. coastal	–	–	1219	–	–	–	–	–	5330	–
2. W. *gebel*	–	–	–	–	–	–	–	–	–	–
4. Central coastal	–	–	1866	–	–	–	–	–	–	–
5. Central *gebel*	1622	3024	1947	–	–	–	–	–	–	–
6. E. pre-desert, north	–	–	2651	987	–	525	1447	909	–	–
7. E. pre-desert, south	–	1750	1764	416	–	937	1187	2063	–	–
8. W. Syrtica	–	–	–	–	–	–	–	–	1400	731
All regions	*1622*	*2600*	*1978*	*797*	–	*717*	*1261*	*1293*	*3365*	*731*

Appendix Table 13: *Average size* (m^2) *of courtyard buildings in different regions divided by construction technique.*

	ashlar	ashlar & opus africanum	opus africanum	large orthostats	small orthostats	regular masonry	irregular masonry	coursed rubble/ drystone	mortared rubble	Syrtica group
# of examples	–	–	*1*	*5*	*27*	*22*	*21*	*80*	–	*18*
1. W. coastal	–	–	–	850	–	–	–	–	–	–
2. W. *gebel*	–	–	–	–	–	–	–	–	–	–
4. Central coastal	–	–	–	–	–	–	–	–	–	–
5. Central *gebel*	–	–	–	–	–	–	–	–	–	–
6. E. pre-desert, north	–	–	750	1265	408	381	733	634	–	–
7. E. pre-desert, south	–	–	–	–	659	416	298	506	–	–
8. W. Syrtica	–	–	–	–	–	–	–	281	–	466
All regions	–	–	*750*	*1182*	*603*	*411*	*423*	*549*	–	*466*

Appendix Table 14: *Average size* (m^2) *of farmyard buildings in different regions divided by construction technique.*

	With luxury elements		Farmyard	Courtyard	Open (undiff.)	Open complex	Range	Villa complex
	Total	With plan recorded						
1. W. coastal	5	1	–	1	–	–	–	–
2. W. gebel	1	1	–	–	–	–	1	–
3. Southwest	–	–	–	–	–	–	–	–
4. Central coastal	28	6	–	3	–	–	–	3
5. Central gebel	30	17	–	14	3	–	–	–
6. E. pre-desert, north	3	3	–	3	–	–	–	–
7. E. pre-desert, south	4	4	–	2	1	–	1	–
8. W. Syrtica	3	1	–	–	1	–	–	–
9. E. Syrtica	–	–	–	–	–	–	–	–
Total	*74*	*33*	–	*23*	*5*	–	*2*	*3*

Appendix Table 15: *Number of unfortified buildings of different plan with luxury elements, divided by region.*

	With luxury elements			All (from Table 5.3)		
	Total #	# with size recorded	Average size	Total #	# with size recorded	Average size
1. W. coastal	5	1	5,330	50	38	1,188
2. W. *gebel*	1	1	195	9	7	435
3. Southwest	–	–	–	11	10	929
4. Central coastal	28	7	3,194	94	15	2,201
5. Central *gebel*	30	15	2,580	156	35	2,138
6. E. pre-desert, north	3	3	3,040	365	217	1,038
7. E. pre-desert, south	4	3	671	414	349	655
8. W. Syrtica	3	2	749	487	402	766
9. E. Syrtica	–	–	–	67	66	1,161
Total	*74*	*32*	*2,417*	*1,653*	*1,139*	*881*

Appendix Table 16: *Average size of unfortified buildings with luxury elements and overall, divided by region.*

# of presses	Total sites	Total with luxury elements		Baths	Mosaics	Marble	Plaster	Sculpture
0	1,438	34	2%	9	25	15	12	15
1	103	11	11%	2	3	3	4	5
2	51	9	18%	2	2	2	1	4
3	26	5	19%	2	1	–	–	4
4	14	3	21%	3	1	–	–	1
5	10	4	40%	4	–	–	–	2
6	5	4	80%	4	1	–	–	3
7–17	6	4	67%	3	2	–	–	2
Total excl. 0	*215*	*40*	*19%*	*20*	*10*	*5*	*5*	*21*
Total	*1,653*	*74*	*5%*	*49*	*35*	*20*	*17*	*57*

Appendix Table 17: *Ratio of unfortified buildings with presses to those with luxury elements.*

	Total	ashlar	ashlar & opus africanum	opus africanum	large orthostats	small orthostats	regular masonry	irregular masonry	coursed rubble/ drystone	mortared rubble	Syrtica group
1. W. coastal	3	–	–	1	–	–	–	–	–	2	–
2. W. *gebel*	–	–	–	–	–	–	–	–	–	–	–
3. Southwest	–	–	–	–	–	–	–	–	–	–	–
4. Central coastal	5	–	1	4	–	–	–	–	–	–	–
5. Central *gebel*	19	4	4	11	–	–	–	–	–	–	–
6. E. pre-desert, north	3	–	–	3	–	–	–	–	–	–	–
7. E. pre-desert, south	3	–	1	–	–	–	2	–	–	–	–
8. W. Syrtica	2	–	–	–	1	–	–	–	–	1	–
9. E. Syrtica	–	–	–	–	–	–	–	–	–	–	–
Total	*35*	*4*	*6*	*19*	*1*	–	*2*	–	–	*3*	–

Appendix Table 18: *Distribution of unfortified buildings with luxury elements, divided by construction technique.*

	Towers	Compounds	*Total*
1. W. coastal	–	–	–
2. W. *gebel*	–	3	3
3. Southwest	–	–	–
4. Central coastal	–	–	–
5. Central *gebel*	–	1	1
6. E. pre-desert, north	10	1	11
7. E. pre-desert, south	3	1	4
8. W. Syrtica	–	–	–
9. E. Syrtica	–	–	–
Total	*13*	*6*	*19*

Appendix Table 19: *Fortified buildings with externally projecting towers, divided by region and building type.*

	Towers	Compounds	Unknown	*Total*
1. W. coastal	1	–	–	1
2. W. *gebel*	1	–	–	1
3. Southwest	–	–	–	–
4. Central coastal	–	–	–	–
5. Central *gebel*	–	–	–	–
6. E. pre-desert, north	24	1	1	26
7. E. pre-desert, south	4	2	–	6
8. W. Syrtica	–	–	–	–
9. E. Syrtica	–	–	–	–
Total	*30*	*3*	*1*	*34*

Appendix Table 20: *Fortified buildings with batters, divided by region and building type.*

	Towers	Compounds	Unknown	Total	*% of total known sites*
1. W. coastal	1	–	–	1	0.7%
2. W. *gebel*	–	1	–	1	1 %
3. Southwest	–	–	–	–	0%
4. Central coastal	–	–	–	–	0%
5. Central *gebel*	–	1	–	1	0.7%
6. E. pre-desert, north	7	1	2	10	3%
7. E. pre-desert, south	3	1	–	4	4%
8. W. Syrtica	–	–	1	1	5%
9. E. Syrtica	–	–	–	–	0%
Total	*11*	*4*	*3*	*18*	*2%*

Appendix Table 21: *Fortified buildings with external yards, divided by region and building type.*

	Towers	Compounds	Range/block	Unknown	*Total*	*% of total known sites*
1. W. coastal	–	–	–	–	–	–
2. W. *gebel*	2	–	–	–	2	2%
3. Southwest	–	–	–	2	2	15%
4. Central coastal	–	–	–	–	–	–
5. Central *gebel*	1	–	–	2	3	2%
6. E. pre-desert, north	17	–	1	2	20	7%
7. E. pre-desert, south	3	–	–	–	3	3%
8. W. Syrtica	2	–	–	–	2	11%
9. E. Syrtica	–	–	–	–	–	–
Total	*25*	–	*1*	*6*	*32*	*4%*

Appendix Table 22: *Fortified buildings with enceintes, divided by region and building type.*

	Total #	Minimum size (m^2)	Maximum size (m^2)	Mean (m^2)	Median (m^2)
1. W. coastal	1	594	594	594	594
2. W. *gebel*	–	–	–	–	–
3. Southwest	–	–	–	–	
4. Central coastal	–	–	–	–	–
5. Central *gebel*	1	1,780	1,780	1,780	1,780
6. E. pre-desert, north	6	120	1,300	668	728
7. E. pre-desert, south	2	160	540	350	350
8. W. Syrtica	–	–	–	–	–
9. E. Syrtica	–	–	–	–	–
Total	*10*	*120*	*1,780*	*708*	*609*

Appendix Table 23: *Minimum, maximum, mean and median total areas for fortified buildings with external yards, divided by region.*

	Total #	Minimum size (m^2)	Maximum size (m^2)	Mean (m^2)	Median (m^2)
1. W. coastal	–	–	–	–	–
2. W. *gebel*	2	1,600	1,800	1,700	1,700
3. Southwest	–	–	–	–	–
4. Central coastal	–	–	–	–	–
5. Central *gebel*	2	400	5,330	2,865	2,865
6. E. pre-desert, north	18	374	7,340	1,212	792
7. E. pre-desert, south	2	484	625	555	555
8. W. Syrtica	2	729	825	777	777
9. E. Syrtica	–	–	–	–	–
Total	*26*	*144*	*7,340*	*1,264*	*813*

Appendix Table 24: *Minimum, maximum, mean and median total areas for fortified buildings with enceintes, divided by region.*

	Total #	Minimum size (m^2)	Maximum size (m^2)	Mean (m^2)	Median (m^2)
1. W. coastal	122	324	8,100	2,157	1,977
2. W. *gebel*	10	375	3,025	1,673	1,683
3. Southwest	5	1,620	5,200	2,610	1,890
4. Central coastal	2	2,250	3,024	2,637	2,637
5. Central *gebel*	81	550	8,000	2,346	2,021
6. E. pre-desert, north	31	340	3,480	1,767	1,600
7. E. pre-desert, south	–	–	–	–	–
8. W. Syrtica	4	460	2,500	1,491	1,501
9. E. Syrtica	5	1,089	3,600	2,033	1,600
Total	*260*	*324*	*8,100*	*2,150*	*1,974*

Appendix Table 25: *Minimum, maximum, mean and median total areas for fortified buildings with ditches, divided by region.*[3]

	With 1+ press(es)		Tower	Compound
	Total	With plan recorded		
1. W. coastal	5	4	1	3
2. W. *gebel*	1	1	–	1
3. Southwest	–	–	–	–
4. Central coastal	2	2	2	–
5. Central *gebel*	17	6	4	2
6. E. pre-desert, north	6	5	3	2
7. E. pre-desert, south	8	8	2	6
8. W. Syrtica	–	–	–	–
9. E. Syrtica	–	–	–	–
Total	*39*	*26*	*12*	*14*

Appendix Table 26: *Fortified buildings with presses, divided by building type and region.*

	All fortified with 1+ press(es)			All fortified (from Table 6.4)		
	Total #	# with size recorded	Average size	Total #	# with size recorded	Average size
1. W. coastal	5	3	415	138	19	401
2. W. *gebel*	1	1	841	84	71	498
3. Southwest	–	–	–	13	6	578
4. Central coastal	2	1	195	6	4	205
5. Central *gebel*	17	6	551	153	45	365
6. E. pre-desert, north	6	6	725	289	183	346
7. E. pre-desert, south	8	8	890	92	80	579
8. W. Syrtica	–	–	–	19	12	381
9. E. Syrtica	–	–	–	16	2	400
Total	*39*	*25*	*682*	*810*	*422*	*423*

Appendix Table 27: *Frequency and average size of fortified buildings with presses and overall.*

[3] In the case of the two examples in which a single ditch surrounded two buildings, the area was divided in half.

	Towers with 1+ press(es)			All towers (from Table 6.5)		
	Total #	# with size recorded	Average size	Total #	# with size recorded	Average size
1. W. coastal	1	1	120	138	8	172
2. W. gebel	–	–	–	84	34	211
3. Southwest	–	–	–	13	4	374
4. Central coastal	2	1	195	6	4	205
5. Central gebel	4	4	283	153	31	195
6. E. pre-desert, north	3	3	335	289	151	211
7. E. pre-desert, south	2	2	301	92	52	266
8. W. Syrtica	–	–	–	19	7	167
9. E. Syrtica	–	–	–	16	1	400
Total	*12*	*11*	*278*	*810*	*292*	*220*

Appendix Table 28: *Average size of fortified tower buildings with presses and overall, divided by region.*

	Compound with 1+ press(es)			All compounds (from Table 6.6)		
	Total #	# with size recorded	Average size	Total #	# with size recorded	Average size
1. W. coastal	3	2	562	138	5	650
2. W. *gebel*	1	1	841	84	31	862
3. Southwest	–	–	–	13	2	988
4. Central coastal	–	–	–	6	–	–
5. Central *gebel*	2	2	1,087	153	8	1,042
6. E. pre-desert, north	2	2	1,521	289	27	1,124
7. E. pre-desert, south	6	6	1,086	92	26	1,213
8. W. Syrtica	–	–	–	19	3	921
9. E. Syrtica	–	–	–	16	–	–
Total	*14*	*13*	*1,053*	*810*	*102*	*1,029*

Appendix Table 29: *Average size of fortified compound buildings with presses and overall, divided by region.*

	With luxury		Towers				Compounds			
	Total	With plan recorded	central lightwell	range lightwell	block	unknown	courtyard	doubled	irregular	unknown
1. W. coastal	14	1	–	–	–	–	–	–	–	1
2. W. *gebel*	8	7	4	–	–	1	1	–	–	1
3. Southwest	1	1	1	–	–	–	–	–	–	–
4. Central coastal	1	1	–	–	–	1	–	–	–	–
5. Central *gebel*	14	11	1	–	–	7	2	–	–	1
6. E. pre-desert, north	33	31	15	2	1	9	2	–	–	2
7. E. pre-desert, south	22	21	9	1	–	1	6	2	1	1
8. W. Syrtica	1	1	1	–	–	–	–	–	–	–
9. E. Syrtica	–	–	–	–	–	–	–	–	–	–
Total	*94*	*74*	*31*	*3*	*1*	*19*	*11*	*2*	*1*	*6*

Appendix Table 30: *Number of fortified buildings of different plan with luxury elements, divided by region.*

	With luxury elements			All (from Table 6.5)		
	Total #	# with size recorded	Average size	Total #	# with size recorded	Average size
1. W. coastal	–	–	–	9	8	172
2. W. *gebel*	5	5	355	36	34	211
3. Southwest	1	1	320	4	4	374
4. Central coastal	1	–	–	5	4	205
5. Central *gebel*	8	8	201	35	31	195
6. E. pre-desert, north	27	27	245	173	151	211
7. E. pre-desert, south	11	11	273	56	52	266
8. W. Syrtica	1	1	144	8	7	167
9. E. Syrtica	–	–	–	1	1	400
Total	*54*	*53*	*254*	*327*	*292*	*220*

Appendix Table 31: *Average size of fortified tower buildings with luxury elements and overall, divided by region.*

	With luxury elements			All (from Table 6.6)		
	Total #	# with size recorded	Average size	Total #	# with size recorded	Average size
1. W. coastal	1	1	225	6	5	650
2. W. *gebel*	2	2	1,438	31	31	862
3. Southwest	–	–	–	2	2	988
4. Central coastal	–	–	–	–	–	–
5. Central *gebel*	3	3	607	9	8	1,042
6. E. pre-desert, north	4	4	1,661	28	27	1,124
7. E. pre-desert, south	10	10	1,169	27	26	1,213
8. W. Syrtica	–	–	–	3	3	921
9. E. Syrtica	–	–	–	–	–	–
Total	*20*	*20*	*1,163*	*106*	*102*	*1,029*

Appendix Table 32: *Average size of fortified compound buildings with luxury elements and overall, divided by region.*

# of presses	Total sites	Total with luxury elements		Inscription	Bath	Marble	Plaster	Sculpture
0	771	80	10%	14	3	1	24	57
1	29	12	41%	2	–	1	5	8
2	5	1	20%	1	–	–	–	1
3	3	1	33%	–	–	–	–	1
4	1	–	–	–	–	–	–	–
5	1	–	–	–	–	–	–	–
Total excl. 0	*39*	*14*	*36%*					
Total	*810*	*94*	*12%*	*17*	*3*	*2*	*29*	*67*

Appendix Table 33: *Ratio of fortified buildings with presses to those with luxury elements.*

	Total	ashlar	ashlar lower & other upper	opus africanum	very regular masonry	regular masonry	irregular masonry	coursed rubble/ drystone	mortared rubble
1. W. coastal	10	–	–	9	–	–	–	1	–
2. W. gebel	6	3	1	1	–	1	–	–	–
3. Southwest	1	–	–	1	–	–	–	–	–
4. Central coastal	1	–	–	–	–	1	–	–	–
5. Central gebel	6	1	3	–	–	1	–	–	1
6. E. pre-desert, north	28	1	1	–	14	8	3	1	–
7. E. pre-desert, south	16	1	–	–	4	10	1	–	–
8. W. Syrtica	1	–	–	–	–	–	1	–	–
9. E. Syrtica	–	–	–	–	–	–	–	–	–
Total	*69*	*6*	*5*	*11*	*18*	*21*	*6*	*2*	*1*

Appendix Table 34: *Distribution of fortified buildings with luxury elements, divided by construction technique.*

الزمني للاستيطان الريفي خلال الفترة قيد الدراسة وذلك استنادًا على الأدلة الفخارية. ولا يبدو أن الاستيطان الريفي في إقليم طرابلس قبل القرن الأول قبل الميلاد قد امتد إلى ما وراء الظهير الذي يحد مباشرة مراكز الحضر الساحلية. لقد كانت المراكز الريفية الصغيرة في الواحات وقمم التلال المحصنة منتشرة في أنحاء الإقليم، وكان الرعاة شبه الرحل يستغلون اللاندسكيب، لكن عدا ذلك ظلت غالبية مناطق الريف غير مستوطنة.

ومع ذلك، فإن الظهور النسبي المفاجئ للمباني الحجرية عبر ريف إقليم طرابلس في القرن الأول الميلادي يُعد شاهدًا على انتقال واسع النطاق نحو استيطان واستقرار في أجزاء كبيرة من المنطقة خلال هذا الوقت. يتبع ذلك مناقشة في الفصل الرابع عن المباني العسكرية المعروفة في الإقليم وتقديم تصنيف جديد لها، ثم يليه في الفصلين التاليين يتم التركيز على أدلة هذا الاستيطان والاستقرار الذي جاء في شكل مبان زراعية "مزارع"، في حين يعرض الفصل الخامس (مزارع "مفتوحة" غير محصنة) والفصل السادس (مزارع محصنة)، ويقدم كل منهما تحاليل للشكل والحجم وتقنيات البناء والخصائص الأخرى لهذه المباني في تسع مناطق جغرافية مختلفة من ريف إقليم طرابلس، يعقبها مناقشة للأنماط التي تم ملاحظتها.

يوضح الفصل الخامس تنوع كبير في شكل المزارع المفتوحة "غير المحصنة" ونوع البناء فيها، مما يعكس أوجه التشابه والاختلاف في طبيعة تلك المزارع والمستوطنات وتطورها في أجزاء مختلفة من إقليم طرابلس. هذا وتدعم الأدلة المعمارية للمزارع المفتوحة بشكل عام النتائج السابقة التي تؤكد الثراء الكبير والازدهار لمناطق الساحل والجبل خلال القرون القليلة الأولى بعد الميلاد. استندت هذه الثروة على الإنتاج والتصنيع الزراعي، بالأخص زيت الزيتون والنبيذ، وتمثلت في مبان كبيرة ذات أفنية courtyard buildings شُيدت في الغالب بأسلوب البناء الروماني المتبع في شمال أفريقيا المعروف باسم *opus africanum*. على النقيض من ذلك وفي الفترة الزمنية نفسها، كان شكل البناء الأكثر شيوعاً في منطقتي مشارف الصحراء وإقليم سرت Syrtica هو مبنى المزرعة من نوع farmyard building الذي قوامه فراغات كبيرة مغلقة غير مسقوفة تناسب حماية الحيوانات. رغم وجود دليل واضح أيضًا على اعتماد الزراعة المستقرة هنا، إلا أن شيوع هذا النوع من المبان الزراعية ذات الملحق المخصص لتربية الحيوانات يشهد على الأهمية الاقتصادية والحضارية المستمرة للرعي إلى جانب الزراعة في حياة الناس الذين يعيشون في هذه الأقاليم.

يبدو أنه قد بدأ التخلي عن العديد من المزارع المفتوحة "غير المحصنة"، في وقت مبكر من القرن الثالث الميلادي، لصالح المباني المحصنة، والمتمثل في الانتقال من المباني الشبيهة بالأبراج tower-like buildings في مناطق مشارف الصحراء إلى المواقع المحاطة بخندق في منطقتي الساحل والجبل. وكما نوقش في الفصل السادس، فإنه في الوقت الذي يوجد فيه العديد من الخصائص والميزات المرتبطة بهذه المزارع كان لها أدوار دفاعية، فقد أكدت الدراسة الحالية إمكانية أنها كانت تخدم أيضًا أغراضًا أخرى الأمر الذي مكنتها من الاستمرار لتكون مفيدة ومناسبة لأنواع من الزراعة والأنشطة الرعوية نفسها التي كانت تمارس في المزارع المفتوحة. إن تشييد المباني المحصنة الرائعة والمشيدة بشكل جيد، والمزدانة غالبًا بزخارف والمتبوعة بمستوطنات كبيرة، يشير إلى مجتمع طبقي متزايد، حيث تمتلك نخبة من الناس الوسائل والرغبة في إظهار ثروتهم ، فضلاً عما يصاحبها من مكانة وسلطة.

يتم في كل فصل أيضًا تقديم تحليلات إضافية للعلاقات المتبادلة بين المزارع الفردية وأنماط الاستيطان، إضافة إلى تقديم موجز ومناقشة حول كيفية توافق الأنواع الأخرى من المباني الريفية (مثل المقابر والمعابد والكنائس والفراغات المسيجة والسدود التعويقية، إلخ...) مع المشهد الكلي. في الختام يقدم الفصل السابع ملخصًا للنتائج الرئيسة للفصول السابقة، ويبحث بإيجاز كيف يتواءم ريف إقليم طرابلس مع ما نعرفه عن الاستيطان الريفي في أجزاء أخرى من شمال إفريقيا والبحر الأبيض المتوسط خلال العصر الروماني والفترة المتأخرة.

يشتهر إقليم طرابلس بمعماره الرائع العائد للعصر الروماني في كل من مواقع الحضر والريف، وقد استحوذت مباني المدن الساحلية في لبدة الكبرى وصبراته وغيرها على اهتمام الرحالة والعلماء وخيالهم لقرون عدة، وتعد دليلاً على الحضارة الغنية والثروة الكبيرة لهذه المدن القديمة. وتختلف عمارة ريف إقليم طرابلس واستيطانه عن ذاك الذي في المدن في نواح عدة، ولكنه لا يقل أهمية عنه. وتعد الفيلات الساحلية الفخمة والقصور الشاهقة والحصون العسكرية والأضرحة الضخمة دليلاً بارزًا على وجود أعداد كبيرة من الناس الذين لا يكافحون فقط من أجل العيش ويصمدون في بيئة صعبة على الحواف الجنوبية للإمبراطورية الرومانية، بل كانوا أيضًا ينعمون بالازدهار. ومع ذلك، فإن أغلب المباني الريفية لم تكن تقريبًا مثيرة للإعجاب، فهي أبسط من حيث البناء وتحمل القليل من الزخرفة، مما يجعل تأريخها صعب للغاية أو يكاد يكون مستحيلاً بدون أنواع أخرى من الأدلة. ولهذه الأسباب وغيرها، لم تحظ مباني المزارع الريفية، لا سيما المباني الصغيرة غير الملفتة للنظر، بالاهتمام نفسه الذي حظيت به التراكيب العمارية الأكبر حجماً والأكثر إثارة للإعجاب. ورغم ذلك، تعكس هذه المباني، كبيرة كانت أم صغيرة، سواء فخمة أو بسيطة، سلسلة من الخيارات اتخذتها قصدًا الشعوب القديمة التي شيدتها، وتحمل الكثير من المعلومات التي تخبرنا عن تاريخ الإقليم واستيطانه.

جُمِعَتْ في هذا الكتاب بيانات متعلقة بعمارة وإنشاءات لأكثر من 2400 مبنى ريفي، تخص في المقام الأول مبان زراعية من كافة أنحاء إقليم طرابلس يرجع تاريخها إلى ما بين القرن الأول قبل الميلاد والقرن السابع الميلادي، وقد تم تحليلها على مستوى إقليمي، ولذا فإن الهدف الأول من هذه الدراسة هو تقديم هذا المصنف الذي تم تحديثه وتوليفه مع البيانات الموجودة حول عمارة وتشييد المباني الريفية في إقليم طرابلس. يحتوي المصنف على بيانات أتت من مسوح سابقة منشورة، وأخرى جديدة تم جمعها من صور الأقمار الاصطناعية. وقد أتاح التوفر المتزايد لصور الأقمار الإصطناعية المجانية، ذات الدقة العالية على وجه الخصوص، إجراء مسوحات جديدة عن بُعد نُفذت خصيصًا لهذه الدراسة، وأضافت هذه المسوحات إلى المصنف مئات المواقع الجديدة، وعكست الفائدة الهائلة لمسح الأقمار الاصطناعية في شمال إفريقيا. وقد جرى توحيد كل هذه البيانات تحت معيار واحد، وإنشاء تصنيف جديد لأنواع الإنشاءات قابل للتطبيق في جميع الموقع التي في أرجاء الإقليم، وأتاح ذلك، ولأول مرة، عمل مقارنات ذات مغزى بين المباني والمستوطنات عبر إقليم طرابلس خلال الفترة قيد الدراسة بطريقة أكثر منهجية وعلى نطاق أوسع مما كان ممكنًا في السابق.

الهدف الثاني من هذا الكتاب هو استخدام البيانات التي تم جمعها لتقييم تطور وأهمية الأنواع الرئيسية للمباني الريفية التي شُيدت واستُخدمت في إقليم طرابلس خلال العصر الروماني والفترات المتأخرة. ركزت أعمال التقصي السابقة في ريف إقليم طرابلس إجمالاً إما على تأثير الجيش الروماني أو أنماط الاستيطان المتعلقة بالأنشطة الاقتصادية، لا سيما إنتاج زيت الزيتون والنبيذ، ورغم أن بعض المسوحات سجلت وناقشت المباني التي شكلت هذه المواقع والمستوطنات، إلا أن العديد من الأسئلة المهمة حول البناء والتطوير والاستخدام والأهمية الاجتماعية-الحضارية للمباني الريفية في هذا الإقليم لا تزال غير معالجة بشكل كافٍ أو ظلت تماماً دون إجابة. كيف كانت المباني في أجزاء مختلفة من ريف إقليم طرابلس متشابهة أو مختلفة ولماذا؟ ومتى تم تبني أشكال وتقنيات معمارية معينة في أجزاء مختلفة من الإقليم ولماذا؟ وإلى أي مدى يمكن تفسير هذه الأشكال من خلال العوامل الاجتماعية-الحضارية أو الوظيفية أو الاقتصادية أو البيئية؟ تهدف هذه الدراسة، من خلال التركيز على الهياكل البنائية نفسها، إلى إضافة بُعدًا جديدًا في فهمنا لدور مباني المزارع وغيرها من التراكيب البنائية في اللاندسكيب الريفي rural landscape وربما حتى حياة الأشخاص الذين بنوها وسكنوها.

تضع الفصول الثلاثة الأولى من هذا الكتاب سياق المادة العلمية، مع عرض نقاش حول الخلفية التاريخية لإقليم طرابلس، وأعمال التقصي السابقة والأسس المنهجية والأدلة على العمارة والاستيطان لما قبل العصر الروماني، والتسلسل

إعمار الريف
العمارة الريفية والاستيطان في إقليم طرابلس (المدن الثلاث) خلال العصر الروماني والفترة القديمة المتأخرة

نيكول شلدريك

جمعية الدراسات الليبية